Battleground
of Desire

Peter N. Stearns

BATTLEGROUND

OF DESIRE

THE STRUGGLE FOR

SELF-CONTROL IN

MODERN AMERICA

New York University Press

New York and London

NEW YORK UNIVERSITY PRESS
New York and London

Library of Congress Cataloging-in-Publication Data
Stearns, Peter N.
Battleground of desire : the struggle for self-control in
modern America / Peter N. Stearns.
p. cm
Includes bibliographical references (p.) and index.
ISBN 0-8147-8128-4 (alk. paper)
1. United States—Social life and customs—20th century.
2. Self-control—United States—History—20th century. 3. United
States—Social life and customs—19th century.
4. Self-control—United States—History—19th century. I. Title.
E169.12.S82 1999
306'.0973—dc21
99-6177
CIP

New York University Press books are printed on acid-free paper,
and their binding materials are chosen for strength and durability.

Manufactured in the United States of America
10 9 8 7 6 5 4 3 2 1

For Meg,

with great love

CONTENTS

| vii |

Contents

All illustrations appear as an insert
following p. 210.

PREFACE

"I really lost it" is a phrase we often hear and use today. The "it" may refer to our temper, our mastery over grief, or another currently expected inhibition. We might use this expression when apologizing for deviating from standard restraints, angling for approval, or warning our listener against provocations that could result in a similar outburst. Whatever its intent, the phrase recognizes some kind of impulse control as part of social relationships in modern American society.

This book is a study of what "it" can mean in a society that has redefined many proprieties over the past century. However redefined, self-control remains an integral part of all organized human groups—whether a hunting-and-gathering band or a complex industrial civilization. Accordingly, teaching personal restraint is a major goal in raising children. No society can allow impulses to be randomly vented, so every group has explicit or implicit definitions of inappropriate anger or sexuality or presentations of the body. The form of these definitions can vary widely. For example, the Japanese worry less about public drunkenness among males than Americans do. Northern Europeans are stricter than Americans are about not tossing litter on the streets. The French feel that it is appropriate to get angry when they feel jealous, whereas Americans tend to check with others about showing any signs of jealousy to make sure they have not behaved or spoken offensively. A number of hunting-and-gathering groups, such as the Utku, an Inuit band, are so strict about hiding their anger after infancy that some do not even have a separate word for the emotion. The permutations are many—and endlessly fascinating—as people seek definitions of behavior that will allow a group to feel that its members are operating within an acceptable range and also to label deviance based on distinctive, even contradictory, mechanisms.

Just as standards of self-control can vary, they also can change in response to different social needs or shifts in larger cultural norms. For

instance, the advent of Christianity in southern Europe altered definitions of appropriate sexuality, and ultimately, it also led to new hostility
to homosexuality. In seventeenth-century England, increasing commercial competition seems to have led to greater restrictions on male friendships, constrained now by rivalry and jockeying for position. And in
eighteenth-century Europe, as part of the initial development of a
modern consumer society, definitions of the appropriate clothing for
major social groups began to yield to less differentiated standards.

During the past hundred years, Americans have undergone many
changes in the definitions of impulse control. For a long time, they were
a "people of plenty," as historian David Potter put it when describing
the national character, dependent on abundance in justifying the American purpose. But a century ago, many Americans saw abundance turn
into indulgence, or threaten to do so, with the onset of more extensive
consumerism. As a result, the principles preached by the middle class in
the nineteenth century encountered novel challenges between the end
of the century and the 1920s. These led to tensions between a new
insistence on self-restraint—sometimes according to the older rules,
sometimes according to novel expectations—and a new delight in personal gratification. We live still with these tensions, sometimes seeking
to tighten restrictions—as in the invention over the past twenty-five
years of categories such as sexual harassment and date rape—and sometimes urging greater relaxation in the interest of individual freedom and
mental health.

A contemporary history of the introduction and evolution of new
definitions of self-control both opens unexpected windows on the past,
by exploring the changes and their causes, and sheds new light on our
own standards and conduct. In recent years, a number of historians and
sociologists have been looking at different aspects of behavioral history,
studying manners, sexuality, emotions, and concepts of the body as a
means of determining why contemporaries act as they do. Tracing the
origins and development of current issues in areas such as self-restraint
is essential to understanding why we are what we are, and it can also
serve as a springboard for reform. Self-control is an established feature
of organized society, and any particular pattern is a construct of it, a
product of a set of beliefs and assumptions and of that culture's social
framework. Just as the history of a person shapes what kind of mature

adult he or she becomes, so a society's behavioral history conditions its responses. Present-day Americans may lack adequate self-control, or more probably, they may define adequacy in some questionable, counterproductive ways that are part of a system of restraints formed from debates over the Victorian system that were begun at least a hundred years ago.

Standards of self-control are only that—norms, not necessarily descriptions of real behaviors. Depending on their personality and circumstance, the members of all societies vary in their adherence to expectations of self-control. In complex societies, differences in social position and subcultures produce an additional range and even alternatives to the officially approved definitions. The resulting order allows leaders to condemn deviations and affects the behavior even of self-appointed rebels. In the contemporary United States, worries about the state of our collective standards and about our adherence to them loom large. They inform editorial critics who carp about a decline in civility. More important, they penetrate the daily life of those people who wonder how they can follow society's instructions to stay slender or who try to figure out the standards for appropriate sexual behavior. Our worries about self-control are different from those of our counterparts in the past. It is important, therefore, to find out how our particular anxieties took root and how they express the tensions in our contemporary standards and the longing for what we recall about the previous, nineteenth-century system.

This book, then, is about a battle that most Americans fight, though often without being aware of doing so. It sketches this battle in terms of the way it has emerged from the past, using history to describe the complex relationship between older systems of self-control and current patterns and to better understand some of our unexpected strengths and unappreciated dilemmas.

The subject is ambitious, as ventures into components of a national character must be. It argues for deep, though evolving, connections in American values over a two-century span, in contrast to the frequent fascination with superficial shifts—often little more than journalistic labels—from one decade to the next. The treatment unfolds through both general analysis—why we have retained older concerns in the radically altered context—and particular histories. This is also a history of a topic that some of my contemporaries do not believe really exists. "You're writing about American self-control?" an acquaintance asked. "I didn't know we had any." This remark, only slightly tongue in cheek, is, in fact, typical of a complex pattern. We worry about restraint in others and also in ourselves and exaggerate our deficiencies as part of our motivation. This, too, results from a challenging national past.

A history of self-control focuses on commonplace behaviors and the expectations applied to them—how we want to look and smell and what we teach our children about appropriate emotions. It also looks at links among disciplinary categories often examined in isolation—just sex or just hygiene. But this behavioral history has wider implications as well. Systems of self-control are politically relevant; for example, we regularly test our candidates for office to make sure they display some of the self-mastery now defined as essential, and we scrutinize more of their personal lives than ever before, to the same end. Our own political reactions are conditioned by the restraints we are urged to impose on ourselves. Some of our key institutions—the armed forces, offices, and sales outlets that employ the contemporary majority—also participate in the system of self-control, either supporting it or seeking alternatives. The window on the present offers a broad view.

ACKNOWLEDGMENTS

A wide array of colleagues and students contributed to this book at various stages of its development. My research assistants for the final segments of the project included Jennifer Rode, Luke Brindle, Ken Billet, Damon Zick, Megan Barke, Darrell Meadows, David Yosifon, and Derek Davision, and I am very grateful to them. A number of scholars offered extremely useful suggestions, some of which are noted in the relevant sections. One of the readers, Kevin White, made several helpful suggestions. I also benefited from my students' work in my New Topics in Social History class at Carnegie Mellon. My thanks also go to Noralee Frankel, Lisa Sigel, Scott Sandage, and Elizabeth Lasch-Quinn for imaginative and constructive reactions. Karen Callas was both diligent and unflaggingly cheerful in helping prepare the text. I'm also grateful to readers for the NYU Press and to Niko Pfund and Despina Papazoglou Gimbel, whose various contributions have improved the book. Various members of my family went beyond tolerating my distraction; thanks particularly to Clio, Deborah, and Cordelia for various useful suggestions. I can only begin to thank Margaret Brindle for what she has brought to my life.

PART I

The Issues

The Heart of the Matter

In the late eighteenth century, those Americans beginning to form a new middle class worried about proper norms of behavior. In 1759 John Adams, the future president, described in his diary his concerns about his physical twitches—too often shrugging his shoulders and moving the muscles of his face—and resolved to acquire a more disciplined grace. From 1775 onward, he and other Americans began consuming a new etiquette literature, spearheaded by the work of British Lord Chesterfield, that spelled out the rules for comporting the body and maintaining other elements of self-restraint. Advice ranged from the broad—"the general rule is to have a real reserve with almost everyone"—to the newly particular: "All men's breath is nauseous, and some men's intolerable." In the same period, again beginning around 1775, writers began to talk of women's natural virtues, their "superior delicacy," "modesty," "natural softness and sensibility of . . . dispositions"—"destined by their very constitution, to the exercise of the passive, the quiet, the secret, the gentle and humble virtues." This was another, gendered, aspect of self-control cherished by many through the nineteenth century and beyond.[1]

In the 1920s, a number of opinion leaders—some self-appointed, others genuinely popular—began writing about the need for freedom from repressive nineteenth-century standards. Ben Lindsey, a widely published Denver judge, argued that a host of ills resulted from outdated attitudes toward heterosexual sex and jealousy. He thus advocated sexual openness and the abolition of Victorian evasions such as red-light districts and double standards. He even praised divorce, at least as a way station until fuller enlightenment prevailed. "It may be that the faster the divorce figures increase from now on till we get rid of the old order, the old maladjustments, the better." Soon other Victorian staples, including norms of posture and definitions of ethereal love, began to be attacked or jettisoned as well.[2]

By this time, experts were crafting new rules for personal conduct, in a rebellion against the powerful standards that had been established in the late eighteenth century and lasted for at least a hundred years. Change, however, was complex. It was in the presumably decorous nineteenth century that law courts recognized the validity of unrestrained emotions such as jealousy, by excusing several prominent murderers of adulterous wives and wives' lovers: "Jealousy, which defies and bears down all restraint . . . vents itself in one result, which seems to be inevitable and unavoidable," as one successful defense attorney put it. And it was the courts of the twentieth century that progressively eliminated this line of argument, by invoking restraint: "The idea that a spouse is ever justified in taking the life of another—adulterous spouse or illicit lover—to prevent adultery is uncivilized." In addition, as the problem of sibling rivalry was introduced and quickly soared to a high place on parental worry lists, nervous parents in the 1920s accepted a new category of children's behavior that had to be brought under control. More broadly, acts based on a double standard of sexuality or the idea of wives as property became less valid, which was a major stride toward gender equality but a new constraint on male behavior. As part of the twentieth-century pattern of self-restraint, modern Americans began to limit themselves in new ways even as they were told that they were gaining unprecedented freedom of self-expression.[3]

Charting the relationship between nineteenth- and twentieth-century rules of behavior provides an important vantage point on reactions even today as we continue to refine and amend the contemporary model. Liberals and conservatives alike point to the contrast between Victorian order and more recent freedom (or license), agreeing on the magnitude, though not the quality, of the change. In the process, however, they have oversimplified both past standards—which were not, in fact, uniformly repressive—and the trends of our own age. Precisely because a behavioral history illuminates the codes we live by, it must refute some common stereotypes.

There are, to be sure, some important contrasts between the Victorian approach and the one that began to emerge in the early decades of this century. Moralists' laments, though not novel, increased in intensity during the 1920s, reflecting a growing relativism in moral standards. College-age youth seemed newly devoted to hedonism. Indeed, such crimes as the child murders by Leopold and Loeb caused even advocates of the new values like Judge Ben Lindsey to comment on the "modern misdirection of youth." A college newspaper editor noted, again in the 1920s but voicing sentiments that remain current seven decades later: "We have very few convictions about anything," and a University of Denver student claimed, "There is no absolute right or wrong." Two psychologists of that decade found that "college students were only half as likely as their parents to judge behavior on the basis of right and wrong." At the same time, however, arguments based on models of psychotherapy, citing individual powerlessness over various drives, began to modify Victorian moral condemnations of deviations from good character. Likewise, whereas newspaper obituaries in the nineteenth century routinely emphasized character attributes, with men remembered as patriotic, brave, honest, industrious, or devoted to duty and with women described as patient, affectionate, virtuous, and innocent, twentieth-century notices more commonly focused on achievements—education obtained, careers pursued, and wealth amassed (categories that by the 1930s began to be applied even to women). Moral commentary receded. Yet the contrast, despite these relatively clear-cut distinctions, was not absolute, as character attainments still carried some symbolic freight in a society that continued to believe that one's personal worth, or lack of it, undergirded one's social and economic place.

The task of comparing two different but related ethics is further complicated by the elusiveness of some twentieth-century norms. There is no question that in the past several decades Americans (with the exception of some important religious minorities and individual critics) have become much warier than their nineteenth-century counterparts about proclaiming rules and castigating deviations. In fact, a significant constraint that many contemporaries have come to accept is the need not to appear judgmental. Even the history of the word judgmental is revealing: until the early twentieth century, judgmental was an adjective referring to rendering judgment, with no pejorative connotations. But in the new regime of the twentieth century, the idea of forming an opinion about other people's personal beliefs or behaviors began to seem intolerant, an unwarranted interference. And so the term began to imply criticism, most often used as part of an injunction to stop: don't be so judgmental. By the same token, a judgmental person was thought to be flawed. In essence, Americans, particularly young people, concerned with being up-to-date, passed judgment on judgmentalism. A new norm was introduced, but in a way that made norms harder to identify and articulate. Tracing the history of actual patterns of self-control as Americans moved from the greater clarities of the Victorian world requires grappling with this complexity as well, which makes superficial evaluations impossible. One recent sociological inquiry looked at how Americans combine nonjudgmental tolerance with a subtle commitment to standards in their own lives, a double-think combination that is the very fruit of the historical evolution central to my study.[4]

This book is also about widely accepted regulations of personal behavior in an age that sometimes seems to see itself as lacking norms. Self-restraint and many of our beliefs about the twentieth century do not readily cohabit. Yet most of us follow all sorts of rules, sometimes because we are externally constrained but often because we are governed by self-control. Certain rules are new—like the greater intolerance of jealousy and judgmentalism—but others, despite the rebellion against Victorianism, maintain or even intensify nineteenth-century standards—like our frantic effort to avoid bad breath. This book focuses on certain areas of impulse control as they have evolved during the century now coming to a close.

Despite its many facets, the basic argument is not complex. Americans in this century have adopted rules for personal behavior that are somewhat different from those that their middle-class counterparts preached in the century before. Although contrasts between Victorian strength of character and its related repressiveness and our contemporary values are often overdrawn, they do reflect some real distinctions in what kinds of restraint were valued and how they were achieved. Explaining why a different regime arose in this century and what the manifestations and consequences have been draws together a number of strands of American behavioral history and helps us better understand ourselves. Contemporary Americans must contend with a mixture of cultural signals, pointing to both individual release and powerful group norms. The novelty of the mixture adds to its inherent tension, which is why anxiety about appropriate standards surfaces so frequently.

The topic is a broad one and, in a literal sense, new, for historians have not probed personal restraint as a twentieth-century subject. Nonetheless, from a host of established findings, I have selected such diverse subjects as child rearing and cleanliness, smoking and smut, along with new research on changing patterns of restraint in such areas as posture and addiction. Established conceptual frameworks also figure in—indeed, we must dip into them at the outset, for according to one common interpretation, we already know what the trends are, and the historian of the subject should, at most, add some discouraging detail. In fact, more nuanced arguments are often more useful than complaints about moral decay, and we introduce several approaches as part of the larger context for the topic itself.

The Downward Spiral

Many commentators would argue that this book's topic is an oxymoron, or at least that its definition misses the point. Instead, not different rules but, rather, progressively fewer rules should be the target—and although historical analysis might be helpful, the resulting tragedy should really be staged as a morality play.

This approach is understandable, even if the central argument here points in different directions. The Victorian regime of personal regulation was strict, and remnants of it still survive. Although nostalgia for a past order enhances the contrast, enough change has occurred for overlapping generations in the twentieth century to have quarreled about appropriate behavioral standards at several key points. The grandparents of parents aghast at their children's body piercing in the 1990s had complained about the habits of the 1920s flappers.

Indeed, laments over moral decline and permissiveness have been heard throughout the century. In the 1920s they were against the new public behaviors of women and the changes in how sexuality was discussed and represented. These concerns resurfaced in the 1960s, when child-rearing experts were blamed for undermining proper discipline, which led to the conditions in which youth protest and aberrant lifestyles could flourish. The notion of moral spiral has revived once more in the

1990s: Even a recent editorial links the increases in per capita crimes of violence, illegitimate births, and teenage suicide to the context altered by the outlawing of school prayer in 1962. A *New York Times* article notes the rampant boastfulness of athletes, politicians, and business leaders, ready to call themselves superstars at the drop of a hat. George Will more broadly condemns the disappearance of civility, symbolized by tattooed, violent athletes like the basketball player Dennis Rodman. The honest frontier coarseness of people struggling with the elements to carve out a new land has given way to "a land where plenitude inflames the sense of entitlement to more of almost everything, but less of manners and taste." The United States has become a "slatternly society—boom boxes borne through crowded streets by young men wearing pornographic T-shirts and baseball caps backwards; young women using, in what formerly was called polite society, language that formerly caused stevedores to blush. 'What next? Whatever.' "[5]

The complaints about the deterioration from the good old days of careful rules and etiquette come most frequently from the conservative side. Robert Bork's book *Slouching toward Gomorrah* relates Americans' waning self-control, including sloppy posture, to a society that has lost its backbone, indulging in welfare frauds and an orgy of illegitimate sex and bastard babies. The conservative tradition has always emphasized human imperfections as part of the argument for order and hierarchy. But in the current climate, liberals often agree with them, complaining about a loss of self-control toward family members, epitomized by the widely assumed increase in the abuse of children. Feminists blast males when they use sexual harassment as a power play. Although some people may assume that men have always behaved like this, others argue that a permissive culture has just made them worse. One's political orientation does in fact determine what facets of the decline of self-restraint one emphasizes—reactions to the idea of environmental controls are a case in point—but the basic claim nonetheless overrides politics: American morals are loosening.[6]

Not surprisingly, formal scholarly judgments frequently concur, giving editorialists and political commentators more grist. In the 1970s Christopher Lasch's discussion of the rise of narcissism, including the collapse of parents' discipline of their children, provided one interpretation of the sea change in American character, which President Jimmy

Carter used as a means of explaining the national "malaise." More recently, historian Richard Bushman traced the decline of manners, which, he argues, young Americans shun as elitist and undemocratic, with the result being an effacement of both beauty and the governance of unruly impulses. He regrets the disappearance of rules for behavior and of service personnel, like theater ushers, responsible for enforcing them. Standards, contends another scholar, James Morris, have gone by the board: "It's all capitulation. No one wants to make a judgment, to impose a standard, to act from authority and call conduct unacceptable." "Americans are becoming slaves to the new tyranny of nonchalance."[7]

Historian John Burnham attempted to put this general notion on solid historical ground. In a book entitled simply *Bad Habits*, Burnham traces the decline of Victorian controls and the rise of new latitudes for drinking, smoking, drug taking, sexual promiscuity, swearing, and gambling. He sees the righteous Victorian middle class as having been undermined during the late nineteenth and early twentieth centuries by a combination of temptations emanating from the lower classes plus commercial exploiters like the liquor companies who helped destroy Prohibition. Although Burnham's causation may be open to question—he never quite explains the internal motivations of the Victorians who yielded to these wiles—many observers would accept his basic findings. America has now succumbed to indulgences that were held at bay a century or more ago. In a study of patterns of family abuse, another historian declared:

> Exercising self-restraint has become countercultural. External controls imposed by police and the courts can of course help to reduce husbands' violence, just as less formal community oversight sometimes restrained violent husbands in the past. But creating within men the ability to exercise self-control will require a reorientation of modern culture.

Like other culture critics such as Lasch, this author really does not know how to escape from the prison of modern impulsiveness, for Americans have become too far removed from their earlier values and rules to recover on their own.[8]

The problem with these models of steadily advancing anarchy is, quite simply, that in some respects they are wrong. Some behaviors have clearly loosened—swearing is a case in point, though George Will over-stated the case. The use of profanity to boost book and movie sales and then, gradually, television, aided by legal rulings that altered censorship in the 1950s, helped create a climate in which men began to swear somewhat more freely, and since the 1960s, middle-class women have joined in as a badge of liberation. Even here, though, some rules remain. Almost all middle-class adults (aside from the minority who do not normally swear at all) are able to adjust their language habits to the setting in which they find themselves. Speeches before unfamiliar audiences, interviews, and initial dealings with strangers thus require a restraint that is readily acknowledged. But there has been a noticeable change, and the growing coarseness is an accurate, if editorially freighted, historical model for the twentieth century.[9]

Some equally clear models work in the opposite direction. We no longer need to be reminded by prominently placed signs not to spit. But in the nineteenth century, such warnings were commonplace (and frequently ineffective) in stagecoach stations, trains, and public squares. (This norm developed gradually. The *Omaha Herald* published tips for stagecoach travelers in 1877, including suggestions like "don't swear," "never attempt to fire a gun or pistol while on the road," and "spit on the leeward side of the coach.") One major American sport, baseball, grew up in an age when spitting seemed to a required ritual. The (charmingly?) nostalgic spitting habits of contemporary baseball players should remind us by contrast how much a common impulse has been restrained in most public and private settings. Similarly, chewing tobacco and the public spittoons that accompanied it—staples of nineteenth-century life, though shunned by the "best" elements—have virtually disappeared.[10]

So we swear more and spit less. Although we could argue that we should work on swearing, the model of steadily expanding license does not work here. My guess is that most current culture critics, sincerely offended by swearing, would nevertheless not opt for an exchange with bygone saliva habits.

Even the common assumption that our century has been characterized by increasing frankness, in contrast to the repressions of the past, is somewhat doubtful. Matters concerning sexuality are unquestionably more open, which will be a major topic in our later exploration of redefined restraint. To be sure, few of us discuss bestiality (despite evidence from the Kinsey report that it was not uncommon in the 1940s). But if many sexual taboos have eased in mainstream middle-class conversation, many observers would contend that limitations on the discussion of death have increased. In the twentieth century, death was moved from the home to the hospital, where its primary caretakers were doctors who vowed to fight it, rather than the pastors and family who in the nineteenth century confronted it directly. A host of euphemisms developed to avoid having to refer to death directly; thus child-rearing experts in the 1920s, concerned about shielding children from direct knowledge of such an unsettling human experience, urged evasions such as "grandma's gone."[11]

So we discuss sex more (though not as thoroughly as we might imagine), and death less—a real change, but hardly one that marks the twentieth century as an age of feckless candor. We need a different model to understand what constraints remain, which have really vanished, and what processes of replacement have occurred.

Broader factors must be considered as well. Despite the recent flurry of comments about deteriorating self-control, a number of interpretations of contemporary America have pointed to the increasing regimentation, not the liberation of impulses. To wit: much of our leisure is dominated by standardized commercial outlets. Is a society that seems to derive some of its greatest pleasures from visits to the highly, if subtly, regulated Disney Worlds truly wanton? Whereas the "man in the gray flannel suit" image was particularly applicable to the 1950s, when corporate employment and suburban conformity were striking because they were newly pervasive, constraints on middle-class male behavior have not disappeared. Interpreting behavioral trends in twentieth-century America thus must reconcile clashes of view between anarchic self-indulgence and mindless robotry. And although the latter image of a population manipulated beyond most precedents is also too simple—twentieth-century Americans do have their rebellious outlets—it does have roots in some of the most fundamental transformations of our age.[12]

The advance of service occupations in the twentieth century has powerfully defined personal values. Most of these jobs, in turn, have strengthened efforts at discipline, as these jobholders are prodded to develop new skills of salesmanship and personnel relations. Factory regulations in the nineteenth century imposed a novel sense of speed and time, key constraints to be sure. But they impinged less on personality styles than did the keep-smiling injunctions of sales gurus like Dale Carnegie or the efforts to mollify anger ranging from foreman-retraining programs in the 1930s to Total Quality Management schemes in the 1990s. In sum, significant portions of most workdays are now marked by levels of emotional restraint not widely attempted in the nineteenth century.[13] Changes in group relations, including new rights and roles for women and minorities, have created other constraints against which conservatives themselves have struggled in their blasts at political correctness but which they forget when they generalize about civility and manners.[14] Other programs of human control, ranging from more extensive (and often more directive) schooling to the quintessentially twentieth-century process of regulating (most) impulses on the highways simply reinforce the basic point: no historical schema positing systematically decreasing personal restraint captures the reality of our age. Few studies have tried to paint a complete picture, preferring instead to generalize on the basis of more selective behaviors.

Dealing with the past hundred years in terms of the evolution of patterns of personal regulation and self-control—stressing the mixture of intensifications and relaxations—is not a declaration of war against the contemporary culture critics, conservative or liberal. Indeed, their dismay at examples of license is legitimate, whether the abuses occur occasionally or as part of general behavior patterns. Even their sense of deterioration can be honored, for in a number of respects most twentieth-century Americans have abandoned rules that were widely accepted in the mid-nineteenth century. But the larger historical evolution that the critics sometimes cite in claiming that change means a progressive abandonment of restraint, no more and no less, needs to be rethought.

Frequently in fact, whether wittingly or not, the culture critics are seeking to use an oversimple historical pattern as part of an ongoing disciplinary effort. Arguing, amid a national vulnerability to beliefs in moral decline, that Americans are becoming increasingly licentious helps keep many people in line, or at least anxious about their behavior. We can be surprisingly ignorant of the many constraints that we accept. This may, of course, be salutary, at least in diverting potential discontent. But it is misleading, and without preempting a final assessment, this book is predicated on the belief that on balance, it is best to be aware of the fences that surround us so that we can better choose the balance of freedom and constraint that works best for us as individuals and as a society.

Victorian and Twentieth-Century Styles

In contrast to judgments that point simply to increasing indulgence or growing repression, a more realistic historical evaluation contains a mixture of change and continuity, a shift between nineteenth-century and contemporary standards, toward a blend of new constraints (wedded to some older staples, modestly redefined) and new latitudes. Before turning to these more detailed developments, we offer an overview of the general trends, in part because the patterns are so often misstated. Against a backdrop of successful Victorian standards, twentieth-century Americans have been building a set of adjustments that permit their participation in an affluent society along with personal controls that seem to facilitate social interactions and also satisfy a still-active individual and social conscience.

The Complexities of Nineteenth-Century Self-Regulation

Self-appointed mentors to the nineteenth-century middle class emphasized character, believing that people were capable of controlling all sorts of impulses, from sex to slouching, by the power of reason. They also argued that children could be instructed in the new proprieties, that no impediments such as original sin supervened. These beliefs took shape gradually, from the initial discussions of new standards in the eighteenth century to the impassioned attacks on traditionalist Protestant clergy regarding their harping on damnation in the 1830s and 1840s. The standards also led to new child-rearing rules that de-emphasized the use of fear or shame to discipline and instituted educational systems that deployed explicit morality to a far greater extent than schools do today. Self-control was a necessary ingredient in the behavior that respectable Victorians expected in polite conversation, in uses of emotion, and in courtship and marriage.

Character and self-control were not the only features of Victorian restraint. Economic and sanitary innovations required other kinds of impulse management. Thus adherence to clock-based time became more important than the more variable rhythms of body and will. People had to learn to get to work punctually, and they also learned the tyranny of time in school and even in precisely scheduled recreational activities. They even learned to schedule visits to the toilet—a constraint unnecessary in farming life as late as the 1950s, when the great outdoors was still always available. This was a powerful new discipline, compared with the looser constraints of an agricultural society, and it was increasingly assimilated by the middle class and others.[15]

The wider reaches of Victorian self-control were part of the early industrial society's legacy to its more mature successor, but they were only supplements to the central emphasis on self-mastery. Just as the Victorian system was different from twentieth-century patterns, so it responded to social and familial needs somewhat different from those of contemporary society. Exploring the system therefore provides a baseline by which contemporary patterns can be judged historically to see what they have preserved and how and why they have changed.

First, like all behavioral codes, the Victorian system was not always followed, despite the nostalgic idea that Victorians were actually what they preached (aside from the fact that the committed middle class was itself a minority). At least a handful of housewives were adulterers, sometimes flagrantly so. Up to a third of all courting couples in the respectable middle class had sex before marriage. Other women found ways to evade other standards: for example, even though respectable women were not supposed to get angry, their justifiable wrath against drunkards fueled many temperance meetings. And even though excessive drink caused some men to fall from respectability, a growing number of housewives took opiates without acknowledging the resulting loss of control. None of this is either surprising or a condemnation of the nineteenth-century middle class. Rather, the standards of restraint were intended to help identify and reprove deviance, even within the ranks. But the real tension between behaviors and norms must be identified before jumping to conclusions about the deterioration of twentieth-century habits.[16]

One historian has tried to deal with the tension while rescuing the superiority of the Victorian system by noting the social utility of hypocrisy.[17] Deviation there was, but it did not jeopardize rigorous norms because it was supposed to be hidden from public view, for example, through the double standard in sexuality. That the twentieth century may take a more open view of otherwise shared behaviors is a more subtle distinction that requires further attention.

Gender itself was another complexity of the Victorian system of self-control. Both men and women were held to standards, but to different ones. Men were most commonly defined as requiring strong character, encountering temptations but having the ability to resist them. That is, men were naturally sexual but could and should learn constraint; they were naturally angry but should learn to deal with the emotion appropriately. Sometimes—though not invariably—regarded as less rational anyway, women were claimed to be constructed to observe many of the necessary restraints. They had to adhere to respectability—the penalties for deviance were severe in terms of social and familial disapproval, with less tolerance than for males—but they should be able to do so naturally. Thus truly feminine women should have no inherent anger and should be able to take the lead in keeping sexuality in check by their lack of serious desire. Of course, many women knew differently, as their many comments about their daily battles with temper showed. Men, however, according to the code, faced truly difficult struggles. They had, for example, to avoid becoming angry at home, but if they were too passive, they would be regarded as sissies. Juggling control and masculine vigor could be confusing, with the mixed signals a real dilemma in growing up male. Indeed, some analysts have wondered whether this confusion was not one reason that Victorian values ultimately had to be replaced. But the pressure on women was in many ways greater, for any deviance was a sign of a natural flaw, with no credit given for strength of character in surmounting inner turmoil. Furthermore, the standards for women were in many ways more unrelenting. Although the gender divisions do not detract from the idea that the Victorian system was rigorous in principle, they do complicate the overemphasis on character factors.[18]

Most important in terms of their system as prescription, Victorians hedged their bets for both genders. Consciously or not, they used structural arrangements to prevent a potential weakness of character or lapses from true femininity. While advice writers insisted on the innocence of children and attacked the remnants of the Puritan belief in original sin, more than a hint of the earlier concerns about human frailty could still be detected. Accordingly, the importance of overcoming rampant sexual desire was underscored by social arrangements that limited contacts between adolescent males and females. Serious courtship usually did not begin until the early twenties for middle-class women and five to ten years later for men. Then, indeed, character might be tested, as we will see, but the crucial period of puberty was hedged with additional, structural safeguards. Even after puberty, a large portion of Victorianism depended on the domestic seclusion of respectable women, which helped limit the challenges to standards of sexual and emotional control. The same principle was used for another seemingly rigorous standard, the insistence on an erect posture. Victorians liked a disciplined body. But they did not in fact have to insist too much, for voluminous clothing, including buttoned vests for men, stays and corsets for women, plus straight-backed furniture left respectable people few alternatives: arrangements more than strength of will kept a person's posture in line. Likewise, abundant grief was welcomed in the Victorian emotional lexicon, as it was a sign of the embrace of death amid love, but potential excesses were cushioned by careful mourning arrangements and protocol. Here, a full statement of guidelines was bypassed entirely. In addition, there was a constant temptation to seek additional arrangements that would reduce the demands on character. The recurrent quest for prohibition, for example, showed the limits of any hope that reason could control an excessive taste for drink. In this case, to be sure, the targets were not only male but disproportionately foreign or lower class, but the connection with other structural arrangements still was important. When we look back on Victorian rigor, we need to have in mind more than a reliance on character and moral education, more even than the elaborate codes of manners. We must remember that Victorians also liked to regulate, to organize the social environment, often seeking to make sure that proper behavior would not rely primarily on character at all.[19]

Finally, Victorian self-control was rarely absolute, even in statements of expectations and even aside from blatant compromises such as the double standard that partially released male sexuality. The most demanding agendas were atypical—as in the unusual efforts to deny any female interest in sexual pleasure or to shroud piano legs because of their evocative qualities. Specific emotions might be proscribed for men or women, but some leeway was granted: jealousy was unfortunate but understandable in women, given their weakness and dependence on love. And there were legitimate outlets for great passion. Women could pour their souls into maternal affection, men into anger against social injustice, and both genders could unite in a soaring love. Victorianism did not ban emotional excess per se. Although sex offered fewer legitimate outlets, here too there was an assumption of pleasurable if desirably moderate expression in marriage, and there was plenty of discussion as a new level of fascination took hold. Children, too, could be held to strict standards of physical control, warned not to wriggle or slouch and dressed in confining outfits, but they were monitored far less than might be imagined, and boys particularly had many opportunities to develop their own, separate codes. Even aside from the variables of real behavior, Victorian rigor should not be exaggerated, for in some categories, constraints were blended with opportunities for fervent expression.[20]

Even our initial glance at the Victorian approach to self-control suggests some of the issues in assessing not only nineteenth-century middle-class life but also the diverse options available to twentieth-century descendants faced with a different set of social needs. A simple movement away from high principles of character cannot possibly describe the trends of our age, for such principles did not constitute the only pillar of Victorianism. Modifying gender divisions, for example, inevitably raised problems apart from the direct attacks on outdated repressions. For instance, altering social arrangements governing the frequency of interactions between men and women, which perhaps was not initially intended as redefining standards of restraint, had an impact. Victorianism was not the triumph of proprieties that some contemporary culture critics like to claim, as it, too, displayed gaps between expectations and realities; it, too, contained subtleties and internal contradictions.

Finally, Victorian standards of self-control included a feature that survived into the twentieth century: a deep but ambiguous relationship with religion that became distinctively American. One of the innovations of Victorian standards was the movement away from denominational religion. In its place, propriety and good physical health, not the avoidance of hellfire, became the official sanctions for sexual restraint. Too much or too early sex would cause mental disorder, impotence, infertility, acne—the list was striking, and strikingly secular. Prescriptive writers often invoked moralism, launching in fact the association between personal health and upright behavior, but without a detailed theological accompaniment. Strong religious overtones remained, however, as Victorians still sought to please God—in modern Protestantism, an unusually benign God—and to achieve spiritual rewards. Indulgence in grief was thus cushioned by a new belief that loved ones would be reunited in heaven. Love itself, as Karen Lystra has shown, had deliberately religious-like qualities for an age that rejected traditional theology but sought spiritual connections. By the late nineteenth century, the importance of American religion—though also its changing qualities—began to distinguish the United States from other industrial societies in which more straightforward secularism gained ground. Instead, American religion helped provide structure in a fluid society, and it was not, as in Europe, encumbered by ties to the state. The result was a religious context for standards of self-control in a society otherwise increasingly this-worldly. Prescriptions in the twentieth century moved still further from a narrowly religious base, but the quest for moral satisfaction continued to link the goals of personal standards to the unusually high levels of religious activity and professed belief in the United States.[21]

The Twentieth Century's Adjustment to Abundance

As the twentieth-century system of impulse control gradually began to emerge from Victorianism around 1900, it combined adjustments in restraints designed to accommodate consumers' increasing affluence with their continuing need to demonstrate personal discipline. Whereas Victorians focused on behaviors, blending the emphasis on character with protective arrangements, the twentieth-century system required greater flexibility, conditioned by the need to compensate for personal indulgence. This dual system—relaxation and personal regulation—by itself accounts for some of the taboos of the twentieth century: a new revulsion against homosexuality, for example, even in the face of loosening heterosexual restraints. It alone explains why twentieth-century Americans so often worry about falling short of their own goals for self-control while also feeling hemmed in by restrictions on their freedom and impulses.

The twentieth-century system of discipline amid abundance generated more specific trends, which together created a new system of restraint. Several characteristics were intermixed, including the legacy of Victorianism itself, preserved in some groups and individuals up to the present day (for example, the sexual and gender standards of Protestant fundamentalists) and adapted, consciously or not, by many others. Just as Victorianism in fact blended several strategies, so the constraints of consumer America are made up of diverse components.

We have already established the negative point, that no embrace of license emerged to replace Victorianism, by either the standard setters (with rare exceptions) or middle-class Americans. Although some changes did facilitate certain excesses—in sex, for example—others imposed new limitations in principle, requiring new behavioral constraints or new guilt, or both. Victorianism did fade, but the simplest alternative is not a useful guide to twentieth-century history or to American society at the century's end.

Rather, it makes more sense to see patterns of twentieth-century self-control as a combination of four trends, all responding to changes in the larger environment, such as consumerism and the rise of the service sector, and overlapping in their impact on both prescriptive statements and actual members of the growing middle class. These distinct trends capture a reality that is not necessarily more complex than that posed by Victorianism properly understood and whose basic unity was a marriage between affluence and moralism.

1. Intensification and Selection. Some standards established in the Victorian period simply endured, often with new rigor. This is the simplest pattern, unsurprising given the power of Victorian norms but surprising in light of the frequent claims about the moral decay of our age. At the same time, certain restraints eased as twentieth-century prescriptions operated selectively on many recent traditions.

Cleanliness is an obvious example of intensification. The nineteenth-century middle class set new requirements for bathing, soap use, and clothes cleaning, as well as the health basis on which they officially rested. Health concerns became even more important in the twentieth century, justifying an ever-widening range of personal constraints. The clearest result was that habits inculcated for nineteenth-century respectability became more demanding; bathrooms and cleanliness products became more ubiquitous; and definitions of good housekeeping became more ambitious.[22] The restraints involved were so deeply ingrained that they rarely felt like restraints—instead, they were simply the obvious accoutrements of civilized behavior. Intensification here also extended into related areas such as a more self-conscious control of personal odor.

Intensification also applied to personal violence. Twentieth-century Americans worried greatly about violence in their society, sometimes with cause but sometimes (as in the 1990s) when actual violence rates were declining. Nonetheless, injunctions to avoid violence, an important part of middle-class etiquette in the nineteenth century, continued to be extended. Middle-class boys, for example, engaged in less schoolyard fighting than had been the case before, as a combination of stricter parental instruction and more adult supervision cut into Victorian boy culture.

The demands for punctuality also escalated. Timepieces became more precise and ubiquitous, and daily schedules more complex, particularly for women and activities-rich youth. In this context, worries about allocations for sleep increased, an interesting change from the greater nineteenth-century nonchalance. But the constraints of time themselves now seemed so obvious that after childhood, specific injunctions were no longer required.

In sum, there was no wholesale rebellion against Victorian standards for personal behavior and presentation. Some norms were relaxed, however, amid varying degrees of effective change. Prohibitions against masturbation were a case in point: whereas the earlier repressiveness was attacked, deprecations based on earlier taboos lingered. In other areas of sexuality, Victorian strictures endured with even more strength, but almost never with full force. The emphasis on male sexual aggressiveness (an eighteenth- and nineteenth-century theme in Western culture, as opposed to an earlier focus on female predators) was revived in the essential Victorianism of some later twentieth-century feminists. School dress codes formed another area of change amid continuity. Although

Victorian levels of formality were progressively abandoned, the idea of regulation was not, with schools upholding their right to declare certain styles beyond the bounds of respectability. Late in the twentieth century, along with other reversions to older ideas, the enthusiasm for outright school uniforms was born again. Likewise, earlier in the twentieth century, some Victorian standards gained new support: against increasing odds, a variety of authorities sought to preserve proper posture, offering new reasons for traditional goals that faced novel impediments given changes in clothing and furniture. Finally, but only in the 1960s, the battle was abandoned, and with rare exceptions such as the military, slouching reigned supreme.

This first set of trends—a mix of enhanced intensity and reduced emphasis occasionally carried to the point of outright rejection—is not surprising. Societies never completely cast off their recent past. The Victorian legacy remained not only in its continuation but also in its capacity for revival. The standards that did intensify serve to remind us that we still do insist on a variety of restraints for ourselves and others, particularly in the presentation of the body, and many of these are deeply rooted in the past.

The challenge in analyzing these trends is determining whether the balance of changes is more than random. Why, for example, did the demands for cleanliness increase while the pressure for an erect posture finally faded, albeit only after an intense struggle? Victorian emphases were tested according to a new set of goals. Those that fit the prevailing criteria of health and interpersonal relations largely passed muster and sometimes were enhanced, particularly when new expert services and a new range of products (soaps, deodorants) could be added to the package. But others were evaluated according to the greater acceptance of personal pleasure—hence some of the shifts concerning sexuality. Here is where Victorianism partially, though rarely entirely, eroded. Finally, the twentieth century created a new set of norms for presenting the self as relaxed. Achieving an easy demeanor posed real demands of self-control, and they bumped against certain Victorian rigidities. In short, selectivity operated according to certain organizing principles. On balance, Victorianism more closely resembled ongoing middle-class behaviors and restraints than is often acknowledged.

2. More Self, Less Structure. In crucial respects, twentieth-century standards of self-control depended less on detailed rules and supportive social arrangements than did those of the nineteenth century. What one authority calls a process of "informalization"[23] calls for careful assessment: although Americans became more informal in a variety of ways, this very process involved an important and, in some ways, an increased awareness of restraints. Only after 1970 did the popularity of combining structural arrangements with character demands return to wide favor, with a series of new regulations, but even this surge barely dented the heightened reliance on personal discipline.

The ultimate failure of Prohibition was a major blow to the idea of supplementing personal controls with formal—in this case, legal—arrangements. Even though restraint was still desired, it now depended more on self-mastery, supplemented by education and social pressure. This model was not, to be sure, absolutely uniform: the number of legal restraints on drug use rose noticeably in the twentieth century, greatly reducing the use of opiates and interacting with growing interests in other recreational drugs. In general, however, a movement away from supportive structures toward more reliance on individual impulse control would describe the developments in various areas more than the outright decline of Victorianism. This might indicate a belief that some Victorian standards had been successfully internalized, and it certainly reflected a distaste for various nineteenth-century rigidities.[24]

The prolonged debate over posture was triggered by looser, more revealing clothing and more comfortable furniture. That is, if people were to hold themselves erect, they had to do it themselves: their personal effort must be intensified. In this case, the campaign was finally dropped, but only after a controversy in which twentieth-century standard setters tried desperately to outdo their Victorian counterparts in educating and cajoling—precisely because the environment became less formal.

Although the twentieth century was hardly devoid of ritual, certain organizing ceremonies became less important because of the continuing rejection of stiffness and formality. Mourning rituals steadily faded, and a variety of new experts directly attacked them as wasteful, inefficient, and misguided.[25] Likewise, the etiquette surrounding the process of grieving became far less elaborate. Along with these changes, the management of grief was left far more to the individual, for the standards for control actually escalated. Not surprisingly, many people found the new task overwhelming and cast about for new alternatives that would provide support in the absence of social rules and arrangements.

The biggest change in the structures of sexuality and related emotions was the more varied and informal mixing of the genders in school—as high school and then college attendance became more common and was almost always coeducational—in work, and in many public leisure activities. Environmental arrangements to guide sexual restraint were reduced as well. Along with the greater acceptability of seeking sexual pleasure, this dilution of sexual restraints prompted an effort to devise new rules for impulse control—an effort that continues, despite great debate and frequent confusion, to the present day. The attendant emotions also required new self-regulation—hence the attempt to develop new internal motors to keep jealousy at bay as social interactions between men and women augmented the challenge to possessiveness.[26]

Many of the changes associated with less restrictive social interactions and dress and with less elaborate codes of manners required new attention to children. Childhood, including early childhood, became a crucial time for instilling appropriate self-control, particularly in emotional life and caring for the body. To be sure, a few innovations in new environmental arrangements helped support this effort. For example, children were more typically shielded from death, in part because of the movement of the final moments from home to hospital. But the greatest emphasis was on instilling internal rules that would allow children to grow into adults who could adjust their self-presentation even when the context seemed open-ended and in the absence of elaborate etiquette guides. Correspondingly, accusations of childishness and immaturity, along with assumptions that adult failures in self-restraint reflected an inadequate upbringing or a troubled childhood, were increasingly invoked in commentaries designed to keep behaviors under proper control.

The need to know how to restrain oneself, to be "mature" without seeming stiff or hidebound, and to vary the restraint according to the context was a crucial ingredient in the twentieth-century system of self-control. This trend led to some of the confusion about self-control itself, for the standards were less uniform and the desire to seem relaxed pushed individuals away from real or imagined Victorian rigidities. The trend also, however, accounts for some of the most important enhancements of the demands for self-control.

3. New Personal Rules. Not surprisingly, just as some Victorian standards declined in salience, so developments in the twentieth century produced novel demands for personal restraint. Two kinds of innovations were important: those that responded to social issues that had not previously been identified and those, more unexpected, that were designed to counterbalance relaxations in other areas.

From the 1930s onward, Americans were formally pressed to learn and internalize new levels of impulse control behind the wheel of a car. Some pressures had built up earlier, but the light traffic and the mechanical limitations of the cars themselves limited those needs. For the past seventy years, however, driving has created new efforts to impose self-restraint. On another front: starting in the 1960s, Americans were made aware of a new environmental etiquette that pushed toward more self-control in the use of energy and the disposal of wastes. During these decades as well, new racial patterns encouraged yet another set of manners, designed to reduce overt racism.

At the same time, some important new restraints, deeply felt though not always followed, resulted from a different kind of need: Americans had to find additional ways to demonstrate their personal discipline amid the greater material abundance that surrounded them and the loosening of some older moral codes. Middle-class Americans had to show their capacity for moral discipline, by either restraining basic impulses or worrying about their failure to do so. Restricting their intake of food in order to remain slender or dieting in order to compensate for prior excess was a new restriction of this sort, born in the 1890s. Here was a crucial area requiring daily attention that had been absent from the Victorian lexicon.[27] In the nineteenth century, Americans rarely worried about being overweight, as physical exertions helped keep off the pounds, and health and aesthetics often advocated plumpness. The diet battles of the twentieth century, and their service as a moral category, thus constituted a fundamental change, their intensity again warning against any glib generalizations about permissiveness. The quest for moral demonstrations was extended to other health crusades, shaping their vigor and frequent intolerance: the amazing cultural shift concerning cigarette smoking, starting in the 1970s, is a good example.[28] Here, as in dieting, a Victorian-like moral fervor was attached to a new behavior category, producing important changes in habits and outlook.

Aside from failures to live up to standards accepted in principle, not all efforts at innovation caught on. An attempt to limit middle-class work zeal was ventured in the 1970s, stemming from feminist attacks on men who neglected their family obligations because of work and male-liberationist echoes in warnings about a narrow, production-oriented, health-damaging masculinity.[29] Terms like workaholic were coined to try to shame practitioners into restraining themselves. But the effort failed, mainly because work values were too deeply ingrained in an approving culture and because economic uncertainties made attempts to reduce one's personal work commitment too risky after the 1960s. Many women preferred to follow a similar work scheme rather than to protest it, although important issues remained. Overall, work remained an area in which excess was culturally approved, just as it had been in the nineteenth century.

False starts, however, should not distract from the main point. Americans have needed new areas of restraints to deal with contemporary issues such as pollution and to provide moral ballast against greater indulgence. Although the current demonstrations of personal virtue differ from those of the Victorians, they are at least as compelling.

4. Compensatory Outlets. Victorian behavioral goals were supported on the whole by middle-class recreational culture. In the twentieth century, behavioral expectations are routinely countered by a very different culture, that delights in contradicting the prevailing values, providing release but also tempting spectators into excess. Emerging in the 1880s and 1890s, this tension most clearly signaled the end of the Victorian system.

Middle-class people in the nineteenth century expected their reading matter, for example, to support the moral codes which formed part of the regulatory apparatus that underpinned character. Victorian mentors disapproved of recreations that were purely escapist or frivolous; circuses, for instance, seemed a bit too distracting for children, though adults might attend. Much leisure was family focused. Reading aloud helped drive home points about the dangers of sexual temptation or about emotional norms while reinforcing family solidarity against the less controllable outside world. Sports gradually gained favor because they could be construed as supporting self-control as well as physical health. Boys could learn to keep their emotions in check as part of being gentlemen on the playing fields, yet they would not lose their emotional intensity as a result. And piano lessons provided both discipline and social grace for girls.

Some people found a different path, patronizing leisure activities that contrasted with normal constraints rather than complementing them. Others gained release by reading about, even morally protesting, working-class behaviors that were loose and spontaneous. Discussions of prostitution, for example, might titillate while ostensibly expressing outrage and illustrating the dangers of deviance. By the later nineteenth century, insistence on a supportive recreational culture began to break down more explicitly. Children began to read racy stories forbidden by adults, which featured coarse language and violence. Clearly, moralism no longer monopolized children's literature. Adults in the bigger cities began to go slumming to see shows, seeking in working-class recreational culture an excitement and vigor their own approved outlets could not provide. All this, of course, was part of the transition to the new period.[30]

Much of twentieth-century leisure involves representations of activities far different from those in humdrum daily life. For instance, middle-class people view exhibitions of nudity or near nudity (as in the 1930s burlesque shows), and (at least after the 1950s) they look at displays of increasing sexual innuendo. They see athletes get angry and aggressive, taunt their teammates, and also engage in the male-to-male touching, all contradicting the approved constraints of work and personal life. They accept as heroes entertainment figures whose excesses fill the pages of fan magazines and the on-air time of reveal-it-all television shows. This trend began early. By the 1920s, athletic heroes were compensating for various deficiencies in real life, including the erosion of literal Victorian values and opportunities for individual success but also the requirements of personal restraint. Babe Ruth, for example, was celebrated for both his athletic prowess and his notorious abandon in eating, drinking, and sex. Watching others and fantasizing about them have become important ingredients of contemporary life precisely because the values illustrated are not those by which most persons live.[31]

This final conclusion is confusing. It can lead culture critics to assume a level of abandon that does not exist, even though some, eager to reinforce moralisms and score political points, should know better. Such abandon certainly can tempt some spectators to cross the line and participate in dubious sexual practices, gambling, or other "bad habits" that violate accepted norms but whose violation is obscured by their appeal and glitter. Attacks on the deviant values of racy children's books; claims in the 1940s that comic books were leading children to violence; more recent blasts against television violence and sex and the lyrics of rock songs all reflect the ambiguity between known restraints and a fantasy culture of excess.[32]

For most people, however, a few excursions aside, the culture is fantasy, not an illustration of collapsing standards governing personal impulses. In fact, this kind of fantasy may suggest just the contrary. Surrounded by remnants and intensifications of Victorian strictures, pressed by needs for self-control amid informality and by whole new categories of demands, middle-class Americans may need alternatives as a form of vicarious release. This is a major challenge in assessing the management of impulse as the Victorian system declined.

Tensions and Divisions

The intertwining of these four trends provides the basis for understanding what the twentieth-century system of self-control has become and how it continues to operate. Unraveling its complexity requires some analytical agility and real appreciation of how many Americans have actually juggled the diverse requirements and compensations against the Victorian backdrop. How does a culture that sets new limits on anger simultaneously manage its indulgence in vicarious violence? How can sexual constraints, both old and new, be balanced against the growing permissiveness of television and movies and the omnipresence of more revealing clothing? Why have Americans become so compulsive about personal cleanliness? Why, in an indulgent age, have most American adults turned so fiercely against smoking, a consumer product supported by all the manipulative resources of modern advertising? These are some of the areas we shall explore in the following chapters.

Three pervasive patterns suggest how the twentieth-century system has endured, sometimes despite real strain. First, the trends shaping twentieth-century definitions of self-control have created important differences and disagreements. Although the expansion of the middle class—the inclusion of a wider array of people with rural or working-class origins and from a greater variety of ethnic backgrounds—has guaranteed greater diversity, the complexity of these trends has compounded the result. That is, different middle-class people may choose different ways of managing their impulses, none of the ways involving sheer indulgence or license. For example, self-consciously expressive sexuality combined with particular attention to achieving a slender, disciplined appearance may compete with stricter monogamy but also less rigid dieting. Victorian respectability, in contrast, did not have this kind of range. Instead, the twentieth-century system depends on mutual tolerance—the lack of judgmentalism that itself can restrict human impulses. It also depends on the fact that no major variant shuns impulse control; rather, the variations pertain to emphases and forms of demonstration, not to the need for considerable discipline. The camps are close enough that any one of them can make the others feel defensive and guilty.

Overall, granting the several possible combinations, twentieth-century self-control operates with more obvious tensions than the Victorian system did—indeed, it seems to welcome tension as a means of demonstrating success. Victorians talked about facing down temptation, but as we have seen, they sought to organize away many temptations. With fewer formal rules, open attacks on repressiveness, and, above all, a deliberately indulgent spectator culture, twentieth-century Americans must grapple more directly with contradiction and excess, adding new categories of virtue that may help demonstrate successful self-mastery. Although these tensions supplement group differences, they also operate *within* most middle-class people—a more important point.

The interplays are numerous: surrounded by unprecedentedly abundant and sensuously advertised food, we worry about dieting. Despite our fascination with speed and at least representations of danger, we value longevity and treat health as a moral achievement. Because of conflicting pressures, we oscillate, as individuals and over time, in how we lie about our sexuality—whether to maximize or minimize. Despite strict injunctions to keep their emotions under control, twentieth-century Americans value emotional ties to the family and have even invented a demanding category of intimacy—which ironically, in many cases, makes the family a less comfortable refuge. Sometimes the potential tensions are rejected as too complicated, as when the quest to combine good posture with a relaxed pose was discontinued. A similar choice explains why many people refuse to accept constraints on tanning invoked for the usually valid moral goal of maximum health. Overall, however, the contemporary system requires choosing among alternatives, which places a premium on a person's individual capacity to balance and on the need to check with others to make sure that the balance reflects adequate restraint.

Finally, the complexity of the twentieth-century system helps explain the pervasive cultural fascination with themes of the inner life and silent adjustment. The contrast in twentieth-century literature with the more plot-filled, event-laden works of the extended Victorian era is apparent. We read about what, sometimes partly unknowingly, we experience, that is, our need for subtle internal adjustments. The same complexity helps explain the fascination with psychological therapy. People who have a hard time living up to standards of grief restraint or who find the pushes and pulls of cues concerning anger or sexuality confusing may need some guidance in adjusting their internal signals. Therapy, created in response to the results of Victorian repression in Europe, gained ground particularly in the twentieth-century United States because of the demands of this new system of self-mastery.[33]

The contemporary system of self-control blends the pressures of a consumer society, with its multitude of goods and spectacles begging for indulgence, with the needs of a moralistic society whose conscience owes much to Victorian precedent. This difficult reconciliation accounts for the divisions in respectable if mutually wary camps within the middle class that choose different emphases, as well as for more widespread anxieties and a preoccupation with the inner space in which a balance must be sought.

| T W O |

Models and Guidelines

Presenting the emergence of a new system of self-control in the twentieth century as directly contributing to the evaluation of current behaviors and concerns builds on a number of intriguing hypotheses about the relationship of past and present social norms. This chapter discusses these connections in order to define further the targets for analysis. The focus on restraint touches on some sweeping characterizations of Americans past and present that need to be made more precise but that also deserve continued consideration. We then describe the subtopics of this particular study, their timing, and the groupings involved.

This chapter thus contains two sets of guidelines for our examination of self-control in modern America: a conceptual package and several specific elements. After discussing these components, we can engage the fuller exploration of the changes that have led to our present standards.

The Available Frameworks

The simplest model currently fashionable focuses, as we have seen, on a model of steadily increasing indulgence, and it does not work. We should note that in less conservative periods, a scholarly version of this model acknowledged the growing liberation from Victorian repression, under the heading of "modernization," a distinctive definitional twist but equally counterfactual.[1] Several more sophisticated interpretive schemes, however, do help establish a preliminary conceptual foothold on a century of change.

All societies impose constraints by means of cultural rules concerning emotions, sexual behaviors, body representations, and social roles. The degree of elaboration and the explicitness of these rules vary, in part because of their different enforcement mechanisms. Colonial American society, for instance, relied heavily on both religion and, in some regions such as New England, community monitoring, which reduced the array of explicitly articulated standards associated with child rearing, compared with those of later periods. Historians of this period often note the range of excited tempers, neighborhood feuds, and coarse behavior tolerated in this society—tolerated because direct community supervision could usually keep them in bounds.[2]

The Civilizing Process

Some scholars have applied to the United States the "civilizing process" model, first developed for early modern Europe by the sociologist Norbert Elias. Elias contended that the increase in government power and the more demanding elite culture beginning to take shape in the Renaissance led to a progressive disciplining of the European upper classes in terms of etiquette—more refined eating habits, for example—and emotional norms. An important study of American manners applies the same model to the nineteenth century, essentially using the more detailed codes first discussed by people like John Adams in the eighteenth century. Impulse control became more refined, and by the end of the nineteenth century, some of it had reached the urban lower classes, resulting in declining or at least shifting patterns of violence. This "trickle down" historical model argues that the upper and middle classes first sought to control their own behaviors in the interest of pleasing their peers and distinguishing themselves from other groups. Then the lower social classes gradually accepted some of these changes in the interest of conciliating their betters and encountering fewer problems with public authorities.[3]

The civilizing process model works well, descriptively at least (the causation is a bit fuzzy), for the Victorian period in both the United States and Europe, with its more exacting middle-class behavioral codes. A key question, however, is locating the twentieth century, the topic of this book. Some scholars would accept the model up to our own age but then contend, as John Burnham did, that a series of factors began to reverse the process: thus the stark contrast between Victorian rigor and modern relaxation. But there have been some attempts to rescue

Elias even for our own, messy age. To do so, some observers stress the continuity between Victorian and contemporary methods of surveillance, including institutions invented in the Victorian decades, such as credit checks. Credit institutions began in the nineteenth century to provide information not only about people's financial conditions but also about their drinking, gambling, and sexual habits and even husband-wife relations. The ability to check on these behaviors has expanded with time, along with some belief that "proper people"—that is, financially responsible people—should be able to keep their habits under control. Society in the twentieth century has added new sources of surveillance, such as found in public schools and the military and, more recently, computerized data banks, while still hoping that people will learn to internalize the basic norms—to be aware of how others might judge them—so that a process of self-surveillance will strengthen the institutional controls.[4]

Continuity is not the only element in using the civilizing offensive dynamic to explain how modern people restrain their impulses. Two supporting concepts are democratization and informalization. The idea of democratization should be clear: in contrast to Burnham's notion that the greater contact between the middle and lower classes pulled the former down toward cruder behavior, the proponents of a civilizing democratization model see increasing numbers of lower-class people in the twentieth century accepting more demanding standards. But this does not have to be an all-or-nothing proposition: since the late nineteenth century, middle-class people have gone slumming in search of excitement, and their habits were modified even as immigrants and urban workers accepted still more controls in a continuation of the dissemination process of the later nineteenth century itself. Thus middle-class people increasingly accepted the somewhat bawdy heritage of popular vaudeville in their entertainments, and after a transition period, workers learned to keep quiet in movies, despite the traditional habit of audience raucousness.[5]

In the United States, the democratization of behavioral controls applies to the efforts at Americanizing immigrants in the early decades of this century, which sought, and to some degree achieved, more homogeneous discipline. Middle-class people relied less on manners as a means of separating themselves from the lower orders—the nineteenth-century pattern—while insisting that all decent persons be capable of controlling themselves. More important still was the steady expansion of the middle class itself, as more white-collar jobs were created and greater consumer prosperity and suburbanization spread to even the blue-collar segment. Around 1900, when not even half the nation could be classified as urban, the self-identified middle class made up, at most, only 15 percent of the population, a figure that rose to 85 percent after World War II. Here were both the bases and the motives for a broader acceptance of at least some middle-class standards.

Democratization must, of course, be tested, which is one of the tasks of the following chapters. One problem, however, with some comparisons of the nineteenth and twentieth centuries is a social apples-and-oranges issue: twentieth-century Americans in general are compared with the nineteenth-century urban middle class, a culturally vital and expanding but minority group whose virtues may be further inflated by nostalgia. That is, inner-city boom boxes are juxtaposed with the sedate behaviors of nineteenth-century upper-middle-class operagoers, which really proves nothing at all. In theory at least—which is what the democratization extension of the civilizing process concept might imply—overall discipline might have grown more exacting in the twentieth century because of the people's greater adherence to more demanding behavioral standards even while the descendants of the old, core middle class were loosening up a bit.

The second element of the civilizing process, informalization, applies to the middle class, both old and new, so it can accompany the democratization process but still explain changes in definitions as well as their dissemination.[6] The argument is that because of the rigorous application of norms during the nineteenth century to a gradually widening group, the basic codes had been internalized by the twentieth century—for example, the reduced need for a public warning against spitting. Enforcement of the codes now required neither the emphasis nor the formality of the Victorian age, particularly as the lower classes became more disciplined. At the same time, shifting management styles and less definite divisions between public and private spaces (as women developed new leisure and work forms, among other changes) encouraged more nuances in acceptable behavior. It was possible to talk openly about sexual pleasure, for example, without fearing that overt assault would be the consequence; barriers could be maintained with less formality and fewer social distances.[7]

In this way, the habit of "social kissing" as part of a greeting developed between male and female friends in the middle class. Although the social kiss demonstrates more than casual acquaintance, it is carefully planted on the cheek, showing that there is no sexual intent. The gesture is informal but in fact highly regulated and, as such, encapsulates some of the complex contrasts between nineteenth- and twentieth-century norms.[8]

Another instance of informalization involves the changing rules of dress, where Victorian rigidities have obviously declined. A neophyte manager or academic department head invited to a Saturday meeting with peers and superiors might assume he needs to wear the same formal attire as required on a normal workday. In fact, however, Saturday dress is deliberately casual, as the novice learns after one embarrassing experience. Again, there are rules, but they call for informality. During the 1980s, the same pattern was extended in American offices to the proclamation of an informal dress day once a week. There was no impulsiveness here, no real increase in individual options, just a retreat from the uniform clothes discipline of the earlier corporate office. Less burdensome dress codes were now safe, but the challenge of being "in the know" was in some ways heightened. People had to be casual—it was a rule—in order to fit in.

Thus a modified model of the civilizing offensive may well apply to twentieth-century behavior, accommodating a combination of change and continuity and also accounting for some of the complexities of the twentieth century. The model is rather general, however, and it has not been modified for specifically American conditions, except for a few notes about less rigid social hierarchies in the United States and a wider search for popularity. The model is most commonly used, in fact, for European societies. It covers a number of trends, and it provides a framework that helps tease out some of the subtleties of contemporary norms, but it needs some careful fleshing out.

One other twist could be added. The French philosopher Michel Foucault, a critic of modern methods of discipline and no partisan of the Elias model, also saw strong links among the eighteenth, nineteenth, and the twentieth centuries in their common emphasis on strict behavior codes not necessarily modified by informalization. Foucault wrote of the spread of "total institutions" like prisons and hospitals, which clearly increased their hold in our own age, and powerful cultural manipulations in such areas as sex, which also link the various phases of the modern era. His additional suggestion pertains to the creation of unwanted behaviors by the very forces that seek to codify them. Thus the insistence on separate men's restrooms as a means of regulating toilet habits in public helps create a more formal gay subculture, which then requires further disciplinary efforts (like the "Pervert Elimination" program by the National Park Service earlier in the twentieth century) to try to eradicate the by-product. Prohibition encouraged new forms of drinking, which finally undermined the movement altogether. These links, then, are another way of accounting for some twentieth-century complexities while acknowledging basic continuities within a longer modern pattern of control.[9]

The Distinctiveness of the Twentieth Century

At the same time, a conceptualization based on stronger contrasts between the Victorian age and the decades since the 1920s also resonates well without replicating the oversimplifications of the moral decay model. This framework, variously stated, was built for American patterns specifically, even though it rests only lightly on detailed empirical research.

Five decades ago, David Riesman offered a compelling distinction between emerging contemporary patterns and essentially nineteenth-century traditions. His argument was historically vague—he did not stipulate when the change began or why, nor did he really care about testing how widely his Victorian model applied—and even his contemporary evidence was sketchy. Rather, he saw a major transition between an "inner-directed" past, in which Americans developed internal goals and followed their own consciences with strong bent toward individual achievement, and an "other-directed" present, in which the dominant orientation was to what other people thought. Contemporaries increasingly turned their personal antennae to the opinions of peers, seeking above all to fit in and avoid deviance. Although he tried to be neutral, Riesman could not conceal his preference for inner-directed behavior.

But judgments aside, his model offers three features for the subject of changing patterns of self-restraint. First, it meshes with some key findings about contemporary Americans—for as we will see, the data on sensitivity to others are richer than what Riesman was able to adduce. Second, it stresses a major change from the nineteenth and early twentieth centuries to the present. And third, it posits restraint in both cases: inner-directed people have an internal compass that can keep their impulses in check, and other-directed people have conformist needs that provide a different but not necessarily feebler basis for impulse control. Here Riesman's approach differs dramatically from the simple deterioration model and from Christopher Lasch's criticism of narcissist trends. Other-directedness might redefine what behaviors need to be restrained as well as how such restraints would be imposed, but it would definitely not recommend license.[10]

More recently, several cultural historians have drawn up a similar statement about the movement from the nineteenth-to twentieth-century standards. They stress the contrast between the Victorian emphasis on character and the switch beginning in the 1920s to the development of personality. The statement overlaps with Riesman's model, particularly in its description of the nineteenth-century desire for clear standards of behavior that would be ingrained in individual conscience, thereby providing a guide to proper behavior and a basis for assessing oneself and others. Character means impulse control first and foremost: impulses come from within and so can be suppressed or targeted by the individual. "Good character" is still invoked today—we require character, not personality, references after all—but the term has acquired a slightly dated, old-fashioned quality as the twentieth century has progressed. Personality, the more recent orientation, is a more flexible construct. It emphasizes particular self-expressions and the importance and validity of individual identity. Impulse is not given free rein, although the idea of firm, objective standards has lost favor. Self-gratification has become a valid goal, but the personality approach insists on conveying a pleasing, winning image to others that can impose some real constraints. The tension between expressing oneself and molding an identity to establish oneself successfully with others is an important complexity, differing from the more demanding but also the more straightforward controls implied in the nineteenth-century concept of character.[11]

The contrast, and also the twentieth-century complexity, is apparent in imagery. When Victorians posed for photographs (restricted also by the available technology, which required the subject to hold still for several minutes), they presented a stern, controlled face: their character was expected to shine through their rigid, uncompromising expression. By the 1920s, as can be seen in yearbook pictures, this rigidity had begun to soften in favor of more spontaneous poses. Formal portraits were supplemented by candid shots. But the result was not really spontaneous, for personality had its own injunctions: now one should be caught smiling, the face carefully composed to indicate friendliness and the capacity to relax and be open to the world.

The transition to personality, linked to Riesman's other-directedness, though defined slightly differently, helps pinpoint the time of the change as the early decades of the new century. It also reveals some of its causes. Some definitions of the transition emphasize the role of films, as well as new photographic technologies that enabled close-ups. As Hollywood extended its reputation as the capital of mass culture and as millions of people began to go movies regularly, more and more ordinary filmgoers began to think of themselves as would-be actors, as people ready to pose. Other historians have stressed more formal cultural changes that undermined Victorian assumptions about character. Jackson Lears underscores the impact of Darwinian and then Freudian findings. With human beings now animals transmitting their characteristics through heredity as part of the evolutionary response, the ability of individual characters to mold their behavior would seem limited. Bad behaviors like alcoholism or even criminality (so modern criminologists argued) might be congenital, beyond personal control. Subsequently, experimental psychologists discovered a multitude of irrational fears among young children, a far cry from the belief that they were readily moldable beings on which Victorian assumptions of character had rested.[12] The existence of unconscious impulses further quashed the idea of a rationally directed life for adults. Although these cultural influences do not fully explain the new model for individual formation—the idea of personality—they do suggest the importance of relaxing some of the unrealistic rigidities and allowing more scope for idiosyncratic qualities and self-gratification. Other cultural factors might be introduced. Turn-of-the-century literati like Oscar Wilde, in England, were defining a modernist style based on self-realization and self-expression, further overturning the idea of objective standards in art and applying similar notions to personal life. If Victorian ideals of firm control and self-improvement were becoming less valid because of scientific findings, the cues provided by bohemian artists could help establish an alternative, modified by certain restraints such as the increasingly explicit hostility to homosexuality. Again, the concept of personality was not a commitment to behavioral laissez-faire but, rather, a validation of self-crafting that would be constrained by the need to use others as a mirror of successful self-presentation.[13]

In the 1960s, a variant of the character-personality periodization brought another crucial change, according to some formulations. Proponents of this approach are not steeped in historical perspective and ignore the issue of earlier transformations. Although they may assume the fashionable mantle of postmodernism, their evidence is typically impressionistic or narrowly drawn. Accordingly, the pollster Daniel Yankelovich sees a decisive move to self-fulfillment in the generation of the 1960s, a rebellion against self-denial, which then created a quest for a new balance through personal commitment. Philip Rieff, reaching slightly further back in time for the ultimate influence of Freudian thought, similarly sees a collapse of older ideals by the 1960s as the idea of denial became irrelevant and therapy replaced moral guidance in an "irreparable break" in the continuity of Western culture. These comments, like the more historically sanctioned character-personality shift, offer important insights. The emphasis on relative recency was obviously colored by the drama of the 1960s, but this drama has now dimmed, thus clearing the way for a broader perspective. Both the time of the asserted change—with the 1960s as the immediate cause rather than the exacerbation of new trends started earlier—and the claim of a complete overturning of past values do not, on balance, play out successfully.[14]

Even with this caveat, the available models of change and continuity—from the civilizing process concept to the emphasis on dramatic new twentieth-century styles—deserve attention in several respects. First, they help point the way to an analysis of what actually happened during the transition from Victorianism to contemporaneity. In a society that frowns on boastfulness, it is important to acknowledge intellectual debts, so what follows in this study uses the ideas as well as the factual findings of others and would have been impossible without the signposts already put in place.

Second, the usable models are plausible, and correctly stated, they not only stimulate thinking but also describe some of what has occurred to shape currently dominant notions of self-control. The models are not entirely mutually contradictory, although they have different emphases and judgmental spins. Elias's civilizing process model, modified by the idea of change due to informalization, can be blended with the idea of a transition from character to personality, even though the frameworks were developed separately and cannot be harmonized completely.

Third, the models, however manipulated toward greater consistency, do not quite do the job, even aside from the special empirical problems of the Yankelovich variant. At the theoretical level, a combination points correctly to stronger links between Victorian and contemporary constraints than critics of moral decay would acknowledge. A combination also recognizes major innovations during the twentieth century, although it does not sort out what persisted amid what shifts. Furthermore, the causes of both persistence and change remain incomplete and abstract. Informality needs more explanation than the partisans of the civilizing process provide, bent as they are on salvaging the theory's applicability to our own confused age. Purely cultural causes of a shift to personality do not suffice—apart from the fact that the whole idea of personality remains rather amorphous compared with its much more definable Victorian predecessor. Indeed, we will see that a better model can be derived from seeing twentieth-century norms as adding a personality overlay to a strong, continuing emphasis on character, that a new combination, not a replacement, best describes the resulting complexity.[15] At a practical level, we simply need more specificity—more case studies of change and continuity, more facts—before we can establish an adequate idea of how we seek to control ourselves and how our quest has emerged from earlier patterns. The theories point in intriguing directions, and they correctly emphasize the importance of figuring out how society tries to cope with impulse as a means of understanding how individuals and larger interactions relate to each other. But first we need to get closer to actual forms of self-restraint as they evolved from Victorian ideas.

The Organizing Principles for an Interpretive Framework

One reason that standards of self-restraint are easier to criticize than to examine is the diffuse targets they present. Even solitary moments may require control standards—thus the nineteenth century's frantic insistence on preventing masturbation, sometimes leading to the placement of bizarre monitoring devices in boys' bedrooms so they would not be really alone.[16] Conversely, isolation in our century—the confinement produced by Walkman headsets, for example—might be a means of getting away from demanding codes of social interaction as people seek a cocoon even in the presence of others. Obviously, we cannot look at every aspect of this subject, though one of the pleasures of undertaking the study has been thinking about some of the hiding places of self-control.

Because the topic is ambitious, we must refer to several hypotheses and principles of organization when introducing it, which we present in advance so as to provide guidelines that the following material will help demonstrate. First, we must define more explicitly the range of topics, for the following chapters contain case studies illustrating the larger whole. Second, we must determine a chronology in order to clarify the timing of the basic changes before we explore them in more detail. Third, we must specify the sources and populations that we are examining.

Applications of Self-Control

Most twentieth-century Americans practice self-control throughout the day, not necessarily more than ever before but in some distinctive ways. Such self-control includes, for example, restraint behind the wheel of a car on the daily commute—an area that Americans, despite many individual excesses, have learned to regulate comparatively well.

Because no study of restraint can possibly include all venues, we offer differing levels of detail on various facets, with particular concentration on the changing rules for emotional and sexual behaviors, for obligations toward physical health, and for the presentation of the body. These areas are important to family and work life and to recreational outlets. They also open our explorations of the way that changing standards have affected the experience of parents and children and of some of the disease entities, like addiction, created in the nineteenth and twentieth centuries to deal with problems of self-control. All these topics have both public and private manifestations. Some have already benefited from important research, like the evolution of indulgence and restraint in cigarette smoking. Others, like the defense and then abandonment of posture standards, are new items of historical study that reveal much about changes in definitions of propriety. A third category, which includes sexuality, is an established subject of scholarly interest and contains byways (a history of foreplay norms has recently been written, for instance) and complexities that will lead to further inquiry. Whatever their presence in the existing scholarship, all these topics gain perspective from their juxtaposition with injunctions for self-control or a felt need for release. All, in sum, shed light on the central subject, along with additional insights from other behavioral categories such as interracial manners or e-mail etiquette.

The development of new norms for control over emotional and bodily impulses, along with the persistence of certain older rules, can also be traced to wider economic and political forces. These rules reflect the influence of an increasingly affluent, consumer-oriented economy, and in turn, they also have helped determine the specific emphases of this economy. They relate to changing political patterns, particularly in subperiods of the twentieth century such as the present, when the taste for larger social agendas has declined and the focus on individual propriety has gained more attention.

I had in mind three criteria when choosing illustrations of changing patterns of self-control: The first criterion was that the illustration had to convey some of the areas in which the goals for personal life have shifted, along with their possible impact on deeply private but also common behaviors. The second criterion was that the illustration had to link these areas to broader issues in political and economic life. And the third was that the example had to avoid the most common data traps of the simple deterioration or advancing repression schools of thought, by including a sufficient range of illustrations to capture both the seeming relaxation and the clear tightening of standards.

Chronology

Concern about impulse control has fluctuated over the past hundred years: it was high in the 1920s during with the debates about Prohibition and then fell somewhat during the Depression; concern surfaced again in the 1960s and then revived more recently. Each episode has been marked by claims that the crucial divide occurred rather a short time ago, for instance, that people were better behaved in the 1950s (according to the shocked witnesses to the sexual revolution and the youth protests of the 1960s) or even the 1970s (according to some commentators today).

Rules also have fluctuated; indeed, the perception of recurrent ebbs and flows of change are not entirely wrong. During the 1950s, for example, we heard public pronouncements concerning wifely propriety that would seem ludicrous merely two decades later and would have appeared at least somewhat aberrant even in the 1920s. For instance, a high school home economics course instructed women to have dinner ready for a hungry husband, to make themselves attractive and happy, to defer any problems in recognition of the husband's trying day, and to keep the children cheery—"speak in a low, soft, soothing and pleasant voice. Allow him to relax and unwind." "Make the evening his. . . . The goal: Try to make your home a place of peace and order where your husband can renew himself in body and spirit." More interesting, however, than the turnabouts on gender, which are familiar, is the pattern of uses of nudity in advertising and related public art. Coming after the abundantly clad Victorianism, representations of nudes from the 1880s to the 1920s—sometimes startling by American standards today, particularly in their featuring of women's breasts—became commonplace only to retreat until the 1960s, when nudes or near nudes were portrayed fairly often once more (though at a pace that lagged behind that of western Europe). Calculating the progress of self-control and license over the past century and a quarter is not as straightforward as might be imagined: even a model of steadily intensifying trends does not always work well.

Based on current editorial attacks on American civility, the principal periodization that this book criticizes involves the assumption of substantial continuity in self-control goals and good character into the

1950s—the last decade in which Americans really "behaved well"—followed by a plunge into behavioral anarchy. Some traditional elements did reappear in the 1950s, but they did not stop the fundamental currents of change that had already been under way for several decades. Even though journalists may continue to point to the 1960s as the watershed, almost all relevant scholars agree—whether they are seeking non-Victorian controls or detailing the advent of bad behaviors—that the main changes occurred earlier.

Indeed, despite all the fits and starts, including the addition of new agendas for liberation and control such as those provided by the civil rights and feminist movements, there is a pattern. The self-control norms of the nineteenth century—the norms that began to emerge after 1750 with the self-scrutiny of people like John Adams—responded to important social needs. They began to yield to a new set of needs by about the 1880s, even though the demand for demonstrations of impulse control persisted. Between this time and the 1920s came the transition to the more familiar twentieth-century rules, which have been augmented amid significant but not fundamental fluctuations to the present day.

Dating the main break between Victorian and contemporary styles about a century ago agrees with the character-to-personality conceptualization and also the idea of the civilizing process framework's being modified by new elements of informality. These formulations, and specific studies on sex or emotion,[17] similarly see a buildup of discomfort with Victorianism around 1900, followed by an explosion of innovation in the 1920s. Our discussion of changes in self-control adds more detail about and some larger reasons for this periodization and also asks, Why did Victorianism loosen its hold?

The standards that became characteristic of the Victorian decades had begun to take shape earlier. They were designed to enable an increasingly self-conscious middle class, eager to distinguish itself from the urban lower classes and new immigrant populations, to identify respectable strangers. In addition, they served a population aware that earlier, face-to-face community supervision had become less effective in an urban society. Even for the rural majority, the proliferation of commercial transactions—mainly after 1800[18]—required broader social and economic relationships. New rules for self-control, supplemented by elaborate social regulations, also were vital to a middle-class population that was pioneering new kinds of birth control (which began in the 1790s). Establishing a family in an urban economy and providing education and appropriate job and marriage opportunities for the children required care in the outlay of resources. Having fewer offspring was helpful, but reliable artificial mechanisms were not yet available.[19]

The resulting culture of self-control was extremely powerful, which is why we remember it and still use elements of it. Among other things, this culture offered new methods of parenting and provided children with lessons they would retain and pass along even when they might consciously seek to rebel or at least to innovate—another reason for its continuation well into the twentieth century. The nineteenth-century middle class also changed some of its religious views, such as their waning belief in original sin and therefore in the legitimacy of using fear to discipline children. Even so, the link of Victorianism to religion added some traditional sanctions to the power of the new norms.

Despite the efficacy of this self-control regime, however, the context for Victorianism was ultimately altered. The principal changes were innovations in work organization, such as the rise of the corporate form and new kinds of job requirements.[20] Although the decline of entrepreneurship was a blow to middle-class identity based on expectations regarding work and success, it did open the way to a search for satisfactions that might supplement the rewards of work. At the same time, a more affluent economy generated new pressures and opportunities to consume. The current stage of consumerism, which started in the last decades of the nineteenth century with the spread of department stores and new products like the bicycle, was not compatible with Victorian controls. It is not clear which came first—work changes or the rise of consumerism—but they quickly joined, prompting a rethinking of the nature and goals of self-restraint. Other innovations were added. Women, better educated and less burdened with children, began to chafe under the strong gender separation that had become part of Victorianism. Although they did not reject the old system of controls entirely—some feminists invoke its remnants even today—they certainly led the way in its reformulation, including their gradual adoption of artificial birth control devices.[21]

New economic organizations, the rise of consumerism, and new gender interactions changed the early commercial and industrial society, and standards of self-control had to change in response, leading to even more shifts. Some transitional mechanisms signaled the new thinking: for example, the rise of red-light districts was an admission that Victorian-level sexual control was impossible but also a hope that deviations could be kept separate from proper society and that a double standard would preserve the purity of respectable women.[22] Other changes were more direct, for instance, the advent of more blatant sensuality in advertising and middle-class entertainment. Around 1900, the first direct attacks were made on Victorian repression by people outside the bohemian fringe. But there was an immediate, disciplinary corollary. Some of the new demands for control also extended well beyond Victorian concerns, for example, the modern American quest for slenderness after roughly 1895.[23]

The half-century watershed—prolonged because Victorianism had worked so well—featured a complex interplay of factors. Some of these changes helped provoke a defense of older values, including complaints about "feminization" in the schools and the activities of the revived Ku Klux Klan in the north in the 1920s, eager to protest a vanishing value system as well as to attack racial minorities.[24] Adaptations and adjustments, however, were more common than revolutionary cultural breaks, despite the pronouncements of self-styled modernists. Some of the juxtapositions were striking: this period was deeply affected by the Comstock laws, passed in 1873, that limited the dissemination of information about sex and birth control, but this quintessentially Victorian legislation came at the same time that middle-class expectations, including a quest for female orgasm, were shifting decisively. By the 1920s, innovations predominated. The watershed decades thus generated the essential causes of these change, headed by a new commitment to consumerism, which gradually produced the new behavior codes. Both the codes and their causes were still in place as this most complex transition period drew to a close.

Our focus on the turn-of-the-century decades as the key break also helps establish a certain rank order in the four trends constituting the heart of the new twentieth-century style. The development of a compensatory recreational culture was one of the first movements away from Victorianism, and it speeded up during the transition itself. Not surprisingly, the need to create new forms of self-control to compensate for new indulgences followed quickly—to wit, the new attack on corpulence in the 1890s—while at the same time, the late Victorians became more adamant about cleanliness and rigid posture. Other new rules, like those governing telephone manners and traffic codes, took shape in roughly the same period but depended on outside stimuli, such as new technologies, that were less chronologically precise; indeed, the process is continuing still. The relaxation of Victorian regulations came last. In the 1890s, some easing was evident in certain areas—posture, for example—as a simple outgrowth of new consumer comforts. But the full turn to a greater emphasis on individual impulse control and attendant new concerns in child rearing, as opposed to Victorian rules and supporting structures, were awaiting the 1920s and then the failure of Prohibition. At this point, middle-class Americans had to choose between which standards to keep and which to jettison.

The primary chronology of this book emphasizes the break around 1900, accompanied by a long and complex transition and spiced by surprising continuities. Later fluctuations responded to less significant, though still interesting, stimuli, a conclusion that has a second corollary, almost as important: The basic structures originating in the late nineteenth century and maturing rapidly by the 1920s have persisted in broad outline to the present day. We are still reacting to corporate organization and a service economy, to rising consumerism, and to reduced gender inequality, although the structures emerging in the 1880s have solidified. Likewise, the new system of self-control that responded to these basic structures is still largely in place, sometimes with intensifications of its own. Thus the demands for slenderness, first heard a bit more than a century ago, are still a part of American lives, but the definition of slimness itself has narrowed: the first Miss America of 1921 had a twenty-five-inch waist, but by the 1990s, her counterparts were five inches taller with a waist three inches smaller.

Very recent changes in self-control can usually be related to earlier developments, which is one reason that complaints about sudden increases in incivility or license are usually off the mark. We have more in common with our ancestors of the 1940s or the 1920s than we might imagine, and our moral problems—if that is what they are—date back even further, with closer links to the basic structures of the American version of an advanced industrial economy. Within this chronological framework—within the framework of the argument that seeks the beginnings of fundamental changes in the decades around 1900—we must deal with the phenomenon of fluctuations. Why did nudity recede for a while after the 1920s? What did the revival of stricter gender standards in the 1950s mean in terms of the broader efforts to define appropriate self-control? To what extent have efforts to control grief and to label excessive grief as a problem needing therapy been modified by more sympathetic approaches since the 1960s?

Are we turning, at the end of the twentieth century, to substituting formal regulation for self-control, and if so, why? The increasing number of attempts not simply to denounce smoking but to use the law to limit it, plus new categories of illegal sexual offenses, suggest some disillusionment with reliance on personal restraint. The combination of criticism of Americans' declining civility and the country's new interest in regulation underscores the need to relate current issues of self-control to a broader chronological perspective.

Sources and Divides

Most of the materials used in this study are prescriptive pieces—advice manuals written for parents, etiquette books, articles, and manuals on sexual conduct, health literature including posture and diet studies, and laws and government comments concerning expectations about driver behaviors or drinking. Together, these materials provide a great deal of information about standards of self-control. Indeed, the nature itself of these materials began to change around 1900, reflecting the need for new statements of standards and new kinds of experts. By the 1920s, the new types of literature were in place, with every indication of a receptive audience.

Victorian definitions of restraint, themselves novel when they emerged in the late eighteenth century, produced a rich prescriptive literature. Before this period, detailed advice about behaviors came mainly from clerics' sermons and tracts. Then, new manners books and a new breed of moralists and etiquette writers—sometimes ministers or their wives but, if so, writing in a nondenominational mode—picked up the challenge of defining the proper middle class. The proliferation of materials mirrored the needs of people unfamiliar with their urban set-ting and eager to acquire relevant knowledge from outside authorities to have access to rules.

This prescriptive literature continued into the 1890s—the decade in which the last Victorian-style child-rearing manual was written, for example[25]—but the rate of productivity fell after the 1870s. This decline indicated both the beginning of change and the familiarity of the audi-ence with the established behavioral rules. At the turn of the century, through prescriptive manuals and also new periodicals such as the widely read *Ladies Home Journal*,[26] innovative advice proliferated. Again, the torrent of materials suggests a new audience, filled with entrants into expanding middle-class jobs, and a realization that with the shifting standards, new advice was needed. The popularizers were changing, too: they referred to science more than morality; they defined their up-to-date status in terms of criticisms of Victorian homilies; and doctors and psychologists assumed greater importance. This kind of expertise prevails yet today.

Prescriptive materials, whether Victorian or twentieth century, reflect expectations, even though their recommendations were not and are not always assimilated.[27] Indeed, one problem with some interpretations of these materials is the assumption that Victorian norms describe reality, whereas we should judge our society primarily by its perceived behaviors. Fortunately, key studies and research data provide evidence of the actual adherence to standards in both periods, indicating deviations from norms, claims of intended compliance, and also behavioral changes in desired directions. Prescription remains the main focus of this book, however, for it was and is part of daily life, if only to provoke guilt and anxiety, and it is the easiest element to trace.

Another variable, apart from the blank spots in the available evidence (for example, think of a history of the rates of masturbation, regardless of the prevailing behavioral standards), is that different groups react differently to recommended norms, and some even maintain distinct cultures of their own. Catholics, for example, picked up some Victorian cues in an attempt to accommodate to American Protestantism and also borrowed an unusual moralism from nineteenth-century Ireland. None-theless, they had their own standards of self-control, particularly until after World War II, including their discipline of children.[28] In addition, various racial minorities did not subscribe to middle-class standards, though most were touched by them, at least after 1900. Well into the twentieth century, African Americans continued to be held to much greater restraints than those applied to whites, and the penalties for "uppity" behavior could be violent and extreme. This was the context in which a new assertiveness, originating in the civil rights struggles, raised intriguing tensions with conventional recommendations of self-control. We shall concentrate, however, on the middle class, which was expanding in the twentieth century. This was the group that most clearly articulated the standards for the whole society, especially amid the democratization that formed part of the new self-control system. Nonetheless, divergences and varied responses existed at all points and played a part even in the middle-class story.

In addition to distinctive racial contexts, three other criteria—gender, social class, and cultural group—cause variations in standards. For instance, although recommendations for restraint by both men and women have usually differed somewhat, distinctions between the genders were a fundamental feature of the Victorian system. They began to blur somewhat in the twentieth century without, however, disappearing, and in fact, subtle new gaps actually widened.

Social class, sometimes combined with ethnic affiliations, produces variations in standards of self-control. In the Victorian era, middle-class people often assumed that the working classes were incapable of much self-control, which justified their differential treatment. This did not mean, however, that the lower classes did not absorb some of the standards, and as we have seen, by the late nineteenth century, some of the gross distinctions, for example, in murder rates or public brawls, began to yield to more general discipline. By the 1920s, with the growth of affluence and the expansion of middle-class jobs, combined with the cessation of mass immigration, class counted for less. This period was the peak of the homogenization of American society's middle-class norms, despite the persistence of important differences. This was the time when Catholicism and Judaism lost prominence as distinctive cultural markers in areas such as birth control or accepted emotional standards. Since about 1960, however, class distinctions have reappeared, combined with the cultural differences among the new waves of immigrants from Latin America, the Caribbean, and Asia. More diverse reactions to norms of restraint help explain why many middle-class people began to call for stricter behavioral regulation and/or to lament the moral decay—a key factor in several of the new trends in the final decade of the twentieth century. In sum, social class always contributes to an understanding of self-control and its norms, but its impact shifts with time.

Finally, though more in the twentieth century than in the Victorian decades, different cultural groups formed within the middle class. These might be based on class and ethnicity or on regional divergences. Some scholars have also referred to a general division between "heartlanders" and "moderns," reflecting different degrees of acceptance of and resistance to the newest set of standards. The emergence of a strong evangelical minority, particularly vocal in the 1920s and then sporadically after World War II, constituted an extreme of traditionalism, sometimes outdoing Victorian recommendations of restraint. But religious affiliation and related geographical location were not the whole story. Institutional differences also built on and exacerbated regional and other factors. For instance, by the late twentieth century, the American military had clearly set itself apart from mainstream American society in the sexual morality it tried to enforce—as in the attempt by the air force to ban adultery—as well as in standards of courage, hierarchy, and insistence on honesty. Landmark cases, such as the attempt to prosecute a female pilot for disobeying orders concerning sexual relations with a married civilian and then lying about her behavior, highlighted the gap between this institution and the more subtle—some would argue, simply looser—standards of self-control in civilian ranks. Differentiation is thus a complex process. Larger cultural divides—degree of religiosity or military commitment—can lead to different patterns of self-control. But many people select their cultural affiliations because of prior choices regarding their own disciplinary preferences—how "modern" they want to be—in a system that embraces a new range of options.

As a result, different individuals contain different clusters of attributes. A study in 1997, for example, showed that women who wished to alter their appearance through breast implants, when no medical factors were involved, were also relatively likely to have had sex before age twenty, to have had multiple sexual partners, to dye their hair (4.5 times more likely than the nonimplant group), to have more than seven alcoholic drinks per week (three times more likely), and to avoid becoming overweight. These women operated, in sum, according to health, beauty, and sexual criteria different from those of their more passive, or at least more traditional, counterparts, and they doubtless regarded themselves as more up-to-date. Distinctions of this sort complicate the assessment of changing standards, not to mention their impact on actual behaviors. This is a complexity that cannot always be explained without detours and qualifications. Although such distinctions do not prevail over the culturally dominant system of values, they must be acknowledged, particularly when explaining why the behavioral results differ from the recommended outcomes.

The Main Targets

This study uses various indices of self-control but does not probe every possible manifestation. It certainly seeks a broader compass than that used by some contemporary critics who assume, for example, that outfits and apparent sexuality cover the whole topic. This book emphasizes one major set of changes between the Victorian era and the present while acknowledging a several-decade transition and then several important fluctuations, including some of the new approaches that have surfaced in the past twenty years. Finally, the study concentrates mainly on middle-class expectations, weighing them against behavioral evidence and paying some attention to gender, class/ethnic, and cultural differences. The result, admittedly, is a challenging framework, but it does not obscure the main focus. For a full century, Americans have been building a system of restraint designed to accommodate new material aspirations while preserving their desire for demonstrable personal discipline.

The contemporary system has been less fully spelled out than its Victorian predecessor, but it is no less defined in fact. Its principles include a strong dose of Victorian moral goals, which have often been transmuted to new targets. The result is a combination of change and continuity not yet captured in available formulas, often bent on showing a fuller Victorian collapse than in fact occurred. The Victorian system is connected with some general changes in contemporary Western societies—hence the utility of several available models—and also with specific American components. For example, a Victorian remnant, bolstered by the nation's commitment to religion, produced a society that became known for its consumer indulgence and Hollywood sexuality but was also a center of unusual moralism. A national penchant for extravagance translated into an often-internalized seesaw between indulgence and self-criticism. The resulting tensions and the novelty of the system overall help explain why Americans so often scurry to check their responses against the views of their peers or media experts. Middle-class Americans have their own ways of seeking moral discipline amid unprecedented abundance.

PART II

The Victorian Legacy and the Beginnings of Change

THREE

The Victorian Style

It is easy to show how the Victorian approach to self-control differed from our own, whatever the judgment of the contemporary state of American morality and civility. According to the educational reformer Horace Mann, expounding the importance of the moral character of teachers in the late 1830s,

> If none but teachers of pure tastes, of good manners, of exemplary morals, had ever gained admission into our schools, neither the school rooms, nor their appurtenances would have been polluted, as some of them now are, with such ribald inscriptions, and with the carvings of such obscene emblems, as would make a heathen blush. Every person, therefore, who endorses another's character, as one befitting a school teacher, stands before the public as his moral bondsman and sponsor, and should be held to a rigid accountability. . . .
>
> One of the highest and most valuable objects, to which the influences of a school can be made conducive, consists in training our children to self-government. . . . So tremendous, too, are the evils of anarchy and lawlessness, that a government by mere force, however arbitrary and cruel, has been held preferable to no-government by mere force. But self-government, self-control, a voluntary compliance with the laws of reason and duty, have been justly considered as the highest point of excellence attainable by a human being. No one, however, can consciously obey the laws of reason and duty, until he understands them. Hence the preliminary necessity of their being clearly explained, of their being made to stand out, broad, lofty, and as conspicuous as a mountain against a clear sky. There may be blind obedience without a knowledge of the law, but only of the will of the lawgiver; but the first step towards rational obedience is a knowledge of the rule to be obeyed, and of the reasons on which it is founded.[1]

Mann's approach suggests several pillars of Victorianism: children were by nature pure, but their innocence needed protection so that their capacity for self-control would develop smoothly. In addition, parents as well as teachers should instruct children how to control their own impulses so that they would not behave improperly. Thus the task of educating children became, at least in principle, far more onerous than ever before because of the mutual requirements of character. Finally, careful education was the route through which childish innocence could be translated into adult good character, with "self-governance," the mastery over wayward temptations, the core quality. Academic goals paled by comparison.

This link between education and the goal of good character showed up in many places. Books designed to teach children to read, such as the famous McGuffey texts, were almost completely devoted to moral lessons, enjoining obedience to parents, good behavior, probity, and, for boys, a desire for advancement and, for girls, firm family values. President Charles Eliot of Harvard, like many other middle-class Americans around midcentury, viewed askance such developments as school sports, even though their justification was that they built character. At one point, after a successful college season, he contemplated dropping baseball, his reason reverting to the rigorous Victorian conception of upright character. "Well, this year I'm told the team did well because one pitcher had a fine curve ball. I understand that a curve ball is thrown with a deliberate attempt to deceive. Surely that is not an ability we should want to foster at Harvard." A different world, indeed.

Definers of Victorian virtue reacted to other distractions with similar distaste. For example, it was chicanery as much as frivolity that caused the circus to be dubiously viewed, and of course, showmen like P. T. Barnum, with his elaborate deceptions, almost deliberately defied Victorian norms. Too much stimulation of the senses—that is, almost anything that smacked of pure pleasure seeking—risked being judged out of bounds, particularly for children. And even though childish innocence was revered, the Victorians also recognized the possibility of vicious impulses. Hence the widespread concern about masturbation could lead to institutionalizing obdurate boys. Less dramatic was the advice about the uncleanness of the genital organs, the first step in planting suspicions about sexuality that many hoped would take root in both genders, but particularly women.[2]

The Victorians' emphasis on character and discipline should not be exaggerated, however, whether in praise or ridicule, to the extent that their standards of self-control seem like museum pieces, in contrast to norms we could recognize today. The Victorians were, after all, working on problems that concern us still. Impulse restraint could, for example, be turned to adaptability. Benjamin Franklin had already written about the need to adjust the self to the situation, advocating a controlled presentation that recognized the capacity to moderate emotional and bodily currents in the interests of adjusting between private and public, commercial and familial, settings. Although literal Victorians were not quite so frank, they too advocated an ability to dominate impulse without losing its motivation. This was the reasoning behind the common plea that men learn to master their anger but also be sure to retain its spur, as a goad to action. In its complexity and manipulation of internal drives, this kind of advice was not entirely distinct from twentieth-century personality ideas—indeed, it lay at their origins, in an age concerned about getting along with strangers and bending impulses to the requirements of success in a commercializing environment. Victorians, like contemporary Americans, were grappling with a surge of individualism accompanied by a need for identifiable discipline.[3]

At the same time, some Victorian standards contrasted with twentieth-century norms in unexpected ways, the unexpectedness being a function of common oversimplifications in interpreting the nineteenth century and our own age alike. Many nineteenth-century politicians, for example, were far more unrestrained in their emotional outbursts than their contemporary counterparts can afford to be. As a candidate, Abraham Lincoln was easily roused to anger during political debates, sometimes using his temper to detract from points made by his opponents. More than once he had to be restrained by Republican colleagues, and he was often cited as "looking savagely into the crowd" simply to find a single heckler. All this came from a politician known not for fanaticism but for his untiring efforts at compromise. Bitter personal attacks and frequent fights were common parts of the political process in the nineteenth-century version of American democracy. Politicians routinely referred to robust passion, as when John Tyler tried to describe his feelings about Texas annexation: "my blood becomes so heated in my veins as to scald and burn them in rapid flow."[4]

The key points are these: Victorian approaches to self-control were indeed different from our own, as standard references to character and the easy efficacy of moral education suggest. But they were not entirely different, partly because we have carefully preserved certain nineteenth-century emphases and some broad functions of self-control, in societies increasingly urban and commercial. Finally, Victorian distinctiveness consisted of more than blanket repression, for different definitions of control led to areas of surprising intensity and even passionate spontaneity.

A Framework for Self-Control

Victorians stressed the inculcation of guilt to undergird proper control and behavior in specific areas. Colonial Americans, perhaps particularly in New England, used shame, called for the disapproval and ridicule of others to reinforce their discipline of children, and put adult deviants on display for community notice. Protestant preachers often emphasized the sinner's guilt in the eyes of God, but more concrete behavioral discipline relied on both group supervision and public shame. By 1850, however, the shift to guilt was widespread, with shame an inevitable but less significant accompaniment. Attacks on the traditional concept of honor and on related practices like dueling as a means of fending off shame also heightened the emphasis on character, with guilt as its sanction and an admission of guilt the condition for resuming normal social contact. Displays of prowess could no longer absolve a person in the eyes of society. Naughty children were no longer paraded before others (or, in the most up-to-date circles, even frequently beaten). Rather, the nineteenth-century punishment of choice was to send errant children to their room to think about the consequences of their action and to suffer separation from their presumably loving family circle. They would be restored to this circle when they acknowledged their guilt through a sincere apology. Similarly, public punishments shifted from stocks and open floggings to isolation in prison, where prisoners would have a chance to contemplate their guilt as well as experience moral exhortations by officials and the salutary discipline of hard work, afterward emerging, one hoped, with character restored.[5]

The reasons for this shift to guilt were several. Socially, it reflected the growth of commerce and cities, which exposed Americans not only to more strangers but also to new values and temptations. Thus the establishment of an inner compass was vital, for the supervision of others became less effective. Guilt also appealed to a society in which economic individualism was prized. Entrepreneurial zeal did not easily coexist with the older community valuation of shame, and in fact, personal demonstrations of worth might be a useful motivation in an innovative, commercial economy. Culturally, guilt reflected the growing emphasis on familial love—particularly mother love—the deprivation of which was the foundation of guilt. Guilt also mirrored the new stress on personal privacy, which made older methods of discipline seem undignified. Finally, because the middle-class majority was now less persuaded of the validity of hellfire threats, Victorian guilt was intended to replicate some of the disciplinary functions previously performed by a more intrusive religion.

Guilt, or the desire to avoid feeling guilty and to be included in a loving family, was enhanced by the overlap between morality and health concerns. The nineteenth-century middle class hardly invented worries about disease or a sense that illness and morals were linked. In the eighteenth century and earlier, serious illness might call forth frantic efforts to combine prayer and available medical help, and epidemics typically induced anxious canvassing of the ethical status of the larger society, with preachers urging repentance and wondering about God's newest punishment for sins. Gradually, however, these traditional impulses were redefined. First, divine punishment of a society began to seem outdated, even cruel. Changes in mainstream Protestantism pointed to God's goodness, not wrath, and major disease outbreaks became occasions for scientific inquiry and public health response rather than compensatory prayer. But the notion that many health problems could be overcome or even prevented by sensible behavior became popular. Although doctors might help, and these shifts in belief were part of a growing faith in progressive science, medical remedies did not rapidly improve. Nonetheless, individual conduct did replace divine judgment in the moral calculus of health, particularly when the most severe epidemics began to diminish, thanks to better urban sanitation.[6]

Infant mortality was therefore no longer taken for granted: children did not have to die, even though death rates remained quite high until after 1880, even in the middle class. In Victorian culture, children were innocents, giving and receiving familial love. Their deaths were met with an outpouring of grief, and the new belief in heaven as a place for a later family reunion thanks to a loving God. But a child's death also was thought to be avoidable, and a search for blame began. Women's magazines began to castigate their readers for feeding children the wrong food or clothing them improperly; hence, children's health problems and parental guilt were newly linked. In adolescents and adults, health effects began to supplement and even outweigh religious rewards and punishments in explaining the consequences of different behaviors. Masturbation, as we have seen, gained new attention as part of an effort to instill sexual guilt in a group that required unprecedented levels of self-restraint to limit the birthrate. But now the professed sanctions for masturbation shifted from divine wrath and damnation to a range of health consequences. Finally, specific diseases, including some that were frightening but conveniently disproportionate among the lower classes, began to take on particularly adverse moral connotations, suggesting that the victims might have caused their own afflictions through intemperate, uncontrolled behavior. This was especially true in the running commentary on drunkenness and, later in the nineteenth century, in the discussion of venereal, or sexually transmitted, diseases. But it also applied to tuberculosis, often associated with wasting behavior.[7]

Health and individual restraint were joined, with health a measure of and justification for personal morality. This shift used some traditional thinking but reduced its religious content, heightened the individualistic element, and, above all, authorized the moral evaluation of disease. Victorians started to believe that many health problems could and should be brought under control, a key step in the new esteem for science and ultimately for doctors who backed their diagnoses with scientific claims. This same belief opened the way for the suspicion that ill health might have something to do with the good sense, even the morality, of the individuals involved—or in the case of hapless young children, that of their parents. The new beliefs facilitated the gradual establishment of doctors as at least supplementary moral monitors, evaluating behaviors in terms of health consequences for a social group convinced that disease and debility measured more than purely physical states. This change showed first in the authority that doctors claimed in discussing appropriate sexuality—the "medicalization" of sex—and it expanded later. Because sexual misconduct was held to have health consequences—mental illness or sterility or a shorter life—doctors, eager for new attributes as they sought further professional recognition, regularly commented on such moral issues as premarital sex or sexual frequency.[8]

Both the new uses of guilt and an implicit association between health and goodness were related to an effort by the urban middle class to vaunt self-control as part of its own identity. Democracy advanced in the nineteenth-century United States, particularly with the granting of universal (free) male suffrage in many states in the 1820s. Many middle-class people sincerely believed in democracy and even supported its extension to African Americans and women. Many also tried to bridge class divisions by recognizing the common rights of citizens, though class tensions nevertheless worsened after the Civil War.

The need to build a separate set of behavioral rules was equally keen, intensified—sometimes in the same individuals—by the changes occurring in political life. In Europe, this movement was initially advanced by the need to distinguish middle-class values from those of the presumably more licentious aristocracy. Although this was not an explicit concern in the United States, it spilled over from the often-copied behavioral manuals written in England and even translated from French or German. More relevant in the United States was the need to identify the lack of respectability in members of the urban, rural, and immigrant populations and, likewise, to be able to gauge one's own respectability, by means of a common adherence to certain restraints (or at least a rhetorical recognition of their validity combined with a willingness to conceal deviance). Here, along with the quest for religious-like substitutes and the need for new clarities in a rapidly commercializing economy, was a source of the avid audience for new manuals outlining appropriate child-rearing standards and adult manners as part of class formation.[9]

Sometimes concern about strangers was extended to nativist attacks on immigrants or hostility to working-class protests. But overt reference to class was complicated in the United States by democratic political ideology, which was why behavioral rules were so important in helping people separate safe strangers from unsafe ones and in explaining why some groups, because of inadequate personal controls, did not deserve social support. The counterpart of the reliance on etiquette and control of behavior was the fear that some people might learn the codes in order to deceive—the fear of "confidence men" prevalent in Victorian America.[10] Concern about being deceived was linked the need to identify values and behaviors in a society in which economic transactions and even school attendance involved strangers. Even middle-class people themselves might fall short, which is where frequently cited tales of individual failure due to drink or sex or some other behavior requiring control came in, along with the mechanisms of credit checks that similarly assumed that personal conduct measured financial worthiness. But rules were made to detect deviance as well as to instill proper virtue. Less obvious but even more important was the need for intimate conduct rules to operate amid social divisions and to help justify these divisions. By the late nineteenth century, Americans had accepted political democracy and yet established a legal difference between middle-class and working-class families in the refinement of feeling they might claim in seeking divorce, with workers held to a more purely physical definition of abuse than those who could assert a more nuanced capacity to control their feelings. Thus in many states, middle-class spouses could claim mental cruelty as grounds for divorce, arguing that a lack of love or proper emotional control from the husband or wife made civilized family life impossible, but court rulings explicitly denied this claim to the presumably cruder working class.[11]

Victorian principles of self-control defined proper conduct amid economic change and urbanization; they helped deal with problems of strangers and implicit class division; and they acknowledged the new beliefs about health and what they symbolized. These principles also reflected a quest for religious assurance even as traditionally religious arguments lost favor. During the early decades of the nineteenth century, there were fierce debates over religion and religious values. In places like Boston, newer and less secure members of the middle class sought new religious rigor, as opposed to the rationalistic, Unitarian approach of the established business class. Various sorts of revivals drew wide attention, and a significant minority of the American population retained or renewed their commitment to a traditional Calvinist ideology, replete with references to original sin and damnation, though with meeting styles that were far more emotionally expressive than those of colonial Puritans. Most of the mainstream churches, however, tended to tone down some of the older theologies, particularly the widespread use of the fear of damnation and adherence to the idea of original sin. The goal was an active religion, but one consistent with dominant middle-class beliefs in secular progress and childish innocence.[12]

The progress toward this goal was gradual. Family advice manuals regularly included sections on religious goals, assuming that these were part of people's lives. Many people, particularly women as Protestantism was feminized, used religion to bolster their self-control by providing additional sanctions and also group monitoring. One Methodist convert, Rachel Stearns, explained the importance of small-group meetings at her church:

> If we have been gay or trifling, or anger and revenge have had a place in our hearts, we do not wish to go, if we stay away, then the others will think there is something wrong. . . . I am thankful that I have placed myself under the watch-care and discipline of a church where when I do wrong they will tell me of it.[13]

These specific religious invocations did fade over time, however, just as the religion highlighted in the family manuals offered generalized comments on God's love rather than specific sanctions or commandments. A religious element persisted, but it sought a place in a more secular outlook.

The result, apart from the enduring religious divisions that gave subcultures a rationale for self-control, was a combination of active religious interest and declining religious motivation. Furthermore, even though they supported the softening of Protestant theology, many middle-class people seem to have developed a thirst for greater spiritual reward and demonstrations of virtue that could recall older values in new forms. At the same time, during these same decades a more commercial economy took hold, affecting rural as well as urban producers. More people actively sought profits rather than localized subsistence and exchange;

the use of money expanded; and international trade increased. With some exceptions in coastal cities and in the South, colonial America had lagged behind Europe in commercial development, but now it was catching up with a vengeance. The suddenness and rapidity of this change and its coincidence with religious upheaval help account for the unusual vitality of religion in American life and for the distinctively strong penchant for moralism.[14]

The quest for virtue could be found in many places. Individual non-denominational reformers attracted disciples, particularly from the middle and artisanal classes in the cities, to programs of austerity designed to fend off sin and compensate for evils of commerce. Sylvester Graham took advantage of a number of anxieties in advocating a wholesome, pure grain diet to avoid the sullied products and motives of a profit-seeking economy while also insisting on rigorous sexual discipline.[15] Restraint and virtue were closely linked (with implications for the intertwining of health and morality) in a society uncomfortable with its own acceptance of economic motives and eager to remain committed to higher values. More broadly, the American middle class embraced with unusual vigor the transatlantic ideology of the sanctity of the family. Belief that the family could provide an alternative to the tawdriness of commercial motives—a "haven in a heartless world"—echoed in England as well as the United States, with some resonance in other parts of Europe. The belief responded not only to commercialization and early industrialization but also to the new need for birth control. Americans seemed especially anxious to make the family a symbol and to argue that women needed to be protected but also instructed as the guardians of private virtue. The Victorian system of self-control thus had to defend the near-religion of the family while feeding the larger American quest for spiritual ballast in a rapidly changing economy.[16]

Along with the traditions of Puritanism—not national in scope but unusually influential because of the voice of New England divines and intellectuals and the presence of an evangelical minority in various regions—the need for a moral counterweight underlay some of the intensities of Victorian standards of self-restraint. It is well known that in the nineteenth century the United States industrialized more swiftly than almost any other country. This achievement occurred in a society that had been less exposed to a commercial economy previously. Not surprisingly, the result was an anxiety that was hard to express directly given the widespread commitments to progress and mobility. When other issues were added, such as the arrival of new types of immigrants like the Irish and Germans, the demands on moral symbolism pushed the American middle class to some extreme uses of otherwise common nineteenth-century bourgeois virtues.

Temperance was a case in point. It had not been a Puritan issue, for strong drink was appreciated as a gift from God, but now it acquired religious-like fervor. Middle-class opposition to excessive drink become a nineteenth-century staple in Western societies, combining a distaste for the damage that alcohol could cause to individual and family with a realization of the demands of the factory system. Temperance movements sprang up throughout the Atlantic world. But the American attachment to them was unusual, leading to vigorous campaigns and extensive legislation at the state level (Maine was the first government anywhere to enact temperance laws) and, ultimately, in the nation as a whole. The so-called temperance movements used the same vigor to try to ban drink altogether, and some of the earliest laws were linked to the religious revivalism of the 1830s and 1840s, in which pledges of abstinence were part of "renouncing all the ways of sin."

Of course, the issue was debated, with opposition directed against the efforts at legislated abstinence. But for important segments of the American middle class, temperance expressed the need to demonstrate self-discipline and personal rigor, as opposed to a substance that could sap the capacity for individual control and wreak havoc on the all-important family. Temperance provided a means of attacking the corrupting influence of strangers, including immigrants who seemed wedded to strong drink and the working classes more generally. It gave women a moral and emotional outlet, demonstrating their claims to leadership in virtue over an issue that wedded public action to private discipline. The movement's vitality pushed reformers to espouse abstinence and prohibition, and not just restraint—an example of the linkage between self-control and moral absolutes. Drinking became "that horribly demeaning vice, which saps the foundation of reason and makes man a beggar, a brute, a criminal, and everything, in turn, which is loathsome and abominable in the estimation of the virtuous mind." This combination of real concern and demonstrated symbolic virtue, plus the tendency to push to extremes, was a hallmark of American Victorianism—the product of several factors. In many ways, this combination survived the Victorian culture that generated it.[17]

The Main Points

Beneath the umbrella of general invocations of character, Victorian self-control was aimed at four interrelated targets: probity, emotions, sex, and the body. In all areas, advice givers and many ordinary middle-class parents and moral temperature takers sought restraint over impulse. Specific campaigns, like temperance or Graham's nutrition and purity movement, were based on the belief that respectable people should maintain control over their mental capacities and desire for indulgence.

Probity

Throughout the nineteenth century, lessons for children and for adults alike taught honesty in social and financial dealings. Impulses to lie, cheat, or evade were severely condemned—as President Eliot's reaction to the deceptive curve ball suggests. Honesty seemed vital to a society in which the respectability of strangers had to be established and in which commercial transactions and profit motives were increasing in complexity and intensity. A good person was trustworthy. There was no margin, in principle, for temporizing.

This belief in probity informed much of the middle-class hostility to gambling, in its condemnation of lower-class interests in lotteries and betting. Besides wasting money, gambling also reinforced the idea that one could get something for nothing, sidestepping the need to make a serious, disciplined effort to win reward. The legal attacks on gambling produced illegal responses, and the common association of criminals with urban gambling activities simply tightened the strings of middle-class disapproval. The whole system rested on dishonesty.[18]

Lying was condemned. Manuals for parents frequently stressed the importance of making sure that children were punished for lies so that they would learn early on the importance of telling the truth. Praise for honesty in difficult circumstances was the counterpart: children who faced up to a misdemeanor and told the truth would be praised as well as punished. It was in the reading books and school histories of the nineteenth century that the reference to George Washington's successful moral battle after he had cut down the cherry tree originated—"I cannot tell a lie." Word use reflected this insistence on telling the truth. The term white lie had been introduced in England in the eighteenth century as a presumably constructive evasion in the interests of social ease. The concept reflected the increasing rigor of manners and smooth personal relations, which made evasion more attractive, since the truth might hurt. But it also picked up on the much older idea of a beneficent or at least harmless "white" magic that contrasted with black. Although most commentators, both English and American, in the nineteenth century recognized the term, they condemned it. White lies were lies, and so no better than black.[19]

Likewise, when manuals for secretaries began to be written later in the century, they stressed personal honesty and accountability. Here the standards of self-control clearly coincided with the pressures of expanding commerce. The secretarial force was growing larger (though it was mainly still male), which meant the need to rely on strangers for relatively intimate, if subordinate, business support. Secretaries managed a whole range of affairs for their superiors, including some financial transactions. In this context, it was not surprising that manuals devoted long sections to the insistence on probity, but the insistence also fit the longer-term Victorian principles of self-control when both truth and money were concerned.[20]

Emotions

Victorians tried to keep a tight rein over potentially damaging emotions, although they did not, as we have seen, insist on emotional control at all times. Family manuals urged parents to be good models for emotional control by avoiding both anger in punishment and the use of fear in discipline. Children's stories provided tale after tale of girls who came to a bad end because they were jealous or boys who won credit because they used courage to overcome fear. Similarly, etiquette books talked about the importance of keeping emotions, like anger, in check and dealing with others' emotions, like grief, with suitably restrained if sympathetic rituals. Good character included the ability to control emotions that might damage others or expose oneself to impulses that might lead to false goals or unrespectable behaviors.[21]

Not surprisingly, envy came in for much adverse comment, particularly in the later decades of the nineteenth century when advertising and consumer outlets were becoming more popular. Ministers blasted envy as a sin that would lead to excessive behavior and damaging competition with neighbors and friends. Secular editorialists excoriated the "fictitious social values" to which envy could lead and urged restraint. A *Ladies Home Journal* columnist warned: "To envy the rich . . . does not bring us one step closer to the fulfillment of our desires." Editor Edward Bok added:

> I do not want you, my dear woman, to be envious of the possessions . . . of one woman in this world, be she rich or poor. To say "Oh, I wish I were rich" is to express discontent with the judgment and dispensation of an All-wise creator, who knows far better what is good for you than you do.

Envy destroyed the contentment that came with solid values and real self-control. It might also lead to social deception, pretending through purchases that one was something other than what one was—"spoiling herself for her family and friends by being a sham"—by aping the fashions of the rich, for example. Here, emotional control was linked with honesty, and both were applied to the need for self-control amid the growing temptations of a commercial economy.[22]

Envy also fell afoul of an even more important criterion for emotional self-control, the protection of the family's sanctity. Envy could lead families to overspend and so undermine not only their values but also their economic survival. True contentment, in contrast, meant enjoying the abundant love the family had to offer, regardless of its material circumstances. Other emotions had to be curbed in the interest of the family's uplifting role. Anger must be suppressed. Men might have a struggle here, since they needed aggressive impulses. But women were, in principle, devoid of anger, although in practice this set up an even more demanding standard. By whatever mechanism of control, anger and combat should be kept out of family confines. Children should be punished without anger, which placed constraints on parental traditions. In the middle decades of the century, one magazine article after another highlighted the tragedy of a first marital fight, as if this foretold a downward spiral from which the union might not recover. Jealousy was another emotion that could damage family relationships, though women, as the weaker sex and also responsible for preserving the bonds of love, might be granted a bit of latitude here. Overall, however, jealousy introduced a possessiveness and pettiness incompatible with the higher emotional and spiritual purposes of family life.[23]

From childhood onward, appropriate emotional control was an integral part of character training. Through example, uplifting stories, warnings of the dire fates awaiting those who let bad emotions get out of hand, and the rituals of proper etiquette, both reason and restraint should keep unproductive emotions in check. If strong emotional motivations were needed in certain circumstances, as with anger for men, one's capacity for control was tested even further, and the choice of target was crucial. Although women were sometimes depicted as appropriately restrained by nature, many wives and mothers recognized that the desired norms imposed a daily challenge, and they recorded in their diaries their struggles with temper or with envy, cherishing each triumph over impulse.

Sex

Sexual restraint was unquestionably a cornerstone of Victorian standards of self-control. As we have seen, it responded to new middle-class needs to restrict birthrates. Ironically, the resulting ethic retarded the use of new or improved artificial birth control devices, introduced in the 1820s and proliferating after the invention of the vulcanization process for rubber in the 1830s. Condoms and diaphragms, or pessaries, became more widely available, but Victorian standards warned against their use lest they encourage rampant, purely recreational sex. Even by the 1890s, the lack of complete reliability of the devices provided an additional motivation for the continued emphasis on self-restraint, especially for those middle-class couples for whom having an additional child was absolutely infeasible. Middle-class birthrates dropped steadily through the nineteenth century. Compromise methods such as coitus interruptus or the male enjoyment of a double standard, which limited legitimate births while placing additional burdens on lower-class prostitutes, plus the gradually increasing use of new devices, help explain this important change. But real self-restraint by one and usually both parties was the most important single component.[24]

The socialization of children pressed the urgency of self-control. Both boys and girls absorbed the basic gender message: decent women do not show much interest in sex and were responsible for restraint, even when men, naturally more lusty, might importune. Men were less constrained but were obligated to accept women's guidance. And even though men were less confined by definitions of sexual nature, they received additional caution through the attacks on male masturbation—"self-abuse." As late as 1910, doctors were warning of the catastrophic results of this practice. An Indiana clinic claimed that the results of drink or opium, though devastating, might be reversed; that is, a man could recover "by his own volition or return of moral courage." "But not so with the man who has destroyed his vitality by vicious and unnatural self-debasement or excesses," which sapped potency and also destroyed the "reserve mental force . . . until the victim is absolutely unable to control his thoughts, his passions or his downfall and complete sexual ruin." This annihilation of the capacity for self-control would lead finally to "imbecility or the madhouse." Obviously it was critical to avoid this collapse by exercising willpower in the first place, although some doctors claimed that treatment could intervene (and that many weak men were flocking to their doors). These attacks on masturbation did not, of course, completely counter the assurances about men's natural sexual power, but they could affect later reactions to arousal, supplementing the more straightforward insistence on self-mastery in the interests of respectability and fairness toward women.[25]

Despite the widespread emphasis on restraint, assessing the demands for sexual self-control is complicated, for several reasons. First, as noted before, Victorians were capable of extreme statements about abstinence and the health and moral dangers of virtually any sexual activity. Some of the silliest statements came from British moralists like Lord Acton, but American faddists like Graham and Kellogg contributed widely read American cautions. Their enthusiasms were close enough to wider concerns to make some sense, but they were not typical of most advice or behavior. The same applies to some of the most extreme actions against masturbation, which did, however, receive some public support in the form of institutionalizing young offenders. At the other extreme, Victorian standards were loudly defied by some utopian radicals, like Max Lazarus. Although most utopian communities were in fact quite prudish, an extension of middle-class convention, a few promoted promiscuity and a dissociation of sex from marriage. Even though these views were exceptional, they did illustrate one complicating feature of the Victorian sexual climate: the interest in sex increased. The subject was widely discussed, though presumably veiled from children's eyes and ears. Somehow, therefore, Victorian middle-class people had to combine real control in practice with an undeniably considerable, and novel, fascination with the topic.[26]

Overall, Victorians moved to define self-control in ways that did not require absolute repression. Sex was clearly not an appropriate interest for the young. References to sex were to be avoided, and the sex organs should be surrounded with some combination of reticence and disapproval; they, particularly male organs, were dangerous. The concerns about masturbation, even when moderately expressed, drove home this conclusion for youth. Sex should not occur outside marriage, and it should be restrained even within marriage for the sake of good health, moral purity, and the birthrate. Because of their more active sex drive (and because men operated more widely outside the home, they faced a greater range of sexual temptations and opportunities in nineteenth-century society), men had the greater task of control though women's guidance, facilitated by a natural feminine delicacy regarding sex, could help a great deal. Couples should avoid sex before marriage, and they should not stray once wed. Spouses did have legitimate sexual needs, however—here, mainstream Victorian advice sidestepped the extremists—and sexual pleasure, if not overemphasized or too frequently indulged in, could be part of a good marriage. Sex deliberately for pleasure alone might seem dangerously indulgent. But marital sex that brought pleasure once a week or so was fine, even healthy, for men and women alike. Thus when middle-class women born after 1870 evinced a growing awareness of orgasm and its desirability, the heightened interest in pleasure constituted a significant change but not a complete departure from the Victorian norms.[27]

Victorian standards of sexual self-restraint had some important ramifications apart from their paradoxical impact on public policy concerning birth control. The definition of love that emerged early in the nineteenth century emphasized its totality and also its spirituality. Indeed, its soaring intensity alone could unite two genders otherwise held to be so different. Love is the "richest treasure of our nature, the most human, and yet the most divine, of our aspirations," perfecting both genders through the "mystical and holy" union it provided. Courting couples picked up the message in their mutual letters: "It [true love] is to love with all one's soul what is pure, what is high, what is eternal." "To love you . . . and to sink my life in the Divine life through you, seem to me the supreme end of my existence." The same intensity encompassed sexuality but relegated it to a lesser, clearly controlled space in the larger dimensions of the relationship. This is a key example of the general Victorian style, juxtaposing compensation with repression. What must be held back in one area, such as respectable courtship, could be released through the new stipulations of love and its priority in the lives and unions of young adults. This redefinition of love, though intended to subordinate sex without eliminating it, led to a greater separation of casual sex from other emotions—a trend in pornography and also a concomitant of the increasing male use of prostitutes.[28]

Victorianism also helped make sex a new basis for cursing, though beyond the pale of respectability. Before the nineteenth century, swearing had a largely religious framework, with the great oaths threatening religious punishments or defying God. Anglo-Saxon words for sexual organs and acts existed but had no particularly bad connotation. When sex was described in eighteenth-century pornography, elaborate and benign metaphors were used, like machine for the male apparatus. In the nineteenth century, as religious oaths lost force, sex, now more closely monitored, took their place, and words like fuck, cunt, and prick began to take on new meaning. They were described increasingly as "dirty words," the term dirty reflecting the moral connotations of cleanliness as well as the new anxiety about sex. Interestingly, in the twentieth century, words with sexual connotations were used still more frequently to berate and condemn, even as accepted sexual codes in some ways eased—an important index of the ambiguous relationship to Victorianism that we later explore. Even in the nineteenth century, dirtiness could be a stimulus to excitement, as the new word use in Victorian pornography suggested.[29]

Victorian strictures on sex were powerful, affecting language and perception as well as moral lessons and public policy. Because they played such a strong role in child rearing, they easily survived simply because of intergenerational momentum, and well beyond the moral and birth control needs that had provoked them. We must remember, however, that full repression was not what the most commonly disseminated standards intended, at least for adults, and that sexual control was only one facet of the broader definition of character.

The Body

Besides sex, Victorian restraint was extended to other aspects of the presentation of the body. These extensions might supplement, but also might complicate, any focus on sexual prudery, for they had significant additional functions. Two broad categories emerged, in both of which Victorian advice literature moved well beyond the standards current in colonial America at least before the 1750s. First, discipline of the body for health purposes became crucial, a part of the growing belief that health could be acquired and that its acquisition had moral as well as physical attributes. Second, control of bodily impulse became a sign of character itself, demonstrating to oneself and others that one's rational capacity was in full command, taking precedence over spontaneity or even comfort. Neither the health nor the demonstration functions of bodily control had explicit aesthetic goals, but they did in fact call attention to the role of careful presentation when dealing with others and could include a concern about appearance.

The most important redefinition of bodily hygiene pertained to the growing approval of, and ultimate insistence on, regular bathing. The idea of cleanliness next to godliness was a Victorian notion, reflecting both religious change and the gradual apotheosis of soap and water. People began to require more time for bodily care, and parents had to teach a new constraint to their children, launching an ongoing battle with the childish desire to get dirty.

In 1800, bathing was rare in the United States, as most people were convinced that the practice was harmful to their health. By the 1840s, however, recommendations of regular baths became common, along with improved facilities in middle-class homes and the better hotels. A reversal of views about health helped this transformation, along with the emphasis on individual responsibility for health. Early arguments stressed the positive effects of bathing on removing noxious humors from the body and skin. Almost all the early discussions distinguished between bathing as an obligation, perhaps somewhat unpleasant (particularly because cold water was recommended), and bathing as a sensual pleasure, which should be avoided. Even when hot water began to be accepted and available, the dominant advice urged short baths to limit languor. At first, soap was ignored, except when dirt was excessive. The purpose was health and, to an extent, regular discipline, which nicely fit the goals of Victorian self-control. As the habit of bathing became popular, with the middle class leading the way, germ theory added to the health arguments and so focused attention more on dirt and not just skin hygiene. By the early twentieth century, baths at least twice a week were widely recommended, to combat "invisible" dirt as well as to create a clean appearance. In sum, bathing had become, like other aspects of Victorian control, a "sign of refinement," and the norms were gradually internalized. "For many people the regular morning bath is at first a trial, then a pleasure and finally a need." Here was a classic pattern of change: a new, rather demanding requirement, essential to health and respectability, that was gradually converted into a habit and even a pleasure. Only the requirement of inducting each new generation of children into the bathing club posed a recurrent burden. Arguments for baths as relaxation began to be added to the list of benefits, a sign of acceptance though also a signal that the goals were reaching beyond the classic Victorian lexicon.[30]

Other habits of hygiene augmented the discipline of the body. In the later decades of the nineteenth century, doctors started recommending exercise as an antidote to artificially constricting fashions (for women) and a sedentary life. Concern about the nervousness that middle-class life created— the disease called neurasthenia in the 1880s—prompted additional recommendations of exercise for mental as well as physical health. Prescriptions for ideal womanhood began to split between more traditional canons of femininity and the addition of an exercise regimen. Here, as with bathing but later in time, the initial interest intensified, adding to the discipline required for bodily health. Temperance activities, although wider ranging in their social and moral implications, also had a physical and health component, as the lack of proper self-control clearly contributed to a ruined body. Important also was the growing concern about toilet training for young children. The traditional nonchalance, in which children were expected to be soiled until they were old enough to have different habits explained to them, began to change by the middle of the nineteenth century. New types of clothing replaced simple, unisex shifts, and these could be kept clean only if children were toilet trained at a younger age. Novel standards of smell and disgust attracted attention as well, which was helped along by the gradual adoption of indoor plumbing. A crucial component of Victorian discipline, and particularly bodily control, now was introduced early in life, with the additional expectations of mastery over toilet habits. The same methods of bodily control could feed the larger adherence to Victorian character norms and guilts and their attendant neuroses.[31]

Another aspect of the Victorian self-discipline of the body was the many injunctions to regulate one's stance and face. Twitches and other spontaneous body movements were frowned on, as John Adams noted in his diary as early as the 1760s. Instead, people should demonstrate their self-mastery by holding still and straight, for their outward appearance would readily display their good character to others.

The range of potential criteria in this category could be vast. The etiquette literature constantly attacked laughter, for example, from the late eighteenth century until a relaxation at the end of the nineteenth century. Lord Chesterfield's manual set the tone: "I could heartily wish that you may often be seen to smile, but never heard to laugh while you live. Frequent and loud laughter . . . is the manner in which the mob express their silly joy at silly things." The goal here was socially important, in a society concerned about personally proved distinctions as older differentiations gave way, but Chesterfield was convinced that it was not hard to attain: "Laughter is easily restrained" by realizing its absurdity and imposing rational control. The advice echoed in succeeding decades. "Frequent and loud laughter is a sure sign of a weak mind, and no less characteristic of a low education." It also was ugly, physically revolting as it contorted the face. The noise was offensive as well, particularly when issuing from women. Books for children warned against the vulgar habit of laughing in school. Extrapolating from laughter, later-nineteenth-century etiquette writers also inveighed against telling jokes, which could so easily fatigue their auditors and might lead, however unintentionally, to personal affronts. Puns were singled out for attack because they assaulted the language that was vital to communication: The "habitual punster . . . saps up your honest words and turns them into traitors before your eyes." Probity and the restraint of humor were linked. Women, again, were particularly pressed to shun wit and accordingly were viewed as humorless when they internalized the advice. The general message was clear, as a popular phrenology book put it: "Laughter is at all times ungraceful, therefore, you will observe, that vulgar people are most addicted to it: well bred persons manage this passion better, they seldom do anything more than smile."[32]

Erect posture was another goal of proper bodily control, emphasized at first to oppose the languid fashions of Britain's aristocracy. This also was protection against "vulgarity," as an upright position contrasted with the bent poses of many workers, caused by years of physical stress on the job. The absence of good posture might also denote sexual looseness, as in the dandies who frequented less reputable parts of town. Fully defined, bodily controls of all sorts were combined, and so complete mastery was important to health and sexual restraint as well as social respectability. Posture sat at the core of restraining unwanted bodily motions generally. "Writhe not your limbs in every shape / Of awkward gesture, like an ape, / No twirl your hands, nor bite your toes/ Nor keep in motion as you sit / . . . Nor lean upon another's chair. / If you must cough, or sneeze, be still / In doing it, as possible." Posture injunctions were mainly directed to children and women. "She who is desirous of presenting her personal charms in the most becoming and agreeable manner, must pay a proper regard to the orderly disposition of her whole figure, and to the general carriage of the person." Careful walking and the control of limbs were important to men as well, as the *Young Man's Companion* noted in 1866: "Awkwardness of carriage is very alienating. . . . Can anything be more inelegant than to swing the arm in such a manner?" and twitching of any sort never fails to "excite a mean opinion." Doctors and scientists increasingly picked up the same views. Evolutionists argued that good posture distinguished whites from "all the less civilized races of Men." Doctors nagged parents who ignored the frequent curvature of legs common among children, and they also attacked premature posture control that might limit the development of the limbs. A host of devices were introduced to improve health, as well as appearance, by straightening the spine.[33]

Living up to these widely urged standards of body control could be at least as challenging as attaining sexual respectability, if only because the standards in principle required constant vigilance against spontaneity. The standards pertaining to body control were even newer than those imposed on sex, for the latter built on traditional Christian morality, whereas the importance of so visibly dominating the body engaged a novel set of behaviors, never before widely encouraged except as part of some special monastic regime. Combined with the attention to cleanliness, the category in some ways pitted the middle class against their bodies, in the interests of visible restraints that would demonstrate respectability in a mixed urban society. Clothing, for example, was beginning to decline as a social indicator, because factory-produced garments gave the lower classes an opportunity to vary what they wore—though middle-class critics greatly exaggerated the resulting trends toward homogeneity. In this setting, a person could still prove breeding by control beneath the clothes, by a disciplined bearing that shouted good character. But these very standards, again perhaps even more than sexual controls, raise questions of impact: how could the middle class even pretend to act on the new demands of laughter restraint or flawless management of gesture and limb?

Rigor and Flexibility

Victorian norms of self-control became a real struggle; achieving good character was serious business. Furthermore, the rigidities urged on the body could apply to other daily conduct. It was little wonder that when depicted, Victorians preferred to look stern. Failure was easy, and even though community monitoring waned, there was a ready audience for news of business or personal collapse—and of course the two areas seemed closely related.

The urgency of the standards of restraint was reflected in the earnest culture with which Victorians surrounded themselves. Earnestness—ridiculed by late-Victorian writers like Oscar Wilde—reflected their reliance on guilt and the equation of character with health and success, plus the official rejection of humor. Self-improvement was the watchword for personal and family reading and entertainment. Attending lectures was a popular pastime, and then concentrated mainly on education, temperance, and sexual abstinence.[34] Reading taught lessons about the dire consequences of character deficiencies. Young people were given fantasies that translated ordinary norms into more dramatic formats. Story titles suggested the range: "The Ruined Son," "It Should Be Love," "A Mother's Love," "Ten Nights in a Bar-Room," "A Boy's Own War." Boys thus read about heroic acts in which courage surmounted fear, and girls were regaled with tales of sacrificial love rewarded. An essentially fantasized ideal of loving families pervaded literature for both genders. Indeed, until the 1870s, there was little for young people to read that did not have a strongly moralistic content. Tentative efforts in other recreational areas, such as sports for boys, by the 1850s, or exercise for girls, by the 1870s, were framed in terms of their service to health (including good body control) and virtue. Piano playing, a virtually obligatory social grace for girls, taught skills that would draw the family together and also had ancillary benefits, such as the frequently emphasized need to sit up straight and discipline the hands.

The wider culture did, to be sure, permit a few outlets. Stories about the consequences of depravity or the looseness of lower-class or ethnic groups might provide some titillation within an ultimately didactic context. After about 1800, as long as virtue triumphed or vice led to ruin, both fiction and crime reports could be exciting, even sexually suggestive. Beliefs about the irresponsibility of African Americans or urban workers could entertain even as they confirmed middle-class convictions of righteousness, and some of these uses of the "other" began to show up in stage shows such as minstrelsy. Crime and disaster reports even in approved newspapers often used surprisingly sensationalist vocabulary, which could provide moments of excitement that did not need to be internally censored. Later in the nineteenth century, the same held true for accounts of "natives" in exotic imperialist settings—the origins of images that made the *National Geographic* magazine both respectably informative and provocative well into the twentieth century.[35]

Even more purely moralistic reading suggested a certain amount of flexibility. A favorite theme of fiction was young men who deserted their selfless mothers, and virtue, for years of degeneracy, only to find the light and return to mother, religion, and morality in one redeeming swoop.[36] Particularly for males, who were theoretically charged with the more difficult tasks of impulse control, Victorian culture provided for the possibility of redemption. Still, in contrast to the recreational patterns that began to take shape at the end of the nineteenth century, there was no large sense of cultural alternatives that were also respectable or at least permissible. Victorians pressed home the moral lessons not only in overtly prescriptive literature but also in nearly every other venue. Alternatives did exist—a lurid "penny press" was established in the 1830s—but one of the prime purposes of Victorianism was to persuade the respectable middle class to shun such materials.

At the same time, the power of self-control should not be exaggerated. The demands were great, but they did not require restraint across the board. In suggesting several areas of flexibility, the Victorian system becomes more understandable—that is, its tenets could be obeyed because they were not uniformly repressive—and the contrasts and continuities with twentieth-century patterns become more nuanced. There are several points to make here before addressing the question about the acceptance and impact of those standards that clearly did place heavy burdens on self-control.

The gendered qualities of self-control standards provided a bit of flexibility simply because they presented somewhat different images. Men might learn from the outpourings of enthusiasm for female love, including maternal love. They also had some options in handling grief, where Victorian tolerance applied particularly but not exclusively to women. In fact, men might sometimes join women in passionate expressions even if they sometimes pulled back, living up to other control suggestions, for example, about avoiding tears.[37] Women, held to tougher norms, also learned from what men were being told. Anger might be unfeminine, but the fact that men were urged to use anger to attack injustice was a lesson available in appropriately righteous causes such as temperance, which women joined and ultimately began to lead. The idea that men had stronger sex drives might be accepted and even turned to women's moral advantage, but it could also provide the basis for arguments that women's drives, too, deserved more consideration and that men who abused Victorian beliefs by double-standard behavior should be called to account.[38]

For men and women alike, though in differing ways, Victorian standards also provided important outlets for expression that might compensate for restraint in other areas. For example, sexuality should be limited, but the intensity of love need not be. Harriet Beecher Stowe, when writing to her husband about some clergymen who had been revealed as licentious, showed how the combination might work for women:

> What terrible temptations lie in the way of your sex—till now I never realized it—for tho I did love you with an almost insane love before I married you I never knew yet or felt the pulsation which showed me that I could be tempted in that way—there never was a moment when I felt anything by which you could have drawn me astray—for I loved you as I now love God.[39]

Men, though not supported by such a restrained gender ideology, could have similar views. Women and young men were also given cultural approval for extremely close friendships with people of their own sex. Young men formed vibrant friendships that included ardent expressions of love and ample physical, though not necessarily sexual, contact. Women's letters to their friends poured out a passion that included physical elements. This outlet for intense love suggests how complex Victorian psychology might be, but it also shows that constraint could be matched by opportunities for vigorous expression. And of course, marriage provided an approved direct outlet for some sexual satisfaction as well.[40]

Other aspects of emotion were factored into the Victorian equation. Strong approval for grief and its rituals allowed both genders, particularly women, to relieve feelings that sometimes went beyond the specific loss. Men might have to restrain their anger at home, but they were encouraged to invest passion in their work and in politics. The overall criteria for discipline of the body also offered some leeway. People were enjoined to hold themselves still and erect, but the growing approval of exercise, in part to facilitate good posture, meant that this discipline was not needed all the time. A few criteria, to be sure, never wavered: there were no areas in which respectable Victorians could relax their probity (except for women, insofar as weakness might be an excuse for minor lying) and few in which sexual restraint could legitimately give way. But the overall pattern mixed control and the acceptance of intensity in potentially constructive ways.[41]

In addition, Victorian prescriptions for self-control usually were fairly general. The one exception was etiquette books, which became increasingly detailed about proper eating habits, dress, and social niceties. This expansiveness reflected the needs of the major cities' emerging upper middle class and the growing influence of European styles and aristocratic forms after the 1840s. The middle class as a whole might learn something from these books—about the appropriate way of leaving and receiving calling cards, for example, or about the proper deportment at funerals—but they were not necessarily heavily engaged. Among other things, they could not afford the elaborate clothing and place settings that the experts recommended. This was true into the twentieth century. The huge tomes written by authorities like Emily Post included sections on how to greet royalty or meet the pope, which might have influenced the middle class but hardly described its main interests. Most other prescriptive literature was far less specific. Family manuals and advice books for youth were usually fairly short, making a few general points but assuming that intricate regulations were not required. The contrast with larger, more elaborate marital and child-rearing manuals in the twentieth century was striking.[42]

Important norms might thus be sketched surprisingly quickly (by twentieth-century standards), almost in passing. Except for a few doctors who attacked the effects of women's clothing and parental habits, arguing that many children suffered from curvature of the spine, posture injunctions were usually not elaborate. A page or two sufficed to tell people that they should sit erect and walk gracefully. No special training was needed, nor were parents expected to have to harp at their offspring. A few issues did command greater attention, such as sex and the recurrent attempt to convince parents that they should control their anger and use of fear in dealing with children. For complex issues or areas in which traditional habits (as in child discipline) were being expressly attacked, a whole chapter in a prescriptive manual might be required. In other matters, however, although clear standards existed, they were not usually belabored.

There were several reasons for this. There was no clear alternative culture of self-control, so there were no models to compete against—a brief, confident statement should suffice for those already eager to be respectable. The absence of a countervailing recreational culture—the fact that approved reading and entertainment illustrated and supported, rather than defied, the accepted norms—provided part of this framework. The whole idea of character argued for people to be able to control themselves appropriately without detailed regulations. Parents could therefore teach children to be obedient, to love their parents, and to be religious; they did not need to be told how to control themselves in every conceivable situation. Nature, furthermore, was benign. Because the standards for posture used the body's natural contours, it was argued, they need not war against them. Children, as we have seen, were by nature innocent, requiring guidance but not remediation. It was also assumed that young people could keep learning, that character was not fully formed in early childhood. Thus the plethora of moralistic tones that were addressed to youth, with every expectation that character lessons were still taking hold.[43] This relieved pressure on parents and reduced the heft of explicit child-rearing articles and books. All these assumptions gradually changed, however, during the late nineteenth and early twentieth centuries, when a far more explicit approach was required.

Even though Victorian advice givers did care about consistent character and probity, their rigors were selective. Self-control mattered most in regard to responsibility for money, reproduction, health, social class relations, and the family ideal. It might be more vaguely sketched, or merely implied, for dealings with social inferiors or even sexual activities unrelated to procreation (except for the invective against masturbation). This was not an inconsistent system, but it encompassed some quiet differentials in emphasis.

Other ingredients contributed to the assured but generalized prescriptive style. Victorian advice writers believed in character, but they also believed in making sure that it was not normally asked for too much. Generations still influenced by the lessons of original sin backed up their invocations of self-discipline with systems that minimized their necessity.

Temperance laws and regulations of tavern hours were designed to reduce the need for self-control when drink was concerned, though the overall impact was debatable in the nineteenth century, and the legislation varied. Because no laws were involved, the different arrangements help explain why rigorous posture standards were not elaborately detailed. Posture injunctions could be fairly nonchalant (except for doctors' warnings, because they focused on real or imagined back problems and tried to use hyperbole to advance their health role through the general norms) because so much clothing and furniture did part of the job. Women's fashions concealed their legs while constraining the lower back, particularly when women wore corsets. Men's tight vests could not prevent a determined slouch, but they tended to remind their wearers of good carriage at least from the waist up, particularly when sitting. Parlor furniture encouraged good posture as well. Chairs were made of wood and had stiff backs. Only the rocking chair, which drew considerable attention because of its relaxed qualities, might encourage a lounging posture, and so it was usually not found in middle-class homes until later in the century. Indeed, the anti–rocking chair sentiment countered the more traditional colonial tolerance.[44]

Sexual constraints depended at least as much on arrangement as on willpower, at least until the courtship period. Young men spent relatively little time with women outside the family. Social gatherings and community fairs allowed the sexes to mix, particularly in smaller towns and particularly before 1860, but adults were present to supervise, and close contacts were rarely formed. Members of the two genders worked apart, and they usually attended different schools after the primary grades. Instead, they socialized with each other—hence the intense same-sex friendships—and young men provided the hundreds of thousands who flocked to the all-male lodges characteristic of the period (and largely gone today). It is little surprise that men like Daniel Webster professed an almost complete ignorance of women and also great trepidation when economic circumstances finally permitted courtship, usually in their later twenties. Exceptions included contacts with servants and other lower-class women. But interaction with respectable women was highly circumscribed, thereby reducing the need for advice manuals to comment in detail on norms (except in more scientific or pseudoscientific discussions about sexuality).[45]

Aside from attacks on the use of fear with children, arrangements to support emotional restraint were harder to find. Gender rules could help support the norms. For instance, a docile, submissive wife might make it more difficult for males in the family to become angry. In fact, a recent study of Oregon suggests that as a result, abuse in middle-class homes declined in the later nineteenth century. There were other informal structures as well. When at home, husbands, at least those in the upper middle class, might spend considerable time in a separate room, the library. Wives and children were careful not to disturb them until the rigors of the working day had worn off. Children who frolicked around their mother knew it was best to withdraw to their own area when their father was home, thereby reinforcing the image of an anger-free family.[46]

Finally, in part because character was touted rather generally, with few specific guidelines for restraint, the Victorian standards were transmitted and received with a number of interesting gaps. Again, sex was the most obvious exception, except for women who absolutely defied the injunctions or men who dallied with prostitutes or the like. Sexual norms were meant to be observed scrupulously, at least when both genders were involved. In contrast, homosexuality was not explicitly discussed; indeed, a full terminology was not compiled until the end of the century. Sodomy was a sin and a crime, though only occasionally pursued. It did not command general attention and was not used to enforce standard character norms. Although what we now call homosexuality was surely not condoned, it may have been so abhorred that comment seemed unnecessary (as with bestiality today). But given the extensiveness of homosocial physical contacts, the absence of even veiled, explicit standards is interesting, with one result that we can only guess at the amount of bisexuality among youth and even adult friends. Women might write to their friends: "I wanted so to put my arms round my girl of all the girls in the world. . . . I love her as wives do love their husbands . . . and I believe in her as I believe in my God." And men to men: "Our hearts were full of that true friendship which could not find utterance by words, we laid our heads upon each other's bosom and wept, it may be unmanly to weep, but I care not, the spirit was touched."[47]

Gaps in the monitoring of children were at least as suggestive, particularly in regard to boys. In many respects, strict controls were expected but in fact, many urban and small-town middle-class boys roamed surprisingly freely after school hours. The middle-class "boy culture" was full of fights and dares. It borrowed adult standards, particularly in tests that would elicit bravery and the anger to fight back; the word sissy helped codify a widely held set of norms. But this culture was not restrained: it ignored cleanliness and posture controls, it shunned elaborate emotional constraints; and it even, through boasting and tall tales, stretched the injunctions of honesty.[48]

Similarly, school discipline was often loose and inconsistent, hardly bent on enforcing self-control. Schoolmasters had to suffer elaborate pranks and mockery. Punishments enforced posture along the school benches, and well into the twentieth century, school pictures showed that schoolchildren or their superiors wanted to display an erect stance for the record. The emphasis on rote memorization was discipline in itself and possibly, as some pedagogues argued, excellent moral preparation for self-control in later life. But the constraints were incomplete, as collective rowdiness then was far more common than in the middle-class schoolrooms of the twentieth century.[49]

Likewise, emotional norms were not advocated across the board, except by individuals who, because of personality or the internalization of character goals, might extend their reach. For men, particularly, the injunction to keep anger at bay was not specifically applied to work or public life. This is why politicians, with no inconsistency, could so openly display passion and even fight. This is why many employers, some of them carefully decorous at home, used anger as a whip in dealing with subordinates at work. Shop rules existed, of course, but they were directed at the working class, and although they regulated impulse, at least in principle—for example, by insisting on punctuality—they did not recommend a specific emotional style. As a result, swearing, shouting, and even outright rage were not uncommon on the factory floor or in the shopkeeper's dealings with his assistants. At times, the bosses easily outdid even protesting workers with displays of wrath. During a strike in Fall River, Massachusetts, one mill owner, infuriated at having to discuss conditions with his labor force, repeatedly got excited, pounding on the table and cursing, demanding violent police reprisals, and firing his own gun in the air. Around 1900, Chicago workers found their employers frequently "raging like tigers," even in dealing with individual operatives who had incurred their wrath. Character either did not apply in these settings or yielded to higher imperatives of economic mastery.[50]

The incompleteness of the application of self-control opened the way for greater latitude in practice than some of the general invocations of restrained character might suggest. It even helped certain individuals to live up to important restraints. Thus the boss who vented his anger at work might find it easier to remain calm at home. In dealing with subordinates or operating in public spheres, effective self-control standards were partly a matter of individual choice.

This does not mean that the standards were hollow or easy to live up to. Character and its attributes in appearance and behavior were important. Members of the Victorian middle class liked to feel virtuous. Real effort went into socializing children in some of the norms of self-control, including the appropriate management of sexuality and the body. Opportunities for middle-class congratulation were enhanced by stories of failure, in which men fell from their social rung because of drink, gambling, or debauchery or women lost the support of their family because they were caught with a lover or came home pregnant but unmarried. Even more generally, the pervasive sense of moral superiority over the lower classes, immigrants, and blacks confirmed the importance of good character and the special claims of the middle class. Poverty, after all, was due more to an absence of self-control than any other factor. If the lower classes curbed their sex drives, treated their children with greater care, and monitored their spending impulses, they could accumulate some savings and possibly rise in the world—this was the flip side of the rags-to-riches stories. According to this view, differences in character were the crucial social variable. The insouciance of minstrel-show blacks might be fleetingly envied—they provided examples of greater spontaneity than the middle class could afford—but in the end, stereotypes of this sort confirmed class pride in maintaining and, by contrast to the other, achieving virtue.[51]

Impact

Finally, the standards counted in real life, which is hardly surprising given the passion with which they were set forth and the various settings and cultural supports involved. Some lessons had to be repeated during the nineteenth century and later, such as the explicit attacks on parental uses of fear, which suggests that some of the new restraints were difficult to accept. And of course, there were many instances of individual or even collective failure, in part because some of the standards were so demanding. Adultery by middle-class women was probably uncommon, because it could be detected so easily given the confinement in which most women lived, because the consequences could be so dire, and because of intense childhood socialization. Nonetheless, some women did have extramarital affairs, and about which some of them wrote with great enthusiasm.[52] A few women had intercourse during courtship, with no apparent remorse, although a larger minority felt great guilt despite the imminence of marriage. Middle-class men, far more commonly, might abuse female servants or use prostitutes. This double standard began to create a bifurcated male sexual ethic, in which "good" girls and even wives had to restrain themselves but men had to demonstrate their sexual stamina with whores in order to prove their manhood. Theft, family fights, and heavy drinking also occurred.[53]

Yet even deviations might reflect the standards. The norms were enforced through stories about the consequences of failure, and the stories could be true. Indeed, the importance of deviance in solidifying mainstream values is often found in the study of society and culture, and it certainly helped support Victorian self-control. In addition, many of the more systematic deviations were carefully concealed so that they would not shatter the veneer of respectability. Hypocrisy protected individuals—like the young men who visited prostitutes—but it also confirmed the validity of the standards of restraint.

Many people struggled hard to control themselves. Lucilla McCorkle, a southern minister's wife, wrote in her diary: "Self-denial—in food & clothing & keeping the tongue. early rising—industry—economy—cheerfulness & sobriety—keeping down & quelling the spirit of malevolence, fault finding—covetousness or rather jealousy." Charlotte Gilman reflected on these goals: "The task of self-government was not easy. To repress a harsh answer, to confess a fault, and to stop (right or wrong) in the midst of self-defence, in gentle submission, sometimes requires a struggle like life and death." The hold of self-control could reach deep: a Pittsburgh girl admired a friend who said, "Oh, the dickens," but quickly added, "Since even the mildest oaths were discouraged at home, I never dared use such a vigorous expletive." At an extreme, of course, the effort to restrict their emotions could cost women their health, and psychosomatic disorders like hysterical paralysis were an indication of the rebellion against the curbs on impulse, but at the cost of further passivity.[54]

Men wrestled, too, although they were not as likely to put their struggles on paper. The oft-told story of Abe Lincoln walking miles to pay back a small loan symbolized the effort of many men to be honest and to be seen as honest in financial dealings. By the end of the nineteenth century, the need to adopt a less domineering style with children did gradually lead to a new kind of middle-class father, less the patriarch and more the pal.[55]

Middle-class efforts at self-control produced some pressure points, however, that no amount of regulation or evasion could ignore. Courtship was an example. It occurred after adolescence. It was surrounded by an intense disapproval of premature pregnancy, including the examples of presumed lower-class indulgence, and prepared by the strictures for both genders against childhood sexual explorations. It was framed by a definition of love deliberately designed to elicit elaborate statements of passion that were not overtly sexual. But surprisingly, courtship itself was not supervised, particularly in the middle decades of the century. Courting couples did kiss and touch, even as they declared religious-like devotion. They fantasized about each other quite openly. Men and women alike had to fight against their desires (despite claims by people like Harriet Beecher Stowe that they felt none). Some gave in, often suffering from guilt and recrimination afterward. Some others held back for years but then let go when a wedding finally could be scheduled. But more did not give in at all because both parties agreed that respectability superseded temporary pleasure.

The system rested on restraint and guilt, with parents hovering in the background. A girl responds to some minor "liberties" by her suitor: "Surely, thought I, he must have mistaken my Character." Self-control, indeed, counted for more than claims of the female lack of passion, as both men and women noted. The rare lapses normally brought remorse from both parties, though with gendered differences. After she had probably had intercourse, a Wisconsin woman observed: "I own I think you to blame in some degree. That is, for not accepting my first denial. . . . We have both done wrong. I have done much the greater because I should have acted the part of a true, noble, Christian woman." "I failed in the full possession of my reason and judgment, thus giving strength to your desire." But "we made firm resolves and the next opportunity showed how they were kept." This last couple were able to contain themselves during the several remaining years before their marriage, showing that although the system was flawed, it worked.[56]

Another common crisis: dealing with servants. Although the norms for self-control did not clearly apply to many workplaces, servants posed a special problem. Some wives blithely used servants as outlets for their anger—much as their husbands did with workers, particularly when racial differences made the mistreatment seem trivial. But servanthood had distinctive qualities that could encourage greater restraint. Servants lived in the home, that center of emotional rectitude, and they interacted with women, brought up to suppress their anger. Yet servants frequently seemed infuriating when they defied their employers, failed to live up to standards of cleanliness, and worked slowly. Their conditions of employment and their diverse backgrounds hardly motivated a consistent embrace of middle-class ideals. Consequently, many wife-employers grew angry or had difficulty turning the other cheek. It is not surprising that the tensions of dealing with servants—how awful they were, but also how embarrassing the resulting shouting matches—peppered middle-class conversation throughout the century or that, toward the century's end when household appliances became more abundant, many wives preferred to alleviate the problem by ending the practice of live-in servants.[57]

Marriage itself posed a problem because, like courtship, it was defined as a mixture of control and ardor. In principle, the standards of self-mastery and domesticity urged restraint of anger, some sexual activity (but how much and with what degree of pleasure were left unclear), plus mutual friendship and even love. We simply do not know how most marriages worked out in practice. A few obviously failed, with angry quarrels and disputes over sex. Even the growing trickle of divorces reflected a lack of self-control or of sufficient love. Many men, ardent friends with other men before courtship and also ardent suitors, preoccupied themselves with their work, retiring to the library when at home, and avoiding the difficult emotional juggling act. Because their behavior was proper and controlled, it was difficult to criticize. After all, being a good provider, not the ability to display emotions, was the ultimate Victorian criterion for a good husband. But men of "good character" who limited family involvements by oversimplifying the equation and omitting passion left many wives somewhat adrift, needing to throw themselves into motherhood, friendships with other women, or reform activities that might vent some of their feelings about men in general. Restraint, more than its defiance, was surely the most common problem in middle-class married life, but the issue of balance was not always resolved. The continuing need to limit sexual activity in the interests of birth control—abstinence was still necessary in the 1890s—though it might be mutually agreed on, could add to the tensions of daily married life.[58]

Determining how closely certain standards were observed is difficult. Posture standards were widely accepted, but as we have seen, they were supported by physical arrangements as much as by self-discipline. In fact, they were not normally viewed as a problem. The injunctions against laughter deserve further inquiry; surely they were not taken literally. Yet during the nineteenth century, foreign visitors often found the American middle class rather humorless. Furthermore, the desire to appear serious, as in photographs for posterity, suggests that these standards, too, had an impact.

Most tellingly, key standards measurably changed behaviors. Sex, especially, reflected the admonitions to maintain a good character. In the second half of the eighteenth century, the sexual habits of American young people had been loosening as community controls began to unravel and new commercial opportunities expanded their horizons. This increasing commitment to individualism often was interpreted as authorization for individual pleasure seeking. The result was a rising rate of illegitimate births, the most quantifiable evidence that sex outside marriage was becoming more common. The insistence on sexual restraint as a badge of civilized conduct thus was designed to encourage the use of birth control amid the declining community enforcement; that is, the goal was to reverse the behavioral trends by insisting on self-control, particularly by respectable women. And the effort paid off, more in the United States than in any of the Western societies that had undergone the eighteenth-century "sexual revolution." Even though interest in sex remained high and slips did occur, the number of illegitimate births fell by about 50 percent (rates of illegitimacy to rates of all births). Concealment or abortion may have contributed to these figures, but in the best Victorian fashion, abortions were outlawed in the early nineteenth century precisely to reduce this option for sexual irresponsibility. The acceptance of control, therefore, was the key factor.[59]

Victorianism succeeded in a society in which the material and symbolic rewards for self-control were quite real. It caused strain. It harbored internal tensions. It produced individual defiance and failure. Its success depended heavily on arrangements new to the period—like the growing social separation between men and women or, culturally, the assumption of women's superior innate virtue—as well as on self-control. The goals of restraint were used to assess other individuals and other social groups. Self-control affected basic human behaviors, from the presentation of emotion to the restraint of the body to reactions to sexual desire.

The various aspects of Victorian self-control presented a mixture of opportunities for subsequent development, and their complexities helped predict later change. The standards could be maintained; in fact, their flexibility moderated the repressive costs. They could be extended to other groups and not used only for the middle class's self-definition. These standards could also loosen, particularly in the more demanding applications. Certain pressure points, like courtship, could be restructured. But the standards could also be tightened in key respects, clarifying some of the imprecision and closing some of the loopholes. This perhaps was the most unexpected face of Victorianism: the wide areas of behavior left untouched because of assumptions that generalized good character would prevail or the belief that more vigorous emotions and physical expressions were required.

FOUR

Transitions

Between 1880 and 1920, Victorianism was substantially redefined and, in some respects, decisively rejected. A full statement of the characteristic twentieth-century patterns of self-control did not emerge until the second quarter of the new century, but the process of implicit reevaluation was launched well before this point. This chapter discusses some of the signs of transition before looking into the causes of these changes and more fully evaluating these innovations.

Because these decades were transitional, the signals were mixed, so this is not a story of steadily advancing experimentation. Some elements of Victorianism remained intact, and there were striking shifts as well. Certain changes clearly represented attempts to accommodate old values to new needs. Finally, and most revealingly, innovation included important new standards of control that satisfied the quest for character in novel ways and with a novel vocabulary. Even in our overview of the intermediate decades—but with some spillover into the 1920s—the complexity of the relationship between Victorian and contemporary goals and methods of self-restraint shines through.

Commonplaces

One important though hardly surprising change involved the signs that elements of Victorian self-control were becoming so widely accepted that they no longer needed to be constantly reiterated. For example, laws and regulations continued to limit spitting in public places, but in fact it no longer was a big problem and so the public postings were withdrawn. Most Americans learned in childhood not to spit, without special assistance from advice givers. In addition, the greater acceptance of the germ theory, particularly between 1910 and 1920 when the influenza epidemic demonstrated the theory's relevance, quietly increased the pressure against spitting: the United States became a society of diminishing expectorations.

The same trend applied to the advice about using fear to discipline children, which had been a staple of family manuals since the 1820s. The need to warn against this Christian/popular tradition, to use images of death and damnation or visions of bogeymen to keep children in line, was a deep-rooted tradition. And the use of fear surely persisted, as it was definitively undermined in American Catholic culture only after World War II. Even more recent studies of isolated rural areas show that parents are still using frightening animals or other objects of terror to stop their children's crying. Nevertheless, the most blatant practices did recede, even in many immigrant groups, and by the 1920s the middle class and those who offered advice in its name clearly felt that the problem was in hand. Advice manuals began omitting this long-standard section. A new kind of concern took its place, however. Not only should fear not be used, but in the view of twentieth-century experts, children were so fragile that even courage should not be strenuously invoked. Children's fright was common, but now instead of urging boys to buck up, parents should sympathize while exploring every means possible to avoid potential scares. Thus although the validity of Victorian advice remained, it had been internalized, and so attention turned to other parental tasks.[1]

Compromises

Some developments reflected a desire to retain basic Victorian virtues while acknowledging that accommodations to a more complex modern reality also were necessary. The recognition of vice districts, the redlight sections of major cities, was an example after the 1880s, when police officials and policymakers conceded that certain activities would take place no matter how many laws were passed. The value of self-control remained high, however; respectable people should not engage in such practices or at least should keep it secret. But there were impulses, particularly male impulses, that could not be denied. The solution was to situate the necessary outlets in a single, lower-class section of town apart from the main business district, though usually close to it and carefully screened from the respectable residential areas. It could be further assumed that most of the people who used the prostitutes and gambling dens were not respectable anyway—they were Asian immigrants, workers, and other low types. But the districts did afford some middle-class men new opportunities for double-standard sexual behavior, and with this, the recognition that sexuality could not always be controlled in strictly Victorian terms gained ground.[2]

"Slumming" was a similar and related compromise that helped the middle and upper-middle classes in the larger cities modify their leisure behavior without admitting that their standards had loosened. Leisure could still be respectable. Indeed, in the late nineteenth century, efforts increased to isolate certain cultural traditions as deserving subdued spectator response rather than the rowdiness endemic among more popular audiences just a quarter-century earlier. In this view, Shakespearean plays now were highbrow museum pieces at which middle-class aficionados could display their good breeding, free from both boisterousness and lower-class attendance. But the desire for more exuberant entertainment and spontaneous behavior took some of these same people to ethnic and working-class sections of town to hear lively music and watch stage shows like the popular vaudeville. This effort to milk lower-class culture continued into the 1920s, with the popularity of visits to Harlem. In sum, although standards still existed, they no longer defined whole behaviors.[3]

Another kind of compromise, traced by historian Jackson Lears, was the merging of health criteria and consumerism. Middle-class Americans continued the process of acquisition during the later nineteenth century, and they were also surrounded by an unprecedented amount of advertising. Materialism, however, continued to connote false gods and a potential lack of control. It was no accident, therefore, that also in this period, accounts of kleptomania, the uncontrolled theft of consumer items, created a new category of deviance. A problem for the middle class, then, was combining a new interest and opportunity with a sense of appropriateness and restraint; merely not being a kleptomaniac would not suffice. In a sense, this issue became fundamental for the twentieth-century style of self-control, but a specific accommodation around 1900 was both revealing and important in itself. New goods could be bought without compunction if they improved health and if they also coincided with appeals to both a scientific cachet and a sense of nostalgia for a purer life in days gone by. Thus shredded wheat was touted as both a natural food—"Mothers, do you not know that children crave natural food until you pervert their taste by the use of unnatural food?"—and the product of the "most hygienic and scientific food laboratory in the world." Consumers could safely indulge in not only the widening array of health products but also new kinds of toilet tissue, secure that higher goals were being served: harsh toilet paper, for example, caused irritation that "is not only a source of discomfort but also a possible seat of infection." Lucky Strike cigarettes made "the red blood leap and tingle!" "No other tobacco gives you that old tasty yum-yum out-of-doors smack you get from Lucky Strike."[4]

New Arenas

Along with compromise, the application of essentially Victorian manners to new settings helped form the pattern of change during the turn-of-the-century decades. The arrival of more female clerical workers, for example, imposed more home-style etiquette on certain work sites, such as federal civil service offices, beginning as early as the 1870s. Male workers reduced their swearing and expressions of anger on the job while also trying to control their use of sexually suggestive words and gestures. This was not necessarily difficult, as the standards already existed, but it did represent an important extension.

Manners crept into the workplace also in the training given to department store clerks, most of whom were female and of working-class origin. To please a middle-class clientele, clerks had to be taught habits of cleanliness, neat dress, and courteous response. Again, the basic ideas were not novel, but they now went beyond older self-control standards to include careful responses even to angry, unreasonable customers. The main point was the application of norms to work and to additional groups of Americans.[5]

Technology might also require innovation in applying established canons of courtesy and restraint to unfamiliar devices. The telephone is an example. Here was a device that could bring contact with strangers into the home and for which there was no clear precedent. The reliance on party lines in rural areas and small towns was another cause for concern, as conversations could be overheard or lines monopolized by a single user. Finally, telephone operators, again recruited from the ranks of lower-class women, helped determine telephone use in these first decades. The response, predictably enough, was the inclusion of phone habits in the standard etiquette books, along with special training programs for operators. People needed to learn what greeting to use, how to identify themselves, how long to let the telephone ring, how to handle wrong numbers without irritation—minor matters, perhaps, but requiring additional lessons in self-control, for spontaneous reactions might be inappropriate. These, too, were more habits to teach children. The rules that were worked out accorded with established forms of etiquette—anger at a person calling a wrong number was clearly unacceptable, for example. By the 1930s, the growing use of automobiles required another, more significant extension of self-control norms in which, again, innovation combined with some of the ideas of restraint that had been emphasized during the nineteenth century.[6]

Permissiveness

Along with continuities and successful internalization, compromise, and extensions to new settings, all part of the persistent Victorian standards, the transitional decades witnessed some striking changes. These shifts, in turn, had two different trajectories: they either reduced previous self-control goals and the arrangements that had helped bolster them, or they introduced demanding new norms.

As an example, social interactions between young men and women became noticeably more common, and male friendship and solidarity correspondingly declined. With more and more middle-class youth of both sexes attending high school, and a minority even going on to college, coeducational schooling became a factor in these interactions. After 1910, the new practice of dating began to replace courtship and included a wider array of social activities, an intertwining of courting and consumerism, and a greater distance from regular adult presence. The nineteenth-century custom of close male friendships waned at the same time, particularly between people in their twenties. Attendance at male lodges, which had once been extraordinarily popular, began to dwindle to such an extent that after 1920 lodges formed an insignificant part of middle-class social life. Obviously, these changes meant the reduction of some of the principal structural arrangements of Victorian life that had moderated the need for active sexual self-control. At the same time, a rapidly growing hostility to homosexuality—plus the introduction of the term itself—presented a new constraint in the dealings of men with one another. The idea of sleeping in the same bed with another man—a commonplace in nineteenth-century hotels—or male-to-male touches or embraces became taboo—another striking reversal of Victorian beliefs and practices that eliminated one of the outlets for passion (whether or not actively sexual) that had implicitly supported the traditional system of restraint.[7]

Between 1880 and 1920, the use of nudity in public advertisements suddenly soared. Little flesh had been respectably exposed during the classic Victorian decades. Indeed, yards of cloth—up to eleven hundred yards for one dress for a wealthy woman—were needed to cover the respectable female form. But by 1880, changes in fashion began to modify this requirement. The newly popular use of corsets and bustles accentuated elements of the female form. Skirts became shorter—by 1905, the Sears catalog advised at least two inches above the ground. Exercise and bicycle riding dictated less restrictive clothing for both genders, at least in some public settings. Looser shirtwaists and bloomers were less confining. As early as the 1860s, female theater stars displayed a fair number of their charms, and even though they were not fully respectable, the fashion leadership of such stars began to be established. Plays like the *Naiad Queen* in the 1860s had women wearing tights to portray soldiers, and the *Black Crook* was touted as a breakthrough that was respectable because it was ballet, even though the costumes were quite daring. Women began to take new roles in circus performances, including bareback riding, for which again costumes might be quite scanty. New publications, including erotic "cigarette cards" and the *Police Gazette*, showed women in revealing poses or even in the nude. Some New York bars pictured nude women in their exterior signs, and an 1885 advertisement for German Bitters showed a woman with her breast exposed. These extremes might have been outside respectable limits, but only because they exaggerated the more general shifts in norms.

A counterthrust developed after 1900. The Associated Advertising Clubs of the World established a vigilance committee in 1911, mainly to ensure accuracy but also to reduce blatant sexuality. Depictions of products rather than sexual fantasies reflected the new realism of commercial art, but the idea of associating sex with sales did not disappear. The endorsement of products by Hollywood stars kept the linkage alive, and specific images, such as an ethereal but definitely nude female torso for a brand of club soda, maintained eroticism only a slight distance away from literal representations. The first Miss America contest, in 1921, introduced the swimsuit competition that would become the pageant's oft-debated hallmark—and the idea of having a woman revealing that much of her body to be celebrated for beauty made perfect sense in what had become a distinctly un-Victorian framework.[8]

By the end of the transitional period, even envy began to be praised. What had long been reproved was now valued as a logical component of consumer behavior. Criticisms of immigrants and women for lacking self-restraint and overspending did not disappear, but they diminished considerably, for spending was now a good thing, not a target for control. After about 1915, publications directed at rural women acknowledged the legitimacy of the desire to be stylish, to envy the easy fashionableness of urban women. Instead of curbing envy in order to delight in rural values, the new wisdom advised that the emotion be indulged so that rural women would learn to dress just as well. Agricultural extension offices began to offer assistance in making currently popular garments like kimonos, shirtwaists, and bloomers, and the most popular lecture of the Cornell Extension Service in 1924 was entitled "The Well Dressed Woman." More generally, a 1911 article in the *Saturday Evening Post* recommended spending as much as possible on creating a good appearance, under the heading "The Sin of Homeliness, the Duty of Every Woman to Be Well Dressed." No longer was the problem extravagance but, rather, the need to cast off old notions of dressing only to one's station in life. Simon Patten, an economist at the University of Pennsylvania's Wharton School of Business, observed in 1913: "It is no evidence of loose morality when a stenographer, earning eight or ten dollars a week, appears dressed in clothing that takes nearly all of her earnings to buy. It is a sign of her growing moral development"—in part because it might help her obtain a better job or

a better husband. Advertisers, naturally, exploited this new moral compass: "Don't Envy Beauty—Use Pompeian and Have It." Palmolive
asked: "The Envied Girl—Are you one? Or are you still seeking the
secret of charm?" Envy had now become an acceptable enticement for
positive action or positive buying, and it did not need to be restrained.[9]

New Demands for Discipline

The second path of innovation highlighted the unprecedented demands
for self-control, like the insistence on avoiding any taint of homosexuality. Some controls followed from the growing emphasis on fashion,
although they required a real effort at discipline. Others responded to
more complex needs and might entail an even greater struggle. Three
examples illustrate this aspect of the transition period.

Between 1915 and 1919, beauty consultants and advertisers launched
what one historian has called "The Great Underarm Campaign," designed to persuade women to shave their body hair in crucial spots. A
legs campaign soon followed. Since dresses in the nineteenth century
had concealed them, this was, almost by definition, a new issue (though
upper-class women in some other cultures had long shaved or waxed
their legs). Only stage performers had used depilatories; now chorus
girls pioneered in what soon, ironically, became a requirement for a
respectable modern appearance. With more revealing clothing, and also
to demonstrate that showing more body was not an excuse for displaying poor discipline or yielding to the purely natural, women more generally were persuaded to follow this new practice. In a short time,
American middle-class women were in the vanguard of the Western
world as body hair became disgusting and its removal a new if minor
mark of civilization. Advertisers picked up the new concern: "Are your
arms constantly pinned to your sides? Or do you scorn to wear the filmy
or sleeveless frocks that the vogue of the day decrees? In either case, He
is apt to think you lifeless and behind the times. He will notice you
holding yourself aloof from the swing of convention." "When you go
to the beach this summer, are you going to be afraid to raise your arms?
Are you going to shrink from the scrutinizing glance of your friends?"
Here, too, was a new way to do what Victorian standards had done:
separate oneself from cruder people, lower class and immigrant, whose

hairiness suggested their inferior stock and, however irrelevantly, con- noted a lack of hygiene.[10]

The successful campaign to eliminate body hair is admittedly a trivial point, though it continues to require a great deal of time and debate over principle. Its timing and the aesthetic standards associated with it are nevertheless significant. Changes in dress, women's roles, and even sexuality had to be matched by a countervailing discipline in the name of beauty and cleanliness. Hair had to go, save as a means of protesting bourgeois standards of self-control and consumer morality.

More serious, although suggesting some of the same needs for disci- plinary compensation, was another great innovation of the transitional decades: the hostility to fat and to being overweight, and the concomi- tant insistence on slenderness and dieting. In the United States, this movement became noticeable in the mid-1890s, after several decades in which a certain amount of plumpness represented good health and prosperity and in which slender women seemed ugly. As recently as the 1880s, medical experts, citing the concern about neurasthenia, had at- tributed excessive nervousness to a slender frame: "Plumpness, round- ness, size . . . are rightly believed to indicate well-balanced health." The about-face was both abrupt and impassioned. Never before, except as part of a special religious discipline, had attacks on body fat been so intense and widespread as they became by the early years of the new century.[11]

During the 1890s, media images moved noticeably toward slender- ness, including *Life* magazine's famous Gibson girl, stage beauties like Sarah Bernhardt (rejected as homely in an earlier American visit), and the heroines of pornographic novels: "She had a waist naturally small." Echoing developments in France, corsetry was attacked as well: fashion- able women should be truly, not artificially, slender. The *Ladies Home Journal* began carrying regular diet advice columns, presaging one of the longest-lasting themes of the twentieth century. In addition, a moral, as well as a physical, message was present from the outset. "Con- stant work will . . . do more to reduce your flesh than anything else"; "put in plain words that means if women were less lazy they would not grow so stout." Men were targeted also. It was in the 1890s that Bernarr McFadden began staging his bodybuilding shows. His exercise maga- zine, *Physical Culture*, quickly acquired a substantial subscription list, using morally loaded terms like slob (introduced into the language only a few years earlier) to drive the point home.[12]

The rapid currency of these new ideas and commercial gimmicks designed to cash in on the craze was amazing. The Fat Man's Club of Connecticut, formed in 1866 when plumpness was acceptable, closed in 1903. A play called *Nobody Loves a Fat Man* opened in 1907. Fat jokes, as well as insulting neologisms, became common. Edith Lowry, writing in 1919, claimed that in 1900 a woman could grow fat and old in peace, but by 1905 someone always seemed to be asking, "Why don't you reduce?" World War I added a nationalistic element, particularly for men: "Any healthy, normal individual, who is now getting fat is unpatriotic." Along with the diversity of arguments and the speed of their dissemination, what was most impressive about the change was its moral fervor. Fat was not just a problem or a health concern (indeed, medical arguments only gradually caught up with the first phases of the craze); it was repulsive, a disgrace. A 1900 novel caught the mood as the beautiful slender heroine caught sight of an opposite: "It was sheer horror that held Susan's gaze, upon Violet's incredible hips and thighs, violently obtruded by the close-reefed corset." A magazine article caught the same, if novel, association of fat control with character in the 1916 article "Fat is now regarded as an indiscretion, and almost as a crime." The first diet cookbook, introduced in 1900 and selling wildly by 1914, self-servingly added in its preface: "An excess of flesh is looked upon as one of the most objectionable forms of disease."[13]

As they were fighting fat, up-to-date Americans were also learning how to combat excessive grief. They repudiated Victorian standards, not in favor of greater permissiveness but, rather, greater control. The idea of a "modern," nonchalant attitude toward death began to surface between 1900 and 1920, and Victorian mourning rituals were now seen as perverse. Medical advance, not sadness, was to be the watchword: "Perhaps the most distinctive note of the modern spirit is the practical disappearance of the thought of death as an influence directly bearing upon practical life." Science, it was claimed, refuted any idea that death was usually an agony, so the living should be free to get on with their own activities without too much emotional or religious baggage. Traditional views remained, of course: "We are perfected in character in the school of suffering." But the dominant plea was for self-control and innovation: "Probably nothing is sadder in life than the thought of all the hours that are spent in grieving over what is past and irretrievable." People were advised to think about their own health and not wallow; those who could not "rouse themselves" needed "the care of a physician." This was a line of thought that hardened after 1920 when psychologists defined "grief work" as getting one's emotion under control and when even etiquette books turned from describing mourning rituals to arguing that the grieving person was placing unseemly burdens on her friends.[14]

All these new control standards prevailed throughout the rest of the twentieth century. Two points are important. First, any attempt to explain the movement away from Victorian standards must include the causes of both the new constraints and the new freedoms. Second, in anticipating the explanation, note that the new freedoms themselves compelled a counterbalancing discipline. The result was un-Victorian, but it retained an essentially Victorian moralism and the need to find tests of and measurements for personal discipline.

New Battles

Nothing illustrates the complexity of the transitional period better than the new struggle over posture. Here, the old standards were maintained in principle, but the arguments and, above all, the methods had to change, for at the same time, the characteristic nineteenth-century supports for posture were progressively loosened. The result was a new call for willpower to take over the job that the makers of clothing and furniture had once helped perform.

Although actual posture patterns began to loosen, until the 1930s people still liked to hold themselves erect for photographs. Furniture moved away from rigid confinement until by 1910 the parlor was renamed the more relaxation-friendly living room. Couches and easy chairs (again a revealing name) became more upholstered and comfortable. The trend was defended as early as 1883 as doing

> a great deal towards civilizing the people generally. It seems to us impossible for the human race to be good-natured and good tempered if forced to sit in a "bolt-upright" position in the extreme corner of a horse-hair

covered sofa, with arms and back built on the very straightest and most perpendicular principle.

The shift in goals toward easy social relations rather than character was as significant as the new furniture. Along with this shift came the looser costumes and exercise outfits, which attacked structured attire in the name of greater bodily freedom, and new, more supple dance styles replaced the stiff stance of the waltz. Always alert, advertisers and commercial artists began to picture more lounging scenes; the Gibson girl, for example, now posed leaning on her arm or fashionably bent.[15]

Thus far, these changes suggest an important movement away from Victorian standards, like the shift concerning envy or the new patterns of dating. Casualness replaced strict demands of character. But in the case of posture there was a rapid counterattack, precisely because the standards seemed so important and because a new professional group saw an advantage in their defense. Not surprisingly, etiquette manuals long maintained the Victorian trajectory, urging good posture especially at the dining table. Doctors stepped up their arguments that good posture was vital to health, adding a new claim that slouching caused the organs to overlap, impeding proper functioning. Many child-rearing specialists used posture as a means of condemning deteriorating standards overall. Posture was vital not only to health but also for its "moral effect on the whole body." At the same time, the greater demands of school were blamed for harming children, causing them to slump over their reading. "For if the State compels the child to go to school, and to undergo the constant risk of developing curvature of the spine . . . universal education must be considered as at least a doubtful blessing."[16]

Amid these new and old concerns, rescue came in the form of the new physical education movement. Its *American Physical Education Review*, founded in 1898, quickly picked up the posture banners with all their various claims and added that appropriate education and school-based checkups could provide the solution. During the early twentieth century, this new breed of experts generated detailed charts through which various posture ailments could be diagnosed. The move toward actual posture courses in schools and colleges began around 1913. Jessie Bancroft claimed that special lessons introduced into the Brooklyn public schools in that year achieved 40 percent gains in a single term. In

1914, she founded the American Posture League, which endured for thirty years. This new educational and diagnostic approach first showed the child what the problem was, by means of a thorough physical inspection, sometimes including photographs. Then the child learned exercises to correct the deficiencies. The desired outcome was continued self-control in the interest of holding the body properly. A "posture crusade" in the Detroit schools in 1913 graded each child's posture and encouraged competition for improvement; shadow pictures projected each fault onto a screen so that the class could jeer the offender. Finally, colleges like Vassar instituted posture checks for each student during the 1880s and 1890s and began to discuss remedial measures.[17]

This was just a beginning, for the posture counterattack reverberated until after the mid-twentieth century. The origins of the counterattack in the transitional decades are revealing. Habits were changing, but a sense of standards and the need for willpower, now aided by powerful educational efforts, persisted. The result was new and complicated, just as the other changes were.

Prohibition, a last gasp of Victorianism-turned-to-regulation, similarly warred against degeneracy, though in this case the degeneracy was less new and the targets were not middle-class (and working-class) children, but working-class adults. But the advocates of temperance ultimately despaired of self-control and so turned to law. Similarly, after decades of laissez-faire, in which the widespread use of opiates was permitted, though hardly admired, laws were enlisted to attack opium products that sapped character and health alike, giving birth to the requirement of prescriptions.[18]

A Time of Struggle

Various combinations of persistence and change were tried during these transitional decades. Some Victorian values emerged intact, even more widely and deeply shared. In other areas, innovation superseded traditional ideas. Yet these changes were balanced to some extent, in part deliberately, by new areas of discipline. And some behaviors simply led to a civil war between tradition and change.

One other shift deserves mention. Schooling was extensively altered and not only because it became increasingly widespread, with more and more of the population going on to high school. In addition, the professed purpose of education shifted toward key skills and academic achievements rather than overtly moral goals. Statements of nineteenth-century moralization began to look old-fashioned and judgmental, only partly because they were commonly linked to Protestantism in a society now more religiously diverse. Schooling was thus defined now in terms of its role in providing a skilled labor force plus access, for those appropriately placed or talented, to the higher rungs of the educational system. Even rote memorization was passed over in favor of more open-ended conceptual challenges in which students were taught to think creatively and solve problems. Novel forms of testing sorted students not by character level but by presumed intelligence. The establishment of the College Board early in the new century also led to more demanding tests for college admission. And the colleges themselves turned away from older moral and religious goals as new discoveries in the sciences and social sciences justified a research faculty and greater academic concentration. No one, of course, advocated amoral schools and students, but the purposes of school had now changed decisively. One implication was that character training had to come earlier, before the school experience, and the list of parental responsibilities lengthened accordingly.[19]

The schools still offered training in self-control, but the vocabulary had changed. For instance, the use of schools both to monitor and to teach posture and hygiene brought morally relevant training in self-control to more children, not fewer. The identification of new categories of juvenile offenders (for girls, primarily offenders against sexual morality) actually made the regulation of youth stronger in some respects. Extracurricular activities, particularly sports, which were intended to impose self-discipline through monitored experiences, and claims about improving character underlay the intense and distinctive American commitment to these nonacademic aspects of high schools and colleges. Fitness campaigns, particularly for young people, also used education as a disciplinary means, and they were assumed to develop character and health simultaneously. During these same decades, scouting and related movements began, aimed at middle-class youth and concentrating on the use of crafts and outdoor experiences to promote traditional character virtues. Discussions of curricular changes in the interest of good citizenship, and particularly the introduction of social studies courses designed to inculcate national values, soon restored moral education from yet another angle.[20]

Schools, like the wider society, changed, redefined themselves, and at the same time continued their quest for traditional values. By 1920 it was clear that pure, unadulterated Victorianism had ended, even though some religious and political groups still were eager to turn back the clock.[21] Nonetheless, demands for discipline and self-control could yet be heard, with new methods supplementing old. On the whole, the reliance on personal commitment, backed by careful child rearing and the ongoing character-building qualities of formal education, became more important, particularly after the failure of Prohibition challenged the formal regulation of private behaviors.

These developments lead us to two questions. First, in regard to the transitional decades themselves, what caused these changes, and at the same time, why were these changes not more extensive? Second, based on this mixture of old goals, innovations, and adaptations, what was the twentieth-century style of self-control as it emerged from the 1920s? How were some of the tensions and contradictions generated up during the transition formulated and resolved?

| FIVE |

Causation

In many ways, the Victorian system of self-control functioned quite well for nearly a century, gaining precision and adherence with each decade from the 1760s to the 1870s. It helped define middle-class identity while providing some guidelines for the socialization of the American population more generally. It was compatible with rapid economic development, and some Victorian habits undoubtedly played a constructive role in motivating and shaping the industrial effort. Even though the system did not fully define real family life, it provided some important emphases. Certainly, it undergirded a successful effort at birth control. But the system put almost unbearable pressure on some people because it highlighted personal flaws rather than larger social and economic forces, and it could cause mental and psychosomatic disease. Whether these costs were higher than those associated with other systems of social control is debatable. The fact that opponents of the Victorian system later claimed peculiar repressiveness does not prove the case, in part because, as we have seen, the system permitted some relief. Its downfall was, therefore, by no means inevitable.[1]

This chapter explores those factors that help explain why the system changed. To date, most explanations have not been satisfactory. Furthermore, some accounts of change have not, in fact, assessed the causes at all (see chapter 2). In any case, no single factor predominated. Rather, this was a complex change containing a great deal of continuity and compensation, so it is not surprising that several different elements were involved, including some interesting countercurrents. Amid a host of contributing factors, however, some basic changes in the economic system can be identified as complicating and, in certain ways, undoing the Victorian approach.

This chapter shows how several changes combined to redefine the middle-class system of self-restraint. Because major change cannot be replicated in the laboratory, it is difficult to assign precise weights to the principal factors. In addition, the redefinition was both substantial and incomplete, so the causes of continuity in the face of change are as important as the causes of the change itself.

The turn-of-the-century decades saw several major alterations in American life, as historians have long noted. Government action was not a major player in redefining self-control, because while American government was growing stronger, the state was still comparatively weak, unlikely to affect private habits. The transition to a new system of self-control did, however, have some relationship to Progressivism and, of course, to educational reform. The Progressives showed some of the same eagerness to invoke character while also regulating deficiencies that we see again today. The rapid growth of immigration and its new sources from southern and eastern Europe help explain why the middle class was anxious to reassert certain Victorian elements, lest American civilization be lost; this was one source of continuity within a rapidly fluctuating context. The nation's growing world power was not a major factor in the redefinition of Victorianism, however, and even World War I, though exposing middle-class men to some novel habits, does not seem to have played a huge role in the American redefinition of Victorianism except in a few categories such as cigarette smoking and swearing. During these decades, the nation moved to industrial maturity, with a population that was more than half urban. Although this transition did not cause the introduction of a new system of self-control, it did provide a framework for it, and the new system was in turn part of the economic maturation process, the shift from a farmer-entrepreneurial to a corporate economy and from the predominance of production to that of consumerism.[2]

The principal factors that reshaped Victorian ideas about self-control were not transient. Rather, they continued to fuel the new system for many decades, indeed, until the present day. A new cultural climate, including new sources of behavioral expertise, was added to the fundamental changes in the economic system and its orientation. The specific factors included the change in disease concerns toward a greater preoccupation with degenerative ailments and the emergence of modern birth control technology. Nonetheless, devotion to a neo-Victorian moralism informed the American transition as well.

A Civilizing Process

As we have seen, once the process of control had begun, according to some theorists, the force of modern constraints on impulses became stronger.[3] This approach is useful in explaining certain aspects of America's twentieth-century style and its relationship to Victorian ideas, and a closer examination of the change process helps translate a vague force into specific operating factors. First, some elements of Victorianism endured. For example, it still was necessary to deal with strangers and to reconcile an emphasis on individualism with the group requirements of industrial life. Second, other elements were defended in new ways or recalled in certain situations. Even when posture requirements virtually disappeared, for example, manuals on how to conduct oneself in job interviews continue to insist on the importance of holding oneself erect and not twitching.[4] Third, some Victorian components had been so widely accepted that people no longer needed to be reminded of them. The expansion of the middle class and its subordination of other groups testified to the success of some Victorian controls in affecting the whole society, for example, permitting the growing awareness of time to oppose the natural rhythms of the human body. Thus, persistence, internalization, and dissemination all contributed to the twentieth-century approach to self-control. The twentieth-century style was different, however, and not only because people could now be trusted to maintain some basic elements of self-control. Both the continuities themselves and the special features of American efforts at restraint, including a moralism that still astounds European visitors, need to be explained.

Internal Stresses and Outside Attacks

Another explanatory approach reverses the continuity argument by emphasizing the contradictions that ultimately brought down the nineteenth-century middle-class system. To what extent did the Victorian system, over time, defeat itself? A fuller understanding of the Victorian system suggests some additional reasons. They do not explain the change but, instead, suggest why the middle class, eager for some simplifications and escapes, was responsive to more basic causes and why some aspects of Victorianism changed more than others.

These shifts and continuities highlighted several tensions. Men, for example, schooled in Victorian control, were told both to be angry and not to be angry, depending on the setting, and this complexity now began to be sorted out. The tolerance of fighting among boys gradually diminished as family harmony seemed to take greater precedence over the Victorian delight in preserving the aggressive spirit. Middle-class men grew more shocked at rage in the workplace, particularly when it might contribute to economically damaging labor unrest. Indeed, the industrial psychologist Elton Mayo, investigating the shop floor in the 1920s for other reasons, was moved to recommend anger restraint techniques when he saw how his class values were being subverted by the emotional realities of factory life.[5]

Men also had to rethink their attitude toward sex, especially in regard to the combination of injunctions of prowess and of respectability. But the basic movement away from Victorian sexual controls was due to other factors, and the extent that confusing signals were resolved was really a side effect. Only in the extent to which the male double standard behavior prompted other kinds of challenges to Victorian sexual claims did nineteenth-century sexual respectability lead to changes.[6] Another conundrum prompted reevaluation: Victorians approved of expressing grief, but they also introduced a heightened sense of time. One of the contributing elements, therefore—though not, again, the basic cause—in the reevaluation of grief in the early twentieth century was the new consideration of time and efficiency.

Self-control in the nineteenth century depended on a supportive recreational and reading culture designed to illustrate virtue. But as we have seen, the stories of virtue's triumphs and vice's disasters also provided glimpses of an exciting alternative style of life. Victorians, men and women alike, avidly read about crimes. In the United States around 1800, fictional and journalistic crime accounts began to center on the theme of beautiful female murder victims, complete with sexual scenarios. Likewise, depictions of working-class life stressed gambling, drink, and degeneracy. African American men became known for their abundant sexual urges and ample equipment. Bohemianism was another target, with artists and intellectuals representing the dangers of drugs and promiscuity. In other words, Victorianism conjured up an alternative style of life that could be viewed as more exciting than the prosaic demands of daily morality, even though Victorian authors carefully pointed out the ill effects of a life of hedonistic pleasure. In the end, in approved fiction, morality did win out, and for reasons carefully spelled out.[7]

Here, Victorian tensions may not have been a cause of new escapist fare, but they supplemented the real spurs to change. It was no accident that early on, nudity was used in the *Police Gazette.* It was no accident that when respectable middle-class people sought a new level of spontaneity in their entertainments, they turned to working-class and ethnic subcultures, for Victorianism had already guided them here in illustrating the perils of vice or the guileless happiness of simpler people. (Obviously, the guilelessness was a stereotype; the Victorian middle class held African Americans to a complex combination of happiness and emotionality in sex and religion but to no emotion whatsoever in their deference to whites.) The rise of a non-Victorian entertainment culture was partly shaped by the romantic novels, crime reports, and minstrel shows. The Victorian package did not unravel by itself, however; middle-class interests themselves had to change first.

The greatest tension in Victorianism pertained to gender, which clearly contributed to change around the turn of the century, as Victorian rationales and control mechanisms rested heavily on time-bound beliefs in essential differences between men and women. Interestingly, the first movement toward new controls, in the eighteenth century, did not emphasize gender differentiation as much, and it is important not to attribute modern ideas of self-restraint to any particular gender formulation.[8] By the 1830s, however, the idea of virtuous women, with highly focused and in some ways limited emotions, contrasted with the notion of more impassioned men. But at the same time as women were virtuous, they were also supposed to be beautiful, and this supported the interest in fashion that ultimately prompted more elaborate consumerism and devotion to body care in decidedly non-Victorian ways. Most important was the mere fact of male-female contrast, which inspired one gender to push for change in the direction of the other.[9]

The impetus for modifying this aspect of Victorianism came from outside the system. As women acquired more education and demanded more legal and political rights (in part because of the moral power attributed to femininity and in part because of the obvious superiority of male rights), they were able to challenge other features of nineteenth-century life, including the social separation between men and women. But when the separation of the genders was no longer such an important issue, other aspects of the Victorian system of impulse control were jeopardized as well. For example, most women did not protest Victorian sexual constraints, but many could see the unfairness of the double standard. Around 1900, when feminists began attacking this inequity, the question was whether the goal should be new limits on male appetites or new sexual interests for women. As with other areas, once the change was under way, Victorian alternatives helped shape the result.[10]

Some historians believe that outside attack brought down the Victorian system. As noted in chapter 2, John Burnham attributes the rise of new vices around the turn of the century to the combined power of grasping commercial interests, bent on making new money from gambling, sex, or drink, and the sapping effect of lower-class habits that had never been tamed by middle-class discipline.[11] Certainly, advertisers were quick to play on growing consumer interests, as we have seen, and the carefully orchestrated agitation by liquor companies helped undo Prohibition and other regulatory efforts, including sexual censorship. But the forces of commercial and class subversion were not the main causes of fundamental change, for two reasons. First, the middle class retained great cultural and economic power. That is, it needed to be motivated to change, not simply corrupted. Although the middle class did shift, it was in response to greater forces than advertising, and the class also retained the power to ignore certain ploys in the name of older values. Second, advertisers did not shake some basically Victorian concerns—for example, in the moral reasons for good hygiene; rather, they played on them and intensified them, in the process disseminating them to wider groups. Commercial manipulation may have helped redefine Victorian self-control, but mainly in echoing and extending larger forces, including the forces of continuity.[12]

A Cultural Sea Change

More important were the larger changes in intellectual assumptions that helped undermine elements of the nineteenth-century Victorian system. We have seen that the Victorian idea of character derived in part from notions of human educability and a benign environment whose core was reason and rational control. It is important to remember that this dependence on reason and training was not complete, as various implicit and explicit arrangements reduced the burdens on willpower. But there was a faith in human nature, beginning with the conviction of childish innocence.

Starting with the publication of Charles Darwin's *Origin of Species* in 1859, scientific discoveries and artistic movements severely dented these assumptions. Scientists increasingly insisted on the animal origins of the human species and also on the power of inherent instincts and emotions. Psychological theories amplified the attention being paid to the unconscious, though we should note that Freudian therapy assumed the capacity for greater rational control once the components of unconscious experience were identified. Victorian cultural predictions were not shattered, but they were complicated.[13]

At the same time, social scientists began probing the human environment, and here American researchers took the lead. The Chicago school of sociology, for example, followed up on European work in the early decades of the twentieth century by examining the deleterious effects of the urban setting. Studies of crime and poverty called into question the dominant role of good character; that is, social and economic forces might overcome even the best impulse control, and hereditary components, as in animal-like criminals, might make this control impossible.

Modern artists rebelled against Victorianism from another angle, by attacking comfortable bourgeois notions of style and beauty through innovations in painting, literary form, and music. Some of the results were deliberately jarring, designed to convey an irrational universe or the influence of other cultures considered "primitive" or to show the dominance of the absurd. Other genres celebrated the power of the machine. All renounced fixed, predictable forms. Moreover, artists were frequently associated with behavioral experimentation, and some, like Oscar Wilde, associated freer behaviors with artistic modernism.

Evolutionary science and artistic defiance combined in the 1880s to create a new group of writers on sexual subjects. The leading figures were European, like Havelock Ellis, but their writings attracted a substantial American audience and inspired secondary spokespeople who agreed that Victorian views of heterosexuality were hopelessly repressive and that sex itself was far more important than had previously been imagined.[14] Freudian assumptions spread only slowly—one study suggests they gained popular prominence in the United States only after 1940[15]—and they did not fully challenge Victorianism. Evolutionary biology might be attacked or ignored, and it too could be reconciled with Victorianism. Those human races were superior in the struggle for the survival of the fittest that displayed the greatest character and capacity for self-control; that is, animal origins did not require animal natures. Thus the impact of fundamental intellectual innovation should not be pressed too far. In fact, as we have seen, large components of Victorianism survived, including a recurrent belief in the importance of good character in overcoming poverty and bad habits alike.

But the new science and art did help create the modernist rebellion against Victorian strictures, particularly those concerning gender and sexuality, in the early twentieth century. In Europe, the shattering effects of World War I prompted intellectual changes that helped shape a new American intelligentsia. American novelists like Sinclair Lewis and Theodore Dreiser explored the seamy side of middle-class life even in small midwestern towns and exposed the banality of assumptions about the capacities of the poor to pull themselves up by character reform alone. Influential social science studies, like the Lynds' investigation of Middletown, was also influential, again showing that many upright Victorians were hypocrites in regard to probity or sexual self-control. None of this meant that ordinary middle-class people, even those who kept up with the new books, had to change their outlook; but an alternative vision now emanated from intellectuals who could no longer be dismissed as bohemians.[16]

The new scientific assumptions also prompted some practical psychological research that directly challenged Victorian values. Industrial researchers showed that people could be manipulated by work arrangements, such as piped-in music, or by advertisements. As efficiency engineering began to alter assembly-line methods, the emphasis on character receded in favor of arrangements designed to create as mechanistic a labor force as possible. Henry Ford, a great advocate of character building through Americanization, undermined his own assumptions by depriving workers of any effective decision-making role. In this setting, character consisted of little more than accepting robotlike routines without complaining. This was a new tension, only partially foreshadowed in the nineteenth-century factories, between the power of organizations to herd and the continuing insistence on individual self-mastery.[17]

Research on children dispelled many of the assumptions of childish innocence. After about 1890, American psychologists demonstrated how children might be affected by unconscious fears and impulses. A set of studies in the 1920s claimed (wrongly, it is now believed) that most children experienced bitter rivalries with their siblings that their parents must attack directly in the interests of sibling safety and a psychologically healthy adulthood. All these findings, initiated by assumptions of animal origins and the spread of scientific methods, did not argue for new freedom; indeed, their implications could support a modified Victorianism. But the need for control increased. General invocations of character would not suffice, as the new expertise generated long lists of necessary restraints. Furthermore, the responsibilities of parenting were doubled as children moved from innocents to problems, with new frailties and vulnerabilities.[18]

The sources of expertise shifted as well. Moral common sense was no longer the principal qualification of the leading advice givers. Rather, they had to be scientifically trained. They must have assimilated the assumptions, if not the details, of evolutionary biology and the psychology of the unconscious. They must be doctors, social workers, or at least trained home economists or physical education specialists. By the later 1920s, persons who wanted to know about marriage could turn to the new specialists, whose books, magazine columns, and college courses cut through Victorian-romantic assumptions and some of the "nonsense" about love or sexual self-control to explain what was important about mate selection and marital success. Changes in the intellectual worldview, combined with a greater striving for professional recognition as well as new professions or would-be professions, undercut the predominantly moral credentials of the nineteenth century's dominant prescribers.[19]

This same shift in worldview, including the recognition of the power of impulse and the psychological neediness of children, helped create an audience for this new expertise. By the 1920s dozens of new child-rearing manuals and books about sex and marriage, dieting and health, crowded the bookshelves.[20] Other categories of expertise talked about successful salesmanship. For the first time, magazines directed to parents or "modern" men found ready readers, and schools accepted the new materials on hygiene. The Victorian advice literature now gathered dust. Except for etiquette books and newspaper columns of advice to the lovelorn, advice and science or pseudoscience were newly intertwined.

Some historians have argued that the new expertise itself caused the collapse of Victorianism, ultimately generating a new (and far less confident) American personality.[21] This is an overstatement, however, in part because so many elements of Victorianism survived, and not only in the etiquette and lovelorn materials. The middle-class audience itself sought new sources of expertise because of the shift in intellectual climate. Still more important were the changes in economic framework that called for rethinking Victorian prescriptions, though by no means casting them aside. Well into the twentieth century, the most avid users of advice were middle-class people in new occupational sectors who needed to adjust their older standards, in the process absorbing some of the new cultural assumptions as well.[22] Overall, the intellectual innovations that challenged Victorianism contributed to the change but did not decisively determine it, which is why some of the proclamations by the sexual rebels of the 1920s or the psychological behaviorists of the following decades were quickly toned down and modified in their popular assimilation.

Corporations and Consumerism

The nineteenth-century prescriptions for self-control needed to be re-defined, but not jettisoned, because the economic environment in which they were meant to fit began changing decisively before 1900, in a pattern that hardened during the following century. Other factors, including the shifts in gender relations and the popularity of non-Victorian expertise, followed in part from this larger shift in framework.

These changes, though fundamental, were not complex; rather, the middle-class reactions were complex. First, the growth of corporations and, in professions like law and teaching, the organization of larger firms or more bureaucratic educational boards reduced the entrepreneurial quality of business and professional life. Even though the new industries created opportunities for entrepreneurs, and professions like medicine long preserved an entrepreneurial framework (until the huge revolution in medical organization at the end of the twentieth century), by the 1890s the typical middle-class businessman or professional was destined for a career as an employee rather than as an independent operator. Bureaucracy, private or public, not individual competition became the norm, with middle management the most common destination. A few criminal lawyers maintained the older, individualistic flamboyance of their profession, but large corporate offices predominated by 1900, particularly in the bigger cities. For teachers, work and curricula were standardized by rationalizing school boards.[23] Along with these basic changes in middle-class work, the class itself began to expand because of the greater need for managers and support staff. This change, in turn, helped impose certain middle-class standards, both old and new, on a rising number of people.

Women found new job opportunities that both reflected and encouraged their educational advance. Professions like teaching needed additional personnel at modest cost, for which women were ideal. Their stereotypic attributes of docility and social grace, plus low cost, made them ideal grade school teachers and librarians. Although most working women remained subordinate, as in the growth and steady feminization of secretarial personnel, new economic opportunities fed the larger shift in gender relations that challenged key aspects of Victorianism.[24]

The rise of service occupations amplified the results of the change in economic structure. More and more people were needed to sell goods, answer telephones, and staff schools and hospitals. Even though not all the new job categories required skills in dealing with people, on the whole such skills became the hallmark of the service sector and, as this sector increasingly predominated in the economy at large, in the bulk of the middle class.

These economic changes had three effects on Victorian standards of self-control. First, because they expanded middle-class opportunities at a faster rate than blue-collar jobs, they confirmed and disseminated many

Victorian concepts, at least in principle. J. P. Morgan, a well-known banker, announced that "character" was the basis of all his transactions. But even as business leaders like Morgan innovated, even as corporate structures muffled the individual economic voice, older values of self-control were preached to a ready audience of new office workers.

Second, at the same time, the changes called for important redefinitions. The goals of working well with people and using a pleasant personality to sell goods or to operate in a managerial bureaucracy called for different kinds of self-control than did those of entrepreneurial business. Department stores, as we have seen, had to train people (mainly lower-class female clerks) to satisfy customers, but some of the goals were new, beyond traditional etiquette, including turning the other cheek to obnoxious customers. Sports, long justified in the United States in terms of character building, shifted to teamwork rather than individual achievement, to subordinate personal excellence to larger group goals. This reorientation gradually filtered down to child-rearing manuals, calling for more systematic anger control and other innovations. These new standards for displaying emotions and maintaining appearance (including weight control, as undue gains might jeopardize jobs), constituted the single most significant impact of the organizational revolution on the American economy.

To be sure, the changes in management structure were accompanied by anachronistic references to individual will and character as keys to success. Self-help manuals proliferated between 1907 and the 1920s, especially those by such enthusiasts as Dale Carnegie and other sales experts. Appeals to force of mind and proper values, with accompanying control over distracting impulses, remained a standard component in this flourishing publishing area. But change crept into even this neo-Victorian genre. Manuals in 1918 cited leadership qualities, intelligence, ability, enthusiasm, and honesty, but their counterparts just a decade later shifted to more self-restraint, such as the ability to take criticism and acknowledge mistakes along with eagerness to see subordinates develop and a willingness to learn from them.[25]

Finally, third, the organizational transformation caused uneasiness and discontent in much of the middle class during the transition decades. Some men found it difficult to work with women, even when the women were subordinate. The fact that women's socialization made it easier for them to adapt to "people-pleasing" requirements added another potential discomfort, which men expressed by attacking the "feminization" of American society. Systematic lament was limited. The middle class was prosperous, committed to moderate politics. Although a few sectors turned briefly to cultural protest movements like the 1920s Ku Klux Klan, more sweeping protest politics, such as the long-term, public anti-Semitism that gripped European middle-class elements, was not a viable option. The mounting labor unrest early in the 1920s confirmed the middle class's reluctance to use politics to challenge the status quo; it was too dangerous, as the later, pervasive "Red scare" demonstrated. The result was a not usually very explicit disillusionment with some Victorian values and an increasing openness to consumerism. By improving living standards and enjoying more material goods, greater leisure, and commercial recreations, the middle class compensated for the new subordinations required of their working life, but amid some quiet anxiety about values that survived as well.[26]

The growing belief in the dangers of stress, first captured in the neurasthenia craze of the 1880s, linked work frustrations with the new commitment to consumerism. American businessmen, the neurasthenia experts claimed, worked harder than any group in the world, and the nation's economic success hinged on their efforts. But the frenzy took its toll in nervous disorders, insomnia, and health problems. Thus it was imperative to restore the system through appropriate enjoyments and leisure activities. These were not, to be sure, ends in themselves, for their moral validity initially hinged on their role in sustaining successful work. Based on this premise, the shift to pure consumerism was not difficult. Consumerism could also compensate for middle-class women's restricted roles, thereby mitigating their confinement to the home without directly challenging accepted standards of femininity. Indeed, buying and enjoying goods answered a number of turn-of-the-century needs.[27]

This second basic economic change was spurred as well by the need of American firms not simply to produce but also to sell goods and by new methods of distribution—the department store and the catalog operations—and advertisements. Even before the formal acceptance of envy, Protestants began to shift away from their opposition to the materialist goals that they had sustained through the middle decades of the nineteenth century to praise fashion. According to the *Presbyterian Banner* in 1875: "If a woman has no natural taste in dress, she must be a little deficient in her appreciation of the beautiful. . . . Indifference, and consequent inattention to dress, often shows pedantry, self-righteousness, or indolence, and whilst extolled by the severe utilitarian as a virtue, may frequently be noted as a defect."

Signs of the middle class's commitment to consumerism proliferated during the transitional decades. Attractive products expanded beyond fashionable clothing to include home furnishings, like imported oriental rugs, and brand-new products, like bicycles. Advertisements graduated from dry, informational headings to more emotional appeals, evoking better ways of life through particular products. Silk goods, still described in terms of price and utility in newspaper product lists in the 1890s, by 1900 were touted as "alluring," "bewitching"—"to feel young and carefree, buy our silk." Time spent shopping, particularly in the department stores, demonstrated the heightened function of consumerism in middle-class leisure life. The object of shopping, including window-shopping, was less community socialization of the sort associated with market shopping in earlier periods of urban development and more the fascinated enjoyment of the goods themselves. The development of kleptomania in the final decades of the nineteenth century constituted an extreme of the new attachment to acquisition. A small number of people, disproportionately women, became attached to stealing things they did not need as a solace for other limitations or discontents in life. Christmas gift–giving habits also took a more consumerist direction. By the 1890s, Americans began to exchange purchased gifts rather than simple homemade items (characteristic of the first modern phase of Christmas earlier in the century), a transition of particular relevance to childhood reward. The employment of purchased items for emotional guidance and motivation also became more explicit. By the 1880s, girls could purchase an array of expensive dolls, and boys enjoyed new sports equipment, like boxing gloves, and toy soldiers. After 1900, even babies' cribs were filled with store-bought items, to which it was hoped they would develop salutary emotional attachments. By the 1920s, equipping home playgrounds and recreational rooms further intensified the link between children and consumerism.[28]

Consumerism spread to the leisure habits of adults as well as children, and here men led the way in consuming leisure equipment as well as paying for professional entertainment. Buying seats as spectators became a dominant recreational form, whether it was attending sports events, slumming at vaudeville shows, or, after 1900, patronizing the movie emporiums that began to dot downtown areas. Singer Eddie Cantor, recalling the early twentieth century, noted the new excitement that immigrant and working-class entertainment was generating: "Opening night . . . you played to the best people in the country. The Whitneys, the Vanderbilts, the Goulds, the Harrimans, the Astors, they were all there. . . . On the road, we were invited to the finest homes, people considered it a privilege if we talked to them." The automobile rapidly expanded the family's leisure range, and although formal vacations were not new to the middle class, they too acquired more consumer attributes, with the proliferation of resort areas and travel agencies.[29]

Even though key aspects of middle-class consumerism appealed to the older values—buying things to maintain health, to support intensive work, to promote the family—the new commitments also changed certain aspects of self-control. Indeed, this was the greatest challenge to Victorianism, the biggest reason for its redefinition during the early decades of the twentieth century.

First, consumerism appealed to desire, not self-control. Its reach could create doubts about the adequacy of discipline even in other facets of personal and social life. For example, American savings rates, never high compared with those of western Europe and Japan, fell during the twentieth century, with only a few upward spikes. By 1997, the U.S. savings rate was less than 5 percent of disposable income, a drop of 70 percent from 1900 and 50 percent from 1967. This, plus the extensive use of credit facilities and more lenient bankruptcy laws, two other century-long practices, is a trend that economists initially attributed directly to Americans' lack of self-control.

Several other points of friction developed. In emphasizing indulgence and appetite over restraint, consumerism shifted other priorities toward greater pleasure seeking. Whether or not inevitably, consumerism and a more open interest in sex were joined by 1900. Advertisers, as we have seen, found that sex sold. The new spectator interests often involved more explicit sexual references. By the twentieth century, the practice of dating directly linked sexual interest and consumer activities. A portion of women's commitment to consumerism focused on increasing their sexual attractiveness, and men found that certain goods, like cars, heightened their drawing power. Particularly in regard to late-nineteenth-century concerns, consumerism also invoked the value of relaxation. Not only was comfort a good in itself, but now, more broadly, the ability to relax showed a mastery over stress and an openness to new recreational and consumer interests.

It was this initial acceptance of new levels of consumerism that prepared the middle class for new influences from advertisers, recreational promoters, and hucksters of various sorts. Once the importance of acquiring and enjoying goods was established, other voices could further attack the values of self-mastery. Even here there were complexities. Certain impulses might require more, not less, control. Grief, for example, needed to be curbed, as it sold few goods and detracted from the emphasis on life's material enjoyments. Relaxation had its own requirements, even as it attacked some rigidities, literal and figurative, central to the Victorian ethic. In the main, however, the unfolding of a new stage of American consumerism challenged Victorian self-control through its emphasis on greater indulgence and pleasure seeking.

Victorian values had embraced some acquisitive interests, as in the rise of women's fashion in the 1840s. But the new level of consumerism changed basic attachments and interests by 1900. It also created a new kind of fantasy life by contributing to the shift from a culture that at least in principle confirmed moral values to a spectator culture that now compensated for constraints, both new and old. People began to watch what they were not. The compensatory consumerist outlets, supplemented by unprecedented media such as the movies, pushed fantasy representations to unparalleled heights.[30]

The two big economic shifts of the transitional decades were related in many ways. As we have seen, the limitations of most corporate jobs encouraged consumerism in its role of compensation. Especially in the recreational field, consumerism in turn opened the way to more service occupations and more requirements for pleasing people. On the whole, occupational changes prompted an extension of self-control in the interests of group coordination and personal promotion. Whereas consumerism justified specific new restraints, it also attacked key elements of the

Victorian ethic. The overall combination was truly challenging, requiring real agility in response.

The Need for Virtue

These changes in economic structure, particularly consumerism, supplemented by limited new roles for women, had one another causal effect in prompting the necessity of finding new ways to demonstrate or at least claim self-discipline. Although compensatory spectator values responded to constraints, they, too, could help promote self-mastery, which was the most puzzling effect emerging from the transition decades.

This pattern has several components. The first is the continuity of the Victorian idea of self-control. As late as 1997, a popular journalist could write : "Americans are fascinated by character. . . . We talk of character education or character building in children . . . with the belief that we can set up a permanent ethical core." A regional foundation offered grants to public schools in the same year that it set "character education" as its goal. Victorianism thus is still alive, which means that the principal adjustments were not overwhelming.[31]

The second component, enhancing continuity, involved the importance of dealing with the unprecedented waves of immigration in the transitional decades. How could these foreigners be brought into the national fold? One answer was essentially to "Victorianize" them as much as possible, to teach them the same values of self-control that the middle class had, supplemented by new laws like Prohibition when necessary. The success of Victorianism, its association with religious values, and the need to emphasize moral training in a diverse society in which immigrants and racial minorities often seemed suspect were the main components of the surprising continuity plus the frequent recurrence of nineteenth-century self-control values in the twentieth-century United States.

At the same time, another, newer factor prompted an interest in self-control that helps explain the continued attractiveness of the idea of character and also the new disciplinary targets such as dieting. In the early decades of this century, the rise of consumerism was generating unease throughout the Western world. Basing so much of life on acquiring goods not needed for subsistence was bound to raise moral issues. Women's involvement was attacked: although they had been held up as distinctively moral, their growing frivolity could be disconcerting, and misogyny was a factor as well. Consumerism also blurred the divisions of the social hierarchy, another source of concern. People might spend beyond their means or might use consumption to claim parity with their betters. Elements of consumerism might also be tainted by a foreign influence—French fashions, for example—in a time of rising nationalism. For a variety of reasons, a consumerist society seemed to some people, even otherwise eager participants, like a world gone wrong.

Anticonsumerist diatribes and movements cropped up almost everywhere. In some parts of Europe, shopkeepers used the undercurrent of anti-Semitism to attack department stores. Socialist movements highlighted the frivolous spending of the middle class, urging a saner approach to life's values along with greater equality. Intellectuals—France's Emile Zola was a case in point—castigated empty-headed spenders, female consumers, and the capitalists who lured them to their unnecessary wares. Scientific discussions of kleptomania easily turned to condemnations of consumer excess—again, mainly women—and department store enticements. Not surprisingly, by 1900, the manifestations of anticonsumerist manifestations were varied and powerful, from France to Russia, and they have been widely studied.[32]

With middle-class consumerism growing faster in the United States than anywhere else at the turn of the century, we should expect at least comparable levels of moral uneasiness. The rapid growth of commerce earlier in the nineteenth century led to a host of compensatory movements, like the pure-food, sexual abstinence approach of Sylvester Graham, designed to demonstrate virtue amid economic change. Around 1900, Thorstein Veblen's widely hailed book *The Leisure Class* helped clarify concerns about consumer trends, though it was directed mainly to the very rich.[33]

Unlike western Europe, however, and perhaps in contrast to its own past, the United States was unable to turn against consumerism too explicitly. Even the revival of the Ku Klux Klan proved limited. The nation was devoted to capitalism, and attacks on the system's latest manifestations had little effect. Anti-Semitism, though certainly present, was not as widely tolerated as it was in western Europe, and no large, politicized anti-Semitic movements successfully blamed Jews for consumerist excess. In addition, socialism never became widely popular. American politics normally was consensual anyway, which limited its vulnerability to protest—particularly from a group like the middle class, which might be morally uneasy but also had many reasons to defend the status quo. Even criticizing women had some limits in the American context, because their virtuousness had been so highly touted; compared with French use of kleptomania as an outlet for misogyny, American commentary was more neutral.[34]

For a variety of essentially political reasons, then, the middle class found it more difficult to expand its hesitations about its own consumerism. As a result, it was more eager to find areas of its own behavior in which compensatory virtue could be demonstrated. This impulse better fit the larger American value system, which was more prone to attribute results to individual character or failings than to wider social or economic forces. Far more than Europeans, for example, Americans in the nineteenth and twentieth centuries alike tended to downplay the effects of social class structure in arguing that an individual could make of himself whatever he wanted—and that failure was the result of personal fault, not deficiencies in the system. Applied to moral uneasiness, this same self-help approach essentially held that individuals themselves had to find ways to relieve their consciences, without trying to burden the larger culture or the political process. Accordingly, movements that conveyed an anticonsumerist message were comparatively muted.

Consequently, as they recognized their own increasing consumerist commitments, many Americans were open to private crusades that would make them feel better—more moral. Simon Patten, the distinguished Wharton School economist who praised modern capitalism and encouraged women's growing interest in fashion, also defended the importance of dieting. Only by restricting their intake of food could Americans display the discipline and control that would make a consumer economy ethical.[35] That is, selective restraint, even severe self-regulation, had to accompany indulgence. This same thinking was applied to sexuality and other aspects of emotional life, and it continued to uphold the moral overtones of the concern about health practices. The need for virtue increased even as literal Victorianism had to be modified.

Continuity and the search for compensatory discipline were just as salient in the twentieth century as was the new, anti-Victorian expertise or the indulgences inherent in the commitment to a consumer economy. Only their combination can explain the recurrence of moralism in American discourse, even in the 1990s; only this combination can explain why concerns like dieting or, later, smoking, took on such fervency in the American context.

Supplemental Factors

The causative structure that made the decades around 1900 a period of transition from a Victorian to a contemporary system of self-control was centered on economic change. The interrelationship between a corporate—increasingly service—economy and the phenomenon of consumerism created needs both to relax certain aspects of nineteenth-century restraints and to develop some new disciplines. Americans' strong attachment to Victorianism and their need to compensate for indulgence, through personal more than political commitments, added to this mix. Enhancing this process of adjustment were intellectual shifts away from the Victorian framework and the expertise accompanying it, and the realization that some of the contradictions—particularly in regard to gender attributes—of nineteenth-century values might be resolved by being redefined.

Two other general changes helped shape the system that gradually took over from literal Victorianism. Patterns of disease and mortality changed decisively between 1880 and 1920, a development crucial to a culture that already linked health and personal morality. Infant death rates plummeted. The death of a child now was so rare, so horrific, that new precautions were needed. At the same time, degenerative diseases, rather than epidemics or other contagious killers, gradually gained primacy as health concerns. Heart attacks, strokes, and cancer, along with accidents, were now the top killers. Particularly after the great influenza epidemic of 1918–19, attention turned to protecting the body's interior. Medicines, public health measures, and inoculations could largely take care of killers that came from outside the body. The new focus on degeneration inevitably underscored the importance of personal habits, calling attention to the need for new means of disciplining the body and enhancing the tendency to believe that one's health mirrored one's character.[36]

A second development linked to medicine was the greater acceptability and availability of birth control devices. Although the definitive developments took place in the 1920s and 1930s rather than in the transitional decades themselves, the middle class's acceptance of artificial birth control devices gradually gained ground. Margaret Sanger and others began their advocacy during the second decade of the new century, and more and more doctors began to support them. By the 1930s, we know that physician-prescribed diaphragms were widely used by married middle-class women (their availability to the lower classes was more limited), and even Catholics began to accept artificial methods. As the use of artificial birth control spread and as a cultural precondition, couples had to place a new value on sexual pleasure for its own sake and to admit that willpower alone was insufficient to ensure the small family size that most parents sought. Changes in the Victorian sexual ethic both preceded and followed from this historic shift in family practices. Now other questions were raised about traditional self-control strictures, while at the same time the guilt over adding sexual indulgence to consumer indulgence created the need for compensatory discipline in other areas. In this context, it was no accident that women's sexual appeal became increasingly associated with a slender figure, as if additional constraint alone could justify this major breach in the Victorian fortress.[37]

How Causes Combined: Sexuality

The next chapters show how, after the 1920s, the major and supporting causes of a redefinition of Victorian self-control worked in areas such as the presentation of the body and emotional standards. Here we preview the framework in which a new set of sexual codes developed in the behavioral area in which Victorianism changed most blatantly.

A growing openness to more sexually suggestive advertisements and recreations marked the transitional decades. This in turn reflected the greater interest in consumer goods and professional entertainers, which relaxed the prior insistence on an explicitly moralistic cultural context. The interest resulted in part from the reduction in middle-class job satisfaction and the decline of the entrepreneurial economy, which made the acceptance of pleasures off the job more legitimate. The shift also built on the earlier interest in entertaining sensationalism and sexual issues, with the moral lessons that had justified them now muted or withdrawn. Victorian ideas of love, which had embraced sexual expression as a subordinate theme, also were adjusted to fit these changes in emphasis. The active feminist debate about the double standard and women's rights, though rarely challenging the idea of proper sexual restraint, also cleared the way for some innovation. The more frequent public contact between males and females, in schools and in white-collar jobs, altered the context for sexuality. Commercial promoters' discovery that sexual innuendo sold goods and scientific investigations of sexual urges based on assumptions about the animal origins of the human species contributed to this new context. Although science often confirmed Victorian elements, for example, by insisting that women did have lower-level sexual desire, by the twentieth century a new group of American intellectuals opposed Victorianism on the grounds of its wrongheaded, repressive approach to sex. Almost all the major factors in altering the framework of nineteenth-century definitions of self-control applied to sex. It is little wonder, then, that during the 1880s and 1890s, quietly and gradually, middle-class couples began not only to experience a more sexualized recreational and consumer culture but also to show more sexual interest in their own lives. Early in the next century, when more acceptable and reliable birth control became available, this change in behaviors and values accelerated.[38]

The relevant factors did not all push in the same direction, of course. The hold of past constraints was especially strong in the area of child rearing. Even parents who displayed more "modern" openness in their own lives changed the treatment of their children very little, as the continued emphasis on the evils of masturbation suggested. Some changes provoked new needs for self-mastery in the interests of continued respectability, for example, in the reactions of many men to women's entry into the ranks of office workers: language and innuendo had to be cleaned up, and this occurred in the federal civil service in the final decades of the nineteenth century. Above all, the greater indulgence in sexual interests, even to the extent of approving of less restrictive clothing or enjoying the use of nudity in advertising, had to be balanced by compensatory discipline. Virtually no one, aside from a few extreme modernists in the artistic community and "sexologists" like the British Havelock Ellis, urged greater license for sexual impulse in all cases. Many people needed to demonstrate, to themselves and others, a submission to new aesthetic and physical disciplines in order to merit participation in even modest sexual changes and in the declining commitment to procreation. Hence, modern women shaved areas of body hair, and men and women alike began to recognize the relationship between rigorous slenderness and sexuality.[39]

In addition, the growing revulsion against homosexuality provided a new category of constraint, a new definition of deviancy, that helped counterbalance the gradually greater permissiveness for heterosexuality. Modern science contributed to constraint as well as openness by identifying homosexuality as a fixed condition—one either was or was not, in a formulation that was both new and restrictive—and ultimately by branding the condition as a disease. The insistence on an unprecedented stringency to prevent this evil followed, particularly in the warnings directed to boys and young men. The massive shift in views began with European medical writers in the 1880s, who studied cases of "contrary sexual impulse." First claiming that the individuals involved were insane, opinion turned for a time to the belief that homosexuals were born with their condition; then in the 1920s Freudianism encouraged a return to the idea that homosexuality was an acquired disease.[40] The main point was the insistence that people, not specific sexual acts, were homosexual— and fear and revulsion resulted. Although historians have abundantly identified the change, accounting for it is another matter. The suddenness of the shift and its extensive, fearful public reception suggest the felt need for compensatory sexual discipline, for the designation of a replacement category of deviancy. Novel ideas and specific factors such as the growth of committed homosexual groups in expanding cities helped guide the alterations in behavior and beliefs that undid the Victorian acceptance of intense male-male friendships, but the moral utility of innovative stigmas was clear. Sex, newly open in some respects, continued to be surrounded with constraint, even fear. Parents and young people still worried, although their precise definitions of sexual immorality and disease had changed. By the 1920s, college youth, learning about homosexuality for the first time from professors and friends, "worried and thought over affectionate episodes in our past relationships . . . and wondered whether they had been incipient examples" of this new taboo. Guilt and sex remained fast friends.[41]

Changes in the standards of self-control responded to a variety of forces, some of them pulling in opposite directions, and tensions regarding self-restraint and indulgence intensified. No one commentator or advice giver quite captured the whole process of change and continuity. A few systematic proclamations issued from anti-Victorian intellectuals, but for most people, these were but one ingredient in a more complicated context. Innovation often was not noticed. In the 1920s, for example, both popularizers and parents began to express concern about sibling rivalry, seeking new restraints over jealousy in the family, yet while experts argued for novel remedies, no one seemed to realize that the problem itself had been only recently invented.[42] Likewise, self-conscious innovation often embraced a far greater number of traditional elements than its advocates acknowledged, as would be apparent in the new codes applied to heterosexuality. Change and continuity were not random, but their interactions were not easy to discern.

PART III

Twentieth-Century Standards

| S I X |

New Combinations

The factors that led to the revision of the Victorian style of self-control solidified in the turn-of-the-century decades. Signs of transition, including both relaxations and new targets for constraint, emerged at the same time, although the fuller shift in standards awaited the 1920s and ensuing decades. This was the point, for example, at which the new popularized expertise generated a flood of advice literature on child rearing, marriage, and etiquette—symptoms, as we have seen, of both novel sources of behavioral advice and audience demand for clarifications amid change.

This chapter deals with some of the trade-offs since the 1920s and describes themes that will be extended to body presentation and sexuality. Earlier transitions were amplified in the 1920s, and the process of redefining a system of self-control continued thereafter, with the 1950s and the 1970s particularly important to setting additional adjustments in motion.

Standards were loosened in some areas, tightened in others, while new technologies called for additional caution. The underlying framework was a process of regulation and deregulation bent on creating a more relaxed but still disciplined personal style, suitable for the demands of a service economy and a consumer society. Subtle controls guided the emergence of the casual. Although the need for demonstrations of restraint remained, the specific requirements shifted.

This pattern of trade-offs was a mixture of Victorianism, modernist attack, and, above all, a tendency toward increasingly detailed standards. Some of these standards were relaxed, and others were demanding, as opposed to the more general injunctions with which the nineteenth-century middle class had been content. The framework of trade-offs, then, was not a tidy, reasoned process of change but, rather, a welter of specific adjustments. That is, Victorian restraints were transformed but not undone as a variety of forces pushed toward a new set of tensions between control and indulgence. The basic factors that required change, beginning with the new consumerism and work needs and including the continuing insistence on the capacity to demonstrate self-discipline, rebalanced rather than simply moved toward the greater freedom that some popularizers thought they were advocating. Each surge—for example, in the recreational culture—generated not just traditionalist concerns but also specific countermeasures to limit excess and compensate for pleasure. Victorianism was gradually redefined, but its spirit continued to inform many of the resulting adjustments and often radically new functions that self-control was now supposed to fulfill.

Understanding this trade-off process is essential to recognizing how nineteenth-century values survived, even at the end of the twentieth century and even in settings that Victorians themselves would have deemed unacceptable. At a commercially organized speakers' panel in 1997, for example, offering famous people commenting on the ingredients for success, the focus was on recommendations that a Victorian would have readily recognized: study, work hard, accept personal responsibility, treat people fairly, and trust in (a nondenominational) God. Retired General Colin Powell, for example, accounted for his extraordinary career in terms of character: it's "a story of values, it's a story of families." Indeed, the whole idea of a lecture series on the moral underpinnings of success, as well as the virtues stressed, bespeaks the persistence of cherished Victorian beliefs and habits in a society that defined specific personal goals, habits, and problems very differently. A reader writing to Ann Landers attacked the idea that avoiding divorce demonstrated "old-fashioned virtue" and "character." Having been stuck with an unfaithful, abusive, drunken husband, "it took all the virtue, character and courage I could muster" to end her marriage and raise her three children on her own. Not only she but also the children greatly benefited from the decision. This ability to defend modern behaviors in terms of older character values shows the range of combinations possible in a culture that has shifted its standards without jettisoning essential traditional qualities and vocabulary.

The same continuity can be seen in today's self-help business manuals, a quintessential nineteenth-century legacy. In the 1920s, when as we have seen, a spate of new manuals sought to prepare their readers for the corporate world, and again in the 1980s and 1990s, such books insisted that by taking the pertinent actions, individuals could control their economic fate and organizational environment. Hence, in the 1990s, titles appeared such as "How to Be Effective Even without Power" and "Influence without Authority." Well-intentioned but unexamined assumptions forced responsibility on a person's individual capacity for appropriate self-discipline. The list of virtues, to be sure, had changed—this is where the trade-offs came in—updating character as appropriate to a corporate and consumer economy. But the root belief in a correspondence between individual self-management and the desired results held remained.

Liberating and Regulating

Several key adjustments made during the second quarter of the century and after were related only because they maintained the tension between easing up and tightening controls inherited from the Victorian past. Violence, for example, was caught up in new fantasy standards and also the effort to define culturally realistic behavior norms. Redefinitions of lying contrasted with novel constraints associated with the new technology.

Fighting

Violence created one of the most fascinating juggling acts in twentieth-century American culture. Many types of violence had declined by the end of the nineteenth century, thanks to factory discipline, policing, and cultural changes. The frequency of public fistfights receded, and the number of murders associated with barroom brawls dropped off as well. These developments may, however, have led to an increase in family violence.[1] Public concern about violence escalated, spurred by anxiety about immigrant behavior and publicity generated by agencies such as the new FBI, sometimes but not always closely related to the actual incidence. Moreover, the growing hostility to anger reduced the middle class's tolerance of even minor violence. By the 1940s, for example, child-rearing manuals were referring to aggression rather than anger, accompanied by the observation that the boundary line between having a vigorous emotion and acting on it violently was too fragile to maintain.[2] Similarly, one of the claims backing up the attack on sibling rivalry was an explicit fear that young children could cause one another serious bodily harm.

The intensifying insistence on controlling violence was displayed in three ways besides the anxious monitoring of real or imagined crime statistics. Beginning in the 1930s, discussions of physical quarrels in child-rearing literature proliferated. During the 1920s, the literature contended that most children would grow out of fighting and that parental intervention was usually a mistake unless serious injury threatened. Being roughed up would gradually teach children that fighting was not a constructive response and instill some useful manliness in boys, whereas scolding or punishment would build up resentment. At most, parents could arrange preventive strategies or diversions, including plenty of exercise such as boxing. Essentially, this approach codified elements of Victorian boyhood practice, along with the assumption that standing up for oneself was an important quality—developing the "love of a fair struggle." Although elements of this approach remained, discussions of how to break up fights and better control oneself became more prevalent in the 1930s. Thus parents should instruct their children that coercion is a bad way to solve problems. Bullies should not be challenged by junior-grade Davids, as in the earlier approach, but should be actively opposed by adults and, if possible, given "help" to overcome their problems of aggression. The post–World War II advice skated a cautious line between seeking to reassure children, whose self-esteem was precious and who needed love more than criticism, and instructing them how dangerous fighting could be. On balance, parental (particularly maternal) injunctions against fights increased, as did the intervention of school authorities in grade school playground conflicts. The range of middle-class tolerance shrank.[3]

These concerns about children's fighting could also be seen in the movement to limit the violence in previously unsupervised youth activities. Particularly after World War II, university authorities campaigned against the violent and dangerous fraternity hazing of initiation rituals. Discussions of reducing violence in sports were less conclusive, however, for as we will see, there was perceived value in this manifestation. In some cases, improved equipment superseded regulation in a quest for reasonable safety.

Heightened warnings about adult violence within the family was the final site where self-control gained new attention. Concern about family violence was sporadic in the nineteenth century, for larger assumptions about familial love and respectability muted comment, save in broadsides against lower-class habits. The subject drew more expert attention in the 1920s, in part because of the rise of urban social work. The idea of an epidemic of family abuse reached the media's attention early in the 1960s, with both quantitative references and heartrending case stories. Doctors were urged to report symptoms, and the popular media contended that abuse was at least as rampant as ever before. *Time* magazine thus reported in 1962 that if the full range of abuse were known, it would be acknowledged as "a more frequent cause of death than such well-recognized and thoroughly studied diseases as leukemia . . . and muscular dystrophy." Readers learned that families of all classes were guilty: even respectable parents, capable of concealing their violence, formed a large part of the problem. Terms like battered child syndrome suggested a need to become familiar with the issue, to work for better police measures against offenders, and to carefully monitor one's own impulses. In the 1970s, there was a similar increase in reports of spousal abuse, which also helped redefined what constituted abuse. Merely shaking a child vigorously, *People* magazine readers learned in 1982, constituted abuse in terms of both potentially dire physical damage and the pathological adult motivations involved.[4]

This growing attention to problems of violence and the increasingly refined statements about the social and personal control required to deal with these problems responded at key points to evidence that violence itself was escalating, in part because of the availability of more lethal weaponry. Although the warnings about familial abuse dealt with real issues, they also served to tighten the rules under which many spouses and parents felt they had to operate. Advocates on both sides of gun control legislation underscored the importance of personal responsibility. Claims about middle-class violence, illustrated by endless made-for-television films about the subject but rarely supported by reliable statistical data, drove home this point. Violence was bad. It was increasing.

Good husbands and parents must carefully monitor their own impulses, for the problems were not confined to the lower class. As *People* put it, "Any one of us can be an abuser."[5]

Despite the ubiquity and precision of antiviolence standards, American recreational culture featured vivid representations of an extraordinary range of beatings, maiming, and mass destruction. Boys' stories and comic books had played on this theme since the late nineteenth century, and then the impact of World War II and the cold war, combined with more pervasive media and more sophisticated special effects, created a frenzy of film and television violence during the second half of the twentieth century. Calculations of the number of acts of media violence to which American children were exposed through cartoons and other readily available fare reached staggering proportions. Watching death and mass mayhem became a favorite American pastime. Casually violent references—drop dead; I'll kill you—peppered informal conversation. Many critics, of course, worried about the messages being sent and warned that media violence could alter real behavior. And surely some individuals were confused by the clash between opposition and encouragement. Others, however, found the tension useful, vicariously relieving daily constraints by watching wild acts of bloodshed while accepting the injunctions about controlling aggressive instincts in daily life. In a culture more and more defined by the interplay between restraint and abandon available to a nation of spectators, violence served as a linchpin.

Lying and Probity

While Americans wrestled with the complex pattern represented by both violence and restraint, the injunctions regarding probity eased. This, in fact, was the clearest case in which central Victorian standards were relaxed. No self-respecting advice giver advocated dishonesty, of course, and in this sense, norms were retained. Furthermore, in some areas, new control arrangements reduced the need to rely on individual character without reducing the need to avoid swindling or pilfering. And we should remember that Victorian preaching did not prevent malfeasance in the nineteenth century; indeed, fears of confidence games reflected not only the desired standards of respectability but their potential fragility as well.

But there were changes. We have seen that by the 1920s, business manuals dropped honesty as a criterion for success. After a new federal bankruptcy law was passed in 1898, a debtor could be protected against full creditor claims—even more than once—whereas in the nineteenth century, debts, whatever their impact on the individual's ability to survive, had to be paid. Now, however, it was recognized that creditors might press too hard and that repayment might be impossible for reasons beyond the debtor's control. Many thousands of Americans took advantage of the new law in its first years, in the 1920s, again after World War II, and in the early 1980s. Individual or family claims predominated over business use. Critics argued for the older values; a 1959 commentary noted that "honest persons, save in the direst circumstances, or except as they have been corrupted by the plain invitation of the law to take the easy way out, will have no truck with bankruptcy." There is no reason to contend that honesty declined, and indeed, increasingly strict credit reports continued to impose fiscal discipline despite the growing use of loans. But the larger cultural framework and the laws that it generated did ease somewhat. And it is probable, as the critics argued, that with time the older stigmas lost their impact, making more people ready to relax their sense of personal obligation and fiscal restraint. By 1997, 1.3 million Americans were declaring bankruptcy annually (more than graduated from college each year), with credit cards having unleashed desires that many found both overwhelming and unmanageable.[6]

Work constraints were redefined as well. As hiring manuals and job interview advice began to focus on people-pleasing qualities and emotional control, the emphasis on values associated with Victorian-style probity eased. The criteria for good secretaries moved away from honesty and financial exactitude to cheeriness and a calm demeanor. The change reflected the increasing specialization, with accountants now responsible for some of the money management that once fell to higher-level secretaries, and new business systems may have reduced the need to rely on good character. Although no one abandoned references to reliability, there was a rebalancing of personal controls. Off the job site, sexuality generated another set of discussions about lying among adults, with most people urged to conceal affairs. The phenomenon may not have been new, but the recommendations were.[7]

Finally, children's honesty began to be discussed in new terms and, with this, came a shift in etiquette advice. The subject surfaced in the 1940s, and traditional views still appeared. For instance, a Catholic manual held that lying was a violation of God's law, even though it recommended that parents "not go to extremes" while promoting the truth. The principal new assumptions were, first, that direct attacks on lying did not have constructive results and might make children feel too guilty and, second, that children naturally and inevitably lied and so must be given great latitude as they moved gradually, possibly incompletely, to firmer standards. "It is a mistake to apply adult principles about telling the truth to the words of a little child." Parents need not back away from a goal of control over falsehoods, and commentary, particularly in the 1940s, waxed eloquent about the importance in civilized societies of telling the truth. The best strategy was not insisting on restraint directly but demonstrating to the child how a lie hurt other people.[8]

By the 1950s, child-rearing advice had gone beyond maintaining flexibility based on the nature of the child's psyche, although this continued to win attention. Everybody lies, so the new argument went, even though this may be unpardonable. Imagination is good; white lies are socially necessary, lest people be hurt by tactlessness. The issue, therefore, is not absolute rigor but, rather, management of the extent to which lying is used. Too much lying about issues of importance must be addressed, but the rest no longer required attention. By the late 1980s, the latitude had widened still further. "Human societies would fall apart if we insisted on saying exactly what we were thinking, on any and all occasions." Common adult strategies obviously teach children that some lies are fine, as when a woman tells a caller that her husband is not home when he clearly is. And even though etiquette books, beginning with Amy Vanderbilt's in 1952, did not list "white lies" in their table of contents, they did offer a range of responses that could be used to escape unwanted social contact without indicating the real distaste involved. In the new culture, being pleasant might supersede truth telling.[9]

This relaxation in discussions of lying reflected the new research on children and the new demands of social interactions now less protected by formal manners. A nation bombarded by advertising claims might well loosen its insistence on rigorous truth telling, whereas the demands of working smoothly in sales or on management teams might rely on carefully controlled concealments and exaggerations. There is no way to demonstrate that lying itself increased over nineteenth-century levels. But as part of the development of personal standards of self-control and self-evaluation, the framework for dealing with the issue unquestionably shifted.

Driving and Safety

Some developments reflected a need for new control standards simply because of significant innovations in the conduct of daily life. Just as the emergence of telephones produced a new etiquette, so, after some hesitation, did the advent of automobiles. The form of this process in the United States had some interesting features, for assumptions of restraint advanced unusually rapidly, along with supportive regulation.

Initially, cars and discipline did not easily mix. Automobile advertisements stressed speed, and by the 1920s, the fascination with daredevil driving had produced a network of racing venues. With essentially no regulation or licensing of drivers, it was little wonder that accident rates soared; in 1924, more than 26,000 Americans died in car wrecks.[10]

Here, then, was an unprecedented problem area. With cars having become weapons, the absence of self-control could cause tremendous damage. In 1905, newspapers and magazines began highlighting the problems, along with books bearing titles such as *The Increasing Automobile Hazard* (1917). The National Safety Council, founded in 1914, undertook massive educational efforts. Three arguments were made, all of which began to take hold. First, better engineering of roads and cars could reduce some of the problems. Second, regulation was necessary. Third, driver self-management was vital. As *Motor Age* explained in 1916, most accidents had "at least an element of contributory negligence." According to a 1931 "safety week" column, "We have only ourselves to blame. People cause 90 percent of accidents." Education was essential to improve personal control.[11]

Industry leaders, not surprisingly, welcomed the self-control theme but opposed other regulations that might interfere with driving pleasure.

By the 1930s, as accident tolls and the attendant publicity continued to mount, training efforts were extended to driver education programs in the schools. Automobile companies formed the Automotive Safety Foundation in 1937, primarily for educational purposes. But industry did not win on all fronts. Regulation increased in the 1930s, including the beginning of licensing requirements, which dramatically reduced crash rates. Speed limits were introduced, 50 miles an hour on rural roads, and 25 to 50 in the cities. Many suburbs began installing speed bumps, and police departments established traffic divisions and began to arrest reckless drivers. Improvements in road design were supplemented by manufacturing changes. In 1926, Ford introduced safety glass and in the 1950s led other companies in formal safety research. By the 1960s, car design itself was being regulated.

Self-control nonetheless remained vital. Despite their fascination with cars and speed, Americans did begin to discipline themselves. They stopped honking their horns at slight provocations, a reaction that forced the French government, soon after World War II and amid less readily self-controlled drivers, to ban honking by law. Americans learned and largely accepted the necessity of staying in lanes and changing them with care, in contrast to the more individualistic techniques of many European drivers. The majority—68 percent in the 1930s, according to opinion polls—also accepted the necessity of speed limits, again in contrast to most Europeans, who continued to resist generalized regulation into the 1990s. Despite engineering gains—ultimately including restraints like air bags that did not depend on self-control—the principal responsibility remained with the drivers themselves. A 1942 book sounded the older theme: "It is the driver to whom we must impute the responsibility for the hazards presented by these instruments." Insurance companies and safety officials reiterated this message in the 1950s and 1960s: "Driver failure or display of poor judgment [was involved] in 74 percent of all accidents."[12]

Tensions ensued. Americans often used driving to vent emotions and frustrations they had had to bottle up on other occasions. They refused to accept more rigorous limitations—such as a 55-mile-per-hour maximum—that demonstrably reduced accidents and fatalities. Hence the regulations introduced in the wake of 1970s fuel shortages were soon lifted. But safety campaigns and the link between calls for discipline and other facets of twentieth-century self-control did pay off, in a comparatively high national level of driving restraint. For some people, however, this achievement only added to the frustrations produced by mounting demands at work and in their emotional life.

A similar insistence on new levels of personal management extended to other areas during the twentieth century, including the home. Here too, Victorianism was adapted to technical innovations. Many nineteenth-century arguments held individual workers responsible for safety on the job, although gradually this approach was supplemented by regulations and improved mechanical devices. By the early twentieth century, safety organizations, supported by professional home economists, applied the same rhetoric to the household, stressing the need to educate housewives about sensible procedures regarding the new gas-fueled and electric appliances. Industry supported these educational and personal responsibility efforts, extolling the safety of their products when properly used. In another Victorian echo, by the 1930s the commentary added that such problems were most prevalent in working-class and immigrant homes—"Homes in which hazardous conditions are found are usually homes 'on the other side of the tracks' "—because the people involved were irresponsible or at least ignorant.[13] As home fatalities mounted in the 1930s, many agencies, including safety groups, the Red Cross, and insurance companies, doubled their education efforts, exploiting maternal feelings of guilt about anything short of perfection in the home. By the 1950s, the tone had shifted to the need for regulations and devices to deal with problems that no amount of self-control and monitoring of children could resolve. Thus there was more emphasis on mechanisms that would automatically turn off appliances and on "child-proof" bottle caps. Trends in the law toward promoting suits against manufacturers of defective products provided another motive for, and illustration of, the tendency to move away from individual responsibility.[14]

The debate nonetheless continued, as with automobiles and even guns. By the end of the century, the theme of personal responsibility for control had reappeared. In an intriguing rhetorical shift, the U.S. Transportation Department announced in 1997 that car crashes should no longer be called accidents: "If you call something an accident, you are saying it's fate, it's an act of God, it's something you can't foresee. . . .

It's not accidental that one person survives a crash wearing a seat belt and one person goes through a window and dies." Joining this new public awareness campaign, headed "Crashes Aren't Accidents," the Wisconsin Transportation Department changed the title of its annual publication from Accident Facts to Crash Facts.[15]

The increasing technological complexity of daily life, an accepted element of twentieth-century history, thus generally expanded the Victorian emphasis on responsibility and the need for self-control. A distinctive American effort to convert safety issues to moral issues was added as well. Debates abounded, as many people refused to accept the degree of self-management being urged on them and as approaches that would not require personal care were touted as well. On balance, however, the result was an extension of the rules that many Americans expected to internalize.

Unrelated pairings, like probity and self-regulation for safety amid more complex technology, are hard to assess in combination. The partial retreat from the Victorian rhetorical delight in honesty was a crucial change, reflecting the new interest in interpersonal smoothness, consumer hyperbole, and the growing belief in the flaws inherent in children. This was clear evidence that literal character definitions were no longer sufficient. But the concomitant rise of a demanding etiquette for drivers of automobiles, though hardly pushed as hard as honesty had been, imposed daily constraints in an area absent from Victorian strictures. Some of these assessments—those of insurance companies or credit raters, for instance—did link driver behavior to other character qualities, such as drinking and sexual habits and even financial reliability. Measuring up was not always easier, therefore, even as some rules were modestly relaxed. Trade-offs in more explicitly related areas were still more revealing of a need to modify old rules and an equally pressing need to retain personal codes and disciplinary demands.

Guilt and Honor

Beginning in the 1920s, child-rearing experts began to attack the Victorian system of guilt. This was one of several emotional categories in which nineteenth-century intensity yielded to new concerns about the fragility of children's psyches. Along with the new discussions about guilt in childhood, in which Victorian rigor was clearly revisited, came an interesting pattern of relying on honor codes for students—codes that suggested a more refined, internalized set of guidelines than nineteenth-century schoolmasters ever advised.

Writing for the Child Study Association of America in 1932, Dorothy Canfield Fisher and Sidonie Gruenberg, both well-known psychology popularizers, argued that it was "undesirable for a child to develop a deep sense of guilt and of failure." Children should know wrong from right, to be sure, but the emotion of guilt would hold them back from constructive, well-adjusted behavior. According to this reasoning, parents should point out problems rationally without trying to load their children with feelings now labeled "adverse" and undesirable. In dealing with early sexual interests or toilet training, for example, a child should be "protected from an impression that there is anything shameful or disgusting about his misbehavior." Guilt caused worry and distress, and people should be protected from this, lest they suffer from the "repressed energies" that could led to all sorts of mischief. A whole life could be affected, not just the transient adjustments of childhood: a youngster made to feel guilty might suffer "a harmful effect upon his mental health as long as he lives."[16]

Here was a frontal assault on key features of Victorianism. Popularizers took some pride in their modernity: "traditions of guilt and sin" must be overthrown in the interests of solid psychological principles. Guilt could paralyze thought and prevent calm self-control, causing a "merciless kind of self-condemnation" inimical to the confidence desirable for personal happiness and achievement. Articles talked of the "floods" of guilt that old-fashioned parental styles could let loose. By the 1950s and 1960s, accusing someone—a parent or friend—of "laying a guilt trip" showed how quickly these very un-Victorian arguments had entered the common vocabulary.[17]

Advocates of avoiding guilt did not intend permissiveness, however, only a new approach to what they saw as a damaging emotion. Instead of using guilt, parents should watch children closely to prevent behaviors that might require serious chastisement and result in guilt. Guidance should instill a rational conscience, a sense of standards, that would make guilt unnecessary. Toilet training, for example, might start a bit later than Victorians had recommended, so that children could be instructed rather than emotionally bludgeoned. But there was no question that toilet habits must be controlled. Just as Victorians introduced discipline based on guilt—requiring isolation so that a child would think over the wrongdoing, repent, and admit guilt—so twentieth-century parents developed the concept of "grounding," removing privileges in order to induce a reasoned alteration in future behavior, with no emotional "trips" involved. Whether guilt was actually avoided in what still could be a guilt-laden exchange is open to question. In addition, this shift might make parents feel guilty for punishing the child in anger and possibly forcing on her what was now seen as a complex, potentially dangerous emotion.[18]

This attack on guilt generated new arguments between children and parents. It could prevent parents from disciplining certain acts that previously would have incurred punishment, thereby creating a more permissive environment. In areas relating to sexuality, such as masturbation, efforts to avoid guilt did increase, with real if inconclusive effects. Assessing the results of this concern about guilt is difficult, and we will return to the issue in later chapters when we consider continuities in guilt about sex and the generation of new guilts about the body, as in the moral anxiety about fat. In any case, commentators on culture began to note a new atmosphere—Ruth Benedict wrote as early as 1946 that "guilt is less extremely felt than in earlier generations. In the United States this is interpreted as a relaxation of morals"—and the decline of guilt-enforced standards became a recurrent complaint against liberal permissiveness. But the reality was more complicated. Either the new or the old standards imposed on children might provoke guilt, whether or not this was a desired effect. Even the experts were ambivalent: for example, a 1959 child-rearing manual condemned guilt as a cause of frustration and anxiety and urged parents to keep their own neuroses in check in order to produce mentally healthier offspring. A later section noted, however, that this emotion was socially essential, serving as a "silent policeman" against unacceptable behavior.[19]

In fact, even as reactions to guilt and the induction of guilt became more problematic, new standards were being introduced into an important facet of childhood and youth that relied directly on a sense of guilt and a desire to avoid it. In 1890, headed by numerous elite private institutions—including women's colleges such as Vassar—and the military academies, several secondary schools and colleges introduced honor codes. These codes, and others installed through the 1930s, assumed that students could be trusted not to plagiarize and not to cheat on examinations, on the basis of personal responsibility, supplemented by an obligation to report on any offending colleagues. The dual premises of the honor systems were rectitude and a guilt-enforced conscience, and among the selected middle- and upper-middle class students involved, usually at small to midsize institutions, the systems usually worked. Although fewer new honor systems were put in place after 1945, several colleges, such as Dartmouth College, Millsaps College, and the U.S. Air Force Academy installed them as recently as the 1990s. Unpleasant experiences with cheating, larger and more socially mixed enrollments, and students' greater reluctance to report on cheaters in the name of avoiding judgmental and guilt-inducing behavior contributed to the system's limitations.

Still, the approach smacked tantalizingly of Victorianism adapted to the new grading procedures of twentieth-century schools, one that offered both individual obligation and separation from institutions of lesser character. Bryn Mawr College, which moved to a full honor system only in 1954, having earlier distinguished honor-bound social behavior from monitored academics, reported wide commitment to the systems already in existence elsewhere. The principle was personal integrity, including self-report as well as report of others, and advocates argued that most students observed this principle whatever the system. Examinations, most notably, did not have to be proctored. Trust and high ideals seemed natural, as opposed to dependence on outside enforcement that would never be complete. Open reliance on honor would be "of immense psychological value," precisely because it emphasized the reliability of personal conscience. Although elite schools cited reports of cheating at other, lesser, and more anonymous sites, like the state universities, the new commitment—the post-Victorian commitment—to self-regulated behavior was an important development. All else failing, guilt loomed large in the equation: "The majority specified that they also expected a student to feel a responsibility for others, either to request the offender to report himself or, if this failed, to report to the board handling such cases."[20]

The coincidence of a reevaluation of guilt and the novel idea of relying on student honor reveals a fascinating complexity. Victorian schools, for all the talk of childish innocence, had no illusions about student behavior when it could not be monitored. Honor systems assumed a new level of student self-control, therefore, and this usually was observed. Aside from these admittedly atypical systems, American college students seemed relatively restrained in regard to cheating, despite numerous and troubling examples of fraud encouraged by commercial essay-writing firms and, by the 1990s, models available on the Internet. Russian observers in the 1990s reported that American exchange students seemed amazingly honest (or naive) compared with their Russian counterparts when taking university examinations, as they largely avoided bringing in notes and crib sheets, which the natives routinely did.[21]

New expertise, including novel approaches to sexuality, combined with the inducements of a consumer-oriented society, prompted a reevaluation of guilt. The unalloyed Victorian faith that guilt was valid and useful was undermined as Americans adjusted to new levels of abundance. Yet guilt did not disappear, or even necessarily decrease, although its targets were altered somewhat. Even the concern about guilt itself could generate the emotion anew, as parents eager to assimilate the most up-to-date advice encountered new remorse about their own behaviors. And systems that depended on the emotion's power proliferated even as references to undesirable neuroses and repressions attracted larger audiences. New evocations of guilt permeated campaigns for home safety and the American approach to overweight and, later, to smoking. The result was a classic twentieth-century trade-off between change and continuity: Victorianism could be freely attacked for damaging rigor even as new rigors were extended to important facets of the behavior of children and adults alike.

Envy and Jealousy

A shift in the attitude toward envy was a crucial part of the transition period around 1900. The growing commitment to consumerism, particularly in clothing, signaled that Americans of various social classes felt envy. Young women talked about their feelings of inferiority when they could not dress fashionably. Efforts to emulate more expensive dress—

for example, in the wearing of silk stockings—multiplied. Accordingly, advertisers and consumer experts began to play on the emotion. Beginning in the late nineteenth-century, popular interior decoration manuals deliberately privileged either expensive antiques or foreign, usually French, designs for the home, implying that the actual furniture choices that most middle-class people could afford would not be quite up to the most desirable standard.[22]

This trend continued to be attacked by most writers advising on character until about 1915. Using older arguments, often strongly influenced by religious goals, readers were told that material envy was misplaced, a sign of skewed values. But as consumerism gained ground and the more secular generation of popularizers came to the fore, the middle class's actual emotional standards did change. By the 1920s, attacks on envy were the exception, and the positive effects of the emotion in stimulating achievement and a more constructive sense of fashion were widespread. Thus in 1923, the editorial staff of the *Ladies Home Journal*, once a bastion of antienvy moralism, praised American women for dressing so well:

> Whatever their background, they seem all to be inspired with what we are told as a typical and standardized American desire to "look like a million dollars." Some of it may be stupid vanity, some of it may be decadent or degenerate vanity, but justly weighed and charitably considered, isn't most of it innocent vanity—wholesale ambition to look one's best, to achieve beauty and distinction, to assert good taste and cultivated selection in clothes?[23]

Likewise, advertisements sought to attach a desirable social meaning to nearly all products, thereby both legitimating and utilizing envy as a means of selling goods. For example, in describing the charms of "gleaming teeth," Colgate maintained that "there is nothing mysterious about these enviable results. The men and women fortunate to secure them did nothing that you cannot easily do yourself." Perfume and soap advertisements routinely invoked both envy and the desire to be envied: "Do other women envy you?" read a perfume notice, "Or do you envy them? The woman who gets what she wants out of life—the woman other women envy and copy—never depends on youth alone, or a pretty face, or brains." Rather, she buys Houbigant perfume.[24]

Along with this important breach in the lexicon of Victorian standards came the literally simultaneous intensification of the attack on jealousy. Unlike guilt, jealousy was an emotion that had been officially reproved in the nineteenth century, although few details were provided and some stories suggested a certain leniency when women's attachments to love and family were concerned. It was not until the 1920s that popularizers began to attack jealousy in children, in terms similar to those soon applied to guilt but with much greater vehemence. Jealousy was redefined as a powerful but destructive emotion, capable, if unchecked, of causing violence to siblings and at the same time distorting the subsequent adult personality. In 1925, D. H. Thom fired one of the first salvos in what became a major campaign to inhibit sibling rivalry—a rivalry that was both named and widely feared for the first time.

> Few emotions are experienced by man which from a social point of view are more important than jealousy. . . . The jealous person becomes an object of dislike. Often he develops the idea that he is unjustly treated or persecuted, and all too frequently this idea causes uncontrolled resentment and disastrous results.

In 1926 a Child Study Association of America pamphlet similarly identified the inevitability and evil of jealousy, noting that the emotion is "so intense that little but harm can come from rousing it." By 1930 the Children's Bureau was offering instructions on how to circumvent siblings' jealous reactions to the arrival of a new baby, under the heading "nobody like a jealous person. A jealous person is never happy." Ways for parents to reduce jealousy, including giving presents to siblings on a child's birthday and arranging for separate rooms and possessions, were held to be vital to developing a healthy, constructive personality. Childish jealousy "indelibly stamps personality and distorts character"; "we have only to read the daily paper to see the results of ungoverned jealousy in adult life." The advice took hold. Many parents wrote to family magazines about their concerns over children's jealousy, and a mid-1940s poll found that the emotion was rated the third most important issue in dealing with children and the most serious of all concerns relating to personality.[25]

In the 1940s, attacks on jealousy were extended to adults in a variety of personality manuals and magazine articles. Jealousy was a possessive emotion, unfair to other individuals and destructive of true love—a view that modernists like Judge Ben Lindsey had trumpeted in the 1920s. A 1945 booklet for high school girls argued that "jealousy is probably the most common of all the unhelpful attitudes. . . . Why do we act this way? The reason is that we haven't outgrown the selfishness of early childhood. . . . We must grow up." Another account extended the immaturity theme, reflecting how a generation of child-rearing advice now applied to adults: "The jealous lover is a child hugging his toy so closely that no one else can see it. Jealousy is almost always a mark of immaturity and insecurity." In the 1960s the antijealousy arguments were carried to the area of sexuality, with possessiveness now a cardinal sin. By then, however, polls indicated that a majority of middle-class Americans condemned the emotion, claiming that they either had overcome it or learned to conceal it.[26]

The relaxation in the disapproval of envy and the greatly intensified attacks on jealousy formed a trade-off, emerging in the 1920s, of self-control standards in two closely related emotional areas. Americans really did put a brake on their condemnations of self and others when they felt envious, but with some complications, to which we will shortly return. But the battle against jealousy brought an important, extensive new constraint into Americans' emotional lives and personal relationships, with which some people struggled mightily. Clearly, there was no unambiguous triumph for permissiveness.

Yet the contradictory directions made sense in light of the changes' causes. Both changes were based on a new generation of expertise, setting aside older moralisms in the case of envy and operating according to presumed new psychological findings (including careful if, in fact, biased studies of the frequency of sibling rivalry) when jealousy was concerned. On the one hand, the changes in feelings about envy responded to the pressures of consumerism, which in turn led to more blatantly emotional consumerist appeals. On the other hand, the attacks on jealousy flowed in part from particular shifts, such as a smaller family size, which heightened the potential for sibling rivalry. The attacks served as a precondition for greater permissiveness in sexual behavior and gender interaction in a period which men and women were mingling more freely and structural limitations on the experience of jealousy were rapidly falling. Here was a case in which internal self-control was meant to replace the earlier effects of substantial gender segregation, with new training beginning in early childhood and extending throughout adulthood. But the growing concern about jealousy also mirrored the increasing insistence on smooth interpersonal relations, in offices as well as social gatherings. An older interpretation, which saw jealousy as a possibly useful competitive motivation, was explicitly attacked. Jealous students did not get along well, and getting along was a crucial goal. After World War II, in part to prevent jealousy, school systems made reports of grades less open or softened grading altogether; later, public postings of grades were outlawed outright, ostensibly to protect privacy but in fact to limit unwanted rivalry.[27]

As with guilt and honor codes, the divergent trends of envy and jealousy did not reduce the obligations of self-control—they merely altered their targets. Yet there was more to this particular trade-off. First, changes in standards did not produce uniform results. Concern about envy did not disappear, and some of the efforts at compensatory self-discipline were clearly designed to deal with the residuum. Economist Simon Patten, for example, who advised a reappraisal of envy for its constructive features, was also a leading advocate of control in eating. Jealousy certainly persisted, despite widespread parental maneuvering and adult acceptance of standards. Students exchanged grades and suffered jealous consequences even when officials tried to limit the practice. Informal socializing, including multiple dating (what the experts called promiscuous dating), easily outran the insistence on heroic levels of self-control. New institutional modifications, including the practice of steady dating, were introduced to ease the tension, but some individuals found themselves unacceptably jealous at various stages of life.[28]

The trajectories of jealousy and envy intersected in important ways. Envy might be approved, but as attachments to material attributes became more tenacious with the advancing consumerism, a person's appearance or possessions became part of the person himself or herself. Envying someone's grooming or clothes could easily turn into outright jealousy of that person. Because jealousy was the stronger of the two emotions, by the 1930s Americans began to use the term jealousy when the emotion, technically envy, was a reaction to what someone else had. With this development, the open approval of envy became more problematic. Even though it followed from consumerism, it could also complicate interpersonal relations. Not surprisingly, teenagers began to pride themselves on their ability to overcome envy—which they called jealousy—as a badge of their emotional maturity. They were applying the same self-control standards, and the social motivations for these standards, as they did to jealousy, or at least they wished to be able to do so.[29]

These complications, along with some traditionalist elements, inhibited advertisers' use of envy. After direct invocations of envy reached a high point in the 1920s, American advertisers turned to stressing the accessibility of their goods. Too much emphasis on using goods in order to be envied contradicted both democratic values and the desire to get along smoothly with others. Criticisms of motives such as keeping up with the Joneses, a common reference in the 1950s concerning the envy of one's neighbors' acquisitions, made it clear that envy or attempts to be envied needed to be reined in. Envy remained a powerful inducement, and advertisements of prestige goods took advantage of it, but a bit of subtlety was required even here. Overall, in the envy-jealousy trade-off, real change occurred in standards and behaviors, but on balance, given the different levels of intensity and the unexpected complications that applied to envy, demands on self-control rose after the 1920s.[30]

The Key Adjustments

Two sets of trade-offs dominated the shift from Victorian to twentieth-century patterns of self-control, spilling over into other areas, including child rearing. First, behavior was steadily regulated in the sites of middle-class work, requiring more—and sometimes arduous—restraint in dealing with both superiors and inferiors on the job and in meeting customers' expectations of pleasing, unruffled personalities. At the same time, however, the accelerated relaxation of leisure standards provided new outlets for at least symbolic expression. Whereas Victorian recreational culture had been primarily intended to reinforce personal virtues, including work performance—one of the principal areas in which middle-class respectability contrasted with many working-class interests—the twentieth-century middle class moved into a compensatory leisure mode. This result produced tension and recurrent traditionalist complaints, and it may not have provided a satisfactory balance because the new combination juggled tighter self-control with greater, if often vicarious, abandon.

Closely related to this adjustment was the rebalancing of manners and emotions. In sum, manners became more informal while demands for systematic emotional control became more stringent. Middle-class Americans became far more casual than their Victorian counterparts, even though their legitimate opportunities for emotional expression were curtailed. As a result, relationships—especially friendship, but also many marriages—were significantly altered. Here too, the end product was not less self-control than the Victorians had dictated. But even though some key Victorian goals were preserved, others were redefined, as Americans were told to become less stiff but more cautious.

Work and Release

The acceleration of new leisure interests, a crucial part of the transition decades, continued after the 1920s. The same period, however, also saw moves to tighten the self-control expected of middle-class workers, whose behavior had not been explicitly targeted—beyond the norms of general politeness—in nineteenth-century advice literature or institutional arrangements. The rise of corporate bureaucracies and the need for people-sensitive service personnel had redefined this climate, and personnel experts were recruited to supply the necessary guidelines and devices, with the support of applied research from industrial psychology.

The push for new levels of self-control initially extended concerns developed during the nineteenth-century industrialization process. Shop rules had long been used to discipline workers and to teach them to internalize certain of their habits. Thus employers attempted to regulate drinking on the job, theft, fighting, wandering around, dirtiness that might affect products such as cloth, and punctuality. Although they had varied success, by several measurements a more self-regulated workforce had emerged by 1900.[31] In this context, it was small wonder that many employers raised the stakes. Americanization programs sought to extend discipline, including "proper" home habits, to immigrant workers. Lower-class girls used as clerks were, as we have seen, formally schooled in appropriate middle-class manners and dress, leavened by additional docility. Time-and-motion studies, which ultimately led to the assembly line, sought to regulate body movements into a series of maximally efficient, repetitive acts, making human workers as machinelike—as devoid of independent spontaneity—as possible on the job. Industrial psychologists like Elton Mayo, studying shop floor behavior, cast about for more opportunities for manipulation and even described the effect of music on efficiency. The factory's emphasis shifted to regulation and manipulation along with personal restraint to keep workers in line.[32]

Some of the concerns developed in dealing with factory operatives spilled over to middle-class personnel, where they had additional implications. Mayo, for example, while studying a General Electric plant in the 1920s with the aim of improving efficiency, was appalled at the amount of anger he discovered on the shop floor. His solution was to design another set of manipulative techniques: for example, insisting that workers state their grievances several times, believing that with repetition their anger would gradually dissipate into embarrassment, thereby making the issue easier to resolve. But this solution actually forced more self-control on foremen and middle managers than on the workers themselves, as they now were obligated to listen to the workers' anger or other provocative emotions without becoming engaged themselves. Self-restraint was elevated to new heights. Similar tactics were proposed for salesmen, another characteristic twentieth-century employment category.[33]

By the 1930s, the insistence that middle-class workers go beyond promptness and efficiency to careful management of their emotions created new strategies that were used and supplemented from that point forward. Almost all the old rules, first developed to discipline factory workers, continued to apply, though some—like the prohibition on fighting on the job—no longer had to be mentioned explicitly. Many middle-class workers avoided the degrading discipline of the time clock, which meant, however, that they must be punctual—another step in the internalization of self-control. The primary focus now applied to additional constraints, particularly those pertaining to self-presentation in dealing with people.

A key development was the creation of formal personnel or industrial relations departments, a process that began in the 1920s (encouraged by worker-manager interactions instituted during World War I). By the

1930s, 31 percent of American corporations had such departments. One of their missions was employee counseling, predicated on the twin notions that experts might be able to help individuals form more constructive job habits and also that white-collar employees were responsible for keeping their emotions under control on the job. In 1922, Metropolitan Life Insurance launched a service of this sort, initially for outright psychiatric illness but later for any apparent adjustment problem. Counselors themselves were required to maintain careful self-control amid their clients' emotional outpourings—to remain amiable, alert, but not deeply engaged.[34]

Personality testing surged forward in the same period, reflecting the experts' confidence that unacceptable characteristics could be spotted in advance and also that the range of self-control necessary for effective work must be extended. At first, into World War I, the testing focused on aptitudes, but by the late 1920s it included sections to pinpoint the test taker's location on an introversion-extroversion scale. The use of the Humm-Wadsworth Personality Test, first at Lockheed Aircraft in the early 1940s as a means of screening out troublemakers, advanced the effort to determine emotional characteristics, with an emphasis on docility. Doncaster Humm, one of the test's authors, claimed that 80 percent of all problem workers had testable deficiencies in temperament. Industrial psychologists believed that such profiles would prevent unsuitable hires and assignments. Another implication was that workers who were accepted were responsible for maintaining an appropriate personality on the job. A manual for secretaries spelled out these expectations: "The secretary should never forget that in order to please people, he needs to exert himself." The argument was that unsatisfactory middle-class and white-collar work resulted more often from a lack of self-control than from a lack of appropriate skill.[35]

New kinds of training programs extended this notion and its attendant demands. During the 1920s, department stores formalized their efforts to produce salespersons with pleasing, controlled personalities. Foremen were subjected to a barrage of retraining campaigns, converting them from using intimidation to motivate workers to trying conciliation. Engineers were used to design work systems that reduced the technical requirements of the foreman's job, and the successful management of people became more important. Foremen were urged to recognize that "the day of the 'bully' and 'slave-driver' had gone, and the day of the 'gentleman' and 'leader' had arrived." This conversion required unprecedented self-restraint: "Control your emotions—control your remarks—control your behavior." Educational programs—the movement crescendoed from the 1930s through the 1950s, at which point the new norms seemed more firmly established—emphasized keeping one's temper, even when dealing with angry charges, and maintaining a pleasant, calm demeanor, including a smiling face. "Impersonal but friendly" was the watchword of the age, guiding workers to present a carefully controlled facade regardless of their inner feelings. With time, one leading sociologist argued, training programs could so distort spontaneous emotional responses that middle-class workers might not know exactly what their feelings were, as opposed to knowing how they were expected to act. During the 1940s, the peak of the retraining movement, hundreds of thousands of supervisors were given instruction. The new norms spread so quickly that foremen and other middle managers, initially skeptical of the new demands on their patience, began asking for additional help. In turn, "coolheaded" became a common form of approval when operatives rated foremen.[36]

Standards of self-control at work were introduced into the preparations for getting a middle-class job in the first place. The job interview became more elaborate. Interviewers, instructed to keep themselves under careful control, sought to judge personality attributes well beyond manners and dress, although these still were important. Often armed with test results, they rated candidates in terms of restraint of temper, absence of excessive shyness, tact, and humor (but not silliness)—in short, a range of qualities that indicated appropriate emotional stability and a capacity for consistent self-control. In turn, job candidates, frequently schooled in interview techniques or aided by the many advice manuals available for white-collar aspirants, sought to project the appropriate image, including the earnestness, reliability, and competence required in the nineteenth century.[37] Despite the available credentials, including school grades, business interviews typically hinged on personal presentations.

The new work demands produced a variety of outcomes. Some people assimilated the added requirements without apparent difficulty. Some, like flight attendants carefully schooled in friendliness, may have suffered from the restrictions on spontaneity without being fully aware of the impact. As one program leader noted, "If you think about the other person and why they're upset, you've taken attention off yourself and your own frustration. And you won't feel so angry." Identification of self-control demands was complicated by a rhetoric that spoke of not only reasonableness but also liberation. After all, this was the individualistic, emancipated twentieth century. Even so, many middle-class workers noted the strain. A telephone operator made the point in an interview with Studs Terkel: "You can't be angry. . . . You have to be pleasant, no matter how bad you feel." Earlier, in the 1950s, a middle manager told C. Wright Mills that he always went home "frazzled" from the effort to keep peace with people "at all levels."[38]

The best way to manage the new demands for self-control might have been by internalizing the joys of salesmanship, preached to tens of thousands of Americans in the books and workshops of self-help leaders like Dale Carnegie since the 1920s. Here, too, the self was fully adaptable to the situation: no customer response should cause one to lose the friendly, bubbly veneer. But there was pleasure in the act of effacing oneself: the knowledge that the result might manipulate the client, whose control was inferior to one's own. Carnegie described his delight when he refused to show his annoyance while being harangued by a customer, knowing that he had the upper hand despite the need to quell a spontaneous response. The lessons of salesmanship seemed so important to the economy of the twentieth century that they also were taught to middle-class children. Schools and youth groups set up programs to teach the art of people pleasing. In the 1920s, newspapers began to recruit middle-class boys for home deliveries, turning away from working-class street sales; and the boys were instructed in ways to keep their own personalities tuned to the mood of a potential customer in order to cajole him or her into subscribing.[39]

The most explicit efforts to teach personnel the kinds of self-control now sought on the job took place between the 1920s and the 1950s. This was the heyday of salesmanship training, "how to succeed" books, and management courses. By the 1950s, the new standards were increasingly assumed, and the aura of novelty receded. Nonetheless, new and further-reaching personality tests were introduced, measuring even more capacities for self-restraint and careful presentation. The increasing use of women in the service sectors after the 1950s added assumptions about feminine docility and pleasantness to the existing job criteria. Many women workers—flight attendants are a prime example—were pushed hard to create appropriate work personalities.[40]

The steady decline of the union movement beginning in the late 1950s both encouraged and reflected the demands of middle-class work as white-collar jobs began to surpass factory positions by a widening margin. Union workers often knew that they needed to present demands and mount protest in a controlled atmosphere, and they might surpass management in their calm presentations.[41] But union styles, including those of some of the most successful leaders, like the miners' John L. Lewis, had earlier made righteous indignation a hallmark. With the larger middle-class labor force, schooled to believe that spontaneous emotions and jobs did not mix and with management adept at defusing grievances through conciliatory tactics, the base for a strong labor movement was clearly weakened. This, plus other, related developments—including relocations of work to less union friendly regions of the country and the increasing use of women, whom traditional labor movements tended to marginalize—reduced even further the potential resistance to demands for self-control at work.[42]

Finally, new management fads reflected the continuing effort to convince white-collar workers of the need to keep themselves in check, often through flowery rhetoric about empowerment and democratization. Sensitivity training, or T-group, sessions blossomed in the 1960s. Group meetings of young middle managers used elaborate role playing with wide-ranging discussions disparaging authoritarian management styles and inculcating the need for careful self-control, particularly in response to aggression. A better command of one's own feelings was the key: "effectiveness decreases as emotionality increases." Undue repression was attacked: the modern worker should be psychologically healthy. Personnel gurus talked of authenticity in relationships. Yet the basic message was unchanged: "The rationality of feelings and attitudes is as crucial as that of the mind." When T-groups receded by the late 1970s, they were replaced a decade later by the new enthusiasm for Total Quality Management (TQM). Here again, personnel experts seemed to attack older, insensitive management techniques while appealing for suggestions from the lower ranks. Team playing was crucial, which could generate exciting opportunities for wider participation in policy discussions. TQM emphasized the primacy of the customer and included control over counterproductive impulses as one of three major targets. Trainees spent the first of three days learning to identify, in themselves and others, "defending" and "attacking" emotions, which had no place in a successful meeting. "Defending/Attacking behavior is seen as making personal attacks, moving away from issues, and becoming emotional." "These behaviors usually involve value judgments and contain emotional overtones." In contrast, "interactive skills" training was the key, with people greeting the ideas of others with supportive enthusiasm and assuming that the ensuing discussion would winnow out stupidity without the necessity of direct criticism. The message was the same as it had been seventy years earlier: leave the self's rougher edges outside.[43]

Greater self-restraint at work, in a climate in which interaction with other people was necessary for successful job performance, was not, of course, the only innovation during this period. Again, there was a trade-off. After the 1920s, the trends already emerging in leisure, toward more pleasure seeking and at least vicarious release, acquired new vigor. Middle-class Americans were participating in worlds of imagination far different from the controls required during the working day.

The chronological progression is reasonably clear. Victorianism relied on a culture of self-improvement. When not actually working, people should seek reading and recreations that reinforced core values and created a better work and family life. The idea of leisure as contrast or compensation was not entirely absent, however, for Victorianism did not succeed entirely even with the middle class, but the effort to shape a unified cultural context was very strong.

By the 1870s, as we have seen, this formula was beginning to weaken. As more diverse leisure interests and opportunities surfaced, the hold of Victorianism required that many of them be justified in terms of higher goals. Thus sports could be seen as part of character development. Many new consumer interests were presented as improving health or the family. The idea of release for its own sake, though gaining in fact, was still resisted. Some of the new leisure actually, as well as rhetorically, converged with work demands. Thus sports, as defined by the later nineteenth century, joined a worklike concern with speed and record keeping, with rules and enforcing officials, and with personal achievement blended with team goals—all this in addition to the idea of enhancing health and refreshing participants for a future work effort.[44]

From the 1920s onward, leisure, though sometimes embracing pastimes already developed in the Victorian and transitional decades, moved more definitively to contrast with daily life and to feature opportunities either directly or vicariously to shed the mounting demands for self-control on the job. Inevitably, there were throwbacks to older themes. The new fascination with hobbies, particularly for young people, showed the ease with which recreation could be justified when it resembled work and might improve the participant.[45] Sports continued to alternate between a means of improving character and a chance to give excited fans an opportunity to let themselves go. Leisure that was too purely hedonistic continued to spark criticism—especially when the young were involved—and to produce countermeasures designed to demonstrate personal discipline and sacrifice. But there was a change in how middle-class Americans began to seek and welcome the tension between what they enjoyed in their off-hours and what they had to observe on the job.

Gambling provided a revealing case in point. In the nineteenth century, the pursuit had drawn some respectable men into poker games and other betting, more in the south and west rather than the northeast. The conflict with central middle-class values was obvious: gambling wasted money, reflected a desire to gain without work, and jeopardized control of oneself. In the later nineteenth century, as middle-class habits loosened but worries about modern behavior tightened, legislators introduced measures to limit still further the opportunities for gambling. Horse racing, for example, was banned in many states by the early twentieth century.[46]

At the same time, however, gambling was gaining new adherents as a leisure outlet. Gambling centers opened in places like Florida in the 1890s, in association with vacation resorts. Even respectable people tried to escape the pressures of work by gaming. By the 1920s, modest betting had become part of middle-class socializing as husbands and wives began to spend more time entertaining together. Small bets over poker or, more commonly, bridge enlivened the leisure hours. A new etiquette developed, seeking to legitimate the new interest by surrounding it with appropriate self-control. Writing in the early 1950s, Amy Vanderbilt thus approved of social bets as long as they could be handled gracefully. Losers—and one should expect to lose—must be able "to pay off the winners in a necessary casual manner." Well before this, gambling centers had been opened for the most ardent enthusiasts. Bookmaking facilities proliferated in the 1920s, and legal bans on horse racing were largely removed by the early 1930s. The same decade saw the tentative rise of Reno and Las Vegas as gaming centers, with Las Vegas taking off after 1941. Betting rose as a proportion of all recreational spending in the 1920s and 1930s.[47]

Also in these decades, sports spectatorship began to become a driving passion for many middle-class men, from white-collar ranks upward. It was in the 1890s that the term fan began to gain currency, apparently a journalistic abbreviation of fanatic. The neologism correctly identified the kind of surrogate passion now poured into following teams and urging them on. Developments such as sports sections in newspapers and magazines and radio commentary facilitated and extended the interest, and the excitement of a radio account of a crucial game or match became part of male life across class boundaries. But it was in the crowds, in the massive new stadiums constructed for college and professional teams, that the service of sports as a release showed through most clearly. People normally hemmed in by requirements of self-control could shout and emote to their hearts' content in the anonymity of a crowd. "I mean, it really helps you, brother, to reach down to your toes and pull out a yell you been keepin' bottled up inside you for Christ knows how long." Watching sports might recall youthful participation in the games and longed-for skills. But it also served as a symbolic contrast to standard self-control. Athletes should be aggressive. They should get angry, shouting at the baseball umpire in a ritualistic battle that would never be tolerated in normal jobs. They should even be violent, though within bounds. They should hug each other in euphoria, as men were no longer allowed to do in the homophobic constraints of real life. They might weep at a loss. And those who watched them, sometimes sharing their outbursts, could escape for a time.[48]

Other leisure outlets were opened. Cheap fiction, radio shows, and comic books provided men and boys with stories of aggression and violence. Tough-talking Nick Carter served that function in the late nineteenth century, a man who would take no back talk and who attracted women without effort (and without great interest). Superman was deliberately invented in the 1930s to provide a heroic alternative to standard constraints, though he too felt no particular excitement himself.[49]

Movies created their own fantasy worlds, with Hollywood quickly discovering (after a brief flirtation with realism) that escapism was what sold best.[50] As with sports, idealizations might, somewhat ironically, include Victorian nostalgia. Just as athletes symbolized courage and targeted aggression, in the best traditions of nineteenth-century boys' literature, so several films featured cowboys whose righteous anger, slow to kindle, would inspire them to perform great feats. Heroes and heroines courted and even married with great passion, along with vivid representations of mother's love. Radio soap operas, borrowing themes from nineteenth-century romance novels, treated audiences to intense, compelling emotion. Passion beyond control was a standard theme, particularly for women.

Fright offered another emotional outlet to people who normally controlled themselves but who took delight in staged fear and in demonstrating spectator bravery. Amusement park rides, an American specialty, proliferated through the early decades of the twentieth century, for working-class audiences as well as the more daring middle-class youth. Horror films and enactments of violence, though tame by late-twentieth-century standards, attracted large audiences, particularly in the 1930s. The use of fear in entertainment escalated steadily, with more daring amusement park rides after the 1950s and then an ascending series of science fiction and horror movies aimed at a youthful audience. By the 1980s, the popularity of Halloween as an adult, as well as a children's, holiday was revived, providing, as some suggested, a substitute for the now-departed, very real fears associated with the cold war.[51]

Dance styles diverged from nineteenth-century models, featuring frenzied motion—the Charleston and other fad dances of the 1920s—or slow, sensual entwining, both of which contrasted with the ordered, disciplined waltzes of the Victorian age. As in work, the trends launched early in the century tended to become more entrenched. Football violence gained ground over the more sedate, stylized baseball. Movies and boys' comic books became more sensational.[52]

This pattern of trade-offs between work and leisure, with the increasing demands for self-control matched by more opportunities to use leisure for release and artificial spontaneity, created some troubling tensions. Some people confused fantasy with reality and brought to their normal life inappropriate expectations and behaviors. Even more observers, recalling more literal Victorianism, worried about the impact on young people of these contrasting standards—hence the campaign against the corrupting, crime-inducing qualities of comic books in the 1940s and 1950s. The leading popular culture critic of the 1940s and 1950s, for example, explained to a Senate committee that even the most ordinary comic books contained "sadistic, criminal, sexual scenes" that could entice even normal children to "delight" in mayhem. The recurrent attacks suggested divisions in the public but also the need to create anxiety amid permissiveness, a theme that continued through ongoing commentary on media violence, rock music lyrics, and other offerings.[53]

Furthermore, different groups participated differently in different kinds of release. By the 1970s, as public lotteries proliferated, 65 percent of the sales went to a more 10 percent of the population, often racial and ethnic minorities; the middle class's involvement was more limited.[54] Even though fantasy leisure bridged class gaps to a degree and certainly offered opportunities to many professional actors and sports figures from minority groups, visible distinctions remained. Most obviously, save for a few devotees of particularly adventurous sports or outdoors activities, the balance between work demands and leisure alternatives was not even. Most people experienced the world of action and passion vicariously as spectators. This disparity helped make the system work: spectators could shout or cry while still knowing that their normal discipline was not being undermined, because the settings were mere artifice. By the same token, however, the effectiveness of the release might be questioned. Could three hours in a sports crowd on a weekend compensate for forty hours in which one needed to rein in one's spontaneous responses?

Some of the most popular leisure outlets had certain constraints built in. Although sports spectatorship provided release, participation was supposed to be serious business, requiring great discipline. Even exercise became known as "working out," lest it be confused with frivolity or a lack of direction. Sports also were valued because they presumably reduced sexual desire, and coaches frequently tried to regulate sexual activity in a belief that sex and sports did not mix. (All this in fascinating contrast to the ancient Greek view of sports, which assumed that sports beautified the body and so enhanced sexual experience.) Movie audiences became increasingly subdued. Silent films created emotions through special effects; hence, audiences shouted and wept when they saw a moving train heading right at them. Gradually, however, they learned to restrain themselves in the face of vivid stimulation.[55]

In addition, efforts to regulate certain kinds of leisure exuberance surfaced recurrently, reflecting potential new problems and also a reminder of Victorian disdain. After World War II, municipal governments discouraged Halloween celebrations in an attempt to eliminate vandalism, and they shortened the hours during which children could go trick or treating. Indeed, the tricks virtually disappeared. Colleges periodically attacked fraternity parties, and movements to provide alternatives to New Year's Eve carousing spread as well. The service of leisure as a contrast to daily self-restraints clearly had limitations.[56]

A New Standard for Humor

Victorian etiquette, as we have seen, disapproved of laughter, finding it physically revolting as well as a symptom of frivolity. However widely the standard applied in fact, its revisiting at the end of the century was yet another sign of the redefinition of self-control norms that would lead toward new possibilities of release and compensation. As vaudeville and burlesque began to expand, humorous novels and private joke books also proliferated. By the 1880s, it was clear that the middle class was becoming increasingly comfortable with laughter in social settings as well as in formal entertainment.[57]

Manners books caught the transition. Maud Cooke argued in *Social Etiquette* in 1896 that wit was a God-given pleasure that should be indulged. Laughter remained potentially revolting—"few grown people laugh well"—but "moderate laughter" was now acceptable. Another manual made an even more ambitious claim: people who could not enjoy a joke were not pleasant to live with and would not have many friends. So long as jokes were not mean, it was "very unwise" to be disturbed by jests, even when directed at oneself: "Join in the laugh, and refuse to consider your amour-propre." Yet another advice writer urged: "[Humor] takes much of the friction off the wheel of life for ourselves and for those with whom we come in contact. Almost every situation has its humorous aspect. Seek it! Drag it into the light if need be!"[58]

Cautions persisted. Young women should learn to laugh gracefully. Although it was important to convey a sunny disposition, laughs themselves were often ugly, "physical contortions," except when one learned to be melodious. But the warnings were now double edged: girls who did not have wit must learn to laugh. "Man is the only animal that can express mirth in appropriate sound. It is, therefore, a prerogative." Boisterous laughter was condemned, but so now was hollow, affected laughter that revealed an "empty skull and a hollow heart." Natural laughter disclosed good character, "like the jingling of sweet bells." Children, naturally humorous, should be encouraged to laugh as long as they did not get out of hand.[59]

Magazines debated the issue. *Cosmopolitan* praised the spread of laughter in 1906, contending that American character was finally triumphing over British propriety. But Professor Hjalmar Boyesen, in *North American Review*, worried that Americans were "inverting the proper relation" between jocularity and seriousness, with social gatherings turning into little more than strings of jokes and funny stories. The *Educational Review* condemned the modern compulsion to be photographed with broad smiles. Another *Cosmopolitan* piece argued for better proportion: "Life is life and humor is decimal one percent of it, and no more." But novelists, including Carolyn Wells, now took up the cause of humor, noting the tension that perpetually serious people brought into a household. "There's only one thing the matter with Aunt Molly, and that is, that she has no sense of humor."[60]

The authorization to laugh helped support the burgeoning entertainment business, including both radio and movies, which worked hard to be funny. Enjoying humor became an important part of escapist leisure, an obvious counterpart to the strictures for self-control on the job. Humor could also be used to defuse tensions on the job itself. As one personnel manual put it in 1921, "The foreman who can see the funny side of things can often 'jolly along' the slacker or discontented workman, when no other means would avail." Laughter thus facilitated new levels of control in other areas.[61]

As always, this adjustment of Victorianism had trade-offs. Accordingly, crying elicited additional criticism. As part of Victorianism itself, men had been warned not to cry. But with women moving into the workplace, personnel experts had to deal with unprecedented problems of crying on the job, and they clearly found them disconcerting. This, then, was one reason to call for more careful management styles so as to avoid offending women, but women also were asked to live up to new levels of dignity. Crying continued to be debated during the twentieth century, with recurrent efforts to value it as a sign of sensitivity and compassion, but on the whole the strictures increased.[62]

Humor itself became a requirement. As the transitional advice literature indicated, people lacking a sense of humor had to learn to fake it, for even on the job, the absence of laughter now signaled an improper balance of character. With change came an opportunity to use humor as a counterpoise to more serious requirements for self-control in other areas. Yet, the importance of using humor appropriately and knowing when to laugh became norms as well.[63]

More broadly, the authorization for leisure added the requirement of roundedness to the attributes of a successful person. By the 1920s and 1930s, job and school applications began to include sections in which to list nonwork activities. Leisure skills thus became a criterion of worth. Here, as with sex (which was not, however, listed as a performance criterion on twentieth-century application forms), an internal ethic developed. Thus the person whose spontaneous impulse was to snooze away the hours after work did not measure up. The result was a paradox. The most popular leisure activities were spectator "sports," like listening to the radio and, later, watching TV, but the new propriety stressed active involvement. Thus what one listed on one's public statements of recreational pursuits and what one actually did for vicarious release often differed, another case in which "white" lies, even to oneself, sometimes were useful.

Manners and Emotions

Closely related to the complex trade-off between self-control at work and greater openness in leisure, including humor, was the readjustment between formal manners and emotions. As the number of leisure opportunities expanded, formality declined, and this affected the work setting as well. This development, however, left important standards intact and also required that individuals know how formal to be depending on the occasion. The decline of manners was not an increase in random freedom. At the same time, any relaxation that did result was partly counterbalanced by new rules restricting emotional intensity. Here, the intricate Victorian combination of both prohibiting and offering opportunities for emotions was simplified into an effort at self-regulation, but the change could have a personal cost and interacted in subtle ways with the decline of formal manners.

A number of forces pushed for decreasing formality in etiquette. As personnel offices downplayed strict job hierarchies in favor of friendlier interactions with inferiors, undue formality became a barrier. Similarly, salesmen tried to adopt a style that would attract customers on grounds of amiability. On the more strictly cultural side, modernists ridiculed some extremes of Victorian upper-class convention as part of the stiff, outdated apparatus that had not allowed its practitioners to breathe. The growing emphasis on consumerism and leisure led to more flexible manners, as enjoyment replaced convention as the goal of recreational activities.

The shift was significant. In principle, Victorian manners had insisted on systematic self-control. Familiarity was dangerous. A proper person always maintained decorum, based on "forgetfulness of self." In the twentieth century, however, manners often seemed to stress the convenience of the individual, with many behavioral rules falling by the wayside.[64]

Two changes were fundamental. First, the increasingly common interactions between young men and women replaced many of the manners that had been designed to regulate their conduct together. Chaperons, though never as omnipresent in the nineteenth century as later images claimed, became even less visible. Dating had its conventions, but they were far less fully supervised and, on the whole, less stiff than the early stages of courtship had been.[65]

Second, in this age of informal democratization, the upper class began to relinquish its social hold. Upper-class people themselves began to patronize more general entertainments, as we have seen. Classic events, like debutante balls, gradually faded in importance. The elite began its conversion from being the leaders of elaborate social forms to being the leaders of daring social activities and great parties—the precursor of the jet-set roles of the post–World War II era.

The American etiquette literature picked this change up slowly compared with western Europe. The concern with not appearing barbaric or rustic meant that the transatlantic upper class long continued to serve as the mentor in manners. Thus Emily Post, writing in the 1920s, could maintain:

> Best Society abroad is always the oldest aristocracy . . . those families and communities who have for the longest period of time known highest cultivation. Our own Best Society is represented by social groups which have had, since this is America, widest rather than longest association with old world cultivation. Cultivation is always the basic attribute of Best Society, much as we hear in this country of an "Aristocracy of wealth."[66]

Only in the 1937 edition did the author decide:

> In the general picture of this modern day the smart and the near-smart, the distinguished and the merely conspicuous, the real and the sham, and the unknown general public are all mixed up together. The walls that used to enclose the world that was fashionable are all down. . . . We've all heard the term "nature's nobleman," meaning a man of innately beautiful character who, never having even heard of the code, follows it by instinct. In other words, the code of a thoroughbred . . . is the code of instinctive decency, ethical integrity, self-respect and loyalty.[67]

Post's book was still eager to identify vulgar behavior, characterized as an "unrestricted display of uncontrolled emotions." But the idea of a defined social elite, setting the stage for elaborate manners, was waning—though etiquette books did not markedly fade away as a result.

Associated with this change was a widespread reduction in the use of servants, which further limited some of the formalism that had been recommended a half-century earlier. In addition, successive etiquette writers vied with Post and her heirs in hastening the movement away from outdated Victorianisms. Amy Vanderbilt, writing soon after World War II, though adamant about controlled behaviors, rushed to recognize certain changes. In regard to calling cards, for example, Vanderbilt insisted that engraving was essential if the practice was maintained, that mere printing was unacceptable. But the ritual of cards was "known by few, and practiced less and less," although it was "helpful to be familiar with it."[68]

Specific changes took many directions. One shift was the move in most middle-class homes between 1910 and 1930 from parlors to living rooms. According to a 1909 commentator, "guests will receive a far pleasanter impression from the easy and graceful atmosphere imparted to a room by daily use, than from the stiff and formal restraints imposed by the old-fashioned parlor." Comfort and a relaxing atmosphere generally prevailed over Victorian convention. Mary Chambers, criticizing "old-fashioned pomposity" in 1929, termed the result a "revolution": a "happy tendency to naturalness and simplicity in social intercourse." The shift meshed with the decline of formal calling and the onset of more frequent impromptu, even unannounced, visits by friends.[69]

Language became less formal as well, and gradually the use of certain swear words became more common in otherwise polite society. Here too, the formal advice literature lagged behind actual practice; but in the 1920s it was recognized that greetings such as "hi" or even "howdy do" were acceptable alternatives to the stiffer "how do you do."[70] Middle-class Americans increasingly addressed acquaintances, even strangers, by their first names, a clear way to express surface friendliness and a distaste for hierarchy. Emily Post disliked the practice, however, even in 1937:

> Surely there is little to be said in favor of present-day familiarity in the use of first names — because those at the upper end of the social scale voluntarily choose to do the very thing by which those at the lower end of the social scale are hall-marked. The sole reason why so many men and women who work prefer jobs in factories or stores to those of domestic employ is that the latter carries the opprobrium of being addressed by one's first name. It will be interesting to see whether the reversal will be complete.[71]

Post also commented on the practice of encouraging children to use first names for their parents (which she was still criticizing in the 1970s and which did not widely catch on). "We know very well that there are countless people of middle age, and even older too, who seem to think that being called Tilly or Tommy by Dora Debutante and Sammy Freshman is to be present with a cup of the elixir of youth."[72]

Judith Martin, the Miss Manners of the 1980s and 1990s, noted that first-naming had generally triumphed, though she disliked the result. "The widespread use of first names, sports clothing, audio recreation, and other attributes of 'informality' in the work world has assisted in the illusion that no-one really needs to perform a service for anyone else."[73]

As Martin suggested, changes in dress also moved toward greater informality, in this case beginning in the late nineteenth century. Occasions for formal attire diminished by the 1930s, whereas opportunities to wear sports clothes multiplied. Many accoutrements gradually disappeared and, with them, not only restrictive clothing but also the etiquette associated with their use. Examples are the movement away from formal hats for men and gloves for women on most occasions. Instructions about tipping one's hat while on a walk thus became moot, and much less formal hand waves (or, with strangers, no recognition at all) replaced yet another polished Victorian ritual. Spearheaded by school-age youth, the rush to informality led (particularly after World War II) to the growing use of blue jeans and T-shirts and, later still, T-shirts with messages on them. At the same time, the acceptability of a shoe style simply called "the loafer" suggested both the trend and some of the factors underlying it. It therefore had become as important to be appropriately casual as it had previously been to measure up to the demands of formality.[74]

Eating styles also eased in middle-class homes and restaurants. Snacking increased after the 1880s with the introduction of commercially packaged crackers. By definition, most between-meal consumption followed less carefully prescribed rules than family dinners had been presumed to do. Fast-food restaurants began to appear between the world wars, led by the White Castle chain. At first, most of the customers were working class, but by the 1930s the leading chains began to attract middle-class families, a move that accelerated after World War II with drive-ins and suburban dining.[75]

Dance styles moved in the same direction, as we have seen, with prescribed motions replaced by a wider range of permissible gyrations. As always, etiquette writers faced a dilemma in choosing between resistance and qualified approval. According to a 1920 manual,

The modern dances have been freely criticized because of the objectionable method of holding the partner, and also because of the "shaking and wiggling" motions of the bodies of the dancers . . . however this may be, these dances have now won acceptance if not approval, and it has been demonstrated that they can be performed gracefully and without giving offense to the most squeamish chaperon.[76]

Or another comment, in 1923: "Lately there has been a great deal of unfavorable criticism directed against the modern dances. There have been newspaper articles condemning the 'latest dance fads' as immoral and degrading. . . . Dancing, even the shoulder-shaking, oscillating dancing of to-day, is really not intended to be vulgar or immoral at all, despite the crusade of anti-immorality dancing committees!"[77]

The steady decline of the most formal social rituals contributed to the belief that manners in fact concealed real character—an interesting shift that complicates the facile association of change with a loss of basic self-control. A comparison of Japanese and American styles in the 1970s pointed out that the American concern for "authenticity" might be hidden by elaborate manners. Indeed, some observers found the American system particularly demanding in its requiring an appearance of personal "honesty" and an avoidance of transparent hypocrisy while also insisting that certain behaviors and impulses were unacceptable. In this sense, the Victorian regime had limited the needs for self-control by making the rules clearer.[78]

This movement away from formality unquestionably reduced certain kinds of self-restraint, yet these trends must be interpreted cautiously. The greater informality did not lead to an absence of norms or a need for carefully managing the self. First, the outlets for reasonably formal etiquette remained. Most newspapers carried daily columns by Post, Vanderbilt, or Miss Manners, and even though their advice was now simpler, they continued to insist on proper eating habits, careful announcements of visits, and other proprieties. Thus in 1997, Miss Manners, in *Miss Manners Rescues Civilization: From Sexual Harassment, Frivolous Lawsuits, Dissing and Other Lapses in Civility*, observed, "People making up their own rules and deciding which courtesies they want to observe, and which they don't, is exactly the problem. Activities . . . basic to society . . . cannot proceed unless everybody knows and agrees to obey the same specific etiquette rules that provide orderliness and fairness." These periodic claims that Americans were veering away from courtesy reflected both the increasing informality and the traditional belief that proper etiquette and the resulting self-control could have sweeping effects on society at large. Furthermore, these claims were designed to induce guilt and enforce standards, often through considerable exaggeration of the lapses described.[79]

Formal occasions could still be found, however, even proliferating in the middle class and beyond. High school proms, often surprisingly expensive, featured purchased or rented formal dress and, at least at the outset of the evening, appropriate behavior as well. A new interest in home-decorating gurus, such as Martha Stewart, focused more on decorative decisions than on self-restraint. But manners books proliferated in the 1980s and 1990s, covering a variety of behaviors with a good bit of Victorian-standard advice, including revised editions of works written earlier in the twentieth century plus a new book by Emily Post's daughter. Courses in manners for children were held in fashionable hotels, where the clients were addressed as "ladies and gentlemen" and told that the key to etiquette was controlling themselves when dealing with others. In addition, etiquette was taught in business schools and other settings as part of the broader training for success at work. The choice of appropriate clothes, eating utensils, and the like figured prominently, as did arenas in which explicit self-restraint might be required, such as cocktail parties.[80]

Related to this continuity and capacity for revival was the extension of manners training to new areas and the disappearing need for them in other areas. Accordingly, advice on letter writing declined as communication forms changed. But many child-rearing books and etiquette manuals now told parents how to teach their children to use the telephone courteously. Children should understand that when they answered the phone, they represented the entire family. They should practice the correct polite responses on toy instruments. On the telephone, language appropriate to personal greetings, such as "hi," was inadequate, so more formal phrases were encouraged: "Good morning"; "thank you for calling." Children also had to learn patience when calling others, for example, allowing the telephone to ring a sufficient number of times before hanging up. As technology enabled new intrusions into private space and time, the appropriate restraint followed fairly closely. By the

1990s, conventions for the courteous uses of electronic mail were just beginning to develop, as the medium initially encouraged an impressive amount of license that reflected the extent to which, even in an age of informality, other forms of communication had become self-regulated.[81]

New manners also applied to the burgeoning leisure fields. Amy Vanderbilt offered advice about proper drinking habits, as well as when and how to smoke and gamble. Here, social forms had clearly moved away from Victorian constraints, particularly for women, but spontaneity was still not encouraged. One of the reasons for the continuing popularity of etiquette columns, in fact, along with the steady expansion of the middle class, was the need to learn guidelines for seemingly relaxed social activities. Manuals thus combined old advice about recurrent formal settings, such as proms, with the sections on limiting permissiveness in newer areas. By the 1980s, the same trend was producing advice books designed to regulate behavior in multicultural situations, under titles such as *Essential Guide to Gay Manners and Etiquette, Multicultural Manners,* and *Basic Black.* Despite widespread protest about the constraints of political correctness, opportunities for humor were addressed, even explaining the appropriate language, in the interest of avoiding offense. Thus whites should "exercise restraint" in seeking to find out about the black people with whom they worked, and blacks were advised to keep their emotions in check while recognizing that "carefully controlled" anger could be a useful tool in interracial situations. Modern manners were complex, and their evolution did not always eliminate the need for self-control.[82]

The reduction of formality in some areas produced its own ethic. In 1955, sociologist Martha Wolfenstein worried about this transformation of requirements: "Where formerly there was felt to be the danger that, in seeking fun, one might be carried away into the depths of wickedness, today there is a recognizable fear that one may not be able to let go sufficiently, that one may not have enough fun."[83] The obligation to be casual and relaxed, like the growing insistence on a sense of humor, could provide its own constraints, at least for certain personalities or at certain moments. The greater amount of swearing, for example, assumed an understanding that the speaker was not too serious and that the listener would not take offense. Sometimes these backhanded manners required both learning and negotiation. The preoccupation with avoiding the appearance of being judgmental had similar roots in a fairly strict ethic of "nonstrictness."

The continued validity of older manners at least in some settings, applications to new areas, and the cues for casualness and authenticity added up to a complex set of signals requiring considerable skill and experience. The new system of manners was accompanied by a readjustment of emotional norms toward reducing their intensity. Indeed, in many respects, this less elaborate etiquette depended on assumptions that others could be counted on not to intrude with strong emotional claims that might violate a personal space now less fully defended by calling cards and careful modes of address.

Managing Emotions

This process of redefinition began in the 1920s. It was during these years, as we have seen, that personnel experts increasingly and explicitly attacked anger in the workplace. Fueled by this shift, by the 1940s child-rearing manuals were advising parents to guard against anger. The Victorian belief that anger in boys should be both discouraged and encouraged as a motivation in business and public life no longer held. Anger now became too dangerous to tolerate, so a variety of strategies were suggested to avoid anger-producing situations, to teach children to identify the emotion, and to learn to ventilate their anger safely. "The more [the child] releases the anger, the less of it will remain, provided it has been handled in an acceptant way that doesn't make new anger take the place of what has drained off." The goals were to prevent any sense that anger could be constructive, to inhibit the formation of an angry personality (to "prevent emotional sores from bursting"), and to show that anger was an infantile emotion that adults must leave behind. "For anyone to pout, sulk, rage or indulge in other displays of violent emotion is to confess . . . inability to face the actual problem."[84]

Mother's love, that quintessential Victorian emotion, was also reassessed in the 1920s. Psychologists and other experts argued that parents and children had inherent conflicts that made a mockery of excessive love claims. More important, experts now claimed that mothers risked suffocating their children with excessive displays of emotion. Scientific child rearing, not "superheated" passion, was required. "It is too bad that freedom of expression, so admirable, perhaps, for one member of the family, may at the same time be so disastrous in its effects on another. Motherlove, for example. Some sort of control is indicated, unless the technique of sublimation has been well developed," wrote one popularizer in 1928. Even though behaviorist psychologists were energetic in their critique and the tone moderated somewhat by the later 1930s, the message remained: women's spontaneous maternal instincts needed careful management. As a 1952 manual put it, the mother and child relationship was "often too intense and precarious."[85]

This general attack on emotional intensity from childhood onward linked it directly to the new informality of manners, with the strictures against jealousy an essential part of the more informal relations between men and women. Without strong warnings against displaying jealousy, the new frequency of social interchange might have been socially unendurable, whereas during the nineteenth century, the control of contact between the genders had limited the need for elaborate advice in this area. The new system of dating entailed frequent changes of partners, and group norms opposed responding jealously. Even after marriage, despite the fact that until the 1950s and 1960s, most white women stopped working outside the home, new habits required jealousy to be controlled. Sociologists reported not only more frequent entertaining of other couples in the 1920s but also flirtation and physical contact short of explicitly sexual advances in many seemingly respectable gatherings. Sitting on the lap of someone else's husband, for example, could enliven a party, but again, this was not a valid basis for jealousy. Clearly, a new set of rules had replaced the more stylized manners, and its demands on self-control could be rigorous. This change accompanied a greater candidness regarding romantic and sexual interests, such as in the open marriage movement during the 1960s, in which, again, emotional rules urged spouses to accept philandering without jealous possessiveness.[86]

Grief was another newly limited emotion directly connected to the informalization of manners. Here, as we have seen, the attack on Victorian intensity began early. Grief was reevaluated in part because of the increasing pressures of middle-class employment and the appeal of consumerism. Job patterns and more extensive schooling made elaborate interruptions for mourning difficult. At the same time, while funerals became more commercial, it became difficult to use grief as an emotional basis for selling goods. Pleasant emotions and enjoyment clearly better fit the new consumerism and worked against the indulgence of grief. Grief was also downplayed because of the growing success in reducing mortality rates, particularly among children and child-bearing women. The change here was toward fighting death rather than mourning it.

Attacks on grief began to appear in mainstream magazines by 1905. One argument advocated a scientific approach to death as a natural, not usually painful event that required no great emotional outpouring in response. Patriotic articles during World War I added the view that grief might undermine the military effort, that death in battle should be accepted calmly. Victorian attitudes were now judged as excessive. An article in the *North American Review* in 1907 explained: "We could never understand why old women should, as they unquestionably do, love to attend funerals, or how anybody could be induced, except as a matter of duty, to make a business or profession of the handling of corpses." Other articles insisted that Victorian attitudes had been "vulgar and morbid": "The best psychology of life is equally the best psychology of death." The campaign continued for some time, recommending professional help when grief was prolonged or uncontrolled. "When a woman cannot rouse herself . . . from her grief there is need of the care of the physician." From 1934: "Modern knowledge . . . offers to the intelligent person to-day a conception of living which is a positive answer to old death fears."[87]

This attack on grief made it easier to loosen the formality attached to mourning and funerals. Special decorations for houses of bereaved families were abandoned, and mourning periods were shortened or abolished altogether. Funeral clothing became more casual. Etiquette books reduced their coverage of mourning situations. Amy Vanderbilt redirected the emphasis away from the appropriate manners in dealing with people who had suffered a recent loss to the need for the bereaved person himself or herself to avoid burdening others with excessive emotion. Vanderbilt praised the decline of mourning clothes and other indications of a somber mood. Furthermore, references to death were to be avoided in condolence letters: "It is quite possible to write the kind of letter that will give a moment of courage and a strong feeling of sympathy without mentioning death or sadness at all." Above all: "We are developing a more positive social attitude toward others, who might find it difficult to function well in the constant company of an outwardly mourning person." Self-control meant keeping under wraps an emotion treasured by Victorians.[88]

Grief, of course, persisted despite the new norms, although professionals now largely regarded it as a problem. Accordingly, "grief work" meant trying to show people how to get out from under it, not to express it openly. This was the context in which after World War II, many Americans formed groups of people who had shared a loss—but strangers otherwise—because only they could appreciate one another's emotional needs. The hostility to grief was revisited slightly after the 1960s, with some disputes over the emotion's utility. By the 1990s, the increasing number of public references to issues of "closure" in cases of loss suggested some modification of the hostile stance, though the term still implied a need to end it that, as one new-style expert argued, could have "a judgmental tinge."[89]

Overall, the attack on intense, intrusive emotions became a hallmark of middle-class values in the twentieth century. Some groups explicitly developed religious or other expressions in defiance of the most widely urged efforts to dampen emotional vigor, indirectly confirming the norms' importance.[90] Political symbolism was intriguingly reshaped. In contrast to the frequently highly emotional nineteenth-century politicians, twentieth-century leaders were subjected to a series of public tests to make sure they could control themselves. Although political debates had become less popular because of their potential intensity, when they were revived in 1960 on television, they no longer primarily involved confrontations between candidates. Rather, journalists asked the questions, designed in part to make sure that the candidates would not respond angrily to provocation. Tears also had to be avoided. In the 1972 primary campaign, the candidate and senator Edmund Muskie's breaking down because of press attacks on his wife removed him from serious consideration—a striking contrast to the permissible emotionality displayed by nineteenth-century leaders like Lincoln. Cabinet members also were advised to keep cool, as style replaced substance. Journalists "are not interested in an answer. They are interested in how you respond. . . . If they are nasty, don't be nasty back. . . . Never get angry. Never lose your balance. Never take the bait." Control was essential to measure up, and a lapse into spontaneity might supersede policy in determining a political fate.[91]

The needs of a management/service economy amid the escalating consumerism worked against emotional intensity. Efforts to promote a friendly but carefully controlled style on the job were extended to other areas. The newly found attachment to the process of acquisition helped replace certain kinds of emotional expression, or at least it was supposed to. Children were now surrounded literally from birth by material objects from which they assumed to derive solace. There was a brief debate early in the century in which traditionalists questioned this trend but were silenced by more up-to-date authorities who believed that things were often the safest targets for emotional involvement. The same pressures, as we have seen, worked against the systematic formality of manners. Indeed, the etiquette books that urged informality in the interest of friendliness insisted on extraordinary emotional control: "Act in such a way that you will feel the emotions you want to feel," always keeping the mind on top of emotions—whether anger or shyness—that might hamper self-presentation. At key points, the resulting trade-off was mutually reinforcing, with informality depending on, but also helping cause, new levels of emotional restraint.[92]

Pressure Points

The trade-offs that emerged throughout the twentieth century inevitably created tensions. Victorian ideas about self-control had produced a number of problems, such as the need to discipline servants amid an ethic that emphasized loving harmony in the home. The twentieth-century style, based more explicitly on tensions in the first place—between casualness and emotional control, work and leisure—had problems as well, though different ones.

Friendship

Friendship posed major trade-off dilemmas. In terms of overall norms and many personal experiences, Victorian friendship had been fairly unproblematic. Etiquette books might warn against undue familiarity, but this advice does not seem to have been widely heeded. Close friend-ships were frequently formed and were certainly widely recommended. Not so in the new, twentieth-century context. Warnings against intensity could easily apply to friendship, as dealing with other people's emotions could seem far more burdensome than before. Casual styles could modify the pursuit of such relationships, and experience at work suggested the desirability of a broader but also more superficial friendliness. By the 1920s, the encouragement of socializing with the opposite sex had cut into some of the friendship patterns of the nineteenth century, whereas the increasing revulsion against homosexuality worked to the same effect, particularly for men. Devotion to consumer activities and recreations also detracted from relying on interpersonal ties.

These considerations noticeably changed middle-class social patterns, despite the many exceptions depending on personality and circumstance. The clearest shifts occurred from young adulthood onward. The close male friendships that had spanned the hiatus between childhood and full maturity during the nineteenth century largely disappeared, replaced by anxiety concerning homosexuality plus the enthusiasms of dating and, from the 1940s to the 1960s, relatively early marriage. Correspondingly, institutions of male camaraderie, such as the fraternal lodges, began to fade in terms of numbers, membership, and range of activities. The process started around the turn of the century and was essentially completed by the 1920s. Women's friendship styles changed in the same ways though just a bit later, but with fewer institutional ramifications except for the growing reliance on dating and then marriage-based socializing. The patterns suggested by diaries and letters maintained Victorian modes, including emotionally intense language, into the 1920s. At this point, more frequent social contacts with men plus the influence of the widely discussed psychology concerning the primacy of heterosexual relationships in normal life created new restraints. Women's organizations survived, but they too began to be less personally structured and more formal in management and the conduct of meetings. Belonging to the "right" organizations, starting with sororities, often took precedence over intimacy. Even students at women's colleges sometimes avoided overly close relationships. A Wellesley freshman explained the new approach: "I have met some very nice girls and of course some pills"; "The social life on this floor has been dull as dull can be . . . to keep ourselves from getting too low, we have had numerous birthday parties and just parties." In a 1933 observation, Frida Sebury showed how these reactions might mature: "Something in me has a horror of female gatherings. I went to our last [alumnae] breakfast and ran away after the second course." Where deep friendships did exist, conflicts may have become more common than before. Finally, when a Victorian-style vocabulary was maintained in female-oriented friendship patterns, it stood out for its exceptional qualities.[93]

These developments took place against a backdrop of concern and new need, which is where the pressure points arose. Some components of the new trade-offs in self-control standards implied a greater need for friends. Many leisure activities moved away from purely family formats— a trend in the middle class—and this could both encourage new bonds of friendship and add to their significance. Most training in emotional control placed a greater emphasis on talking things out with someone. For children, this was a responsibility of their parents. For adults, spouses or friends might serve. The idea of empathy gained attention in this context, to help other people deal with emotions they could no longer directly express.[94] More recently, the interesting phrase "being there" for a friend has similar connotations, along with the implication that one was going beyond the call of duty in serving as a listening post for someone's frustrated outpourings of grief or anger.

The rise of feminism led to new calls for female friendship and to new criticism of men for their discouragement of the same ties. Ignorant of the recent history of close male friendships, feminists and male sympathizers alike correctly identified the current tendency to define friendship somewhat casually and particularly to avoid associating it with intense emotionality or physical contact.[95] The result, for some, was a certain amount of rethinking, though it was not clear, by the 1990s, that any wholesale revisions had been made. Rather, a continuing conflict over definitions, with changes in characteristic styles greeted by hesitations and countercurrents, formed the clearest pattern.

Marriage

Some of the same themes applied to twentieth-century marriage, although this seemed to be one institution that did serve as ballast against overall emotional control and the calculated coolness of the middle-class workplace.

Calls for a redefinition of marriage standards surfaced in the 1920s. The most widely prescribed ideals stressed a companionate marriage, with greater equality between the two partners and more emphasis on shared consumer and leisure enjoyments.[96] Its compatibility with other trends in the economy and in the standards being applied to personal conduct was obvious. Later, when more married middle-class women began to work, they pooled their income with their husband's to enable them both to have higher living standards, a move that also led to more shared decision making.[97]

What did companionship mean beyond shared consumption? One part of the overall effort to reduce emotional intensity focused on appropriate redefinitions of love. Beginning in the late 1920s, the profound and ethereal qualities of Victorian love were extensively criticized. Indeed, a new breed of marriage advice experts counseled against using emotion to choose a spouse, because it would surely mislead. Rather, a careful calculation of shared interests and background should supersede passion. "Science" was a far better guide, generating "less emotion, strain and regret than would otherwise be the case." Few discordant couples were seen as suffering from inadequate love. Avid popularizers like Ernest Burgess welcomed the decline of older romantic ideals. Elton Mayo wrote that love was an "ailment of adolescence" that must be abandoned before real marriage began, based not on love but on "admiration, respect . . . mutual interests, reciprocal assistance, attachment and becoming accustomed to each other." Other outlets as well attacked Victorian love. *Esquire*, founded in 1933 and long the leading magazine for middle-class men, took on this aspect of Victorianism with a string of articles during its early years trumpeting the idea of a "New Love" that would be far less cloying than nineteenth-century romanticism.[98]

But self-restraint in marital emotion was not the only available option. Twentieth-century marriage standards became more complex than those for friendship, in principle and often in experience. The vocabulary of spiritualized love common in the later nineteenth century fell into disuse, just as the most flowery language used in friendship gradually withered. But the goal of intense love was preserved, sought in marriage decisions and, now, in marriage itself. Here, somewhat ironically, the images available in reading and the media preserved and, in some ways, extended Victorian values, in this case not just as an escape from reality but also as a potential guide.

Escapism was evident in the ongoing tradition of romance novels and their equivalents on radio and in the movies. The Gothic motif featured love conquering accomplished women, after which fear predominated as women remained powerless. In these and the Harlequin romances that moved from fear to love, the "new love" theme of accommodation and careful planning was turned on its head, for love was deliberately portrayed as blind and compelling. But the audience could discern the real-life cues, as well as escape, in some of these representations. Radio and then television soap operas, for example, presented deep love as the only valid basis for marriage. Despite countless obstacles, the stuff of endless plots, love should be pursued and would usually triumph.[99]

Widely read popularizations in the 1920s made these ambiguities apparent. Elinor Glyn, an author of novels and screenplays, frequently wrote essays about love that were published in American magazines and collected in a 1923 book entitled *Philosophy of Love*. Marie Stopes, also English, attracted a large American audience by writing about sexuality. Both writers explicitly extended the insistence on love to marriage itself, well beyond the limits addressed in Victorian discussions—when marriage had not been evaluated in emotional terms beyond fairly vague statements about "connubial happiness," and courtship literature stopped short of marriage itself, except for perhaps a rueful remark about how things changed once the wedding was over. In the new approach, presented as an alternative to traditional male dominance, love was not merely premarital, but neither was it merely sexual or a diverting fantasy. Thus Glyn described ideal marriage as "the infinite bliss of the mating of the soul in peace and freedom from anxiety." Love becomes "so infinite that on neither side is there a shadow of difference in intensity. A perfect understanding, a holy meeting upon the planes of the soul." Stopes put the case similarly: "Every heart desires a mate. . . . Nature has so created us that we are incomplete in ourselves." Lovers are "conscious of entering a new and glorious state . . . a celestial intoxication." What was being projected here was a new vision of essentially spiritual intimacy, begun in courtship in the nineteenth century but now extended into the goals of marriage as well. Writers like Stopes and Glyn admitted that marriages often fell short, with men becoming cynical and women wounded, but they insisted that a good marriages would encourage a "physiological and spiritual" merging of both spouses. There was, to be sure, an important element of careful management in these presentations, for marriage partners should work hard to reduce selfishness, to retain an aura of mystery and attraction, "taking pains to be agreeable." But the goal was unrestrained union. These were ideals carried into the films and stories current in the 1920s, making marriage and its assumption of transcendent love the quintessential happy ending.[100]

Many people sought to make marriage an exception to the growing effort to control intensity. Anne Morrow, who married Charles Lindbergh, looked for examples of the "humdrum divinity" of married life, wondering how women could be in love and yet "self-contained." While hoping for deep love, she also accepted the definition of marriage offered by sociologist Ernest Groves, who saw it as a relationship encouraging "the development of the character and personality of both husband and wife." Many women were disappointed to find such a gap between hope and reality. The pressures of housework, the difficulties of meeting consumer goals, and other problems entered in here, but so did the difficulty of finding consistent emotional union. Ione Robinson wrote that after her honeymoon, she felt "as if I'm sitting in heaven and just starting my real life." But two weeks later, she was concerned that "I am nothing" as her husband turned to work and political interests. Another woman defined love as "the absolute willingness to belong forever" and tried to show her husband that she could not have independent interests because "he is all I have in the whole big lonely hellish world." But her longing for passionate togetherness turned to increasingly bitter disappointment, as self-restraint was imposed on her by circumstance and her husband's withdrawal, rather than by choice.[101]

The dilemma of conflicting marriage definitions—which added up to a contest between marriage as an illustration of the goals of emotional management and marriage as an idyllic exception—had gender connotations, as women wanted more emotional involvement (according to polls in both the 1930s and the 1970s, rating their husbands' lack of interest as one of their leading problems) and men saw women's emotional claims as "nagging" (which they rated as one of their chief problems). The standard twentieth-century trade-off, between control in fact and fantasy in escape, did not work well because the fantasy was likely to intrude into actual expectations. By the 1990s, many spouses—by this time women as well as men—began to prefer the emotional context of work, where rules for self-restraint were much more clearly defined, over the messier emotional environment of the home, thereby rearranging their priorities of time and attention accordingly.[102]

Conclusions

Requirements for self-control were widespread and powerful through the twentieth century even as new opportunities for release opened up and, indeed, partly because of them. Their hold was far-reaching: accordingly, in the 1950s, civil defense planners targeted the white middle class for preservation because it alone could be counted on to keep emotions of fear and anger under sufficient control to respond constructively to a nuclear attack. Many results of self-discipline were counterintuitive, however, like the need to turn to strangers in times of grief. In the 1990s, a lawyer instructs his clients about to appear as witnesses on their own behalf: "Stay calm—never lose your temper no matter how hard you are pressed. Lose your temper, and you may lose the case. If you lose your temper, you have played right into the hands of the other side." In a situation in which righteous wrath might seem both inevitable and even useful in pressing for justice, the demand imposed on provoked politicians had come to apply more widely.[103]

On balance, moreover, middle-class Americans learned the rules, one result of the detailed monitoring in early childhood. When an individual could not quite measure up, he or she tried to conceal. Comparative studies show that Americans are especially eager to hide emotions like jealousy and anger that they cannot avoid but know would cause them shame.[104] The trade-offs applied to a post-Victorian world left Americans uncomfortable with license and permissiveness unbalanced by compensatory disciplinary categories. But the converse also was true: assertions of moralism began to seem too rigid, and many demanding standards were dressed up in liberationist vocabulary or leavened by fantasy alternatives.

Understanding the pattern of trade-offs, which are not always obvious to the participants themselves, requires ambitious empirical and psychological claims. New, if subtle, rules for emotional control are directly related to more relaxed manners and more open approval of humor. Spectator participation in representations of violence escalates even as casual violence among males measurably declines. The redefinition of standards in the twentieth century is shaped by this balancing act, this deliberate tension, between vigorous moral constraint and the lure of consumerism, informality, and commercialized leisure. Proving the connection is not easy, for it is not always clear which component came first, as in the intermixture of informalization and the growing disapproval of emotional intensity. But the trade-offs— the deliberate tension between control demands, new or traditional, and opportunities for indulgence—were explicitly connected, often emerging simultaneously. The psychological interplay is thus immediate and direct, which helps explain, as we will see, another deliberate twentieth-century tension, between efforts to see behaviors as controllable, entirely an individual responsibility, and the attraction to explanations, such as addiction, that might take failures out of the domain of controllability. The same framework applied to changes and continuities in the standards for sexuality and the body.

Sexuality

The Clinton Parable

In 1998, Americans were confronted with their capacity to be collectively weird about sex. Democratic President Bill Clinton was caught in an affair with a White House intern, Monica Lewinsky, about which he initially lied. Republicans and associated moralists seized on his dilemma with glee, some of it purely partisan but some quite sincere.

This book and this chapter were not prompted by the Clinton episode, but its illustrative capacity is considerable. Clinton's lies about his activities and the confused American response reflected uncertainty about the importance of sexual truth. This was not a new uncertainty—politicians like Alexander Hamilton had done the same two hundred years earlier—but it may have gained ground amid other changes in standards of probity. Clinton was surrounded also by the distinctively twentieth-century insistence on keeping his temper in check: public pronouncements were eagerly scrutinized for signs that he had yielded to impulse and lost control, and in the main, he passed these tests.

Sex was at the center. Clinton's crisis was caused in the first instance by his own behavior (including a decidedly modern interest in oral sex), but it then captured three features of contemporary sexuality. First was deep division. Americans, collectively and also within the broad middle class, disagreed passionately over sexual standards, with a minority insisting on Victorian-style rectitude and control. This surprisingly literal traditionalism was not the majority view, but it commanded wide attention.

Second was the novel frankness of public representations of sex. Newspapers that as recently as the 1960s had concealed evidence of far more pervasive presidential sexual activities, particularly those of John F. Kennedy, now thirsted for every semen-stained detail of Clinton's activities. The *New York Times*, once a defender of journalistic dignity, seemed to shift its motto from the very Victorian "All the news that's fit to print" to a more contemporary "All the news is fit to print."

The combination of new public license in discussing sex (undeterred by cluckings about protecting children's innocence) and minority prudery was unquestionably American. No other country seemingly could understand how such wide public airing could occur, unchecked by any concern about privacy or dignity of office and, at the same time, why so many people were outraged.

The American majority itself was hostile to the crisis but long unable to bring it to an end. Their impotence resulted partly from partisan machinations in Washington and partly from a contrast between minority passion and majority nonchalance. And partly it resulted from the majority's own desire to appear sexually moral. While most people distinguished between Clinton's failings and his quality of leadership—for which approval ratings remained high—they also remained opposed to adultery. Indeed, only 11 percent rated adultery even sometimes acceptable. Most people also saw Clinton's affair as a clear indication that national morals were deteriorating, and they wanted this trend stopped.

This is the third feature of late-twentieth-century American sexuality. Most people—those outside the traditionalist minority—were willing to downplay the importance of sexual transgression and to urge tolerance. A majority thus granted the possible acceptability of sex before marriage. But their own codes had not, overall, been revolutionized, and during the last decades of this century, a desire to tighten up had been gaining ground. In this regard, media freedoms had clearly outpaced changes in the public's outlook, even aside from the morally avid minority. It was impossible, in this context, for most Americans to press too far their desire to get on with more routine political business, just as it was impossible for Republican leaders not to hope that they could cultivate a more extensive backlash against the Clinton presidency.

Division among Americans, media openness about sexuality, and pervasive if somewhat confused moralism among the majority itself added up to a prolonged public circus concerning presidential behavior. Short-run results surely included another litmus test for politicians: to be sexually unreproachable at least in office and to admit and deplore their own previous sexual straying. Despite real change, and in part because of it, Americans continued to find sex a difficult subject. The larger patterns of the twentieth century translated into far more than the crisis of a single president, for it also included ongoing tensions about personal behavior.

Key Trends

Even when Victorian precedents are understood as a tension between romance and restraint, American sexual standards and behaviors relaxed in the twentieth century. Sexual pleasure was now regarded as important, particularly by the middle class, and the older cultural mechanisms used to resolve Victorian complexities, like the stress on ethereal love, receded (though they did not disappear). With the rise of dating and then the subsequent "revolution" of the 1960s, sexual activity changed, and sexual display became more open, placing sex high on the list of spectator attractions.

These trends differ in many respects from the trade-off approach described in the previous chapter, in that the growing permissiveness was less constrained by new sources of rigor. Yet sex was balanced by both new strictures applied to the body (the subject of chapter 8) and counterweights generated within the sexual field itself. The combination created a discipline different from, but complementary to, that of the nineteenth century. But despite the persistence of prudery, the balancing act was more subtle, the theme of indulgence more heavily emphasized.

The challenges to self-discipline shape all accounts from the 1920s to the present. The revolutionary current that began to emerge around 1900 has been widely discussed. One author writes about the "modernization" of sex, beginning with such opponents of Victorianism as Havelock Ellis. Steven Seidman sees a similar break in popularized advice. He argues that proponents of marriage worried about instability and divorce and advised a more open embrace of sexual pleasure as the way to save the institution. Without question, as we will see, the recognition of the importance of sex became a staple of a new kind of prescriptive literature and an even newer marriage education movement. Paula Fass's study of college youth in the 1920s looks at the battle between traditional moralists and relativistic, permissive youth standards, with the latter gradually but clearly (and, in her view, fortunately) winning out. Kevin White, more critical of the decline of Victorian emotional values and behavioral standards, sees the new preoccupation with heterosexuality and with adequacy of performance as originating in the 1920s. And of course, more recent treatments of sexuality, including discussions of further changes in both standards and behaviors in the 1950s and 1960s, even more clearly signal a "sexual revolution."[1] This chapter discusses the predominant changes, as well as some data and categories not fully covered in existing works. It also seeks to modify—to complicate, in the interest of historical accuracy and contemporary self-understanding—the conventional picture. The trend toward permissiveness was not unqualified. Traditional values continued to operate, not only through prudery, but also through the ongoing commitment to Victorian romantic expectations. The result made the advance of new standards more hesitant and more contested than might have been expected, not only in the initial decades, but throughout the whole century. Furthermore, and this is crucial, new areas of prohibition were devised even by the same popularizers who embraced some version of greater permissiveness in other respects. The redefinition of homosexuality was the first of several such markers. At the same time, standards were created to guide indulgence itself—and in some, though new, hedonistic ways actually replicated Victorian concerns about male restraint and female virtue.

Three other trends, in other words, accompanied the more open indulgence: the evocation of more customary norms, the installation of new areas of concern even as older ones receded, and the creation of standards designed for pleasure seeking that nevertheless could be rigorous in their own right. Tradition and disciplinary innovation combined to dispel any impression that consenting sexual practice was acceptable no matter what, although this idea occasionally surfaced in both the modernist surge around 1920 and again in the heady days of the 1960s. One result of this combination was the continued sense, well into the 1990s, that the United States remained an oddly puritanical island in a larger sea of Western sexuality. We will see that even many sexual "moderns"—adult masturbators, for example—remained sensitive to squeamishness about their own acts.

The new package created several characteristic features of American sexuality. First, diversity was central, amid much mutual suspicion and disapproval; generalizations about even the middle class (partly because it was expanding) became less useful; and new gaps arose between men and women even in the face of important moves to the contrary.

Second, a fissure opened between spectator sexuality and actual behavior: what was passively enjoyed and permitted (over the opposition of the most vociferous traditionalists) was far more daring than what was actually attempted, except in literal self-manipulation as masturbation became more common. Heterosexual behavior changed as well, as we will see, but it lagged behind presentations of sexual delights. One manifestation of the fissure, which became more vivid over time as legal changes unshackled media presentations after the mid-1950s, was the nation's odd international sexual posture. Comparatively prudish in behavioral terms, and even in some areas of representation such as television nudity and topless bathing attire, Americans nevertheless created international sex symbols like those of no other society. From Hollywood's ascent to leadership in sexually suggestive movie stardom in the 1920s, to the success of jiggle-and-bounce shows like *Baywatch* as the world's most widely shared television fare around 1990, the United States and celluloid permissiveness became synonymous. Even within sexuality itself, in other words, the American amalgam was riven by internal conflicts among both groups and individuals. The nation still emitted strong, though now more intermittent and specialized, signals of sexual restraint.

The Problem of Timing

Another complexity, though of a different order, is the sometimes intricate chronology of modern American sexual trends. Middle-class sexual culture began changing in the later nineteenth century, and there is evidence not only of franker discussions of sexuality but also of a more open interest in sexual pleasure by, for example, married women born after 1870. By the 1890s, modernist attacks on Victorian stereotypes, and exaggerations of their repressive qualities, emerged, particularly at the scholarly level but with some popular spillover as well. Finally, though by no means novel, forms of entertainment featuring sexual innuendo and including scantily clad women began to attract a larger middle-class audience, at least on the fringes of respectability. Vaudeville performances and burlesque houses were added to the spectator patterns of young urban men, to some extent across social class lines. Changes in printing technology and taste also made titillating images more widely available, for example, on provocative (and sometimes pornographic) postcards. The possibility of building fantasy images of sexuality and of using vicarious indulgence as an escapist outlet increased, with a greater array of visual stimuli.

In these decades also, the key causes of change in standards and behaviors alike were set in motion. The new phase of consumerism, recognizing the importance of pleasure and sensuality as part of promoting and enjoying the acquisition of goods, got under way. Nude figures were used in advertisements, along with textual references to bodily pleasure. The expansion of leisure worked in the same direction. With more time available, middle-class people began to enjoy pleasure for its own sake, albeit with some anxiety and self-deception. Leisure activities promoted the relaxation of costume, particularly for women, in ways that had sexual as well as athletic implications. Led perhaps by men (a majority of whom, in a 1970s poll, rated sex as their number one sport), both participant and spectator sex were classified with larger recreational interests. Public contacts between men and women expanded, with more coeducational schooling into adolescence and the entry of young middle-class women into office work. Here, the developments were double edged, as we have seen: the same heterosexual atmosphere required new levels of self-discipline, governing both sexuality itself and attendant emotions such as jealousy. Civil service offices in Washington, mixing men and women in the later nineteenth century, required an adjustment in male language and behavior (including control over what later was called harassment) and the emergence of a mutually accepted range of sexual banter and innuendo. At the same time, birth control devices became more widely used by married middle-class women, heightening the possibility of having sex for pleasure alone. Attempts to persuade the American Medical Association to support birth control—in the interest of women's health and in acknowledgment of the inevitability and legitimacy of sexual desire—were shouted down in the early 1900s. Only after World War I, through the efforts of reformers like

Margaret Sanger, did the approval of medical professionals and the technology essential to recreational sex come closer together.[2]

These developments took some time to coalesce, which is why the pattern of innovation in sexual culture was set only in the 1920s. This was the decade in which advice literature began to focus on sex as the primary component of a happy marriage. Margaret Sanger articulated the common claim: "In marriage, as distinct from every other human relationship, the bedrock of lasting happiness . . . in every respect, lies in a proper physical adjustment of the two persons, and a proper physical management of their mutual experiences of [sexual] union." Marie Stopes, the English writer whose books soared to the top of the charts in the 1920s and 1930s, made the same point: "Where the acts of coitus are rightly performed, the pair can disagree, can hold opposite views about every conceivable subject . . . without any . . . desire to separate: they will enjoy each other's differences. Contrariwise, . . . if the sex act is not properly performed . . . all that harmony and suitability in other things will be of no avail." Dr. Isabel Hutton concurred: "No matter how ideal the partnership in every other way, if there is want of sex life . . . marriage cannot be a success." These views prevailed for decades, along with attacks on real or imagined Victorian limitations such as the belief in women's lack of capacity for pleasure and fulfillment.[3]

The 1920s also broadened the practice of dating to replace courtship, again with sexual implications. Courtship itself could be sexually as well as romantically charged, as we have seen, and dating did not differ entirely, incorporating, among other things, the insistence on the female capacity for self-control. But dating was associated with commercialized leisure activities, which themselves could have sexual components, as with movies, and which could lead to expectations of exchange, as with sexual favors in return for the male's financial outlay. Dating began at a younger age than courtship had and, for the middle class in high school and early college, with fewer direct connections to potential marriage; it was supposed to be fun in and of itself. Not surprisingly in this context, dating began to establish reasonably well understood patterns of escalating sexual activity—hand-holding, necking, petting, and the like—though supposedly short of outright intercourse. Later innovations, such as steady dating, increased the potential for sexual intensity. A male culture developed around dating in which efforts to press for sexual activity (or at least to boast of sexual success) became part of a new gendered peer setting.[4]

The 1920s also launched the other main components of twentieth-century sexual culture. When critics worried about the sexual implications of dating and college life more generally, decrying wanton youth and sexual profligacy, compensatory disciplines were introduced. Attacks on homosexuality were popularized and incorporated into child rearing. Parents who were told to loosen some customary restrictions, such as watching for masturbation, were given new worries that they conveyed to their children. Now that homosexuality had been identified, labeled as deviant, and categorized as an orientation incompatible with heterosexual normalcy, the need to restrict any signs of homoerotic leanings became an important parental preoccupation and, by adolescence, a concern of youths themselves. Dress and body imposed new controls as well. In the 1920s, fashionable female clothing was unprecedentedly skimpy, but it presented a boyish, slender figure. Greater sexual interest and opportunity were matched by new regulations and restrictions. This pattern applied to both genders, though with different specifics, with control of the figure (and also body hair) applied to women and greater anxiety about homosexual leanings conveyed to men.[5]

Finally, the decade witnessed the growing availability of sexually relevant ideals and images, with the emergence of Hollywood and the movie star. Nudity in advertising began to fade—a reminder that trends in this area were rarely uninterrupted. But sexual innuendo became commonplace. Attractive women began to be associated with automobile advertisements, with emblems like the "Fisher Body girl" directly linking automotive design with the slender female form. Lingerie advertisements multiplied in newspapers, magazines, and catalogs, featuring the female form while also reminding the reader of the need for aids such as brassieres. Subtlety was not necessarily required. Into the early 1940s, *Life* magazine contained a series of notices for Blackstone cigars that featured drawings of chorus girls straddling the elongated product, with the slogan "extra pleasure in every size and shape." The opportunities for sexual fantasy were endless.[6]

This initial articulation of a post-Victorian—in some ways, anti-Victorian—sexual environment was important, and it intensified over time. For several decades, marital advice continued to underscore, essentially unchanged, the primacy of sexual adjustment; the only shift was toward franker terminology, referring more directly to sex with fewer circumlocutions. Attacks on past repressions continued, for example, in recommendations to parents concerning the sex education of children. The increasing exposure to the new sexual standards, along with their gradual intensification, led to further developments. By the 1940s and 1950s, explicit reports on national sexual habits were published, notably the Kinsey reports. These in turn generated more discussion and, if not without controversy, a sense that efforts at the social regulation of sexual habits were misplaced (with exceptions such as homosexuality, where Kinsey's description had no immediate impact on legal restrictions). As the traditional reticence about public discussion of sex receded, the sexual practices themselves became a more private matter. These shifts in the context help explain why, early in the 1960s and in some cases before the major behavioral changes, many Americans, aware that more shifts might be on the way, began using terms like *sexual revolution* even though the term was misleading in its scope. The same shifts also help account for the pressure to use new birth control technology, such as birth control pills. Initially justified by concerns about population growth, the pill was incorporated into the broader interest in recreational sex and individual rights to sexual expression—and, once widely available, the pill promoted new patterns of sexual activity. Changes in sexuality, then, gained momentum, leading to innovations that confirmed and extended existing trends toward greater openness, interest, and availability.[7]

This intensification proceeded in fits and starts. Trends included not only the heightened sexual interest alone but the periodic revivals of more traditional views and particularly the identification of new counterbalancing areas for self-restraint. Cultural outlets could either stall or reverse field. *Esquire* magazine, founded in 1933, was long associated with new male attitudes toward sex. Its attacks on Victorian romantic love ideals termed them mushy and ridiculous. This image was enhanced by the emphasis on pictures of well-endowed women like the Varga girls series in the 1940s. But after 1960, as part of the move toward greater respectability and a wider female readership, *Esquire* began to criticize promiscuous sexual habits associated with the sexual revolution and to underscore the importance of combining sex with love and with marriage. Self-styled innovators thus did not constantly press forward; the more traditionalist option was always available, as were alternative interests. After the 1960s, *Esquire* began to tout careers and physical fitness as more important than sex. Except in advertisements, in which sexy poses became sexier over time, fluctuating rather than escalating hedonism best describes the evolution of a number of media outlets.

Even the lurches and miniwatersheds in trends did not move in a predictable direction. The clearest break, highlighted by the conservatism of the early 1950s, was made in the sexual frankness and imagery prominent in the late 1950s. U.S. Supreme Court rulings against censorship opened the door to new kinds of publications, such as *Playboy* (founded in 1953), and music lyrics, from the early days of rock 'n roll, began to refer directly to sexual pleasure. As one historian put it, American culture became increasingly sexualized, and at least for a time, sexual expression was equated with personal freedom and liberation.[8] This important chronological divide had at least some behavioral concomitants, especially among young middle-class women. Yet it also produced another redirection when efforts accelerated in the late 1970s to identify new areas of restraint and prohibition, as through the formal introduction of categories of harassment, date rape, and the like.

The basic point is that even though middle-class American sexual culture became more complex and divided in the early twentieth century, a consistent tension has remained. In the 1960s, more of the human body could be publicly exposed, on beaches and in the media, than in the 1920s (except for the formal nudist movement), but phallic cigar advertisements were more common in the 1940s than would have been tolerated in the mainstream media in the 1970s. The new sex manuals and talk shows offered more explicit titles than their marriage-manual counterparts of the 1920s had, but the actual messages and some of the advice were similar. Above all, the components of the overall cultural-behavioral package remained the same: the tendency to become more permissive combined with traditionalism and innovative injunctions for new rigor that can be understood only as the result of a continuing disciplinary tension. At no time did a systematic sexual revolution create a new dynamic; only fantasy imagery tended to spin out of control, opening gaps with widely accepted advice and with actual behavior.

Advice Literature

Advice about sex came from a variety of sources. Marriage and sex manuals offered a different, more subtle set of constraints than sex education materials did, and popular magazines mixed how-to details with reflective comments on sexual goals. Each genre, however, developed a novel, evolving, but definite balance between urging pleasure and pleading for discipline.

A number of historians have recognized the importance of advice literature in tracing the mainstream development of twentieth-century American sexual culture. The literature was abundant, which is itself an interesting development, and sold widely. Marie Stopes's major works had passed the 900,000 mark by 1939, and a resurgence of how-to manuals from the 1960s to the 1980s regularly topped the best-seller lists, rivaling cookbooks and dieting books. During the crucial transition decades, sex advice manuals were supplemented by college and even high school courses on marriage that brought some elements of the advice (if not, usually, the purely technical aspects) to an even wider audience.

The centrality and popularity of prescriptive literature on sex, dating, and marriage were enhanced by two other characteristics. First, the material differed from typical Victorian advice, even granting that the latter's range was greater than is sometimes recognized. Most writers were self-consciously anti-Victorian, flaunting their modern hostility to past repressions. In the process, they exaggerated Victorian prudery as a means of dramatizing their own innovative qualities and making their own sexual standards seem more liberated than they actually were. But this ploy, too, was a sign of change. The manuals underscored the importance of sex, including its centrality in marriage. They denied any particular differences in the basic sexual needs and desires of men and women, although they often highlighted gender differences in other respects. They talked about sexual issues not only explicitly but also with unusual attention to procedures, regarding technical arrangements as vital in ways that Victorians normally ignored. The new manuals embraced the validity of pleasure and, with few exceptions, implicitly or explicitly recommended contraception, again in contrast to most nineteenth-century materials. If nineteenth-century references suggested that Victorians were fascinated with sex, twentieth-century prescriptive offerings demonstrate that twentieth-century Americans have been inundated by it, at least on the cultural level.

The second characteristic of this view of sex was its complexity, and here the continued insistence on various types of personal discipline was central. Approaches varied during and after the 1920s, and some presentations were freer than others. The materials also changed over time. But overall, both at any given time and over the span of eight decades, important internal tensions concerned the ongoing role of self-control in sexual matters. Outright traditionalism surfaced, and even though its hold had weakened, it remained significant. New disciplinary goals were inescapable. With rare exceptions—mainly between the 1960s and 1980s—writers did not advocate unrestrained permissiveness. Quite the contrary: good sex, valid sex, required careful self-discipline, for two key reasons. First, although sexual impulses were natural (as well as good), satisfactory sexual performance was neither natural nor spontaneous. After all, the whole advice genre depended on teaching people that sexual skills were complex and had to be learned. To be sure, some of this inexperience may have resulted from the errors of the past, from unreconstructed Victorianism. But most manualists advised that impulses as well as misplaced conditioning must be brought under control. Second, sex and its pleasures were serious business. A few people touted joy for its own sake and while urging skills enhancement also tried to promote lightheartedness, but most experts were as earnest about their goals and conditions as the Victorian moralists had been. Marriage and self-worth alike depended on the proper employment of the tools of sex, with both frivolity and impulse discouraged.

The Pioneering Efforts of the 1920s

In the 1920s, modernist British intellectuals proclaimed a new era based on freedom from Victorian ignorance and repression, women's emancipation, and birth control. According to Bertrand Russell, "The decay of inhibitions, which has taken place among the young of our own time, has led to the reappearance in consciousness of instinctive desires which had been buried beneath mountains of prudery. This is having a very revolutionary effect upon sexual morality." Russell acknowledged a difference between sex and love, with the latter preferred, and he opposed yielding to "unbridled impulse." But restraint must be different—"the whole problem of sexual morality needs thinking out afresh"—and the real target must be ignorance and any sex that was anything but natural and enjoyable.[9]

Not surprisingly, modernist writings were greeted by reassertions of older moral codes, sometimes embellished by the newly explicit hostility to homosexuality ("always a sexual perversion"). In a 1922 offering, Minister A. H. Gray presented sex from God's point of view. He agreed that birth control was acceptable to a point, that interest in sex was both natural and desirable to the extent that youth who found themselves deficient could not be "commended." But sex was also a problem. Children must be carefully guided, with the goal to provide information in preventing premature sexual activity or "unwholesome curiosity." Masturbation—self-abuse—remained evil, its bad effects sometimes exaggerated but nevertheless devastating. "The habit is *not* natural, and therefore it is *not* hard never to begin it." Men require particularly careful management, because even a casual embrace with a girl on a date can lead to trouble, though fortunately girls are rarely aroused. Sex is a gift from God, part of love and marriage. Any other construction or overemphasis—including the unhealthy and abnormal interests of homosexuality, the salacious literature and media presentations all too readily available, and birth control to the exclusion of procreation—is anathema. "Work off your emotions in positive ways." Gray commiserated with contemporary adults assailed by degenerate messages but noted that proper upbringing could spare the next generation this troubling turmoil.[10]

Neither the modernist nor the modified-traditionalist approach prevailed at this time. Far more common was the effort to combine the attacks on ignorance and the resulting constraints on pleasure, with several targets for self-control. Margaret Sanger and Marie Stopes were typical for the decade, as their popularity as manualists attests. Sanger urged a "clean, healthy" appreciation of sex: "Sex expression, rightly understood, is the consummation of love, its completion and its consecration." Traditional efforts to keep people in the dark about sex and its delights must be banished by enlightenment. But sexual pleasure also required control: "We must learn how to master the instrument of bodily expression so that passion is transmuted into poetry, so that life itself becomes lyric." Control, in turn, was directed mainly, though not exclusively, toward men. First, purely mechanical sex was a snare. Even though the Victorian balance between love and sex shifted with writers like Sanger toward a greater prominence for sex, it basically continued. Loveless sex provided no real satisfaction and might spoil later opportunities. Furthermore, it led to evils like prostitution (now commonly defined as a result of concupiscent women and uncontrollable male appetites) that should be reduced by a mixture of personal restraint and policing. Second, even in relationships framed by love, men were often overhasty; they must instead restrain "the driving grip of sex attraction" through "early training in self-control, . . . to become its master and not its slave." Ardor was essential during courtship, but not at the expense of modesty. Too many young people were now taking too many sexual liberties even while avoiding "the limit." Premarital sex was wrong, risking a loss of self-respect and mutual love, and nonmarital sex was dreadful. Particularly in the early stages of marriage, male self-restraint remained essential, lest the conjugal relation be spoiled forever. The young husband "must not forget that haste and hurry can defeat him more than deliberation and control." Patience was essential to both parties, who should "at every moment" hold themselves "under intelligent control." Mutuality was the key, and the primary attention of husband and wife alike should be toward satisfying the other party, not the self. Sanger praised what later manualists usually deemed as too demanding, "to reach a climax simultaneously with that of his beloved." In this mutual interaction, women's requirements were admittedly simpler and entailed overcoming prudery and releasing basic instincts more than observing restraint. But women also should make their body and appearance pleasing, cleaning themselves carefully before each sex act, and also avoid taking the initiative. Finally, both parties must not engage in "frivolity or levity," instead treating sex with the reverence it deserved as the height of monogamous love.[11]

Sanger thus advocated combining sexual pleasure with a mixture of old and newer constraints. Sex and marriage remained firmly associated, and the recent past was criticized not only for its prudish ignorance but also for excessive male license with prostitutes and promiscuity. Sexual activity should be framed by the appropriate emotions: sex untouched by love was repellent. A more explicit interest in pleasure was coupled with pleas for self-control essential to mutuality, with specific injunctions added: here was a newly important disciplinary category. Finally, attention to hygienic and cosmetic constraints rounded out the presentation of vigorous but carefully schooled sexual expression.

Control themes were even more prominent in Stopes's popularizations, though her basic categories were the same, including the importance of surrounding sexual activity with deep, even spiritual, love. "It should never be forgotten that without the discipline of self-control there is no lasting delight in erotic feeling. The fullest delight, even in a purely physical sense, can be attained only by those who curb and direct their natural impulses." Stopes supplemented the invocations of male restraints in the interest of female pleasure, for example, by remarking that husbands who presumed too abruptly on what they viewed as their marital rights would effectively be guilty of rape. Ideal husbands, in contrast, followed high standards in respecting their wives' wishes and rhythms and engaged in "self-suppression in order to attain their heart's desire, the happiness of their mate, and consequently their own life's joy." Such husbands, capable of difficult self-restraint, also gained "added vitality and sense of self-command." Stopes added more detailed instructions concerning foreplay. She implicitly intensified the demands on both women and men to be sexually successful by arguing that the orgasms the prostitute "simulates" ought to "sweep over every wife each time she and her husband unite." Stopes even revised the Victorian concern about frequency of sexual activity, albeit in the interest of pleasure rather than physical health, by urging ten-day periods of abstinence between briefer periods of "repeated unions." Ignorance and foolish, prudish traditions remained suspect, but impulse and excess were even more dangerous.[12]

Other manuals and related publications in the 1920s revolved around these approaches. Judge Ben Lindsey, a self-professed modernist, spent more time than usual blasting outdated marriage conventions and ignorance. He prided himself on his sympathetic treatment of young people accused of sexual activities, noting that although he did not necessarily approve, he certainly understood. But there were limits. "The girl who permits a boy to kiss her may not be doing wisely, but she can hardly be described as having gone wrong. . . . Actual sex liberties are another matter." "Though I expressed strong disagreement with her course [premarital sex by a young woman], I condemned her not at all." For Lindsey, sex was natural, not criminal, and young people's curiosity was a good thing. But the goals of his advice, as opposed to those of the law, were still the encouragement of restraint before marriage and then sex conjoined with love in marriage. Indeed, precisely because sex was a natural drive, it should not be legally regulated; rather, it should be "governed and controlled . . . by educated wisdom, common sense, self-control and good taste of the individual." In this sense, the disciplinary stakes increased.[13]

Eugenic concerns helped put Paul Popenoe, one of the most widely read marriage advice writers through his books and *Ladies Home Journal* columns, into a somewhat more conservative camp. To Popenoe, marriage was the essential context for sex, if only because sex and procreation must still be linked. Monogamy was natural and modern, scientifically correct, "and libertines who exploit their own inclinations under the guise of Progress are merely arguing their own ignorance and adding to their own mental confusion." Laws must discourage sex outside marriage—a view opposing Lindsey's. In addition, prostitution should be regulated. For young people, sex was simply wrong, whether before marriage or not, because of its implications for the quality of children but also for the sake of the couple itself: "Coitus is constructive if in its proper place, destructive otherwise." "Premarital intercourse almost always represents a purely selfish seeking for excitement and gratification, and the man or woman who goes into marriage with this point of view is severely handicapped from the start." Abortion, however, should be legalized to help reduce the effects of inappropriate sexual activity, and frank sexual instruction was mandatory. Celibacy should be avoided, for it contributed to warped, self-centered personalities. From a eugenic standpoint, Popenoe's concern about social well-being thus led to some distinctive emphases—which he maintained into the 1940s—which highlighted the common mixture of new promptings with a sense that control still was necessary.[14]

Most manuals followed the antiprudery, prodiscipline line even more closely. William Fielding's *Sex and the Love Life* echoed the themes pioneered by Stopes, Sanger, and others. "The ardor and impulsiveness of the male must be controlled, and the erotic energy utilized in preparing (wooing) the female for the joyous consummation of love." Men must never force themselves on their wives; rather, hastiness must be controlled by the primary requirement of consideration for the feelings of their partner. Restraint was essential, along with techniques to arouse a passive partner. Yet sex was vital, and ignoring it produced nervous ailments in the male and hysteria in the female. Women's obligation— presumably natural in this oddly Victorian remnant but necessary whether natural or not—was to hold back: "Modest reluctance and hesitancy on her part, with a prolonging of the love-play which naturally follows, perfect the mental and spiritual state for the acme of enjoyment to be derived, as well as enhance the physical preparation for the act." The rare "robust" wife must restrain herself from demanding too much of her husband and from violating the canons of sexual femininity. At the same time, women must be responsive, active participants. "The woman who believes herself frigid or with an erotic constitution so weak that it is irresponsive, should make an effort to find out what wonders psychic re-education will perform." In sum, both parties needed interest and discipline, avoiding excess. The sex act itself, though essential, should not be attempted more than twice a week.[15]

These general points were supplemented in the manuals and in more specific how-to statements by elaborate discussions of foreplay, which signaled the arrival of a new sex code simultaneously advocating pleasure and incorporating Victorian assumptions about gender and restraint. The discussions of foreplay, in separate articles as well as sections of general marriage manuals—most were written by physicians beginning to establish their key advisory role—highlighted the new commitment to sexual fulfillment, including women's active interest and the conviction that sex was an essential part of marriage. But the activity itself, though now conceived far differently from its nineteenth-century guise, remained complex, which is where discipline came in. Women must be wooed, as in Victorian romance but now with sexual aims; their passions were real but dormant, and men must learn to restrain their own ardor so as to please their partner. Men should master certain techniques, including words of love as well as physical stimuli. According to this new script, both genders had obligations. But men faced the most stringent constraints in the patience required and in the larger litmus test of their wives' ultimate pleasure and satisfaction.[16]

Both general and specific commentaries stressed the continuing gender differences despite the commitment to mutuality. The messages to men were more detailed than those to women, given the concerns about women's enjoyment and the deleterious impact on women of both sexes' prior ignorance. Nonetheless, women had obligations as well. Newly elaborate statements about hygiene and appearance, rarely applied to men, reminded women that sexual indulgence was not free. Beyond this, the common insistence on marriage as the only appropriate framework for sex applied mainly to women because they remained the principal regulators of premarital contact, whose reputation and conception had the most to lose from lapses. Almost as important was the new instruction to enjoy sex, to shed any inhibitions, and to have orgasm and, at the same time, as part of respectable femininity, to be deliberately uneager, slow to respond, and dependent on male initiatives. Attacks on prostitutes for their wanton sexuality highlighted these injunctions. Merely meeting the new insistence on pleasure might be demanding enough, but to do so in terms of the larger balance required real finesse. In sum, sexual discipline was necessary for both genders, but in different ways. Old rules combined with modifications like the redefined purpose of male restraint, plus the new requirements of pleasure and prowess or pleasure and modest reluctance. It is little wonder that in the culture at least, earnestness overrode fun.

Changes and Continuities

From the 1920s to the 1960s, the marriage advice literature introduced a few new variations on the common themes, in some cases toward greater experimentation. College courses on marriage proliferated as people sought guidelines for sexual and marital success. Attacks on ignorance flourished. The leading new manual, Van de Velde's *Ideal Marriage: Its Physiology and Technique*, first written in the 1930s and revised several times into the 1960s, attacked Victorianism as vehemently as had the reformers of the early decades. "Sex is the foundation of marriage. Yet most married people do not know the A B C of sex.

My task here is to dispel this ignorance, and show ways and means of attaining both vigor and harmony in monogamous sexual relations." Appeals for discipline continued, in part because many authors, like Popenoe, persisted through the midcentury decades and others, such as Van de Velde, had themselves been schooled in the first wave of sexual reform literature. Thus Van de Velde maintained the themes of male self-control, manifested in careful "love play." Failures here were inexcusable, even coarse and brutal. The only changes were his suggestion that occasionally women might take the initiative and his somewhat more extensive discussion of birth control.[17]

A new area of controversy involved premarital sexual activity. The predominant emphasis on marriage and monogamy continued, fueling the routine criticism of contemporary youth. Writers like Popenoe never wavered in their insistence that only marital sex was healthy and proper, arguing, for example, that premarital sex "tends to deteriorate character by weakening such important traits as altruistic disinterestedness, the sense of responsibility, and the habit of self-control." But there was some dissent. Ernest Burgess approved of premarital experimentation, although he insisted that actual intercourse should await marriage or at least a prolonged engagement. Activities short of intercourse, however, were not only occurring in fact but were also desirable in that they provided experience. But even in the 1950s, while agreeing with Kinsey's claim that women who had engaged in premarital sex adjusted more easily to marital sex, Burgess observed that "we do not feel that any basis yet exists as yet for counseling premarital sex experience as an aid to the sex relationship in marriage." Another manual, first published in 1930 and arguing from the women's standpoint, approved of premarital sex outright. Teenagers, of course, must be warned about giving in to the temptation of "transient and promiscuous sex relationships," but young working women should be mature enough to handle various forms of sex, including petting, mutual masturbation, and oral sex, as means of giving "direct relief of physical sex tension in a way not to be secured through more roundabout sublimations." Women who used these "new opportunities for sex freedom" would be better prepared for marriage, in part because they would learn to be less passive. Rechanneling "sex energy" through sports and other activities also was important, for some boundaries remained, but the range of initiative was expanding, and even "occasional episodes" of sexual intercourse might be tolerated. However, the issue remained contested. A late-1930s manual repeated the more common message, that "premarital intercourse provides the poorest kind of training for marriage" because of social disapproval, secretiveness, and "unaesthetic circumstances." Both public opinion and the importance of emotional intensity were brought into play: "The physical appetite can be satisfied in a few moments, but the act has little of the satisfying emotional value that it has in marriage."[18]

The earnest approach persisted. A 1942 manual thus introduced sex in light of the growing instability of marriage, arguing that mutually pleasurable marital sex was satisfying precisely because it "excludes selfish indulgence" and also served as "an integral part of spiritual development." Hygiene was emphasized—"never go to bed with your husband without first washing the entire genital area, including the inner and outer labia, with soap and water. And this is just as important in the tenth year of your married life as on your honeymoon." Birth control was obligatory and was the woman's responsibility. During sex itself, women should not be simply passive, though men remained the primary initiators. Men must learn to slow down, but women needed to work hard for pleasure on their own part. It was necessary to "learn to reach your climax together. . . . If all this seems like too much trouble, remember that the happiness of your marriage—yes, perhaps the marriage itself—depends to a large extent on your attitude and conscious efforts." Men must be patient, being careful never to force themselves in what would effectively be the rape of a wife. They must understand that for a woman, "physical love and spiritual love are so closely woven as to be inseparable," so they must assure their partners of this side of the relationship. As in the 1920s, both parties must understand that desire is not enough: "Don't let anyone tell you that 'sex will take care of itself.' The sex act is not so simple or instinctive that it may be entered into without any knowledge; it is distinctly a duty to be informed." Finally, undue frequency was a constant danger, for "sexual emotions take a heavy toll on the physical as well as the nervous system of the body. . . . Overindulgence—the 'over-sexed' mate—is probably one of the leading causes of marital maladjustment." As Ernest Burgess put it somewhat inelegantly, "Problems of sex adjustment in marriage . . . pose a problem for everyone concerned with the education and counseling of parents, and of young people before marriage." Finally, confirming the basic continuity of the advice but also indicating a changing cultural setting, prescriptive writers found it necessary to warn against the "oversexed" quality of media representations. "The bogus Romance of the movies is a common barrier to full satisfaction in marriage. Romance is to be sought not in infantile philanderings but in adult life-partnership."[19]

With the 1960s, the leading manuals started putting stronger emphasis on pleasure and signaling greater approval of various forms of indulgence, in concert with the changes in the overall culture and a new generation of advice writers. *Marriage for Moderns*, first published in 1942 and continuing through a 1970 edition, stressed the complexity of sexual behavior and the need for training and control, along with women's desirably greater passivity and the need for explicit male restraint ("by the sacrifice of his own immediate pleasure if necessary"). In 1962, Dorothy Baruch warned men against confusing their need for care with a surrender of initiative. ("It robs the man of what he most basically wants—to feel his manliness. It keeps the woman from finding what she most wants—to be cherished and desired.") Technique was downplayed in favor of shared feelings of love or empathy that should regulate sexual conduct and lead to mutuality. But even in 1958 Albert Ellis, in *Sex without Guilt*, was repudiating earlier ideas of control, proclaiming the value of masturbation plus the desirability of having young people achieve orgasm through petting and even engaging in intercourse (though in part as a preventive against "sexual deviation"). Ellis praised the greater hedonism and individualism that would ensue:

> Every human being, just because he exists, should have the right to as much (or as little), as varied (or as monotonous), as intense (or as mild), as enduring (or as brief) sex enjoyments as he prefers—as long as, in the process of acquiring these preferred satisfactions, he does not needlessly, forcefully, or unfairly interfere with the sexual (or nonsexual) rights and satisfactions of others.

Gone from this statement were anxieties about male and female differences, concern with an emotional or a marital framework; now pleasure in sex itself became the centerpiece.[20] Insistence on active communication replaced detailed discussions of mutual discipline, and the spate of how-to books placed more emphasis on their technique. Even performance goals were downplayed in this effort to enable everyone to have fun. "Orgasm is not the ultimate criterion of success in a sexual encounter. . . . It is extremely important in our numbers-oriented society to avoid emphasizing numbers in our sexual lives. In the area of sex, more does not necessarily mean better." Finally, in a crucial shift, homosexuality started to be tolerated.[21]

Among the widely sold new manuals, Alex Comfort's *The Joy of Sex* came closest to a discipline-free effort. Comfort deplored the "antique idea" of women as passive and men as performers, instead stressing women's role in "getting him excited to start with, or in controlling him and showing off all her skills." "The main dish is loving, unselfconscious intercourse—long, frequent, varied, ending with both parties satisfied but not so full they can't face another light course, and another meal in a few hours." Of course, antisocial or dangerous behavior must be avoided, and reciprocity and communication remained important. Comfort also urged women to be careful of their looks and hygiene, including control of odors. But his emphasis was on the mastery of varied, sometimes complex techniques, not a balancing act between restraint and expression. Only performance might seem a demanding standard in itself, as Comfort urged not only great frequency but also the desirability of simultaneous orgasm.[22]

Despite their greater enthusiasm for sex itself and their abandonment of older gendered distinctions, most manuals, including the most widely read and reproduced, maintained more components of the older balance than their innovation-minded authors wanted to admit. They talked about the need to avoid "forcing" sexual responses. They talked about carefully controlling permissiveness according to one's own value system while shying away from establishing rules. "The price for greater freedom of choice is greater pressure on the individual for responsibility in making decisions." Warnings against male overeagerness persisted and even increased. "It is important . . . that the fantasies and the sport involved in imagining sexual encounters with others remain playful or, if they become real, that they are done with the person's consent. . . . Even though no harm may be intended, forcing your intentions may be frightening to the other person and could lead to legal difficulties for yourself."

Even masturbation continued to be a matter of concern: "Total enjoyment of your body involves more than reaching orgasm. . . . Always masturbating under an atmosphere that is tense and rushed may lead to sexual problems, such as premature ejaculation, when you become an adult." Birth control received greater attention in an age that acknowledged premarital sex. Thus a contemporary manual stated: "There are no rules that go with petting or making out, and what you do is limited only by your imagination and the limits that you and your partner set"—but in fact, the ensuing text included a considerable list of warnings. Basically, although impulse was given somewhat greater latitude, as in telling men not to worry at first about early ejaculation, awaiting greater experience, the fact was that nature was inadequate: not only techniques but also consideration must be learned.[23]

This balancing act showed clearly in the works of the most popular prescriptive writers, Masters and Johnson in the 1960s, and "Dr. Ruth" Westheimer in the 1980s and 1990s. Masters and Johnson led the parade in attacking outdated notions such as female passivity. Yet they were firmly modern-traditionalist in insisting that marriage was the only appropriate context for sex, thus rejecting most extramarital and group sex (not absolutely forbidden but rarely possible without hurting the marriage and so normally out of bounds). The very title of their pioneering work suggests their intention to combine enjoyment with responsibility. The experts continued to underscore the close attachment between sex and emotion, as opposed to purely performance-oriented sex. Even attempts to have sex too often might introduce the dreaded mechanical element, leading to people's "following directions, not expressing feelings." Masters and Johnson deliberately shied away from words like *obligation* or *self-control*, and they were unwilling to condemn anything outright. But certain norms remained. As another 1970s manual explained, "It must be accepted that rules have always existed with regard to sexual love and must continue to exist. On examining these rules, we find that some of them are entirely arbitrary and irrational whilst others can be fully justified."[24]

Dr. Ruth, writing and speaking from the mid-1980s onward, has returned even more definitively to some older themes. What she sees as the "growing popularity" of marriage makes updated restraint easier to promote, and the dangers of sexually transmitted diseases underscore the warnings that must accompany even legitimate pleasure. Commenting explicitly from a "post–sexual revolution" vantage point, Westheimer concentrates on the importance of lasting closeness as the true goal of sex: the "ideal connection with another human being." This usually means marriage, and it certainly means controlling sex according to higher emotional standards.

Good sex is difficult. It requires patience, tact, and even dissembling in the interests of avoiding attacks over infidelity, impotence, or other issues. Men must learn to control their speed—a long-standing theme that Westheimer believes can at last be resolved by means of a stop-start method "so reliable that in one generation we expect to see premature ejaculation disappear entirely." The idea of discipline, especially for men, is acceptable once more in this context: "The man should have attained good control," and both parties should adopt "a calm approach" when lovemaking begins. A man "can control himself if he carries the idea in his mind," and if he fails, he owes an apology to his partner. Infidelity is dangerous; open marriage almost always a disaster. Of course, most couples will have had prior sexual experience, about which they should largely keep silent. Of course, masturbation is fine, indeed highly desirable even for adult women. Of course, people fantasize about movie actors or other ideals. But the basic insistence on sex as a balance between individual interest and mutuality, between self-expression and the need for physical and emotional regulation, is apparent. Despite some important prescriptive experimentation, particularly in the 1960s and 1970s, the most typical manuals of the final decades of the century maintain an updated version of the twentieth-century commitment to combining pleasure with discipline.[25]

Newsstands

Popular magazines described sex in a way that was distinctly different from that of the advice manuals, but collectively they produced the same tension between caution and indulgence that the manuals established. Some magazines opted for a version of modernist permissiveness when it became feasible, others for skepticism and warning. There also was change over time. Dependent on newsstand displays and the U.S. mail, magazines explored sex very gingerly into the 1950s lest they attract

PHOTOGRAPHS

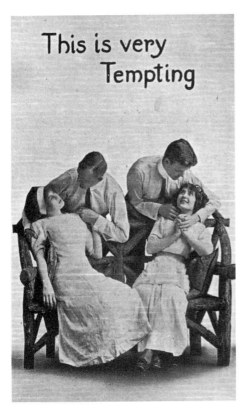

Above and facing page: Suggestive and pornographic postcards became available by the 1890s, thanks to new printing technologies and a changing audience. These three American products might be widely sold at newsstands and other outlets. From a collection by Lisa Sigel, with thanks to Professor Sigel.

HOW GRACIE ENTERTAINED HER FRIENDS.
A WELL-KNOWN WOMAN OF SAGINAW, MICH., PUTS UP AN ENTERTAINMENT FOR A SELECT CROWD THAT IS VETOED BY THE POLICE OFFICIALS.

Above and facing page: The delights of the *National Police Gazette*. Scenes of sin and advertised temptations in sex, violence, and sports. From issues in 1898.

Advertising picked up the opportunity, with symbols (in this case, phallic) that would be attacked today. From *Life* magazine, October 5, 1942.

Scare tactics on bathing and grooming. From *American Magazine,* August 1928, p. 149.

Hygiene and sex: a claim about aging and appearance. From *Ladies Home Journal,*
May 1928, p. 77.

Dental hygiene in the age of the salesman: another new standard. From *Ladies Home Journal*, April 1927, p. 240.

Left: The effort of posture: training for children. From *Parents' Magazine*, November 1937, p. 22.

Below: The Ivy League posture photos. From *New York Times Magazine*, January 15, 1995.

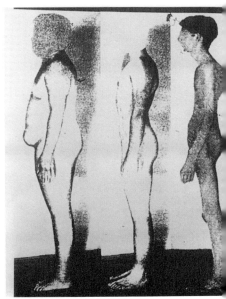

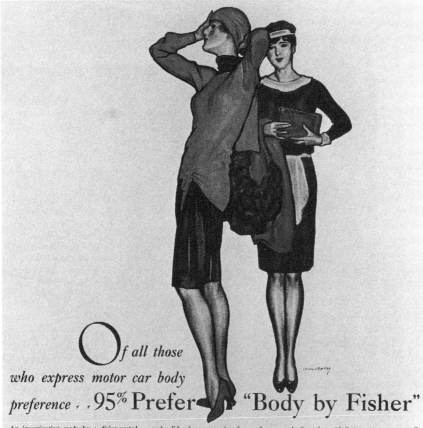

O*f all those*
who express motor car body
preference . . 95% Prefer **"Body by Fisher"**

An investigation made by a disinterested agency and reaching into every county of every state in America, has revealed that the vast majority of motor car prospects select a car with its body attributes foremost in mind. It also established that 95 per cent of all motor car buyers who are influenced by the body in purchasing a motor car, prefer Body by Fisher.

When the American people—who *know* motor cars—exhibit

such solid and pronounced preference for any automotive product, there is only one answer: *That product must be unmistakably superior.* As a matter of fact, the super-quality and super-value of Body by Fisher have been evident from the first. So evident, that Bodies by Fisher were early demanded by the manufacturers of the finest motor car chassis. Inevitably, Fisher thus became associated years ago in the public mind not only with better

bodies—*but with better motor cars* as well.

Note the result: When General Motors gathered the finest motor car in each price class into one great organization, these better cars were already equipped—had long been equipped—with Body by Fisher. That is one reason why today the emblem "Body by Fisher" is the unfailing guide to the better motor car in every price field—a fact which is very plainly apparent when you glance at the list printed below—of cars equipped with Body by Fisher.

CADILLAC · LA SALLE

BODY FISHER

GENERAL MOTORS

BUICK · OAKLAND · OLDSMOBILE · PONTIAC · CHEVROLET

Mature posture and sensuality: the "Body by Fisher" car design campaign in advertising. From *Saturday Evening Post*, November 24, 1928, p. 34.

⊙BESITY BELTS

· · · FOR · · ·

Ladies and Gentlemen.

For full description of these Belts see page .

Prices range from $5.00 to $15.00, according to size and depth.

Any size made to order for Gentlemen and Ladies. I also manufacture Magnetic Shields for Back Ache, Kidney and Liver Troubles, Neuralgia, Rheumatism, &c. Can be mailed to any part of the world on receipt of price.

Manufactured only by

GEORGE BURWELL, Chemist,

176 Boylston Street,   -   Boston, Mass.

Above: An early gimmick, 1892. The belts had more than one hundred electrically charged magnets, plus medicated flannel, covered with silk. The electrical charge was supposed to disintegrate fat. From George Burwell, *Obesity and Its Cure.*

Right: Miracle stories in the battle against weight. Dropping nineteen pounds led to a better job, with self-discipline aided by a commercial beauty kit. From *Ladies Home Journal,* January 1942, p. 44.

LOST—19 Pounds
FOUND—A Better Job

The Success Story of Bettye Baker, of Little Rock, Ark.

"I was overweight, ill-proportioned and unhappy, and that's no way to look and feel at 23," writes Bettye Baker, secretary. "So I enrolled in the DuBarry Success Course. In six weeks, 19 pounds seemed to scoot away."

Before

After

"My first thrill was buying a size 14 suit instead of a size 18. Poised and confident, I went out and got a new job at an increase in salary that will pay for my Course many times over the first year."

It Can Happen to YOU!

Bettye Baker is just one of more than 35,000 women, from 16 to 60, who have found the way to beauty through the DuBarry Success Course. "I wanted a good figure, a clear skin, shining hair," she says, "and every dream came true!" The Course is a practical plan for improving yourself in face, figure and fascination. It shows you how to use at home the same methods taught by Ann Delafield at the famous Richard Hudnut Salon, New York. You get an analysis of your needs—skin, hair, figure, posture, weight —a routine that tells and shows you what to do every day for six exciting weeks. And it's fun!

Get the Full Story—Send the coupon or a letter or postal at once for the book, "Six Weeks From Tonight," and find out what this proved successful way to loveliness can do for you.

Du Barry Beauty Case Included!
With your Course you receive a Case containing 11 different DuBarry Beauty and Make-up Preparations and Accessories selected for your type.

DuBarry

SUCCESS COURSE
ANN DELAFIELD, *Directing*

RICHARD HUDNUT SALON
Dept. S-2A, 693 Fifth Ave., New York, N.Y.
Please send me the book, "Six Weeks From Tonight," telling all about your DuBarry Home Success Course.

Name

Street

City_____State

Above: The idyllic goal of emotional control. *Parents' Magazine,* April 1937, p. 32. *Below:* Harsh reality as warning. *Hygeia,* December 1937, p. 1080.

It is a whole lot easier to understand about human babies when one knows how animal babies come into the world

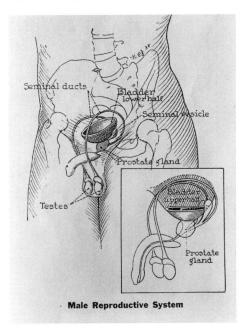

· Male Reproductive System

Above: The careful innocence theme. From
Parents' Magazine, December 1942, p. 25.
Below: The daunting biological approach.
Hygeia, July 1941, p. 527.

The Careful Casual. From *New York Life*, January 1885.

Coeducational lounging at Stanford University. From *Life* magazine, June 7, 1937.

public outcry and censorship. The frequency and openness of commentary increased greatly after the court decisions of the mid-1950s and the rise of blatantly sexualized competition in the form of *Playboy* and its racier analogues. At this point, some magazines began to feature alluringly exposed women on their covers and articles offering the latest wisdom on arousing one's spouse or lover in bed. *Cosmopolitan*'s conversion to glossy sexuality in the 1960s is the most striking example, but others, especially women's magazines, began to include as many articles about sexual pleasure as those on dieting and clothes. However, magazines rarely offered the kind of specificity about techniques and dysfunctions common in prescriptive literature, even in the 1920s. And many highly sexual titles headed articles actually about appearance, cosmetics, or hygiene.[26]

The main point is the diversity of approaches to sex, featuring surprisingly tenacious hesitancy and appeals for restraint of impulse. In 1947–48, for example, leading magazines both lingered over the shocking aspects of the new Kinsey report on American sex habits, with its revelations of extensive bestiality and homosexuality, while also attacking the idea of research on sex unfettered by standards of conduct. Balance, in other words, overrode the journalistic desire to titillate. This duality easily survived the rise of more permissive fare a decade later, becoming an important counterpoint to the new cultural signals emanating from the so-called sexual revolution of the 1960s. A case study of two popular and reasonably typical outlooks, in combination with the advice manuals, suggests some of the characteristic zigzags and continuities.[27]

Esquire magazine was designed to appeal to educated, middle-class men, using two features of modernism almost from its outset in the 1930s. Editorials immediately disparaged Victorian ideas of love and marriage, which constrained individual independence and advocated an impossibly saccharine, hollow ideal. Sexual enjoyment, among other things, should not be so complicated, and *Esquire* articles often implied that it could be aligned with travel adventures and consumerism as a lifestyle issue, in contradistinction to Victorian contexts. Second, particularly by the 1940s, *Esquire* began to feature pictures of scantily clad girls along with cartoons filled with sexual innuendo. Here, surely, was advanced hedonism of the sort that would lead to soft pornography when laws permitted. Indeed, many readers—for example, in the barbershops where the magazine was commonly found—may have read *Esquire* only for this material.

Articles that discussed sex directly were another matter, for from the 1930s to the 1990s, *Esquire* disputed the interest in sex, departing from this line only to acknowledge the sexual revolution of the 1960s and to increase the frequency of its acerbic commentary. During the 1930s and 1940s, *Esquire*'s typical approach to sex was surprisingly cautious. An article might advise more sexual frankness to children, but without forcing the issue. The magazine's goal seemed not to be abundant pleasure but a harmonious life and social responsibility for an innate human drive. Mutual devotion, not promiscuity (viewed as a "deviation from the normal structure of love") was the intent—despite *Esquire*'s frequent gibes at Victorian sentimentality. This approach echoed the prescriptive appeals for mutuality rather than the selfish satisfaction of a purely physical urge. Furthermore, sex should only be one component in mate selection and not a leading one, with considerations like a partner's promptness for appointments given greater weight—a theme repeated in ensuing decades.

Still more commonly in these early years, *Esquire* modified its attention to sexual issues with a far greater delight in misogyny, denigrating independent women and cautioning men to avoid their snares. Both marriage and therefore also sex became dangers that men should ration and control. No sensual delight, however seemingly casual, could compensate for giving women any edge, and men were well advised to stay out of the arena altogether. In sum, sex was a low-priority item, and sexual instincts must be firmly disciplined—not for the mutuality that marriage counselors were recommending but, rather, for the freedom to enjoy masculine worlds of consumerism. In the same vein, articles recurrently attacked the whole idea of women's sex appeal, arguing that sensible men ignored it and women distorted their own lives in seeking it. Other commentary refuted any notion that men were more carnal than women and warned men of wives' frequent infidelity. Indeed, the idea of "wild women" was part of *Esquire*'s agenda to attack contemporary female irresponsibility and the danger this posed to men. In this view, love was a delusion, whatever the role of sex in it. Sex, indeed, must be restricted when selecting a mate lest it make the whole process riskier than it had to be. In particular, a woman's sexy appearance should be largely ignored. *Esquire* also attacked male interest in scantily clad women (despite its own stake in the enterprise) as fundamentally tasteless. Even sleeping in the same bed with a woman was criticized because it followed from a false image of loving, sexual perfection and actually prevented the real goal—a good night's rest.[28]

In short, sex for the *Esquire* of the early decades engendered more skepticism and warning than interest. An article on sexual decline with age summed up the magazine's cautious position: difficulties may be unavoidable or the results of "self-indulgence or stupidity." They are unfortunate but not necessarily tragic if a man has enough mental control to interest himself in other things, not lingering over the past but stepping up to the "good life still ahead." A similar article, on the eve of the sexual revolution, called attention to the frequency of heart attacks during sexual intercourse as the basis for urging again that men learn how to "temper impetuosity in lovemaking." Control was essential to the even more fundamental sense of keeping sex in the proper perspective.[29]

Perhaps partly to protect its identity against new competition, *Esquire* maintained its guarded tone in response to the sexual revolution. At the same time, it abandoned some of its earlier misogyny in light of the newer menace of sexual excess. By the mid-1960s *Esquire* was arguing that *Playboy*-like cheerleading actually reduced sexual pleasure by making people feel self-conscious and holding them to public standards for what should be private, individual acts. "When the ultimate *Guide To Bliss* is written, the book that sweeps away all barriers, inhibitions and doubts, sex, alas, may have come to mean nothing at all." According to this view, the New Hedonism was "more coercive" than the old Puritanism and must be opposed. *Esquire* began pointedly to praise marriage as a context for good sex, promoting the idea of a "truer partnership" and hoping it could survive "modern sexual mores." Indeed, monogamy became the approved subject of several quite sensitive articles. By the 1980s, contributors to the magazine were wondering: "Isn't it time we stopped thinking about sex and started thinking about something else? Like love?" Without pushing the older moral codes, *Esquire* argued that the new permissiveness itself was imposing standards on performance that severely reduced enjoyment—and that the easy availability of erotica was making the whole subject boring. Again, the main problem was that sex was becoming too isolated from the more meaningful aspects of life, notably affection and intimacy. Americans, the magazine noted, were disillusioned about these changes in culture and behavior and were "beginning to question the joys of 'sex.' " By the 1980s, *Esquire* was running a series of articles that looked back on the sexual revolution with disdain. One male author contrasted his premarital experiences with the deep satisfaction, sexual and otherwise, he now derived from his marriage and parenthood. A woman recited her many encounters while concluding that she now thought back on them infrequently, "mostly when I drag my bicycle downstairs and skin my leg . . . [or] when the toilet overflows"—ending with the hope she might get lucky and meet a man with a working brain and hands that are "good at something else besides touching me." Overall, *Esquire* strove consistently for a clear acceptance of sexual pleasure (clearer than in its earlier decades) that could at the same time be defined in ways that would bring under control the many excesses and distortions.[30]

Mademoiselle, first published in 1952, was a magazine aimed at young middle-class women. Like *Esquire*, however, it staked out a position on sexual issues before being challenged by the country's growing permissiveness—and it maintained a redefined version of this position during the decades of cultural furor. *Mademoiselle's* goal was to protect women and their sense of personal control from undue demands on performance. An early article stressed the "crippling anxiety" caused by discussions of frigidity, in turn the product of well-intentioned efforts to propel women toward greater enjoyment. According to this article, most women labeled *frigid* were simply victims of exaggerated expectations; if they could relax, they could easily achieve a "complete response," however that was defined. Similar worries concerned whether they had had an orgasm and had taken too much time to gain pleasure. Another target was the pressure to barter sex for male favor. Desirable men are not after sex alone, and women should feel justified in presenting a "cheerful firmness" in rejecting requests. The magazine cautioned against premarital sex, advising women to stand up to men who might argue that sex would alone prove love. "If Romeo and Juliet were to go to a marriage counselor today, they would be told please to control their actions—and continue their education—at least for a while." *Mademoiselle* contended that most college women insisted on an emotional context for sexual activity, denying that such activity was "nothing but pleasure seeking." The advent of birth control pills was similarly greeted with the confident expectation that they would not prevent most women from insisting that sex be combined with "idealistic romantic love." "Freedom, Yes; license, No." *Mademoiselle* was at the same time careful not to take a rigid stance, arguing that one's own values would lead to various, and equally acceptable, sexual results: the important point was to know what one wanted and to set limits on this basis.[31]

By the mid-1960s, greater sexuality brought more variety into *Mademoiselle's* commentaries. A series of articles by men urged women to loosen up, though not to be loose, and to realize that men judged women by their "capacity for pleasure." Likewise, revealing European beachwear drew praise. Sex, these same authors argued, was part of maturity, and men were not villains for wanting women to perform. The recommendation was "abstinence in moderation." Yet female "swingers" were condemned as psychologically ill, and collegiate sex still drew warnings. Promiscuous women were regarded as a minority; rather, the sexual revolution was described as more a media creation than a real change in standards or behavior—except that it seemed to be heightening male expectations and so women needed to be very clear about what they wanted. Increasingly, the more hedonistic alternative was played down, by male and female writers alike, in favor of guidelines for appropriate control. For example, an article in 1968 declared: "Like all girls, you will hope for a romantic marriage. Romance and promiscuity are simply not compatible." (This appeared next to a perfume advertisement touting the product's ability to attract men.) And in 1969: "Virginity is not outdated. Neither is tenderness—nor courtship and the family circle. . . . The important thing is to make a choice, without being either coy, hypocritical, or stuffy." Comfort's *Joy of Sex* was praised insofar as its pictures conveyed "a great deal of tenderness and feeling" (not exactly the book's main point) but was criticized for exaggeration and potentially dangerous invocations.[32]

In 1973 *Mademoiselle* introduced a regular column, the "Intelligent Woman's Guide to Sex," that tried to combine selective injunctions toward pleasure seeking with warnings against culturally induced excess. The column's author, Lillian Roxon, recommended that women take sexual initiatives, for pleasure increased with greater personal control, but the specific initiatives mentioned included asking a date out to dinner. More commonly, the column repudiated the belief that maximizing sexual activity in any sense maximized pleasure. Real liberation, Roxon contended early on, probably meant "less and more discriminating sex." Even the possibility of celibacy drew an approving comment. Women should feel free to reject and should expect their decisions to be respected. "If I can reject a manuscript . . . then I can reject a man"— even if this goes against the powerful belief that women should try to please. In 1977 the *Hite Report*'s claim that the emphasis on intercourse privileged male over female pleasure was cited with guarded approval. In the same vein, an article in 1978 proclaimed that "with all this fuss about sexual freedom, it's a little hard to stand up and admit it's not what everyone imagines. . . . Perhaps we could all begin to set the record straight—by saying that without love and trust, 'it's just not worth the hassle.' "[33]

The theme of restraint and firmness was strengthened in the 1980s, not in favor of any single standard of sexual conduct but, instead, responsibility for clarifying one's own values and then making sure that others respected the choice. This became the essence of control. Concerns about sexually transmitted diseases—such as genital herpes, which surfaced as a public problem early in the decade before AIDS obscured its threat—enhanced the caution in any exploration of values. "We didn't need herpes to give wham-bam-by-the-way-what's-your-name sex a bad reputation; just a lot of people finding out that being physically intimate with a virtual stranger is lonely as hell. . . . In fact, rather than proving a shortcut to emotional intimacy, sex too often turns out to be a short circuit." Nonetheless, as if to prove the magazine's broadmindedness, articles on the pleasure of offering oral sex to a man appeared as well. On balance, however, *Mademoiselle*'s highest priority was making sure that women knew that they could reject sex and that they should often do so; the tides of sexual pressure could be rolled back. Furthermore, without reviving an older code, it was also bent on insisting that for most women, sex must be disciplined by an expectation of love and commitment, with men pressed to toe the line. "Too much sex, too little love—what ails the American male?" Experiments remained acceptable, however, "as long as we are doing what we want and not being pressured into sex."[34]

Both *Esquire* and *Mademoiselle* insisted on standing back a bit from condoning what was passing for sexual correctness from the 1960s onward. They both worried that men and women alike might lose appropriate control, and they were eager to point both to alternative standards and to evidence that actual behaviors were not collapsing into promiscuity. Emphases of this sort helped maintain many of the tensions between indulgence and discipline that most of the leading prescriptive manuals featured as well. *Playboy* and other magazines kept up a steady drumbeat against restraint or guilt. These publications themselves reflected wider cultural themes beyond growing overall permissiveness. Pornographic stories, for example, shifted from the male demonstrating prowess through multiple conquests, surrounded by sex-starved women (a staple of the 1950s), to the man gaining satisfaction from inducing multiple orgasms in one or more women. But this evolution, though interesting, hardly embraced any disciplinary tension beyond the implicit invocation of demanding performance standards for both genders. Yet most other hedonists continued to oppose any sort of restraint or guilt. Slightly less committed hedonists occasionally introduced some balance. For example, in 1980 *Cosmopolitan* interrupted its hymns to femininity to conduct a poll demonstrating the widespread dissatisfaction among American women with the sexual revolution and the emphasis on orgasm. The magazine itself was undeterred by these findings, continuing for the next decade and a half to feature articles on being sexy and "Driving Your Man Wild." The sexual revolution, in substantial part a creation of the media, had an undeniable bandwagon effect. Yet the larger culture, shaping and reflecting the media as well, particularly beyond the realm of pure entertainment, created immediate countercurrents apart from the fulminations of pure traditionalists. Here, earlier commitments to discipline and control, though not unchanging, were reaffirmed in the standards of sexuality.[35]

Sex Education

A final cultural category was central to the elaboration of twentieth-century standards: the sexual training of children.

The movement away from Victorianism toward a more explicit discussion of sex and a greater interest in dispelling ignorance led to dramatic changes in sex education. Indeed, presentations of sex education goals to parents embraced the most consistent strand of popularized modernism available since the 1920s. Enlightenment, open inquiry, and even the pursuit of pleasure or at least preparation for such a pursuit predominated. Sex education specialists, writing in such venues as *Parents' Magazine*, preached good sense and rational control but were more wholeheartedly bent on attacking repressive myths than any other successful, popularizing group. The idea of restraint was omnipresent but subtle because previous disciplinary efforts had proved to be counterproductive. But the tension inhered in the twin goals for dispelling ignorance: promoting happiness and preventing excess or premature experimentation.

Sex education also introduced another kind of balance between indulgence and constraint, which affected large numbers of children even as it signaled divisions in American sexual culture. Even though advice to middle-class parents mentioned only the most generalized discipline, such as the need for responsible character development by means of knowledge and reason, the schools' actual sex education programs put discipline at the forefront. After the 1820s, just as enlightened parents were told to avoid physical punishments, the schools continued to administer them. Similarly, in the twentieth century, the admonition to free children from sexual fear was in fact constrained by what most hygiene teachers were told to teach. As with other facets of the twentieth-century tension between permissiveness and control, American children were left to work out the precise boundaries for themselves, assured that for most, the choice would be accompanied by anxiety about being insufficiently relaxed, insufficiently restrained, or both.

Translations of Modernism

Writers like Bertrand Russell or Ben Lindsey, at the forefront of the early attacks on prudery, stressed that children should be taught that sex was natural and desirable and not to fear their bodily impulses. It was parents, misled by traditional prudery, who needed guidance. "The very fact that so many parents have themselves grown up with a warped and distorted outlook on sex makes it difficult for them to give good, sane sex education to their children." This was a message reiterated for several decades.[36]

Advice to parents before 1900 either ignored sexual issues or warned against specific problems, notably masturbation, without more general guidance. Even proponents of instruction, on the grounds that ignorance was worse than knowledge, tended to treat sexuality as a "problem" but refrained from offering any details. By 1910, however, child-rearing experts subscribed to a scientific approach that would provide useful answers to children's curiosity. The purpose was both to dispel ignorance and to restrain impulse: "Develop right thinking, control conduct." Traditionalists disagreed. A Catholic commentator argued, "Let the young have less desire, not more information, strength of will, not complete information." President Eliot of Harvard located the problems as "lust in men" and a "complete lack of moral principle in certain classes of women," leaving unaddressed any educational program at all. Groups like the American Society of Sanitary and Moral Prophylaxis, headed by the editor of the *Ladies Home Journal*, were organized to oppose radical doctors and sociologists, and their debates appeared in a number of magazines. *Pearson's*, for example, reported the controversy while favoring some educational efforts.[37]

By the 1920s, the battle had been won by groups responsible for mainstream child-rearing advice, and a suitably restrained modernist program prevailed. By the late 1920s, the standard arguments had been established. First, children's questions about sex were entirely natural and should be honestly and calmly answered. Adults with a healthy ("untrammeled, vigorous, sensitive, reciprocal and glad") sex life would automatically respond well; others would need guidance in order to raise children "free from fear, embarrassment, shame and apology." Joy in sex should be the main goal. Inherent impulses such as masturbation must be permitted, despite older admonitions. No harm was caused by at least moderate practice, whereas repression could have very undesirable consequences. Children also should be explicitly taught "something at least" about sexual techniques. The goal was not, however, complete permissiveness. In addition, the contemporary youth culture was also attacked for its brazenness and false freedom. Education would correct this along with outdated prudery, by producing rational controls over "raw sex impulse run wild." Education would replace futile regulations on behalf of morality, though not primarily to unleash the libido from past repression:

> Soundness, responsibility and beauty in sex living will be developed as the expression of inner fineness. We shall help young people apply to sex expression the same courtesy, tact, good taste, fairness, honor and understanding that they do to all other relationships, instead of trying to safeguard it with merely external fences, such as moral dictums, fears, conventional habits and conventional marriage.[38]

Sex education thus was meant to incorporate the same messages as the advice to adults, that sex was great but must be controlled. The tone differed, however, as popularizing experts more readily targeted ignorance in most parents themselves. That is, adults should hide their own unfortunate vestiges of shame and guilt (another control target) in order to teach the next generation properly.

The goodness and naturalness of sex were stressed. Some authorities recommended occasional nudity, as children would satisfy their curiosity about sex by occasional glimpses of their parents naked. Old ideas about masturbation were routinely attacked and replaced by acceptance of the practice as beneficial "if not practiced habitually into maturity." "You can't have much sexual feeling toward someone also if, discovering it in yourself, it is entirely forbidden and repressed in childhood." Only adult-induced guilt was a real problem in masturbation, though its excess was still discouraged. Evasion and shame were the key enemies— leading, one authority argued, to "unhappiness, neurosis, and suicide" (hyperbole about childhood sex was not a monopoly of the Victorians). Although the main goal was a happy sex life, it also included a battle against "intensely morbid curiosity." Again, control through understanding easily outweighed permissiveness.[39]

By 1940 this approach was supplemented by scientific efforts to determine how and if sex education improved adult sexual happiness. One study, claiming quantitative precision in the best social scientific fashion, demonstrated that husbands had more than a third more "Euphor-units in marital happiness" if well instructed than if not; wives did best, however, with if they characterized their childhood sex training as "rather inadequate," although those with no training were worst off.

These findings did not hamper the effort to provide a "wholesome" sex education to remove "morbid and distorting emotional strains," thus permitting both pleasure and appropriate "self-mastery." At the same time, there was every reason to keep children constructively occupied so they would have less time for curiosity or masturbation. No traumatic prohibitions should intervene, however. Even the desirable goal of confining sex to marriage should not be achieved through moralistic harangues but by presenting one's own marriage as a "sweet picture of domestic content." Sex must be seen as normal, and the additional message that "it is only sex outside of love that is ugly and debasing" must be introduced subtly.[40] By the 1950s, Catholic advice literature concurred with this basic idea of sex education, including its emphasis on dealing frankly and naturally with children's questions. It was distinctive only in urging more frequent references to God and divinely appointed rules and more "chaste thoughts" for both genders.[41]

Not surprisingly, the most triumphant restatements of relevant modernism, with their deliberately vague statements of balance between indulgence and discipline, continued to resound in secular materials. A 1950 offering recommended abandoning purely traditional, misleading constraints "to substitute for the external sanctions of the super ego, the free sanctions of conscience." "The men and women in this new age will believe that sex, like other primary human appetites, is not bad in itself but only when used out of its proper place or beyond its due degree." Even the advent of the sexual revolution created few mainstream materials that sought to improve on this approach.[42]

The Role of Schools in Sex Education

Sex education in the schools was a contentious item early on, and it remained contentious. Modernist beliefs gained by pushing the idea that the schools could be useful here given parental inadequacy. But they could not be given full rein because of the public dispute about whether sex education should be offered and what it should consist of. In one sense, school-based sex education strove to be more values neutral than the child-rearing commentary was, because the values were harder to agree on. In fact, however, through a combination of traditionalism, tone, and innovation, many programs conveyed a much more disapproving view of sex than child-rearing popularizers advocated. Finally, precisely because of its checkered history, including its being used to discourage sexual interest, sex education was a prime candidate for more overtly cautionary service in reaction to the presumed sexual revolution of the 1960s.

When the movement for sex education in the schools began in the 1920s, the biological component of the modernist approach gradually won out and, with it, a mission to dispel myth and ignorance. Because of political pressures and public divisions, other modernist elements surfaced only rarely. Elite suspicion of the masses—the sense that only blatant warnings might suffice for discipline—and working-class and religious hesitation about removing sex education from the home complicated the implementation of programs and reduced their effectiveness. Thus there was no inculcation of joy and little nuanced statement of rational control and its harmony with pleasure. Moreover, certain topics such as masturbation and birth control could not usually be discussed at all. So what was enlightenment for? Although values and intended controls were transmitted, they were largely removed from the balancing indulgence that characterized twentieth-century middle-class culture in other respects. This plus an element of traditionalism—for example, nineteenth-century-style attacks on masturbation were being taught in public school programs into the 1930s, complete with warnings about insanity—painted a far different picture of sex education and of the relationship between schoolchildren and adult sexual standards.

Conversion to the idea of sex education came only gradually in the interwar decades. The Lynds reported unanimity among their middle-class parent sample in Indiana, majority approval in the working class (although in each case, large minorities of grandparents were opposed). But beyond some hesitant references in high school biology classes, only a small number of school districts—possibly as few as 3 percent as late as the 1950s—gave more than a passing nod to sex education or an occasional guest lecture. The dilemmas of the field reflected adult ambiguities, not necessarily adolescent tensions. The few programs that were established were mainly a collection of warnings and admonitions. For instance, a New York curriculum, approved in 1921, noted the need to yield to any significant public opposition. Beyond attacks on misinformation and unnecessary fear, all the programs' goals were cautionary.

Thus young men should know about nocturnal emissions, young women about menstruation, because parental instruction was so "woefully lacking." The reasons? "To prevent morbid and to give healthy attitudes toward sex matters." "To teach people, both by precept and example, to discern for themselves between the wholesome and the salacious"—to use sexual knowledge, in other words, to attack peer culture, movies, and even "dancing and other amusements" in the interest of restraint "and to develop a preference for the wholesome." Teachers should, of course, have exemplary "character and good judgment." The actual curriculum stressed the biology of reproduction but also moral precepts. The family was presented as "a natural unit" based on a spiritual love, in contrast to the mating instincts of lower animals. Love, of course, "endures through a life time," whereas animal sex is "promiscuous and of short duration." Boys must learn about the health consequences of masturbation, plus good attitudes, "the exercise of self-control," and fairness and social responsibility. Girls should also learn "the exercise of self-control." Both must see "morality, rather than sensuality as the dominant factor in social life." And again, should there be any doubt, the primacy of high and spiritual pleasure must be emphasized over "the more gross indulgences."[43]

Individual teachers might take a more modernist view, although even in the 1960s they continued to avoid "certain" questions about birth control, abortion, and "adult sex relations." Several agencies, some federally supported, were formed to support sex education, sometimes recommending it before high school. But even though the programs were criticized for lacking morality and unduly emphasizing mechanics, in fact they rarely did more than combine data about reproduction with warnings about potential dangers and problems. Public support did rise, reaching 70 percent by 1969, and doctors and educators lined up behind the idea. But the justification of sex education, beyond attacking ignorance, continued to focus mainly on using training to regulate sexual behavior.[44]

The 1960s saw both a rapid expansion of sex education curricula to more than two-thirds of all states (although as late as 1981, only two states actually required programs) and a massive conservative campaign against them, spearheaded by such groups as the Christian Crusade and the right-wing John Birch Society (which characterized the programs as "a filthy communist plot"). Although the campaign did not destroy the movement, it did keep the programs limited and often at least vaguely negative about sex itself. One educator, urging the importance of teaching about love as a context for sex and about "responsible decisions"—hardly an extreme hedonist—argued in 1985 that only 10 percent of all schoolchildren received a well-rounded program because school authorities so easily caved in to the opposition of a small minority in the community. Few young people, he contended, were taught anything that would make them feel there was an alternative to guilt even for thinking about sexual pleasures or other normal fantasies. Birth control, in particular, remained a forbidden topic, even though surveys showed that comprehensive programs did increase students' knowledge of the risk of pregnancies and sexually transmitted diseases, as well as the actual use of condoms, and that more ambitious efforts in Europe (coupled with available birth control devices) made serious inroads on the rate of teenage pregnancy.[45]

For the first time outside some private schools, a few programs, in the glow of the sexual revolution, adopted a neomodernist agenda. A New Jersey curriculum in the late 1970s talked openly of pleasure, noting, for example, "Grown-ups sometimes forget to tell children that touching can also give people pleasure, especially when someone you love touches you. And you can give yourself pleasure, too, and that's okay. When you touch your own genitals it's called masturbating." Intercourse itself was only indirectly discussed, but the comment that "when you are older you can decide if you want to have sex" was quite positive. "Most people do, because they like it and it's a very important way of showing that we love someone."[46]

This approach was both short lived and atypical, however. Most programs increasingly attacked damaging sexual behaviors that led to teenage pregnancy and AIDS. The kinds of anxieties directed toward college students in the 1920s were now conveyed to younger adolescents. Schools continued to teach basic reproductive biology, still assuming that such knowledge promoted responsible behavior, while avoiding contraception, abortion, and homosexuality as too controversial. The warnings about disease became louder and became more graphic. A New York City curriculum, revised in 1981, thus insisted on responsibility and promotion of the family, although it included sensitivity to different sexual orientations and mentioned family planning. Far more programs, like one at an Atlanta middle school, simply stated the main goal: "to help boys and girls resist pressures to engage in sex." The increasingly conservative influence pushed for teaching abstinence as the only acceptable approach to be used in sex education, and a U.S. surgeon general who advocated teaching about masturbation and birth control was hounded out of office. In 1997 the federal government was providing $137 million to school districts that taught abstinence exclusively, and the Clinton crisis led to further pressure. Leading motifs, according to federal guidelines, stressed that "a mutually faithful monogamous relationship in the context of marriage is the expected standard of human sexual activity" and, more ominously, "sexual activity outside of the context of marriage is likely to have harmful psychological and physical effects." Fear was now being combined with the more traditional cautionary approach.[47]

Public instruction regarding sex could normally gain ground when aimed—as a 1930s advocate noted—at problems such as disease, abortion, and illegitimate births. The programs reflected the complexity of adult attitudes as they veered toward self-control and discipline without the counterbalance present in child-rearing recommendations to middle-class parents. Demonstrably—as critics pointed out—many American youngsters ignored these preachments. For some, however—even those who engaged in activities they had been taught to shun—the programs might add to a sense of guilt and furtiveness. The programs' emphases also helped persuade adults of youth sexuality run amok, thereby affecting their own attitudes toward discipline (of others if not of themselves)—thus engendering further opposition to more nuanced training. To this extent, sex education both contributed to and reflected the complex tensions of twentieth-century sexuality standards in American culture.[48]

Realities and Fantasies

From the 1920s through the 1990s, Americans did try to implement the basic tension in their new sexual culture. They maintained considerable discipline in actual behavior while changing the precise definition in various subperiods, but they continued to search more actively for pleasure in the recreational sexual culture they sponsored as spectators. Here, fantasies, though usually irrelevant to measurable behaviors, became vitally important.

Sexual Behavior

Sexual standards inevitably raise issues of enforcement and deviations. Victorian commentators, however, found relatively few problems in the middle class, at least once boys had navigated through adolescence without masturbating. The few deviants usually were men who failed to remain faithful to their wives or unmarried daughters who became pregnant. The "other" was abundantly available to illustrate the perils of sexual misconduct—working-class families who had too many children, racial minorities whose undisciplined sexuality caused their low status and justified segregation and neglect.

Only in the later nineteenth century did moralists, including feminists, begin to discern trends of greater indulgence, as indicated by men's increasing use of prostitutes and a growing perceived incidence of venereal disease. This new tension between standards and apparent behavior presaged the twentieth-century situation, in which sexual excess often seemed to outpace self-control. The more complex standards themselves and the effort to combine approval for pleasure in certain contexts with the need for discipline may have contributed to these shifts in conduct. For example, in their Middletown study, the Lynds noted that men conducting extramarital affairs were becoming less secretive, sensing that community disapproval had loosened. This was not a claim that the frequency of extramarital affairs had risen, which the Lynds did not know. Even more important—as the Middletown findings also suggest—was the decline of social enforcement. Birth control became more available, at least to middle-class people willing to consult doctors. Women appeared more often in public, so domestic confinement was less able to support sexual restraint. Dating took young people farther away from family monitoring. More responsibility now rested on self-discipline even as the cultural codes themselves began to favor a balance between pleasure and restraint.[49]

One result was the worry—of traditional critics, of course, but also popularizers—about actual behavior. We have seen that ignorance and outdated repression were often attacked for leading astray youth, particularly males; updated standards would bring more pleasure to marriage but also bring appetites otherwise under greater control. Marital advisers worried about excessive repression but also about men who had indulged hastily and ill advisedly with others and who needed new lessons before approaching the marriage bed. Sex education, particularly in the schools, was directed even more single-mindedly toward correcting existing behavioral excess. The outpouring of concern escalated, particularly with the 1960s and the presumed sexual revolution. But a middle-class gap between conduct and ideal was at base a staple in twentieth-century perceptions.

At the same time, we should recognize that standards, inculcated as part of socialization and still urged on adults, usually have a behavioral impact. It would be surprising to find actual sexual activities, on average, totally departing from the norms being advocated. Conduct did change because of weakened community and legal controls, greater use of contraception, a more sexualized media culture, and the impact of more nuanced advice. But it never, insofar as can be determined in an inherently private domain, totally escaped controls to the extent that some critics claimed. The greatest deviation from standards came through differentiation, the substantial variety developed in different middle-class groups, depending on personality, religion, and other factors in defiance of the more uniform mainstream culture. Few, however, committed themselves to maximizing indulgence and jettisoning restraint, despite some widely publicized experiments during the late 1960s and early 1970s.

We can assess middle-class sexual behaviors since the 1920s from a variety of vantage points. Premarital sexual experience is one. Surveys in 1929 and the 1930s indicated that about 35 percent of college women engaged in premarital sexual intercourse, probably a bit up from Victorian courtship levels. Although virginity was still professed as desirable (but only by 60 percent of college women in one poll), there was somewhat less shame or hypocritical concealment than in the nineteenth century. A 1936 survey of middle-class families claimed that although 74 percent of women born before 1900 were virgins at marriage, only 32 percent of those born after 1910 claimed to be. Kinsey's figures showed a trend toward an earlier age for first intercourse for women, although only 20 percent of all women (regardless of generation) reported first having intercourse before the age of twenty. After the 1930s, college students more frequently used condoms. Language changed as well: "making love" in the nineteenth century meant verbal declarations in courtship, but by the 1920s it referred to the exchange of caresses or more. On a variety of fronts, then, the greater permissiveness of the prescriptive culture joined the apparent generational break around 1930. Still, the extent of this transformation should not be overblown. Observers at the time exaggerated its novelty because they did not know about the large (though disproportionately male), sexually active middle-class minority in the Victorian decades. For women, most premarital sex was with their fiancé and was not intended to be promiscuous. According to the 1929 survey, whereas 35 percent of women learned about sex through premarital intercourse, and 22 percent read about what to expect on their wedding night, 21 percent still professed to have learned nothing about it at all from any source, even their parents.[50]

This growing tension between rising sexual interests and static norms was partially resolved during the 1940s and 1950s by the precipitous decline in the middle class's age at marriage. This unquestionably reflected the drop in the average age of first sexual experience, but it also confirmed the power of restraining standards—a truly fascinating, if transient, reconciliation. More and more middle-class men and women were now getting married in their early twenties. Premarital sex was often immediately followed by marriage, thus instituting a behavior change along with the continuity in standards. And in the population at large, teenage sex and parenthood increased as well.[51]

Sex within marriage also changed as middle-class recreational sex began to diverge from more traditional, male-dominant working-class patterns. Again, the widespread availability of birth control, mainly physician-prescribed diaphragms, reflected the growing acceptance of sex for pleasure. By 1928, a large majority of middle-class couples were using contraceptive devices. Techniques also became more varied, with experiments with different positions for intercourse and the use of oral sex. As a result, more women reported having orgasm, and by the early 1940s, 73 percent of all married middle-class women claimed they experienced orgasm always or often during intercourse. Interestingly, some surveys suggested that the frequency of marital sex declined as men became more responsive to their wives' desires.[52]

Still, there were marked differences between the genders. Women wanted to have sex less often than men did and were far more likely to refuse to have it. Men, now expected to give their wives pleasure, professed a new source of discontent when women failed to report having an orgasm. Polling data showed that men were more unhappy with the sex in their marriage than women were and were particularly concerned about their wives' lack of responsiveness. Traditional cultural differences in assumptions about gender now translated into new disputes, given greater public encouragement to make sex actively pleasurable In some cases, men's grievances were heightened by the belief that they had been patient and restrained, but to no avail. Women, however, had their own complaints, again mixing tradition with innovation. Expecting sexual pleasure but also seeking romantic love and now the new and elusive goal of marital intimacy, women were often disappointed both physically and emotionally. Diary evidence, more than polling data, and indications of frequent sadness reveal the various ways in which the combination of old and new standards created criteria for sex itself and for its emotional context that were not often met. The baby boom's surging birthrate from the late 1940s into the 1960s further complicated marital sex through the intrusion of new levels of infant care. Clearly, to this point, evolution, not revolution, had described middle-class efforts to combine pleasure with restraint.[53]

The 1960s unquestionably brought more behavioral change, but it built on previous trends. Within the middle class, three or four shifts predominated. First, the age of first sexual intercourse fell for both men and women. In the middle class, the drop was not massive, in contrast to that of the urban lower class of all races, but it was important. The majority of middle-class Americans began to have their first sexual experience between the ages of fifteen and eighteen, a pattern that lasted through the 1980s with slight fluctuations. Before the early 1950s, only a large minority of Americans fit this pattern. A cohort born between 1933 and 1942, reaching their teenage years beginning in the 1950s, reduced the average age of first sexual intercourse. And the trend persisted: in 1970, 29 percent of all American women had premarital sex between the ages of fifteen and nineteen; in 1980, 42 percent did so; and in 1988, 52 percent did so. (Only by 1995 was there any measurable break in this trend, as teenage sex declined by about 10 percent over a five-year span.) Although it was the lower age that was most striking, the concomitant increase in the marriage age for the middle class after about 1963 toward the middle to late twenties, meant that the correlation between sex and marriage had weakened.

By the 1970s, couples living together before being married became a rapidly growing, though still atypical, household form. The pattern reflected the continuing association between sex and some emotional commitment, but not necessarily marriage, and cohabitation was less stable than marriage, which meant more shifts in partners This development was a result of more reliable, easier forms of birth control—the pill and the intrauterine device—that no longer depended on discipline near the act of intercourse itself. The percentage of women having sex before marriage clearly had changed, although it had already been fairly high. In any case, the practice became more open, and the link between sex and engagement eased. As part of this pattern and also as a result of the rising divorce rates, the average number of lifetime sexual partners almost surely increased. It also is possible that the rates of adultery rose, at least in the 1960s and early 1970s; certainly, widely publicized cases of open marriage and (presumably) promiscuous communal groups created that impression. Finally, homosexual behavior became more open, beginning with the Stonewall uprising in 1969 and the formation of the gay liberation movement. How much sexual practices and even the number of gays increased, as opposed to the much greater shifts in public awareness, was open to question; again, publicity and perception undoubtedly outstripped behavioral revolution in most categories.

At the same time, there were important continuities or even countertrends. First, it quickly became clear that men's and women's experiences still often differed. The famous poll by Shere Hite was notoriously unscientific, but it revealed that a large number of women were dissatisfied with their sexual experience and its emotional context. Were the poll to be taken literally, rates of women's marital orgasm had actually declined (or the definition had become more rigorous or both); Hite's data had only a minority of women regularly achieving orgasm, as opposed to Kinsey's earlier 70+ percent. Complaints about unemotional sex and a lack of love and commitment on men's part harked back to dissatisfactions promoted by complex standards several decades earlier. Men's complaints also reechoed. A major 1970s survey pinpointed the leading issue: women's lack of adequate interest and of capacity to achieve orgasm. Of course, expectations of ever-mounting pleasure made it easier to be dissatisfied than ever before, but important underlying constraints remained as well.[54]

When the media dust settled, polls revealed an altered but hardly unbridled pattern of middle-class behavior. According to the survey data (dependent, of course, on what people chose to say), American sexuality at the end of the 1980s remained recognizably balanced in most respects. It had continued to evolve and, in a few categories, reflected a decisive break from the 1960s, but an evolutionary pattern emanating from an interest in combining pleasure with discipline still described the trajectory. It also is important to note that the measurable behaviors were less distinctive compared with those of western Europe than the culture was, a point to which we will return.[55]

About one-third of all women still claimed only one sexual partner in a lifetime, and two-thirds had between one and four. For men, the comparable figures were 19 percent and 40 percent, respectively. The number of partners increased with educational level. Few people maintained more than one sexual partner at a given time, and only 25 percent were unfaithful in marriage. It is not clear that adultery had increased or even that the number of partners had risen; rather, the higher divorce and remarriage rates may have accounted for most of the partner changes, at least for women. "Swinging" behavior, or rampant promiscuity, was rare; only 3 percent of all men had five or more sexual partners in a given year.

The striking shift still focused on sex before marriage and relatedly the age of first sex and the range of youthful activity, although on all these counts, the middle class was more guarded than were, on average, elements of the urban lower class, including African Americans. Evolution did continue: 43 percent of men born in the 1930s had had only one sexual partner before age twenty, compared with 28 percent in the 1960s generation; 33 percent of the 1930s male cohort admitted having sex before marriage, compared with 70 percent in the 1960s (figures for women were 31 percent and 58 percent, respectively). Only a small portion of the population had had large numbers of partners as adolescents, and they were not primarily middle class, but the overall minority (10 percent) was larger in the 1960s-born cohort.

Vaginal intercourse remained the preferred sexual mode, although oral sex became more popular after the 1920s. This was a particularly dramatic expression of nonprocreative sex, not frequently mentioned before the twentieth century (save in some experimental nineteenth-century communes) and not even featured in prior pornography as a turn-on. The rise in popularity of oral sex also gained significance in the challenge it posed to the generally intensifying standards of hygiene, as if the expression showed the priority of sex over normal fears of dirt and contagion. The change had massive implications. By the 1980s, 60 percent of all men had had oral sex at some point in their lives, but 85 percent of twenty-five- to twenty-nine-year-olds claimed to have had the experience, with the middle class (as measured by education) in the lead. At the same time, only 17 percent of all women, well below the actual percentage engaging in the practice, enjoyed giving oral sex, thereby reflecting the tensions between internal disciplinary impulses and what now seemed expected of a modern sexual participant.

Masturbation was common, involving well over half the population, with levels rising with education, although more than half, particularly in the middle class, felt guilty about it. In addition, men reported having sex more often than women did. It was not clear that frequency of intercourse had risen for either gender, which is one reason that high if reluctant masturbation levels among adults, particularly men and including married men, were noteworthy. Only 29 percent of married women reported having reasonably regular orgasms, and 42 percent expressed satisfaction with their sex lives, figures not dissimilar to those reported in the 1970s and possibly lower, at least in the category of orgasm, than in the 1940s. In contrast, more than 80 percent of all men had regular orgasms. Gender disparities may also have shown up in areas such as partner reports. The gap between men's and women's partner claims were fascinating, suggesting a greater use of a minority of sexually absorbed women than seemed probable and/or different patterns of prevarication. Men, still in a culture that encouraged claims of prowess, may have been tempted to exaggerate partner and frequency rates, whereas women (particularly when sexual conservatism again became more fashionable in the late 1980s) may have been tempted to glide over youthful indiscretions.

Constraints counted even aside from gender. Only a small minority of men and women alike reported enjoying watching other people having sex. Rates of anal sex were low (despite the fascination with this option in contemporary pornography). The majority of Americans had only one partner in a given year, including a majority (59 percent) for men aged eighteen to twenty-four. One reason that AIDS spread less rapidly since its discovery in 1983 than had been anticipated was simply that the American people were more conventional in their sexual behavior than many observers assumed. Most heterosexuals' aversion to anal intercourse was a specific factor. Some types of activity may have slowed in response to the threat of disease or at least entailed new levels of protection (a whole field of condom etiquette sprang up, showing the role of manners and restraint amid change), but the strongest indications were that in most respects, there had never been a behavioral revolution at all. Daniel Yankelovich professed amazement at a 1980s finding that most Americans, male and female, preferred sexual partners with whom they had emotional rapport and confidence over people who were sexier in appearance and method. Choices as well behaviors, therefore, did not veer off well-defined pathways.

In sum, American sexual activity had loosened, moderately in most respects and dramatically in a few, over eight decades. But the majority of Americans were still considerably disciplined. Most Americans could claim some relationship between their sexual behavior, particularly after marriage, and the guidelines they encountered in the prescriptive culture. Gaps existed, but in some cases, as in the rates of women's orgasm, they continued to reflect a failure to live up to the twentieth century's assumption of pleasure, not an excess of indulgence.

The Compensatory Alternative of Sexualized Media

The tension and restraint that framed the behavioral changes did not apply to the images available for spectator viewing. In the first half of the twentieth century, the available sex-oriented reading and viewing expanded, balanced by past restrictions and occasional traditionalist counterattacks. Then, in the 1950s and 1960s, America's sex spectatorship departed from its previous contours, as evolutionary trends blossomed, or deteriorated, into a virtual public obsession. Traditionalist warnings persisted, but with extremely limited effects; balance, in this area, was largely lacking. But American public presentations still were constrained in comparison with European analogues: for example, outright nudity was not used in advertisements, and (except for cable movie channels or the *Playboy* outlet) explicit depictions of intercourse could not be seen on television. Nor did American women commonly wear topless swimming suits on public beaches. These were not insignificant holdovers of restraint, but they paled before the new abundance of flesh and innuendo now available. Larger disciplinary standards or cautionary constraints were missing, in contrast to the prescriptive standards or to actual behavior.

There were three major departures from reasonably respectable nineteenth-century recreational culture. First, the extent of what could be revealed in the public media greatly widened. Stories about sex, including news accounts, and visual imagery became more explicit. At the same time, more revealing costumes in leisure settings, particularly for women, brought new levels of spectatorship to resorts and backyards.

Second, sexual fare became more routine. Although the nineteenth century did have media outlets, such as vaudeville shows with scantily clad women (apart from the pornography available mainly to the upper class), they were used infrequently, in contrast to more modern suggestive films or television fare. Stories about sexually related crimes were common during the nineteenth century,[56] but in the twentieth century, they have been nearly daily events, at least in the tabloids. A key progression was the introduction of sex into standard news fare. By the 1980s and 1990s, this evolution began to be extended to political figures, with their sexual escapades, real or imagined, becoming headline news.[57] The progression toward sexual presentations in leisure routines drove many ordinary individuals to participate in a panorama of self-revelation on television and radio talk shows, discussing their multiple affairs, adulteries, and deviancies before an audience accustomed to hearing accounts of sex.

Third, escapist sex included reports of real or imagined sexual behavior, and after the 1950s, particularly beginning with the Kinsey reports, observation became part of the sexual culture. After the 1950s, the nation was regaled with stories about sexual revolutions, available along-side suggestive films and magazine covers, and these presentations were less often combined with moral warnings or obligatory unhappy endings.

Four factors caused these new media trends from the beginning of the century through the turning point around 1955. First, modernist intellectuals insisted that sexual stories and investigations no longer be censored. This movement helped lead to objective scientific inquiry, which cut into censorship (even before Kinsey) and also helped create a public appetite for national sexual self-scrutiny.[58] Second, with new technology came the ability to produce highly accessible color illustrations, followed by movies and then television and finally the Internet, at the century's end. Graphic sexual imagery became more common, exempt from most regulation. Third, changes in the law, following to some extent from modernism but also from shifts in wider public beliefs, explain the surge of sex data, including fantasy fare, by the 1950s. Fourth and most important, commercial producers found that sexual suggestion and consumerism could be linked. Advertisements, as we have seen, began to use sex from at least the 1880s, and sex sold even more directly with the rise of the movie industry. Growing consumer abundance was linked to the growing sexual abundance at the level of escapist outlet and fantasy.

The reasons for these trends clearly involved changing public tastes and interests. John Burnham claims that lower-class vulgarity joined commercial exploitation in the growing sexual license of American culture. But in some cases, the changes in taste may have been caused by the other factors involved.[59] Modernist influence came from the top down, as did changes in the law to a great extent, but there were spontaneous expressions of spectator taste from other social sectors as well, which was one reason that sex sold so well.[60]

Changes in both law and the media began the process of spectator escalation after 1910. Court rulings beginning in 1913 held that news outlets had the right to use revealing pictures and accounts of celebrities' activities, a shift that underwrote the rise of the tabloids in the 1920s. Presumably scientific accounts of sexual behavior also received a legal boost in 1930, with a verdict that the book *Hands Around*, dealing with prostitution, could not be banned because its "appeal to passion or lechery is wholly lacking." Advertising, already committed to associating sex with consumer products, became more inescapable with the rise of illustrated magazines and billboards. Calendar art featuring nude or provocatively posed women became standard fare in certain men's sites such as barbershops and garages. Movie stars also were depicted in suggestive (if by subsequent standards well-clad) poses and, along with stories about their frequent affairs and marriages, began to assume roles as larger-than-life sex symbols. Overtly provocative film titles such as *A Shocking Night, Red Hot Dames, Lurid Lips,* and *Her Pucker Price* vied for attention while stars like Mae West routinely paraded their physical endowments and offered sultry come-ons in their screen roles. Even more ambitious fare like *Gone with the Wind* escalated sexual references during the 1930s. Nude or seminude entertainment continued to be available on the burlesque stage. Strippers like Gypsy Rose Lee commanded widespread attention as they moved to the borderline of entertainment respectability. It became steadily easier to see more sexually stimulating fare, in more visually interesting media and with more blurred lines between fantasies and apparently real-life stories about the image makers.

This evolution was not unchallenged. Laws dating back to the late nineteenth century continued to restrict some spectator presentations. Court decisions outlawed certain books, such as *Lady Chatterley's Lover* and *The Tropic of Capricorn.* Bowing to pressure from religious groups, headed by Catholic organizations, Hollywood instituted a tougher code in 1934, which banned depictions of adultery or lustful abandon, although during World War II, U.S. troops were permitted to put images of nudes in airplanes and other military equipment. Purity campaigns continued unabated into the 1950s, which at least delayed the expansion of sexualized spectatorship.

The dam burst in the 1950s and early 1960s as several developments combined. New commercial publishers, such as Hugh Hefner of *Playboy* (1953), began to offer pictures of nudes and stories of sexual exploits. Hefner's empire gradually expanded to other publications, nightclubs, and a much-disclosed personal appetite. Hefner's widely publicized philosophy asserted the value of sexual pleasure in itself, in virtually any form. He admitted the possibility of love in combination with sex but insisted that the linkage was not essential. Other publications, like *Pent-*

house and *Hustler*, followed in the early 1960s, presenting still more graphic imagery and accounts of multiple partners, oral sex, and attacks on outdated pruderies. Kinsey's reports had started to appear in the late 1940s, giving Americans unprecedented detail about their own sexual behavior and its variations. The reports implied that a range of sexual behaviors were natural and should be acceptable, a matter of private taste and not public regulation. This development helped lead to another set of changes in law and governmental monitoring. Rulings by more liberal courts found works previously judged pornographic now acceptable because of their literary merits. This was the judgment that released *Fanny Hill*, an eighteenth-century novel, in 1966. In 1970 the U.S. Commission on Obscenity and Pornography contended that graphic materials, whether literary or visual, might stimulate sexual feelings but did not directly lead to unacceptable behaviors. Rather, they offered "affectionless sex" and should not be proscribed. In this atmosphere, Hollywood and television tested the boundaries of public taste and official response. Television began to show a couple in the same bed. Costumes became more revealing, references to multiple partners and promiscuous sexual prowess more frequent. Rock music introduced more graphic and provocative lyrics, including linkages between sex and violence. By the 1980s, homosexuality was depicted in mainstream films and even television series. Interesting media hesitations remained, however, particularly in depicting male nudes. But by the final third of the century, in terms of amount, range, and explicitness, American sexual spectatorship had been revolutionized.[61]

In this context, the traditionalist protests continued, but with a limited impact. The attacks on rock music and unrated television programs persisted, but the tide could not be rolled back. Only when children's access was concerned was even limited change possible. Thus religious organizations helped remove the graphic male magazines from convenience store shelves in the 1980s, although other newsstands, including college bookstores, ever alert to what sold, maintained easy access to them. The authorities also grappled with the even readier communication available through the Internet. A federal expert in 1997 worked on the difference between depicting an erect penis used to show how to put on a condom and a largely nude actress on the cover of *Vanity Fair*, arguing that the latter might be more clearly regulated because it was for "fun." But aside from the discussion of technology that might allow censorship by parents, the surge continued.

More interesting was the emergence of public standards (sometimes upheld by law) combining the fascination with openly presenting sex with the insistence on exhibiting good character. Posing in the nude disqualified one aspirant for the Miss America crown. Athletes and movie stars might feed the gossip columns with relative impunity, but sportscasters caught in adulterous situations were subject to greater criticism, and politicians might be driven from their trade by unduly open displays of hedonism. A leading Democratic presidential contender in 1988, Gary Hart, thus failed to survive a well-publicized yachting trip with a young woman. The Clinton crisis of 1998 was preceded by recurrent lawsuits and discussions of leadership standards.

Another important development led to some blurring between escapism and sexual reality. Media sexuality became so ubiquitous that some spectators began to seize on the more sensitive efforts as a means of exploring issues of their own. The 1997 television show *Ally McBeal* featured the characteristic short skirts, lovely women, and focus on sex in virtually every episode. But the themes also stimulated fan involvement, including Internet sites and chat groups where people used the show as a basis for talking about their own sexual experiences and other personal issues, intertwining their lives with episode themes. As one commentator noted, the show became "equipment for thinking about love, sex and relationships," particularly among viewers living alone. This overlap remained unusual, however. More shows, such as the promiscuous and improbable prime-time soap opera *Melrose Place* that preceded *McBeal*'s time slot, pushed sex—viewer identification be damned.[62]

Certainly, most of the media surge was unaffected by disciplinary impulses. By the 1980s and 1990s, sexualized humor had become a mainstay in television's situation comedies as sexualization proceeded and as several other comedy subjects became too sensitive for comment. Lust encountering impediments was funny. Temporary male impotence became a comedy staple. Interestingly, because media women were supposed to be sexually ready, "frigidity" was not paraded for laughter. Fantasy was more important than this category of concern. But women's faked orgasms, complete with sound effects, were common on laugh tracks. Humorous birthday and Valentine's Day cards picked up sexual motifs with a vengeance. Reference to declining prowess became a male birthday mainstay, and allusions to sexual desire vied with more traditional romantic sentiments on the February card racks. As before, with the growing use of sexual terms as curses, humor was double edged, reflecting the discomfort with demands for sexual pleasure as well as its embrace. But the theme's omnipresence was unquestionable as it spread into additional areas of spectator entertainment.

In this context, fantasy could run wild. Sexologists recommended it as a secret spice to marriage. In 1976, presidential aspirant Jimmy Carter—trying to be one of the boys despite his born-again Christianity—confessed that he frequently lusted in his heart thinking about women other than his wife. Revealingly, his comments evoked an earlier, more rigorous era of self-control when images as well as behaviors might be disciplined, but they made no sense to most Americans, who did indeed restrain their actions, but in part by letting their dreams run free.

The explosion of sex spectatorship is a familiar aspect of contemporary American culture, with the fascination with sexual imagery and fantasy playing out in the larger tension between discipline and indulgence. Some commentators, however, mistook the culture for the real thing. Barbara Ehrenreich, for example, assumed that men's interest in *Playboy* in the 1960s signaled a decline in their commitment to family and in work values. Historian John Burnham and many editorialists documented the new cultural license and then assumed or claimed, without evidence, that behavior had changed to the same degree. This linkage pushed interpretation too far, for the sexual fare sought in recreational spectatorship had only a limited relationship to measurable behavior or overall personal sexual standards, areas in which change, though significant, was far less extensive. Even the masturbatory use of the new media depictions was, as we have seen, accompanied by considerable guilt. Men did not flee substantial commitment in their sex lives; rather, some of them supplemented their commitment with the private perusal of graphic imagery. Thus, sex spectatorship joined other aspects of the nation's compensatory culture, providing alternatives to discipline and restraint—alternatives that did not contradict this reality but, rather, helped reconcile self-control with the temptations of a consumer age.

Toleration of the new spectator culture was predicated on the conviction that the regulation of imagery was not needed to restrain behavior. Just as swearing now demonstrated the mastery of anger control, so spectator license depended on quiet behavioral restraint in sex. This involved real change, to be sure, but hardly in the direction of unbridled hedonism. Victorians in this area, as in several others, combined personal standards with public restrictions on temptation. The consumer culture had overridden the restrictions on temptation, on the assumption that people could keep their behavior in check. Greater faith in internal discipline and in the capacity of the whole population to adopt something like middle class norms differentiated this approach from the past. Despite some deviations, particularly in assumptions about social homogeneity, this faith was not entirely misplaced. A balance remained. Behavior, linked to widely accepted standards, now deliberately diverged from imagery—just as other escapist recreational staples, like sports, departed from ordinary, controlled behavior and with similar implications of tension but also compensation.

Even so the glare of escapist sexual fare—combined with common exaggerations about behavioral change and with misleading assumptions that media culture somehow described reality—did help generate the final component of the twentieth-century battles over sexuality, the emergence of restrictive innovations that would heighten the rigor of respectable discipline, whatever the fantasy media chose to present. For those uncomfortable with the culture, innovation was all the more necessary in that traditionalist efforts to impose censorship had largely failed. Even the traditionalists put more energy into opposing abortion as a means of attacking contemporary sexuality than into trying to dent the consumer culture directly. More people, uncomfortable with the implications of undue sexuality but not traditionalist, looked for novel means of supplementary control that would not put them on a collision course with popular media fare at all but that would nevertheless highlight the necessity of discipline and restraint.

Discipline and Regulation

Trends in behavior and sexualized media fare often overshadow the focus on prescriptive culture. In fact, the effort to reconcile cultural tensions remained a powerful force, continuing to distinguish the

United States, in sexual matters, from other Western and Atlantic societies. This is why prescriptive advice was so eagerly consumed in the
1990s as well as in the 1920s. The need to reconcile might temporarily
lapse under the pressure of youthful defiance, as in the late 1960s, but
it would resume with a vengeance. This was the context in which important new restrictive efforts developed by the 1970s, significantly affecting
behaviors and personal evaluations and fascinating in their reminder of
ongoing cultural imperatives.

From the outset, twentieth-century trends toward greater permissiveness in sex—both the relaxation of public controls over sexual expression and the easing of private standards in favor of pleasure seeking—
were matched by new definitions of deviance. These definitions, in turn,
had two effects. First, they identified behaviors or groups that were
beyond the pale, that required active remediation and, usually, legal
proscription. Here, innovation generated a familiar counterpart to an
acceptable behavioral range, using deviance to highlight the boundaries.
Second, the additional definitions served to create new anxieties that
constrained permissible sex. For example, child rearing embraced new
freedoms, such as masturbation, but also new worries about current
categories of propriety. Adult heterosexual contact blended a sense of
hedonism, even a sense that active enjoyment was a requisite component
of mature behavior, with nervousness about abuse. These worries joined
with lingering traditionalism to create strange alliances among otherwise
diverse groups concerned about permissiveness. They also produced
internal tension in many individuals, who found it difficult to reconcile
simultaneous praise and blame for impulse.

The first surge of new permissiveness in cultural standards and dating
behaviors was greeted by the new furor over homosexuality. This was a
problem defined as a constant menace to appropriate behavior and a
worrisome potential symptom in childhood. The condition was sick; it
was legally proscribed; it was, in contrast to more traditional beliefs, an
all-or-nothing category precluding appropriate sexual interests. Generated initially by psychological research and terminology, the popularization of beliefs about homosexuality served as a counterweight to the
relaxation of standard nineteenth-century sexual disciplines. For decades,
authorities argued that homosexual impulses could be brought under
control, perhaps with some therapeutic assistance. Accordingly, young

Americans were implicitly schooled to monitor their own interests, to make sure that any subversive leanings were controlled or at least concealed. Here was a new reason to keep an eye on impulse.[63]

The identification of homosexuality as deviant was not an American monopoly, but it is probable that the anxieties about personal behavior and child rearing were greatest in the United States during the middle decades of the twentieth century. Homosexuality was the kind of disciplinary concern that Americans relished as a counterpoise to growing indulgence.

Americans also led in another reaction to sexuality—the rapid spread of male circumcision. Based on various medical and hygienic arguments in the late nineteenth century—including a belief that the practice would reduce masturbation—the circumcision of male infants became almost universal between the 1920s and the 1950s—precisely the period in which the lack of objective medical justification ended the practice among most Europeans. Americans' unusual acceptance of the practice as an antidote to uncleanliness but also dubious habits even as sexual interests were expanding showed the peculiar national importance of counterweights—whether disciplinary or, as in this case, surgically imposed on a population without a voice.[64]

The changes in public standards and private behaviors that became apparent during the 1960s were not initially greeted by the same kind of disciplinary innovation. Indeed, as experts eased their condemnations of homosexuality, urging that legal restrictions be repealed and rejecting the older idea of homosexuality as a psychological disease that could and should be remedied, even this earlier counterweight lost some of its effectiveness. Although hostility to homosexuals remained, key supporters of the older insistence on control, such as psychiatrists, largely withdrew their opposition with the removal of the disease label. Into the 1970s, some people believed that a trend toward permissiveness would steadily increase, without generating new restrictions in the process. In fact, some scholars judged that healthy indulgence had at last replaced repression.[65]

This was not, of course, what happened. Two developments emerged to constrain both the sexual culture and sexual behavior. The first was the revival of traditionalism itself. By the end of the 1970s, certain Christian groups directly attacked the manifestations of the sexual revolution. Their protests focused on highly sexualized media presentations of sex but had little impact except to lead to some voluntary rating systems (R for adult sex and violence in movies, and so on). Another set of activities concentrated on abortion rights, provoking intense political debate and some restrictions on access to abortion, as well as increasing ambivalence in Americans' responses to polls about the legitimacy of abortion. Because most "pro-life" advocates also opposed programs that would disseminate birth control information, their opposition to abortion was clearly intended to increase the requirements for personal sexual discipline. Finally, the traditionalist counterattack helped frame the context for widespread moralism concerning the recrudescence of sexually transmitted diseases in the 1980s and particularly AIDS. Vigorous statements about disease as a punishment for sexual misconduct and about the need for self-control as the primary response to disease accompanied the larger campaign for a moral rollback.

The resurgent traditionalism also caused a new differentiation between the United States and western Europe. In the 1960s, both societies had experienced changes in premarital sex leading to higher rates of illegitimacy. Europe (and Japan) responded by making birth control information and devices more readily available to teenagers, which rapidly pushed down the rates. The United States—true to a Victorian heritage that remained uneasy with seeming to encourage sex, at least in this age group—simply held fast, preferring to rely on self-restraint backed by educational programs bent on abstinence. As a result, after falling from the peak in the 1950s, rates of adolescent pregnancy remained high, except in the middle class. Federal policy did support a modest promotion of birth control among teenagers in welfare families in the 1970s, spurred by sensationalist reports about a pregnancy "epidemic." But these poorly funded efforts faded noticeably in the 1980s, and attempts to use school health programs to facilitate birth control, such as the Adolescent Health Services and Pregnancy Prevention Act of 1978, were almost always rejected. On balance, Americans decided to identify sex, rather than pregnancy, as the main problem when minors were concerned.[66]

The second development, not always distinguishable from the first, involved the new disciplinary standards by which sexual excess could be redressed and new anxieties created in the sexual sphere. Like the measures of the 1920s, they were laden with symbolism—but they were far more direct in their restraint of heterosexuality. Three innovations predominated, all originating in the 1970s or early 1980s: a redefinition of abuse to include sexual activities, a redefinition of rape, and an unprecedented focus on sexual harassment. All these categories were newly constructed, although the problems they targeted were not new and although invocations of rape in the marriage advice literature in the 1920s as part of urging male self-control had set the stage as well. The novelty of these categories, however, especially in stimulating a revival of legal regulation to reinforce personal discipline, was an effort to recreate a balance between restraint and indulgence in the sexual sphere It was no accident that American law and commentary took the lead in developing the innovations, as the programs clearly responded to a cultural imperative in twentieth-century America to maintain a tension around permissiveness. Treating the innovations as constructions does not, it must be added, invalidate them. Rather, they may be judged as entirely appropriate even as they are assessed in terms of their timing and larger cultural role. Whatever the assessment, the innovations restored a more characteristic contemporary tone to American sexual standards without literally reestablishing the specific standards of the 1920s. Sex was up again for debate in public forums and in private evaluations and behaviors.

Child Abuse

The primary attention in the area of family abuse continued to focus on physical beatings of spouses and children and on efforts to protect the victims. The overall campaign to highlight these problems, from the early 1970s onward, extended the definition of abuse to include measures that some parents regarded as normal physical discipline. As we have seen, psychological abuse was often highlighted as a means of calling adults to task for failing to restrain emotions of anger or trying to induce unusual levels of guilt or shame. In addition, the definition of sexual abuse was enlarged to cover abusive acts well short of penetration. Parents were urged to be vigilant against adults, including family members, who fondled children or even spoke to them in suggestive ways. What had been regarded a generation before as unpleasant eccentricities by older male relatives, were now, at least theoretically, legally action-able. Therapists, attempting to help their patients recall past abuse in childhood that had been repressed in memory, often seized on sexual incidents—and in the process, patients were sometimes encouraged to remember episodes that had not in fact occurred. Sex probably headed the list in regard to false memories, a sign of the popularity of this new contest between desire and restraint.[67]

Date Rape

The idea of rape by dates, acquaintances, and spouses was hardly a late-twentieth-century invention, but the campaign against it that emerged, complete with legal apparatus, was unquestionably new. The concept was introduced in a *Ms.* magazine article in 1982, and it spread quickly, answering a practical and moral need in important categories of Ameri-can society outside the traditionalist camp. Date rape was a direct attack on an area in which behavioral standards were changing. The basic argument was laid out in this first article and then elaborated in a steady stream of press commentary, with responses by college counseling serv-ices, women's advocacy groups, and lawyers. Because the "sexual revo-lution" had made it more difficult for women to turn down sexually compromising situations and had encouraged a preexisting male interest in scoring sexually, concern about coercive sex had escalated. As with rape generally, but particularly because acquaintances were involved and the women had often consented to the earlier stages of sexual activity, reporting was very difficult. Often, the women in question had not initially realized they had been raped, because they simply did not apply the new definition to their situation. For their part, the men often were unaware they had behaved unacceptably, considering women's attempts to say no as part of a hard-to-get routine that invited persistence.[68]

To be sure, the concept of date rape applied to more than recent sexual trends. It also was responding to long-standing concerns about rape in general and to agonizing difficulties in reporting, as many victims were treated to demeaning criticisms, with their behavior called into question more than that of their attackers.

Three other aspects of this new concern should be mentioned. The first is its resonance and dissemination. Campus rape crisis centers and students services quickly began responding to the problem, offering advice and legal support to victims, providing detailed information in orientation sessions about the need to avoid any coercive acts in sex. Mainstream newsmagazines like *Newsweek* and *Time* periodically reported on the phenomenon. Sometimes they urged a bit of caution, noting the difficulties in deciding which actions involved force and which were initially consensual and then coerced. But they routinely accepted the basic category and speculated about the many incidents that beset American youth. Specific books and other materials supplemented the drive. The concept became a staple among the age groups in the middle class normally regarded as most involved in sexual innovation.[69]

Second, proponents of the date-rape category, and many victims, emphasized the searing quality as well as the frequency of the newly defined crime. It was rated hard to survive, a "life-threatening experience." Extensive therapeutic support and group discussion might be required for recovery, precisely because of the loss of personal control rape involved. At the same time, the problem was seen as epidemic, involving perhaps three-quarters of all rapes (admittedly, most unreported) and perhaps a quarter (estimates varied wildly) of female collegians.

Third, the category increased the importance of self-control while accentuating the demands involved. The central propositions were the insistence that men accept women's wishes concerning sex and that male restraint was possible at any stage of sexual stimulation. "Men don't physically need to have sex after becoming aroused any more than women do. Moreover, men are still able to control themselves even after becoming sexually excited." This formula harked back to the disciplinary prescriptions of the 1920s; men have a greedier sex drive than women which, however, must be carefully restrained in the interests of responsibility and mutuality. What had been added was the extension of this idea to an advanced state of foreplay (which, earlier, it would have been a woman's task to avoid) and the revival of criminal sanctions to supplement the appeal to disciplined propriety. Sex must be brought under new control, with a recognition that it was often unwanted, undesirable, and illegal.[70]

Harassment

The introduction of sexual harassment as a formal category of sexual unacceptability predated date rape. The initial article about this concept, by Letty Pogrebin, appeared in the *Ladies Home Journal* in 1976. Again, the behavior was not novel; it had been informally negotiated in many coeducational offices since the late nineteenth century. But the loosening of older strictures and the surge of women into the service-sector workplace had created new confusions and sensitivities. Of all the innovations created to discipline contemporary sex, the harassment category had the greatest potential, because of the ubiquity of the settings involved and the inherent nebulousness of the basic criteria. Widely publicized incidents kept the category on the nation's front pages almost weekly during the 1990s. The incidents seemed endless, ranging from a suit by a woman sports reporter against football players who made lewd gestures to her in locker-room interviews, the dramatic confrontations in the nomination of a U.S. Supreme Court justice, the pressured resignation of a U.S. senator, and a host of accusations against President Bill Clinton for requesting sexual favors.[71]

The basic premise resembled that of date rape, that men sometimes touched, whistled, solicited, gestured, and grabbed in ways that were offensive to women. According to Pogrebin,

> The woman victimized . . . can suffer great personal anguish, depression, and physical stress symptoms such as nausea, headaches, and severe body pain. If she's seen as a tool for sexual pleasure, she knows her work won't be taken seriously. She has no job security as long as she's used as a decorative office ornament or a prize to be bartered among clients and customers.

Although the problem was not new, the standards of self-control had to be more stringent and to be backed by legal sanctions.[72]

Masses of women agreed. Articles about sexual harassment drew an "avalanche of mail" from readers who had suffered from experiences for which they at last had a name and against which they could now mobilize support. Along with rape, harassment also generated many new personnel regulations, both governmental and corporate. Like rape, harassment entailed excessive power (usually male, although public discussions admitted some reversals under female supervisors). Whether or not fully defined in law, sexual harassment standards sought to discipline important aspects of male culture, even in entrenched institutions such as the military. Indeed, the admission of women into the armed forces brought unprecedented contact; nonetheless, men were expected to monitor their behavior more closely than ever before. Women's right to wear revealing, alluring clothing gave men no excuse to falter under the new standards of self-discipline. Indeed, the crux of the issue was control, in that women had to "take control of their own bodies and lives," and for this to occur, men must have even greater control over their impulses. Even more than rape, concerns about harassment promised to extend arguments over propriety into other areas, creating organizational anxieties about lawsuits and also personal anxieties about safety and respectability. Not just acts but also words, jokes, gestures, and even eye contact now came into play. Should one flatter an other-sex colleague about changes in appearance? Many new workplace rules said no. Did a romantic e-mail message from a faculty member to a student constitute harassment or merely bad judgment? The definition of harassment favored the student, deeply upset in a cultural context that encouraged (perhaps quite validly) new levels of psychological dismay. How careful must a man now be, given potential monitoring that easily rivaled traditional forms of chaperonage but with a range of behaviors far more amorphous than traditional courtship? The larger impact of the harassment concept revealed twentieth-century disciplinary culture in its worried willingness to extend self-control and also in the assumption that any chink in the armor might lead to a torrent of unacceptable impulse.[73]

Sexuality Reclothed

In the final quarter of the twentieth century, the United States pioneered in reinventing selective prudishness, through a combination of traditional and novel attacks on sexual excess. Earlier emphasis on the individual's right to have sex was substantially displaced by an equal emphasis on the individual's right to reject it. With sex now also burdened by new disease risks, "great sexual restraint" won new praise. New boundary lines had to be negotiated, such as between "professionally pleasant" and "friendly," because the lines between friendly and flirtatious and seductive were too "thin." Between 1989 and 1999, mainstream Americans rethought abortions, becoming markedly less tolerant of them in the interest of women's careers and more insistent on personal restraint.[74]

No consensus emerged around the new standards. Only a very few institutions enforced them to the extent that Antioch College did, with its policy of requiring explicit requests and responses for every stage of a possibly sexual encounter: "May I kiss you? May I place my hand on your breast?" At both the high school and college level and among some adults, individual and collective vows of celibacy and virginity seemed to spread, or at least gain new media attention. "A lot of kids are putting off sex . . . and they're proud of their chastity, not embarrassed by it. Suddenly, virgin geek is giving way to virgin chic." This argument followed from the increased incidence of sexually transmitted diseases, but it also mirrored the larger new desire to restrict nonmarital sex. Clearly, nonsex was becoming popular, as traditionalists and liberal feminists joined forces on key issues of restraint.[75]

Yet hedonism persisted as well. Furthermore, by the mid-1990s, date rape and abuse campaigns had elicited new criticism on grounds of false or unfair accusations. It was the contestation, not an agreement on new standards of control, that remained the main point, after a decade in which permissiveness seemed to overwhelm the twentieth-century American inclination toward disciplinary tension. Different groups of Americans took different approaches to issues such as premarital sex, office flirtation, and even adultery—and except for strict traditionalists, they did not have to feel backward in the process. Contestation also served society at large: it was tension over the balance between permissiveness and restraint, not harmony, that best suited American cultural patterns in the twentieth century. The invention of new regulatory categories obviously was a response to new problems, including new diseases, but it can be fully explained only as the felt need to revive a cultural ambivalence. What the new disciplinary criteria and the revival of legal enforcement had done in the area of sex was to restore individual anxiety and a sense of limitation. Indulgence had to be matched by the appeal to character and self-control.

The growing reliance on fantasy—the clearly revolutionary category of contemporary American sex—itself provided an ironic discipline. To be sure, fantasy presentations roused dispute, and they were bounded by American prudery. But fantasy might also frustrate; except for accompanying masturbation, it was by definition constrained by a failure to materialize. Fantasy might stimulate and inform, but the nation's greatest new sexual investment could also distract from the commitment to real sexual connections. In sex as in other escapist areas, the invention of "virtual reality" through new technology confirmed and extended an existing pattern: the best stuff was a spectator sport.

Conclusions

Sexuality stands out in the history of modern American indulgence, although arguably changes in material acquisition have been far greater. The prominence of sex highlights the real shifts away from earlier standards and its centrality to wider consumer appeals. In contrast to most targets of contemporary disciplinary standards, sex has remained more private, more difficult to assess in a mirror of peerdom—hence the often frantic worry about both adequacy and appropriate restraint and the obsession with public figures whose sexuality seems bigger than life. And sex looms large because Americans cannot agree on the goals to be sought, among themselves and often within themselves.

Complex trends have emerged. Dating behavior entered a new phase in the 1980s as young people began moving in groups more than in pairs, in part to help control sexual and emotional contacts. The intensity of the classic dating regime was now too hard to handle amid pressure to perform but also to restrain, so other mechanisms were devised. On another front, the military in the 1990s—stung by evidence of harassment and infidelity—tried to be more prudish than it had been in its all-male past when regulating the health consequences of prostitution was the primary concern. Military authorities now tried to enforce rules that extramarital affairs might disqualify officers from service, an extraordinary extension of moral standards. Sex therefore seemed to be a unique index of character. The Clinton crisis elicited comments about the need for public officials to exhibit "such virtues as dignity, moderation, disinterestedness, self-mastery."

For all its special qualities, the standards and behaviors applied to sex fit the larger pattern of national self-control as well. Evolution combined with fantasy outlets and compensatory disciplines was a standard pattern requiring a balance between restraint and release much like the mix of mastery and authenticity applied to emotion. Sexuality also joined other facets of physical discipline: the sexy individual was supposed to offer a highly controlled body, and this tension surrounded sexuality with another set of disciplinary challenges.

| EIGHT |

The Body and Health

Standards for the body, hygiene, and health escalated steadily during the twentieth century, and in some areas Americans accepted unusually rigorous norms. The contrast with sexual patterns was striking and deliberate. For many, the change was imperceptible because the standards and the way they were presented made so much sense, but this is simply another way of highlighting how important the changes were, in that they were extensively internalized. The detailed rules regarding personal hygiene and presentation of the body followed from apparently objective justifications, mainly the expertise attached to the maximization of health and the value placed on health itself. But not every health-maximizing principle was equally accepted. Americans turned away from tanning more slowly than experts urged. And although they accepted constraints, they did not accept the specific speed limits on automobiles that would minimize highway fatalities; hence the move away from 55 miles per hour in the 1990s. But not all promptings to fuller control over the body rested on health alone. The acceptance of discipline over the body followed in part from a desire for moral legitimation amid the burgeoning consumerism and an increasingly permissive sexual culture. This, in fact, was one of the great trade-offs of the century: many people justified the new levels of indulgence precisely because they could demonstrate their self-control in their treatment of the body, or at least their commitment to worry about it.

The growing informality of clothing, including revealing attire, was closely correlated with the dissemination of new rules about hygiene and body shape. This equation was already taking hold around 1900, in the transitional decades, and it extended from the 1920s onward. Changes in clothing reflected both consumer interests and sexual suggestiveness, so the moral compensation through greater health and body discipline seemed essential. Instances of particular moralism in the ways that body discipline was presented reflected the national propensity for this kind of justification and the absence of alternative means—through diverse political ideologies, for example—to express hesitations about the hedonism of modern life. In the main, Americans sought individual ways to show that they had not abandoned self-sacrifice even as they had become more affluent and more openly sexual, and the body/health nexus effectively answered this quest. Reliance on individual discipline also increased when the apparent failure of Prohibition led to the notion that the external regulation of health-related behaviors was ineffective or counterproductive. Doctors and medical advice gained influence, but the wider acceptance of health as a talisman for morality provided the opening.

To be sure, many people failed to live up to some of the body standards. Some groups refused outright in key areas, and many individuals found the demands too rigorous. But the importance of standards does not depend entirely on their successful implementation, and as in the nineteenth century, the failures helped illustrate the norms.

This chapter examines four categories of health and body discipline. In the first, personal hygiene, the intensification of standards was unusually effective. Victorian precedent provided a base, and Americans proved unusually open to advice about body care.

The second category, posture, generated an intensive effort to rescue Victorian standards from the pressures of comfort and informality intrinsic to American consumer society. Ultimately, the traditional standards lost out, so we focus our attention on the causes of relaxation and the result in terms of the overall perceptions of discipline.

The third category was not Victorian at all, even though it had emerged during the transitional decades, after the 1890s. Pressures on Americans to remain or become thin grew during the interwar decades and again after World War II, leading to anguished attention to the body amid the inducements of consumer affluence. This, as the posture programs failed, was the clearest disciplinary battleground.

Finally, the moralism attached to issues of health and the body reappeared in the campaigns concerning smoking and drinking that were launched in the 1970s—with amazing, if incomplete, success. Here was abundant evidence not only of the widespread acceptance of demands for new discipline but also of the moral need for programs that would allow demonstrations of self-control and excoriations of those who could not measure up.

The Context

In the nineteenth century, careful treatment of the body and health had become attributes of middle-class respectability and control. Doctors and health commentators had already established themselves as experts, urging norms for the treatment of the body on grounds of health and, often, adding a moral overlay. The expansion of Victorian concerns and doctors' reach enabled bodily discipline to be monitored, particularly after the 1920s. It was at this point that the practice of having annual checkups became part of middle-class routine, especially for children. The apparatus used to determine key aspects of the bodily state, such as scales, became more elaborate. In the later nineteenth century, hospitals started using them, and public scales became the rage soon after 1900, when being weighed was a normal procedure in doctors' offices as well. By the 1920s, scales were common in middle-class homes. At this time, too, doctors also began to use sphygmomanometers (to measure blood pressure) and other devices to probe the body's internal workings. Although these instruments were beyond the ken of ordinary patients, they revealed the latter's success in managing their bodies appropriately. Like confessionals in a more religious age, medical checkups provided a ritual by which the results of self-control could be verified.[1]

Between 1880 and 1920, the number of infant and maternal deaths plummeted, thanks particularly to improvements in living standards and public health. In turn, this change heightened the concern for preserving health because it now seemed more achievable. The death of a child became exceptional for the first time in human history, and at the same time, the conquest of many communicable diseases by means of vaccines and new medicines began to refocus adult attention to problems of degeneration. From the late nineteenth century, the spotlight shifted to problems of the heart and arteries and to cancer. These, along with accidents, were the new leading killers. Major fund drives, particularly for cancer, called attention to both the diseases and the goal of greater prevention and treatment. Above all, the whole idea of degeneration introduced the possibility of individual control, at least when combined with the sense that death before old age could be prevented. Thus, attention to personal habits—rather than public health concerns—increased, with hygiene combining an attack on both the potential sources of premature degeneration and the germs now recognized as unseen carriers. This was another reason for admitting a greater role for doctors and their advice in setting standards for self-control.[2]

Finally, the body as a locus for testing personal restraint meshed with consumerism and the demands of a service/managerial economy without losing its capacity to function simultaneously as a site of moral compensation. Appropriate body control, beginning with more rigorous hygiene, improved the ability to interact pleasantly with others. Appearance was relevant to work, and although it still depended on informed clothing choices, it now included the body as well. Body control also sold goods. A circle was therefore established in which concern about health and physical presentation created new markets for relevant products, and the commercially induced desire for the same products raised the standards for body care progressively higher. Few other areas of self-management offered this consumer potential. At the same time, body care was not simply consumerism. It served the higher goal of health for oneself and one's family. It involved, or could involve, personal discipline and even self-sacrifice, continuing service as a moral counterweight to the indulgence that other forms of consumerism and sexuality entailed.

This attention to the body emerged from a combination of factors. A willingness to spend money on items for hygiene depended in part on the precedents set in the nineteenth century as well as on the increasing importance of medical expertise and regular monitoring. The results— again in contrast to most other areas of twentieth-century self-control— might seem inevitable, hardly a matter of choice. Particularly in regard to hygiene, conscious self-control might not seem to be involved at all, which of course made the pressure to conform all the stronger.

Clean and Sweet-Smelling Americans

A powerful theme in twentieth-century American history is the growing attention to cleanliness, grooming, and the prevention of body odor. In the 1890s, middle-class families often made do with a single bathroom, even in a large house with four children. Half a century later, their counterparts' houses had two bathrooms but fewer children and less overall space, and half a century after that, many of the newer homes and apartments had more bathrooms than occupants. This trend reflected the American penchant for frequent showers and the desire for absolute privacy for those bodily functions that were at once unavoidable and, by contemporary standards, unsavory.

Sweat, for example, was now acknowledged, whereas references to it in the nineteenth century were noteworthy for their absence. Occasional passages in bankruptcy laws did use the phrase "sweat of their brow" as a biblically inspired symbol of worthy labor. An attack on bankrupt businessmen noted a "cold-sweating brow" as one of several physical signs of failure. In a letter from Alice Baldwin to her husband, one intriguing passage speaks of sweat. "How are you on this hot day? I am most roasted and my chemise sticks to me and the sweat runs down my legs and I suppose I smell very sweet, don't you wish you could be around just now." Historians have debated whether this reference regarded sweat as erotic or as ironic, something to be avoided. Overall, however, the subject was taboo, at least in public. It could not be approved, for it contradicted the new interest in bodily control and grooming, but it also could not be condemned, for it was a natural process. So it was ignored, in etiquette books, literature, and most of the popularized medical discussions. Despite cumbersome clothing, the lack of air-conditioning, and exacting social situations, sweating was surely common, but it passed beneath official notice.

Not so, of course, by the 1920s when criteria could be added to the standards of body control. Sweat was desirable now that exercise had become popular, but it also had to be disciplined. Just as other body products had come under greater control, so sweat was now explicitly monitored. New fabrics and less formal clothing, along with air-conditioning, aided more rigorous standards of sweat control, as did products, increasingly available after the 1920s, to reduce sweat and mask its odor. Sweat was now under siege, and telling someone that he or she was sweating was a suggestion that somehow that person's body and emotions were not under proper discipline. Indeed, sweat could even have a political impact: Richard Nixon's moist upper lip seemed to confirm his loss of control in his resignation speech.

Terms like body odor, or B.O., gained new currency useful in advertising and even reached beyond the body itself into the area of personality and character. For example, in regard to underarm smells: "You are going to overcome this bad habit right away." "Carelessness in this regard inevitably lowers the esteem of those about us." "Any personality is enhanced with pearly, well-cared-for-teeth and a winsome smile." "That daily bath . . . affects you physically and mentally. It seems to send your self-rating thermometer climbing." "Never lower your standard of personal daintiness by letting a cleansing bath escape your daily program."[3]

This tightening of grooming standards continued a process begun in the transitional turn-of-the-century decades, including the new attack on several sites of female body hair. The campaign escalated in the 1920s, if only because the manufacturers of relevant consumer products discovered new means to persuade people of the importance of crucial aids. Already the working class had been bathing more regularly, using the growing network of public bath houses available by 1900. Now the movement shifted into a higher gear: with few systematic exceptions, most Americans subscribed to common, and demanding, standards of cleanliness, smell, and manicured appearance.[4]

The campaign for better hygiene was abundantly advertised in all available media. Serial dramas on the radio became known as soap operas. Manufacturers also began to sponsor school programs in order to bring these standards to new groups of Americans, including recent immigrants. As the *New York Times* explained in 1927, "All the soiled and sotted children, backyards, restaurants, and streets of the country are to be sought out, imbued with the desire for soap and scrubbing brushes, and turned loose with appearance and self-respect improved several degrees." A trade association of soap makers, concerned that their product might lose ground because of the new availability of cosmetic creams, lipsticks, and deodorants, began to look to new means of information and pressure. Thus soap makers presented regular, diligent washing as vital to beauty and health and to personal success. Dangers were omnipresent, in the form of unseen germs and microbes that could be removed only by frequent cleansing. Schools must teach that "*all* the children wash their hands regularly after toilet and before lunch." "In 92 percent of the deaths caused by communicable diseases the organism enters or leaves the body through the mouth or nose; and it is the human *hand,* in many instances, that carries it." The fundamental goal was that "the object should be not merely to make children clean, but to make them love to be clean." The issue was hygiene, but also manners: germ transmission was "biological discourtesy"; control a matter not just of health but of "decency."[5]

Industry-sponsored school programs also encouraged teachers to check on their students' home habits. "Have children report on days they take baths at home. The *type of home* will determine whether to expect more than two baths a week." Brushing one's teeth (twice a day) and combing one's hair were other habits to insist on, along with wearing clean clothes. The progression was that each stage of schooling should answer to higher and higher standards. By the ninth grade, children should not merely want to be clean but should feel uncomfortable when anyone around them was not clean and fragrant. "It is essential to make the children *want to do* the things they are taught. . . . The self-activity of the children must be aroused. They must get the beliefs strongly tied up with the emotions. This will help them to establish more firmly the habits begun in earlier grades." And even though the sponsors declared that no child should be unnecessarily embarrassed, in fact public shaming was widely used against dirty and unkempt students. Other hygiene programs, such as screening for ringworm, also drove home the pariah status of deviants. Exemplary children were rewarded, or allowed to serve as monitors during group hand-washing sessions.[6] As one urban poster noted, "A Clean Machine Runs Better—Your Body Is a Machine—KEEP IT CLEAN." It was small wonder that according to a 1938 poll, Americans believed that soap ranked just below bread and butter as a necessity of life.[7]

Clearly, Americans built on the Victorian concern with cleanliness and grooming, including the control of odors, leading the Western world in most personal hygiene concerns. But was this really a movement of self-control, as opposed to simply buying and using the right products? And why did Americans prove so disproportionately interested?

There is no question that appeals to hygiene worked in part because of the massive commercial apparatus behind them. American advertising advanced much more rapidly than European commercials did—almost half a century separated the formation of the first advertising agencies in the United States from that of their more modest counterparts in France, for example. Yet their audience's interest was vital to the campaigns' success, and this interest had distinct roots. Victorian precedent was one, as was the growing need, in the 1920s, for many groups to figure out how to adopt middle-class standards as a means of becoming somewhat more comfortably American or qualifying more readily for service-sector jobs. Also crucial was the association between cleanliness and a sense of moral worth—a need to purify the body in order to measure up, to oneself and others, amid consumer indulgence and more open sexuality. This is why words like *civilization* made so much sense in selling soap products. The fact that cleanliness also seemed, objectively, to produce a better appearance (and therefore sexual appeal) and better health only added to the moral component.[8] By the 1990s, when large and luxurious bathrooms became popular in upper-middle-class homes, the consumerist, sybaritic element gained new ground, becoming a regime of body discipline that justified pampering.

Self-control was part of the demand for hygiene. The school campaigns correctly assumed was that habits instilled in childhood would become routine, important emotionally, and even pleasurable. Accordingly, in adulthood, they would be automatic and not perceived as disciplinary requirements, particularly when supported by commercial products. But the process began with control, imposed on children and maintained by their parents and other adults.

By the 1920s, child-rearing manuals made this point clear. Picking up cues from the school campaigns, popularizers urged parents: "Your best hope of establishing habits of cleanliness is to create a desire for cleanliness." The two keys were, first, the regular washing of young children when they were firmly under parental control and, second, vigorous and even mildly menacing discussions of germs and disease. Gradually, under this regime, even the worst offenders, young male adolescents, would learn routine habits of body control. But effort was involved at crucial stages by parents who had to teach unnatural impulse control to their offspring and, gradually, by the youngsters themselves.[9]

The same pattern applied to more specific features of the hygiene campaigns. Regular toothbrushing, with commercially available powders, first became widespread in the 1920s. Bristle brushes had been available earlier, though the extent of their use is not known. New kinds of brushes, including the first electric prototype, were introduced in the 1880s. The first widely used American dental cream, Dr. Sheffield's Creme Dentifrice, came on the market in 1892, introduced by a Connecticut dentist. By the interwar decades, articles on dental health and, equally important, freshness of breath began to appear in child-rearing outlets such as *Parents' Magazine*, supplemented by product advertisements. Although health concerns were primary, white teeth for appearance (and straight teeth; orthodontics became a specialty in the 1930s) and pleasant-smelling breath were important as well. With smiling increasingly required as part of one's self-presentation, dental campaigns found a ready audience. For truly errant teeth, braces became standard in the middle class, a symbol of regimented mouths made possible by the growth in family prosperity after World War II.[10]

By the 1950s, most Americans regularly devoted considerable time as well as money on body care that would have amazed, though possibly also pleased, many Victorians. Although the idea of hygiene as moral compensation for indulgence should not be overemphasized—in part because its implementation fit so readily into a consumer mentality—Americans' emphasis on personal cleanliness and odor control was unusual. Rebellious youth in the 1960s clearly picked up on the disciplinary content of hygiene and appearance standards, deliberately defying pervasive injunctions about hair, cleanliness, and (sometimes) odor, with the extent of normal control highlighted by their deviance. It was equally revealing that particularly among middle-class youth, the rebellion largely failed, despite the continued interest in defiant dress, hair colors, and body piercing in some quarters: messiness might still be used to shock, but cleanliness and odor control surged back after the 1960s. Overall, in twentieth-century America, management of the body became an essential counterpart of the greater informality of clothing, demanding a deeply internalized effort.

Posture

Insistence on correct posture, another Victorian staple that had been used to measure personal discipline and character, had many parallels with the campaign for hygiene, particularly in the reliance on school-based programs and the intensity with which standards were recommended on grounds of health and propriety. Unlike the campaign for hygiene, that for posture had a different association with consumerism, and it ultimately failed. Whereas hygiene advanced along with more relaxed clothing styles, advocates of correct posture encountered problems with the greater availability of comfortable furniture and alternative body ideals. The posture campaign shows the tenacity of older standards, but in this case, they were unable to retain the link between body management and moral concern.

The Context

Like several other disciplines, including hygiene, posture rested on a combination of Victorian precedents and new anxieties about the loss of moral control in a consumer society. The declining popularity of vests and corsets and the wide availability of upholstered furniture directly challenged posture and prompted new appeals to self-discipline. Professional groups' arguments, though self-serving, were bolstered by long-standing beliefs in the body as a machine and by newer arguments about industrial efficiency, all of which showed up in posture discussions. The use of mirrors, along with the larger trends in sexuality, led to a new interest in bodies and provided additional methods of self-control. Before the twentieth century, home mirrors had been small or, in upper-middle-class homes, usually placed at shoulder level. Now, however, improvements in glass manufacturing made large mirrors more affordable and available, and full-length versions became standard in bathrooms and in many public spaces. Proper posture could improve the resulting images, whereas mirrors (like home scales) added to the pressure to keep the body under control.[11]

The Arguments

Advice about posture flowed from several sources between the 1920s and the 1950s, using traditional standards but with some new justifications and, above all, enhanced detail. Posture remained an issue of good manners, but given the attractions of consumerism and comfort amid the cushioned, inner-springed furniture of living rooms and more casual clothing and dance styles, it was now not just a goal but a problem, requiring remedial or preventive attention.

In the nineteenth century, doctors had sounded alarms about posture, but with little resonance in wider public discussion. Now they linked it to a more general effort. First, posture problems were held to be pervasive, particularly among children. In 1880, Dr. D. F. Lincoln's *School and Industrial Hygiene* claimed that confinement at poorly designed school desks was causing up to 92 percent of all students to suffer deviation of the spinal cord. An 1894 manual noted that "it is seldom that a completely normal figure is met with." "Studies" showed that curvature of the spine was virtually endemic, particularly among girls and women. A popularized tract in 1943 echoed the theme: "We are forever engaging in activities which tend toward asymmetry and derangement of our architecture."[12]

The doctors' second argument was that crucial aspects of modern life were undermining posture requirements. Again from 1943, "In our daily habits of eating, sitting, lounging, leaning or standing, in our clothing itself, especially in shoes, lie influences upon bodily posture, which are . . . abusive." Another doctor, somewhat earlier, documented the deterioration of posture in modern society as the "weedward drift."[13]

Third, diseases like scoliosis and rickets continued to command attention, and bad posture was now seen as causing health problems beyond the back itself. A supplementary argument maintained that anything less than erect posture caused the organs to interfere with one another, impeding the action of the heart, kidneys, and liver. First used in the late nineteenth century, this idea endured until the mid-twentieth century. Posture was essential to "lessen the strain of the structures involved [and] enhance efficient functioning of these organs."[14]

Fourth, medical examination was necessary to detect posture problems. Parents could not do the job, for dangerous deviations might be missed. Only doctors or other trained experts could make the diagnosis and propose remedies. Beginning early in life, regular checkups therefore became an indispensable part of the burgeoning pediatric practice.[15]

Not only the definition of good posture but also its moral connotations persisted. Correct posture was more than a "physical and hygienic advance"; it also was vital to the "moral effect on the whole body." As one doctor put it, just as a healthy person can be identified by his erect stance, so sneaky people, cowards, and criminals can be detected by their bad posture. Correct the physical, and one controls the self.[16] Not until the 1950s did a doctor note that "it is well to remember that the vast majority of co-called postural defects in toddlers need no active corrective treatment as they . . . disappear *pari passu* with the evolution of the mechanism by which postural control is maintained." Doctors were beginning to withdraw from the field of battle.[17]

Physical education specialists commented even more widely than doctors on posture issues, and in the 1890s, posture became a physical education staple. But after two decades, this argument began to shift. The specialists had no explicit disagreement with doctors, but their focus narrowed and the emphasis on available remediation, with professional guidance but through individual training and responsibility, increased. The result set the tone for the most widely disseminated posture commentary and ironically may have limited its effectiveness. Posture remained a problem, even though warnings about the deleterious effects of modern life faded. At most, specific programs might include throwaway lines about "modern daily living" requiring "little muscular strength," along with sincere if also self-serving claims about the universality of the resulting problems. Little moral lament was involved, however, for the focus was on the attainability of correctives. Likewise, the emphasis on childhood—the stage of life over which physical education specialists had new claims as schooling expanded—strengthened. If children were properly cared for, adult standards would be assured, and there would be no need for sweeping remarks about health and character. Finally, childhood issues could be handled through careful attention and the inculcation of discipline.[18]

Amid this more focused effort, assumptions about the relationship between posture and character control continued. Jessie Bancroft, the founder and leading guru in the American Posture League until its collapse in the 1940s, put it this way: "These attributes we claim are attained through the establishment of correct bodily mechanics, otherwise known as 'good posture,' better termed poise, and I would go even farther and say personality. Posture expresses personality." One authority drove home the point by contrasting Jekyll and Hyde: the upright Jekyll, erect in bearing, with noble aspirations, and the groveling, crouching, and therefore evil Hyde.[19]

The ideas of the physical education specialists found their way into more generalized child-rearing literature dealing with children and adolescents alike, becoming commonplace from the 1920s to the 1950s. *Manners and Conduct in School and Out* offered general advice about sitting up straight and holding the legs in front: "The way you sit or work or stand shows culture or lack of it." Some passages were directed toward school settings—how to stand erect when reciting—although other emphases had wider applicability. Above all, the book stressed the importance of posture and the student's individual responsibility for maintaining it.[20]

Other signs of concern include the widely sold government pamphlet, *Infant Care;* by 1929 it was recommending that doctors check posture as part of regular medical examinations as soon as a child was old enough to stand. This emphasis on very young children was new and potentially very troubling, since toddlers almost automatically fell short of ideal posture. Furthermore, the inclusion of posture in the standard child-rearing literature—the pamphlet was a perennial best-seller—was another sign of its growing hold in American culture.[21]

The shift away from simple etiquette toward a medical basis was clear by the 1930s, with manuals arguing that posture was necessary for good health. That is, because bad posture contorts muscles and organs, it impedes their full functioning. At the same time, posture revealed moral qualities: "Posture is a definite index of well being or the reverse, but it is more than a physical index, it is also a spiritual and emotional index." It must not be taken for granted; rather, parents must begin to guide their children in infancy. A number of pamphlets, including one by the Children's Bureau published in 1933 and reissued in 1946, provided illustrations by which parents could evaluate slumped backs, knock knees, bowed legs, and poorly placed feet. Rating scales were based on photographs of normal and deviant postures, allowing parents to grade their offspring.[22]

Concern about adolescents matched that now applied to toddlers. D. H. Thom, a major figure in the child health field, wrote the 1933 government-sponsored report. Adolescence was an awkward age, and many children, particularly girls, often slouched from embarrassment about their sexual development. Parents thus had to be careful not to tease teenagers about their bodies and should help them pick out appropriate shoes and clothes. Thom stressed the physical "importance of good posture habits in maintaining the various organs of the body in the proper position and enabling them to work to best advantage." Other writers maintained the larger correlation between posture and self-esteem: "It will require much bravery on the part of a mother to face the problems that will come as the child approaches adolescence. . . . Many children, regardless of their previous physical care, seem to slump at this time."[23]

Parents continued to be targeted in the 1940s and 1950s. Dr. Benjamin Spock's classic book on child care devoted considerable space to posture, particularly in its earliest editions. Parents' nagging was counterproductive, but posture problems were both common and serious, suggesting either health or psychological difficulties. "Many children slouch because of lack of self-confidence. It may come from too much criticism at home, or from difficulties in school, or from an unsatisfactory social life." The best recourse might be a school service, a doctor, or a posture clinic—places where a more "businesslike" atmosphere could help the child focus. Parents could contribute most by guiding exercise and by providing a reassuring atmosphere in which children felt adequate.[24] Again, posture surpassed nineteenth-century etiquette and character concerns by becoming an index of a person's place in society and individual psychic status.

The attention to adolescents continued. In 1949, Mary Beery discussed her goals as "director of social conduct" at an Ohio high school: Posture is the most important signal available to others to decide what they think about a person. It should be maintained in the home—no sprawling or putting feet up on the furniture—at school, at play, and at work. It required, in sum, constant attention. Walking with a book on the head—widely recommended and a frequent scene in movies made between the 1930s and the 1950s—was a classic posture corrective, especially in dealing with stairs. "People who see you descend in this manner will know that you have confidence in yourself." Explicit instruction in "posture correctness," urged a number of manuals reissued as late as 1960, might be necessary for teenagers.[25]

The role of posture concerns in child-rearing advice was faithfully mirrored in *Parents' Magazine*. From its inception in the mid-1920s, the magazine carried about one article a year on posture issues. As many of the experts warned, most parents dealt with bad posture merely by urging their children to sit up, stand straight, and get their feet or elbows off the furniture. There was more to be done, given the central position of posture in mental and physical health. "Mental slackness is not necessarily caused by a bad walk, but almost invariably when this condition exists, the bodily movements are uncertain." The magazine also carried much posture-related advertising, mainly for insurance companies and clothing firms. For example, good shoes were important. Putting children in front of a mirror so they could see directly the unattractive results of bad posture and the need to start training early were themes the magazine shared with the popular child-rearing manuals. Tests, including standing against a wall, walking straight lines, and mirror observation, helped parents identify the problems. But by the end of the 1950s, the subject was dropped, a decade before most child-rearing manuals tired of the theme.[26]

The new breed of personnel experts, appearing in the 1920s and anxious to provide employers with testable criteria for evaluating job applicants, routinely included posture in their descriptions. Bad posture was held to indicate introversion, itself predictive of poor group skills and also inferior health. Thus posture, along with blood pressure, anemia, and a few other characteristics, should be carefully assessed in physical examinations and visually evaluated by interviewers as well. Accordingly, the literature aimed at preparing applicants for interviews included reminders about careful posture in standing and sitting as a fundamental feature of self-presentation.[27]

School and College Programs

Concern about posture covered far more than proclamations and advice. As with hygiene, active efforts, begun before World War I, were made to carry the message into schools for monitoring and training, and the involvement of physical education specialists provided a cadre of experts with direct access to the students.

The program sponsors, educated in physical education at the university level, used the standard arguments, with even more emphasis on moral benefits than on health. Posture was "a sign of the child's total mental, emotional, and physical well-being." "Experience teaches us to expect enthusiasm for living, initiative, self-confidence, and self-respect from a person with an early erect posture." The converse also held: "It is just as natural and normal to slump when one feels personal and social inadequacy." Experts claimed that many parents simply neglected their children's posture, and the most grandiose posture claims even implied that other family problems that sapped a child's self-esteem would show up in posture.

Many schools either photographed children or, more commonly, had them stand in front of mirrors in swimsuits, underwear, or other minimal garb as experts assessed their stance. The Bancroft test, widely applied, recorded posture in standing and walking, and scales and assessment procedures were available. In the 1940s, an Iowa posture test added sitting to the postures observed. Elaborate forms, printed and widely disseminated, allowed teachers to record the students' performance with regard to spine, shoulders, chest, knees, and feet. Ordinary teachers might be trained to do this job if physical education programs were not available at the grade school level. Posture posters were widely circulated in the schools, and the most ambitious authorities also provided inspirational plays and poems to press the effort. In one dramatization, children were asked to choose among role-playing classmates exemplifying good and bad posture for a variety of jobs. "But it is the career woman who enters an office like this who gets the job." "And this is the soldier for me." "I'd be afraid to take medicine from him" (a role-played doctor who slouched). In the early 1940s, not surprisingly, posture was directly associated with military success and the war effort, and

| 267 |

schoolchildren were told that their posture training was derived from programs instituted in the army. "We need [these programs] to win the war."

A suggested chorus for grade school classes put the program in perspective:

> Perfect posture, perfect posture,
> Do not slump do not slump.
> You must grow up handsome, you must grow up handsome,
> Hide that hump, hide that hump.[28]

College programs were instituted at private East Coast schools. Physical education instruction at Harvard, offered to faculty from other institutions in summer school programs during the 1890s, launched many of the specific initiatives. Harriet Ballantine, a physical education leader at Kenyon College, was also prominent in these early efforts. Even before this, in 1884, Vassar College began to maintain records on the physical condition of each student, including posture data.[29] With further training in posture efforts, these measurements soon became an annual practice, including a final evaluation near graduation. At both men's and women's colleges, each student was photographed in the nude, sometimes at various angles, for posture assessments, a practice that continued at many schools for several decades and that later led to the revelation that these nude photographs had been kept in archives long after the programs themselves had been abandoned.[30]

College practices were widely shared and discussed. A meeting of the Eastern Society of College Directors of Physical Education for Women, held at Vassar in 1921, canvassed a variety of health issues, including posture.[31] A round table allowed various representatives to discuss what kinds of posture measurement charts and machines they used. Goucher College, noting it lacked space, time, and money for a machine, argued that "we waste a great deal [of] nervous energy and valuable time when we lay so much stress on 'Posture.' " The Goucher director recommended general exercise instead. Bryn Mawr, Cornell, and several other institutions admitted they had no machines but pointed to the posture instruction they offered in gymnastics and dancing classes. Simmons and Wheaton referred severe cases to orthopedic surgeons. Vassar, Barnard, and the University of Pittsburgh encouraged posture through efficiency tests and awards, although the Barnard College doctor thought that the posture problem did not warrant special instruction. Smith, Wellesley, and other women's schools, along with Syracuse University, used shadowgraphs, schematographs, and posture tracings. Wellesley used these to "carry to the mind of the student what posture means." Smith graded the tracings, and Vassar conducted a "posture drive" in 1919/1920.

These efforts escalated into the 1930s and 1940s at the women's schools. In 1930, Vassar, with a new physical education director and raising money for a larger gymnasium, elevated physical training to a "liberal art" and began to claim the right to dismiss students if their posture or other aspects of their physical condition proved to be inadequate. "Severe posture defects" were noted as one of the most common sources of concern. Posture problems led to special exercise assignments for about one-third of all first-year students. "A system of records, photographs mostly, shows, particularly to those with posture defects, steps in progress and furnishes an incentive for going on."[32] Two years later, Vassar began its Fundamentals in Body Movement course, required of all freshmen, which emphasized posture training, with additional special exercises and individual counseling for students identified (through the assessment of the photographs) as having curvature of the spine. The course taught not only general posture but also how to get out of a car, put up a suitcase in a luggage rack, and so on. "Fundies" continued into the 1960s.

The proliferation of costly and intrusive posture campaigns at the college level recalled the Victorian role for posture in training a distinctive kind of body control for the middle and upper-middle classes. Women, long identified as having poor posture (either by nature or because of restrictive dress and lack of exercise), received a disproportionate amount of attention. Yet army manuals also contended that posture made the body a more "efficient instrument." "A body that is out of line is like any machine out of alignment." The institutionalization of posture standards was thus the most striking example of the expert counterattack in the early twentieth century.

Even though the most strenuous discussions had ended by the 1930s, the momentum persisted. In the 1940s, the posture photographs taken of students in the elite colleges were given new support by a Columbia University authority, W. H. Sheldon, an evolutionist eager to demonstrate the effect of body type (endomorphic, mesomorphic, or ectomorphic) on personality. By arguing for a variety of "natural" posture types, this approach carried the seeds of destruction for key posture assumptions, but it took a while before the contradictions became clear.

Collectively, the ubiquitous posture programs reflected characteristic ambiguities in the translation of Victorian standards into the twentieth century. On the one hand, school efforts sought a democratization, with opportunities and obligations distributed equally. On the other, the concentration of more advanced posture campaigns in elite colleges suggested that posture remained an area in which the really well bred could distinguish themselves from the lesser classes.

The Collapse of the Posture Campaign

In contrast to the steady intensification of hygiene demands, the pressures and programs for good posture began to diminish by the 1950s. Behavioral trends toward the acceptance of comfort and a relaxed body pose now overwhelmed the countercurrents, and posture ceased being an important issue.

Poses in official photographs revealed the change. Through 1929, for example, many yearbooks displayed students in uniformly rigid poses in both individual and group pictures. Subjects sat or stood straight, with no visible differences, save in uniform, between military training groups and civilian organizations. Even sports team pictures (as opposed to action shots) remained stiff. Hesitant changes first emerged in the 1930s, with casual shots showing people leaning and bending now mixed with formal pictures. Although women's group shots remained more conventional than men's, "beauty queen" and cheerleader poses allowed reclining, even languid, presentations or demonstrations of more athletic grace, suggesting an implicit contrast between the attractive and the formal body. By the 1940s, even faculty were portrayed slumped or leaning, and by the 1950s, all efforts at systematically erect posture had disappeared. If sitting, people leaned on chair arms or tables, and when standing up, they chose among a variety of poses.[33]

Another, though later, symptomatic shift could be found in the nature and advertisement of bedding. By the 1960s and particularly the 1970s, mattresses began for the first time to be advertised for their effect on maintaining posture and supporting the back. Before this point, the selling points of mattresses, relatively thin affairs in any event, were low cost and easy cleaning. Cotton, "sanitized" contents and covers met the demand for better hygiene as the battle against germs and contagions spread throughout American households. At most, an absence of "lumpiness" might be held up. Likewise, posture experts rarely mentioned the relationship between sleep and the spine, although the subject did come up very occasionally in the pediatric advice literature concerning infants' sleeping position. This does not mean that people were unaware of the relationship between bedding and back comfort. With the 1960s, however, standard references to the importance of mattresses in providing support—"deep-down firmness for luxuriously relaxing support," "won't sag," allusion to "ortho" types—began to dominate the newspaper advertisements. With most people's normal posture now slumping—with no character issues involved—it was both proper and sensible to look for compensation in bedding. By the 1970s, explicit references to character-free posture began to replace the vaguer comments about "support," including the introduction of a "Posturepedic" brand name and other attractions such as "patented heavy-duty posture grid foundations."[34]

By this time, in fact, the long posture campaign had slowed down. Schools programs had ceased, except for specific checks for scoliosis (usually in middle school, not grade school). Posture cameras were shuttered, the charts largely discarded. In the 1960s, Vassar College dropped its posture pictures and Fundamentals of Body Movement course, in an atmosphere in which required physical education of any sort seemed outmoded. Indeed, the physical education that remained concentrated more on recreational exercise and athletics. One optional course, "Movement Analysis," was designed to increase body awareness and grace, and although an understanding of anatomy was mentioned in the course description, posture was not. Shifts in posture priorities even affected the military. Reserve Office Training Corps units on campuses had to institute more formal posture training because of its disappearance in the middle-class experience elsewhere. "Sitting at attention" was one newly important device, which caused considerable initial discomfort to recruits unaccustomed to this kind of classroom stance.

New editions of etiquette classics like Emily Post's continued to repeat some older advice. "There is no doubt that a person—man or woman—who stands and sits erect shows himself off to his best advantage." People should sit up straight, a particularly challenging task for women given the need to manage legs and skirts. Sitting properly elicited elaborate instructions, especially in regard to overstuffed furniture. But even Emily Post relaxed a bit when it came to sitting at table. People should not fidget, but they could put their elbows on the table when not eating, particularly to participate better in conversations. Even newer manuals, such as Letitia Baldridge's, written after her service as social secretary to Jacqueline Kennedy, recommended the old standards as essential in polite society. Jacqueline Kennedy herself, apparently, received letters commending her good posture—"good posture attracts an admiring eye."[35]

A newer breed of etiquette adviser, however, took pride in downplaying strict posture and deriding the rigidity of traditional manuals. Amy Vanderbilt, despite admiring Victorian posture, had to admit the inevitable: "Today with fewer and fewer uncompromising chairs being manufactured, we are more or less forced to lounge as we sit." It was now all right for women to hold their legs in various positions when sitting, for the old norms simply did not fit. Sitting at table required little comment beyond not interfering with others; the placement of hands and elbows was a matter of good sense, not rigid rules. By the 1980s, Judith Martin, "Miss Manners," took pleasure in unseating outmoded customs. "A less formal posture . . . is no longer punishable by hanging."[36]

The virtual cessation of posture discussions as a component of social criteria or child rearing undermined the basis for medical attention. By the 1940s, most child-rearing manuals omitted posture considerations altogether (and by the 1960s, this omission had become nearly universal, with the exception of writers like Benjamin Spock, whose careers had begun in the posture era). When posture no longer measured character or social worth, doctors had no reason to claim that a majority of people suffered from posture defects. Even the pseudomedical research on diverse body types supported this shift. William Sheldon and his colleagues actually began arguing that traditional standards reified the pleasures of mesomorphs, making the other body types needlessly miserable. Other beliefs, such as the notion that poor posture forced internal organs to collide and so interfered with their efficiency, disappeared as well. This change was also accompanied by the near disappearance of several posture-related diseases, notably rickets and infantile paralysis, thanks to new nutritional or preventive measures.[37]

By the 1960s, medical comment, diagnosis, and measurement alike had moved away from posture. What had once inspired many articles in the medical and physical therapy journals was now reduced to a few scattered comments. Some of them—like a 1970 piece entitled "A Straight Back—A Nonsyndrome"—were designed to remind practitioners of the irrelevance of older concerns.[38] Even earlier, an article in the *Journal of School Health*, by an academic physician, explicitly refuted these ideas:

> Another favorite focus of misguided concern by school personnel and excessively worried parents, is the matter of posture and fitness. We still hold the notion, research findings to the contrary, that a healthy child should, somehow, perform his daily duties more successfully if he tried to resemble an alert West Point Cadet—preferably at attention. There are no scientific facts to substantiate the benefits of this aesthetic ideal.

That is, posture has nothing to do with character or personal adjustment; it is not related to diseases of the organs; and it does not cause defects such as scoliosis; its only purpose is to make posture a subject of school inspections or training.[39] The claims of a prior generation of physical education specialists were fraudulent and had be stopped. Even orthopedic medicine largely eschewed a systematic approach to posture, its practitioners sometimes arguing that back pain had no more to do with posture than did some of the other diseases so long tied to the posture campaign. In medicine and school health programs, the extreme reversal of previous interests suggest a collective embarrassment at the past naïveté and culturally motivated hyperbole. So great was the reaction, in fact, that doctors may have unduly downplayed the role of posture in back comfort, offering cautions and training only in pronounced cases of scoliosis or, for adults, in the aftermath of accidents.[40]

Child-rearing manuals or developmental studies now mentioned posture only in regard to a need to remediate old parental habits. Parents had long been advised not to chide; now this recommendation took on greater force. Children's posture should not be a matter for discipline of any sort. The same attitude applied to a new interest in making children proud of their bodies. Finally, and most important, parents themselves stopped trying to enforce the old standards.[41]

Parents' Magazine provides a barometer. It stopped carrying articles on posture by the late 1940s, indicating a confused transition. Then in 1958/1959, a few articles appeared, designed to instill the new wisdom. Parents must not nag, for this would merely make children self-conscious or hostile. Short of a structural deformity, which was quite rare, posture would "take care of itself." Doctors must be called in for physical problems, and exercise remained important generally. But there were no absolute standards. Tests were silly, because no two individuals had the same posture, and there was no proof anyway that bad posture harmed health. Posture changed with age, which was part of the process by which almost all children acquired the stance they needed automatically. The most important goal was to make children feel attractive. "A healthy and happy child will assume good posture naturally." Again, the message was mixed, in that some standards remained. But the urgency had disappeared, and with this, the magazine dropped the subject entirely—just as phrenology and other body-measurement fads had disappeared in the past.[42]

The ramifications of relaxed posture involved more than the cessation of effort plus the substitution of material supports (the new mattresses); a certain revulsion against previous standards entered in as well, as the about-face of medical attention showed. Even the youth culture was touched. Long a source of alternative body presentations that defied recommended standards, as in the slouched, vaguely menacing poses of 1950s idols like James Dean, the youth culture could no longer make much headway with casualness alone. To be sure, even in the mid-1990s, a song by the group Nirvana included the ironic comment "I have very bad posture." The juxtaposition of youth posture and the military stance had been an even more prominent visual ingredient of the protest musical *Hair* in the 1970s. But now with adults largely abandoning the posture campaign and lounging around themselves and with teachers standing and sitting almost as casually in classrooms, poor posture had lost most of its defiant power. This development might explain new efforts to find other, more shocking forms of body presentation, such as tattooing and multiple piercing, in the continuing need to demonstrate that young bodies must annoy their parents.[43]

Why Did Posture Fail?

Alone among the major forms of body discipline, posture standards yielded considerably after midcentury. Several factors were responsible. Advancing consumerism certainly worked against maintaining the older posture tradition. Comfort gradually won out against discipline. Leisure activities favored athletic grace over rigorous posture. Changes in leisure technology also increased opportunities for private relaxation—listening to the radio, watching television—when posture standards readily eased. As early as the 1930s, depictions of respectable American families with parents reclining and children sprawled on the floor in front of the radio suggested the acceptability of the informal pose. Leisure and more open sexuality alike placed a premium on a friendly stance, even in public; a rigid posture now seemed stiff and remote. Even though good posture remained necessary for job interviews—again, the new culture of informality had complex rules—service occupations that depended on superficial friendliness might undermine a rigid pose as well. That is, many factors worked against posture and ultimately overwhelmed it.

This general framework, however accurate, does not explain why posture standards lasted as long as they did or why posture programs finally collapsed more completely than other disciplinary regimes. Posture came to depend on particular professions and arguments that had a powerful short-term impact but limited staying power. Physical education specialists turned to more formal sports activities, giving up the posture crusade in favor of other physical-training goals, and the rise of women's sports in the 1960s played an important role in this evolution. Doctors found other emphases that might more readily persuade a public audience. In addition, posture arguments focused too exclusively on children, thus depriving professionals of other potential clients while also reducing any adult sense that posture might compensate for consumer indulgence. And they did not develop a ringing rationale in health: the idea of poor posture's impeding the smooth functioning of the inner organs simply did not catch on, and by the 1950s, even doctors turned away from it.

The posture campaign failed also to take advantage of its interaction with consumerism. Indeed, posture advocates actually muffled their earlier efforts to show posture as an antidote to insidious comfort. The confrontation of posture with the dominant trends in furniture and clothing also diminished as experts stressed the preventive training of children. Hence the idea of discipline through posture appeared outdated, not relevant to the moral needs of an affluent society. Dieting, as we will see, more adequately filled this requirement. At the same time, posture products were not abundant, despite advertisements for corrective shoes and a few other items in the interwar decades. Posture thus failed to benefit from the kind of consumerist support given to both hygiene and dieting.

The result was not a complete collapse of standards but, rather, some of the same complexity we have seen in regard to the rise of a leisure ethic and more open sexuality. Respectable Americans no longer had to hold themselves straight in every circumstance or even worry about their children, but they still had to satisfy two requirements. First, middle-class Americans still had to know how to adjust their stance to the situation at hand. Manuals on job seeking advised: "Enter the room with a straight back and your head held high. Use good posture throughout the interview." Revealingly, "good" did not require further definition. In other settings, however, a relaxed demeanor indicated comfort with one's own body and a genial openness. For example, training manuals for teachers instructed them how to hold their body in an informal pose, indicative of self-assurance without rigidity and of a friendly interest in one's audience.[44]

Fighting Fat

The quest for slenderness and, for men, a greater interest in muscularity began in the 1890s. This was an area of discipline that was not really Victorian at all, although it encompassed older concerns about fighting indulgence and demonstrating virtue. As with hygiene, the pressures for weight control or dieting steadily accelerated, with each generation's putative standards surpassed by the next. Also similar to hygiene, dieting related easily to health, work, and appearance. Like hygiene, but unlike posture, dieting did not complicate the demands for relaxed friendliness in personal relationships or leisure style. Rather, it meshed more readily with more revealing, less formal clothing, combining discipline with apparent ease. At the same time, the quest for slenderness served explicit functions in moral castigation. It did overlap with posture, however, in that dieting clashed with certain elements of consumerism. This clash did not deter the escalation of standards and personal concern, but it did make dieting more complex than hygiene. Overall, the slenderness craze was special, generating more worry and doubt than any other facet of body control.

Intensification

The most important development in the battle against fat, starting in the 1920s, was its intensification. Ladies were first. Until the 1970s, girls were far more likely than boys to be identified as overweight; as the *Women's Home Companion* noted in 1920: "[Boys] usually have better opportunities to be normally active, and also they are not as much disturbed about their appearance as the members of the opposite sex." According to Emily Post, "it is hard for an overweight woman to be dignified." Doctors commented, often with some annoyance, about the women who crowded their offices asking for guidance in losing weight, but they acknowledged the validity of their concern: "The modern desire, particularly of the female of the species, is slimness. It is undesirable to require special clothes, restrict social and recreational activities and be the target of jokes." "Overweight is also a mar to beauty. . . . An excess of fat destroys grace and delicacy. A fat face has a monstrous uniformity. No theatrical producer would hire a plump actress to mirror the real depths of the human soul." Further changes in clothing toward more revealing attire both reflected and encouraged the new female concern. As a diet book put it, it is "desirable to avoid inordinate curves and shapes and protuberances, which do not look well in the more revealing garments." On a coarser level, the word *broad* became current in the 1920s as an insulting reminder to women.[45]

Men felt the moral pressure as well, even though the aesthetic demands on them were not as intimidating. The concern about health in the 1950s, with new reports of male vulnerability to arterial and heart disease, added to the existing framework. Fat boys faced ridicule: "It wasn't fun to have the other boys giggle at the sight of me and call 'Q-ball' and 'Fatso.' " Special books, like the "Fat Boy" diet series of the 1950s, sold hundreds of thousands of copies—just as women's magazines were inundated with diet columns, often averaging more than one per issue. Arguments directed toward men were similar to those for women, except for somewhat less emphasis on appearance per se. As men began to have annual medical checkups, with special warnings about blood pressure and stress, the health criteria loomed large, as did comments about having bodies suitable for work and sexually attractive. Amid the steady bombardments, the concern with fashion increased. In 1994, the director of an eating disorder program in St. Louis commented,

> I have men coming into my office telling me they're convinced they were passed over for promotion because the other guy was slimmer and they look more like a beach ball. Or their wife is unhappy with them because of their appearance. . . . With more men's fashion magazines on the market, more emphasis is being put on the way men look. Now they're subjected to the same concerns about body image that have plagued women for years.

Men remained less willing than women to discuss their weight problems openly and less willing to join weight control groups, but they nonetheless worried about measuring up.[46]

For both genders, the intensification of standards showed up in the unending media discussions and the proliferation of weight-control paraphernalia. Weight-loss stories became a staple, complete with references to moral redemption. Bodies once out of control were brought in line through a combination of personal discipline and a particular line of products or weight counseling; the results were restored marriages and ascending careers. Special weight-reducing machines and exercise regimes proliferated, and common food products, like Pepsi Cola and Domino sugar, began advertising on the basis of weight-control claims, even before special diet lines were introduced in the 1950s. By 1990, the overall diet "industry" was reportedly valued at $33 billion. With doctors now joining the appeals for thinness and actively responding to patients' concerns, this aspect of body control supported a large portion of medical practice as well. As one doctor put it in 1950, "Reducing, or the deliberate effort to lower body weight, may be called the all-American preoccupation."[47]

Scientific findings joined with a cultural eagerness to undertake, or at least to contemplate, greater sacrifice. Thus in the 1930s, doctors began telling Americans that the previously cited figure of 3,000 calories a day was too high; that 2,400, perhaps even 2,350, was preferable. Recommended weights were similarly lowered. Standards for weight gain in pregnancy also dropped steadily until the 1980s. In 1942, a Metropolitan Life Insurance company chart listed 145 to 156 pounds as the desirable weight for a man five feet eight inches tall; his counterpart in the 1959 tables was listed at 138 to 152. During the same time span, the standard for a medium-frame woman of five feet four inches went from 124 to 132, to 113 to 126. Over this seventeen-year interval, the tables dropped by 8 percent, and these stark numerical shifts were accompanied by actuarial and medical findings to the effect that health, or at least longevity, was best served by weighing less than the recommended poundage.[48]

The demands for muscularity to accompany slenderness increased as well. Around 1900, the ideal male body normally included well-developed muscles as well as an absence of fat. By the 1970s, the growing popularity of workouts and beach vacations made more men aware that they should not only avoid fat but also develop some muscles. Even more striking was the increased demand on women after the 1970s to become fit and develop better muscular tone to accompany their slender body, with fashions such as bare midriffs designed to display success.

In some sectors, these norms moved from recommendation to requirement. From the 1950s until prohibited by law after the 1970s, a number of employers fined or fired workers—particularly women—for failing to lose weight. A California policewoman, for instance, was punished and finally terminated for being ten pounds overweight. Flight attendants also were held to strict standards. In the 1980s, the penalties shifted to higher insurance premiums, and a number of companies began offering cheap "weight-management" courses, along with counseling and exercise facilities, as part of "wellness programs." Fat people and work did not mix well, a message stressed by advice manuals. One book noted that fat "can count against [a man] when promotions are being considered. Then, it's the vigorous, ambitious, dynamic man who usually has the edge—not his solid, calm, comfortably easy-going colleague who carries just a little weight too much." A teenager who lost thirty pounds was told that his strength of character ensured that "you can look forward to success in any future undertaking."[49]

Americans picked up the message about the importance of controlling their weight, the consequences of failing to do so, and the steady increase in pressure. A few cultural subgroups implicitly dissented, maintaining older beliefs about eating and the attractiveness of heavier bodies. This approach was especially popular among many African Americans and Latinos, whose actual weights were above national averages. Overall, however—and publications aimed at the divergent minorities included standard diet advice along with the approval of alternative standards—the commitment to this aspect of body discipline was widespread. By the late 1940s, up to three-quarters of the letters concerning beauty tips sent to the *Ladies Home Journal* involved weight control: "I would like to lose ten pounds. Do you have any diet suggestions?" Many middle-class Americans poured over calorie charts and the daily weigh-in on the bathroom scales. As early as the 1930s, jokes about fat people became routinely funny. According to opinion polls, by 1951, 21 percent of American men and 44 percent of women judged that they were overweight, and in 1973, these percentages had zoomed to 39 and 55, respectively—a rise that easily surpassed actual weight gains. In 1950, about 11 percent of all Americans professed to be on a diet, whereas in 1973 the rate was 42 percent. Reports of a virtual obsession with being overweight—beyond "the bounds of science and logic," as one observer noted in 1959—were clearly close to the mark.[50]

Slimness and Character

One reason for the obsession with fat, beyond health and job advice, beyond fashion and media hyperbole, was the role of weight control in forming a sense of personal morality, with character issues part of the diet crusade. A *Cosmopolitan* article in 1954 described a successful businessman whose life was unbalanced, who worked and consumed too hard, never relaxing or spending time with his family. But just in time, he changed his values—and also dieted and lost sixteen pounds. Dieting was part of the moralizing process here, a symbol of ethical balance.

Experts like Dr. Hilde Bruch blamed the obesity problem on "pampered and undisciplined appetites." "Fattened wallets," one commentator remarked, "make fattened Americans. Overweight? Blame our soft, lazy way of life."[51]

This kind of rhetoric had begun in 1900, building on an earlier, nineteenth-century effort to link nutrition and morality in an increasingly commercial world.[52] What was new was the omnipresence of the issue and its link to consumerism. Moreover, the relationship translated into truly vicious characterizations of the overweight, passed off as self-evident. After World War II, women's magazines routinely carried comments about obesity as a sickness, about fat people as objects of failure and ridicule. "Are you aware that fatness has destroyed your sex appeal and made you look older, somewhat like a buffoon whom people are inclined not to take seriously in any area or on any level?" By the 1950s, overweight had been translated into psychobabble, a symptom of maladjustment and immaturity. "Circumstances leading to a high-weight mark usually stem from a fatal character flaw and other psychological manifestations." "Only when you can face up to and come to terms with the reasons causing you to overeat will you be able to slim down and stay that way. . . . Or might it be fear and anxiety about sex that make you keep yourself unattractive." "The obese woman's very dimensions reflect her need for strength and massiveness in order to deny an image of self that is felt to be basically weak, inadequate, and helpless." "Psychiatrists have exposed the fat person for what he really is—miserable, self-indulgent and lacking in self-control."[53]

In this context, fighting fat became a moral issue. By the 1990s, college students rated controlling weight in the same category as refraining from theft or from extramarital affairs. People who ate low-fat foods were accordingly cited as more moral than others. The connection, though new, made sense: dieting had become a demonstration of character in an indulgent world. To be sure, specific diet products were advertised as making it easy to lose weight. But many dieters recognized the need for discipline, and the exercise literature picked up on this, talking of "workouts" and the need to "feel the burn" before any good could be achieved. In the best self-help tradition, diet articles frequently revealed the happy ending: having not only lost weight but also demonstrated newfound character, the slimmed-down person wins deserved new success in business and social life. Key organizations, such as Overeaters Anonymous, incorporated the moral regeneration theme, asking members to confess their eating sins in groups and to seek a kind of spiritual rebirth to achieve their desired body weight. Fat had become close to sin. Control over fat had a symbolic meaning in the United States, and the connections continued to tighten as the century wore on.[54]

This moralistic twist was distinctively American. Many dimensions of the crusade against fat took shape on both sides of the Atlantic and for similar reasons in societies provided with abundant food but sedentary jobs. European doctors and popularizers, however, denied a character dimension. Weight was a problem of health and aesthetics, and no good would come of making it more. Patients should be reassured, not insulted or psychoanalyzed. "An obese person should leave your consulting rooms confident and solaced." With other ways to protest consumer trends and less belief in the importance of individual self-control as the basis for success or as a counterbalance to social ills, Europeans tried to distinguish between vigorous insistence and moral evaluation. Stories about dramatic weight loss were not repeated in European popularizations because the salience of this kind of redemption was less clear. Diet groups were less popular, and there was less interest in a psychological approach or in a need to detail moral failings and to demonstrate moral commitment before an audience.[55]

The Battleground

Maintaining high standards for slenderness, for a complex set of motivations, proved no easy task in a consumer society. Many Americans did not maintain the shapes they sought, and indeed national weight averages surpassed those of other industrial nations, despite what was in some respects a vigorous, well-subscribed campaign for self-control.

The purpose of the campaign was warring with impulse, so it was not surprising that some people failed—particularly as desk jobs proliferated, mechanical transportation replaced walking, and foods grew richer and more appetizing. Some people lost the battle. Furthermore, the American performance was significantly affected by the weight experience of certain groups that did not share the middle-class zeal for slenderness, for they helped determine the national average.[56]

Even for the committed, however, several features of the national culture proved hard to reconcile. At least by the nineteenth century, Americans had developed the habit of eating quickly, and voluminous consumption was praised. At the time, this mattered little, since exertion helped keep weight down, and in any event, plumpness often was preferred. In the late nineteenth century, however, with the creation of snack foods, beginning with packaged crackers in the 1880s—ideal for satisfying cravings rapidly and also suitable for promotion through advertising—snacks became an American specialty, battling with the desire to stay slim. Moreover (and in interesting contrast to both hygiene and posture), children were long unburdened with dieting strictures. Even as warnings to adults increased, overweight children (particularly boys), were rarely mentioned until the 1970s. On both counts— snacking and the unwillingness to discipline children in this area— American practices, compared with those of other diet-conscious societies, were particularly resistant to the newer emphasis on slenderness. One result was, quite simply, the unusual number of Americans who in fact had to diet, rather than keeping weight off in the first place.[57]

Some groups and many individuals nevertheless took the disciplinary injunctions seriously enough to remain or become thinner than their counterparts earlier in American history. Middle-class white women, especially, lost up to five pounds per person, height held constant, between 1941 and the 1960s, with the greatest change occurring after age thirty-five. Men, however, and the American population as a whole put on weight in the same period. Then, in the 1980s, weight gain increased even among white women, with the percentage of obesity rising sharply: the average American adult added eight pounds, height and age held constant. Before this anomalous and substantial shift, the trends suggested a battle fairly joined, with some notable victories and some clear defeats, as widely recognized standards clashed with consumerist opportunities. Even magazines reflected the tug of war, with diet articles coexisting with recipes for rich foods and tempting advertisements.[58]

Dieting, in fact, juxtaposed consumerism and the desire for discipline as starkly as any aspect of twentieth-century society, which is why it is important to emphasize the ongoing conflict. In fact, the strain produced not only some important weight control but also a more pervasive anxiety that served as an additional emblem of the tensions of American consumerism. Even though they were less successful than some other contemporaries in keeping pounds off, Americans clearly worried more and had less confidence in their own appearance. In their actual dieting, this guilt was significant, if sometimes counterproductive. As one observer put it, "Dieting while growing fatter is an inverted spiritual exercise; every time you break your resolutions you eat even more, for consolation and in defiance." Americans were hard on themselves: according to poll data, many were dissatisfied with their bodies and were convinced that they had not measured up to their own standards, in marked contrast to more complacent reactions in countries like France.[59]

Selective restraint legitimized American life in a consumer society. It appealed to beliefs in individual responsibility for adjusting to larger trends. Applied to dieting, one of its most important twentieth-century havens, it produced serious efforts at self-discipline, which in turn resulted in either real limits on weight or moral self-criticism—or both.

The Body, Health, and Virtue

Inconsistencies in the standards that Americans applied to the body were obvious. The most glaring stemmed from conflicts between consumer appetites and the desire for control. The tensions were not substantial in the area of hygiene, in which purchases and cleansing the body meshed nicely. They were prominent in the dichotomy between the relaxation-comfort pairing and posture and ultimately helped defeat the most rigorous posture standards. And they were endemic in the area of weight watching, in which health and aesthetic and moral demands were far too great to abandon standards but where the allure of solace through eating remained strong as well.

Tensions also showed, less expectedly, in the approach to children. Concerns about controlling the body in the interests of appearance, health, and moral demonstration required greater adult supervision of children, because standards of cleanliness and, for a time, posture had to be taught early on. Yet—perhaps partly in compensation—there were odd lacunae; for instance, Americans believed that children should be indulged, with the body pampered rather than disciplined and with childhood held separate from adult standards. Children thus received mixed signals regarding the conflict between hedonism and restraint that carried over into adulthood, with food producing particular tensions between remembered solace and the extension of demands for restraint.

Despite the ambivalence, and even when standards were incompletely honored at best, the twentieth-century emphasis on control over physical impulse created a large reservoir of moral energy. Americans found it relatively easy to believe that bodies out of control signaled bad character or some crucial psychological flaw that added up to the same thing. They also harbored a recurrent impulse to see disease itself as a punishment for insufficient discipline, rather than as a health problem that should be defined only physically. Heart attacks, although sometimes thought to be a symbol of hard work and achievement, might thus be prevented through appropriate applications of the will to observe correct eating habits, relaxation, and exercise. AIDS, as we have noted, clearly punished sexual license. Cancer would respond to individual attention to hygiene, diet, and rejection of smoking. In 1996, a report from Harvard University's School of Public Health contended that 75 percent of all cancers resulted from lifestyle choices and therefore could be controlled. Indeed, the experts came close to claiming that most people who died of the century's most dreaded disease had only themselves to blame.[60]

Arguments for emotional restraint had in fact long emphasized its effects on health. By the early twentieth century, popular health articles made the connection explicit, as tests of blood pressure and heart activity became more common. "Whenever . . . the passions are permitted to overrule the reason, the result is disease; the heart empties itself into the brain; the brain is stricken, the heart is prostrate, and both are lost." By the 1920s, cautionary articles with such titles as "What Strong Emotions Do to You" were common in periodicals like *Harper's* and *Scientific American*. Motherhood also prompted the invocation of discipline for the baby's sake: widely sold books counseled against drinking, smoking, and gaining too much weight. "Before you close your mouth on a

| 285 |

forkful of food, consider, 'Is this really the best bite I can give my baby?' " Constant attention was necessary because of the dangers that surrounded the body. Self-control was being interwoven with health criteria in a variety of ways, with the body both a motivation and a measure of good character.[61]

The idea of disease as the alternative to moral control was not uncontested. Americans also looked for social remedies, as in the better regulation of environmental pollution, and placed huge hopes in medical science to rescue them from illness and disease whatever the cause. Thus the outbreak of AIDS outbreak prompted fascinating claims that scientific research could provide cures if only enough money were invested, along with the moral strictures. By the 1980s, with the interest in genetic explanations and, possibly, genetically based remedies, even for issues such as obesity and alcoholism, the symbolic meaning of disease and practical approaches to dealing with it had been challenged.

The potential for seeing health issues in moral terms remained great, however, for many Americans were eager to seize on a connection between body discipline and health, with both drawn into larger service as symbols of morality in an indulgent society. This combination showed in the unusual energy the United States devoted to the crusade against smoking in the final decades of the twentieth century.

This Is a Smoke-Free Section

Victorian values had challenged smoking in the later nineteenth century—specifically, cigarette smoking, which was newer and therefore less sanctioned and which spread among lower-class groups whose behavior was always suspect. For men, cigarettes were held to be effeminate. The accessibility of cigarettes to young people was also an issue, for smoking seemed to be an act of defiance and a breach of proper etiquette and control. Opponents applied the same thinking to women's smoking, linking it with prostitution. Health concerns were raised, along with the rights of nonsmokers, under a haze of moralism, for the new forms of smoking seemed to signal a degeneration in character. Accordingly, various leaders applied to smoking some of the same arguments used against drinking. Lucy Page Gaston, a member of the Woman's Christian Temperance Union, formed the Chicago Anti-Cigarette League in

1899, which went national two years later. Henry Ford also came out against smoking. By 1909, a number of states had banned the sale of cigarettes, and many school systems forbade public smoking by teachers, on pain of dismissal.[62]

But this opposition to smoking was defeated by popular habits and organized counterthrusts. The increasingly powerful tobacco companies worked against the restrictions. Then in World War I, cigarette smoking became even more popular, supported by the army as a means of providing quick contentment for the troops. The extension of regulatory efforts against drinking, through Prohibition, and their perceived failure also fouled the antismoking climate.[63]

Ironically, by 1930, when the final laws limiting cigarette sales were repealed, the effects differed considerably from the consequences of ending Prohibition. Drinking habits continued to be comparatively restrained even when regulation eased. Prohibition had decisively altered working-class drinking styles, and even when the taverns reopened, their range and impact did not replicate turn-of-the-century patterns. Thus the per capita consumption of distilled spirits, which had dropped by 80 percent during Prohibition, did increase gradually during the 1930s and 1940s but only to 70 percent of pre-Prohibition levels and then fell another 20 percent after a peak in 1951; the figures for beer showed a similar pattern. Only wine consumption increased. Self-regulation, in other words, continued to limit the average use of alcohol, although of course there were many problems of excess and adjustments after the prohibitive measures ended. The use of cigarettes, however, steadily climbed. The average annual production quadrupled between 1930 and 1966, and per capita consumption tripled between 1940 and 1966 (at which point the average American was smoking more than four thousand cigarettes per year). The kinds of restraints still urged on Americans concerning alcohol, including recommended treatment programs or new self-help groups such as Alcoholics Anonymous for those still overwhelmed, simply dropped out of the smoking arena. Advertisements increasingly touted smoking for its pleasure and its enhancement of sophistication and sexual appeal; media presentations did the same; etiquette books, discussing proper provisions for smokers' needs, added their stamp of approval.[64]

Then came the definitive attack, spearheaded by doctors, health organizations such as the American Cancer Society, and government offi-cials. In the late 1970s, after some years of tentative health warnings largely ignored by the smoking public, more definitive findings were published about the relationship between smoking and cancer and sev-eral other diseases. This revelation was supplemented by the antismoking forces' service to the need for self-discipline and to attacks on those incapable of control. After the unusual hedonism of the 1960s and the disillusionment with government attempts to improve society through legislative reform, the new crusade was perfectly timed.

New research on the health effects of smoking began in the 1950s and reached public attention in 1964. By 1978, 90 percent of all Amer-icans had come to believe that smoking involved real hazards. In 1965, Congress passed the first legislation requiring warning labels on cigarette packages. Interest groups like the Action on Smoking and Health (formed in 1967) and GASP (Group Against Smokers' Pollution), with ten thousand members in one hundred local chapters by the 1970s, pushed the cause along. Information on the effects of "secondhand," inhaled smoke began to appear in the late 1970s and was confirmed by the surgeon general in 1984. Minnesota required the provision of non-smoking areas in 1975, and San Francisco prohibited smoking in public places in 1983, after vigorous debate.[65]

As the campaign unfolded, smoking first became unmannerly and then immoral. Between 1964 and 1979, the emphasis was on self-victimization, but with the growing attention to the impact on others, smoking then became socially irresponsible. All the familiar character chords were played. Aside from the required labeling and regulations of public space, this was an issue for individuals, not governments—at least until the late 1990s. Middle- and upper-class people took the lead in abandoning their own bad habits and urging the same on lower-class groups and on the young. The cessation of smoking became an act of self-discipline. Smokers became pariahs, driven to huddle in doorways, appropriately segregated because of their demonstrable lack of charac-ter.[66]

Representative arguments dripped with moral evaluation. Smoking constituted "some element of human frailty or incompleteness in the smoker. . . . Addiction, compulsion, irrational action: these are the mes-sages that waft up with the smoke. . . . People are tied to smoking as

Gulliver was tied to the ground by the Lilliputians." But as with all moral issues, there was hope: "Stopping smoking is no different from any other difficult thing in that it can be more readily mastered with learning and practice." Self-restraint became part of the new manners, "a norm of civility." The fate of children was invoked: parents must cease smoking for the sake of their offspring if nothing else. Even the health warnings themselves embraced character as well as hygiene: smoking was the "single most preventable cause of death," a "pestilence," with smokers nothing less than "merchants of death."[67]

This self-righteous moral framework (not, interestingly, applied to other health hazards like tanning, in which appearance counted for more, interpersonal relations for less) explains the amazing speed of the transformation of American smoking. Even though smoking's health risks were real and unusually great, only this moralism explains Americans' quick, intense conversion and attendant intolerance of smokers, compared with reactions in other health-conscious societies. Some commercial supplements were available to help wean smokers from nicotine cravings, but the crusade did not depend on rampant consumerism. Indeed, its main focus was against the leading agents of consumer hedonism, the tobacco companies, which unquestionably was part of its appeal. First Lady Hillary Clinton railed against an actress who had smoked heavily in a movie comedy, her passion reflecting an interest in making political capital from the attack on smoking, a concern about role models for America's youth, and a desire for uniform inhibition, for deep if selective asceticism. Individuals, especially members of the middle class, did demonstrate character. American behavior changed much more rapidly than did its counterparts in other industrial countries, where (as with dieting) character was less often cited than health and smokers themselves were less stigmatized. At one point, indeed, a group of French politicians was persuaded to modify some antismoking legislation lest it smack of American moral totalitarianism. It was an extraordinary moment for American self-control. The energy deployed, undeniably effective at least until the late 1990s, clearly derived from sources beyond smoking itself: amid the uncertainties of life associated with the end of the cold war and painful economic adjustments, the nation needed an unambiguous test of character, with reviled deviants available to highlight the majority's virtue.

Conclusions

Regulation of the body and physical impulses, aside from sexuality, played a distinctive role in twentieth-century patterns of self-control, standing out from other control campaigns in several respects. Unusual rigor and solemnity highlighted the importance of body discipline in fighting other areas of indulgence, with health the demonstration of good character. Physical discipline reflected some of the same pattern of trade-offs visible in other areas of self-control. Posture yielded to an insistence on slenderness, and dieting may have eased in part because of the new attack on smoking. Yet the general trend toward strict standards of body management and presentation was clear. Furthermore, except again for some aspects of sexuality that the insistence on physical discipline helped counterbalance, there were no compensatory outlets. Americans told to keep their emotions in check could at least enjoy representations on television or in sports. Not so for health and body. Only humor—the fun poked at fat people—might release the tension somewhat. Overall, the moralism attached to physical controls was serious. This partly reflected the conviction that health should be preserved at (almost) all costs, and it partly reflected the sense that health itself, along with proper physical comportment, had become a moral symbol, a demonstration of discipline amid affluence.

Addiction and Disease

Earlier arguments about body discipline and even sexuality concentrated on the American tendency toward moralism in converting issues that could be defined as problems of health or beauty or even efficiency into larger challenges to character. This penchant has never precluded a quest for shortcuts—even beliefs in dieting as moral demonstration, for example, can yield to hopes that this pill or that cream or the other recipe will do the trick with no exertion of character at all. The argument is not that Americans do not seek such escape hatches but that they do it less often than some other people—in the diet field less often than the French, for example—and that they often combine the search for an easy solution with an odd reversion to a moralistic component. This pattern is clearly revealed in arguments about addiction and related disease explanations for character flaws. Americans have long been fascinated with explanations for loss of control, adopted for a society that no longer believes in Satan's minions, precisely because control looms so large in their personal and cultural lives. For the same reasons, Americans cannot agree that explanations displace responsibility. This dilemma arose in the nineteenth century but intensified as part of the twentieth-century quest for discipline, thereby intertwining continuity and enhanced needs.

New categories of mental disorder have proliferated in the twentieth century. During the past fifty years, American psychiatrists have nearly tripled the disease entries in their standard reference compendium. This pattern reflects professional self-interests (therapy for nervous complaints was a key component in the rise of private practice), new research discoveries, and possibly some new, or newly intense, human ailments. In many cases, it also shows a need to soften an inability to live up to modern standards with a designation as illness—beyond the individual's control. The recent research for genes that help explain not only why some people are schizophrenic but also why some are slightly obsessive compulsive enhances the use of disease as an escape hatch. This chapter focuses on addiction and a few related, popular disease-excuses such as nervous breakdown to show how they relate to the considerable demands that twentieth-century institutions and prescriptions place on self-control and to show how a strong moral overtone shines through, qualifying the diseases' service as rational excuses.

Definitions of addiction and other quasi diseases originated in the late eighteenth and early nineteenth centuries, explaining certain behaviors that, in some individuals, exceeded the capacities of the human will. The definitions focused on impulse control above all.[1] The expansion of medical and psychiatric research and expert commentary in the twentieth century enlarged the range of behaviors that addictions might explain while greatly extending popular awareness. Addiction thus linked Victorian and twentieth-century approaches to self-control, confirming the close if complex relationship between the two modern eras in American culture. This linkage centered on a common need to explain unacceptable behavior in nonreligious terms amid demanding disciplinary standards. At the same time, addiction's service increased in the twentieth century because of the growing contrasts between leisure and fantasy life, on the one hand, and standard norms, on the other; the concept explained why some individuals failed to draw the appropriate compensatory lines. A variety of medical experts promoted and benefited from this intensification.[2]

The concept served multiple functions. On the surface, in the nineteenth and twentieth centuries alike, the concept of addiction mitigated the pressure for self-restraint, by arguing that some people simply could not meet the basic goals. Addiction, supplemented by arguments concerning genetic flaws and new types of mental disorder, could excuse, and it could also justify regulation in place of personal discipline. This was one reason that Americans seemed so fascinated with addiction and related concepts that could rid them of the tremendous burden of personal responsibility if they failed to measure up or even worried about failure. Indeed, even though addiction research was by no means an

American monopoly, both the initial scientific idea and its popularization had particularly deep roots in the United States, precisely because
of the preoccupation with self-control as a moral imperative. The idea
of a legitimate escape—a fault-free explanation—had obvious appeal, to
some extent replacing older, now discredited notions of original sin.
Related concepts in the twentieth century, including genetic explanations and certain kinds of references to amorphous mental disorders,
attracted particularly widespread American commentary on the same
basis.

From its origins also, the addiction concept formed a complex relationship with medicine itself. Doctors defined addictive diseases, provided data, and discussed cures, a process that continues to the present
(though recently addictions have been touted by nonmedical professionals who see advantage in hopping on the bandwagon). But against the
most common modern trends, addiction concerns were also periodically
partly "demedicalized," removed from a strict disease category and converted to moral responsibility in cause and cure alike.[3]

The addiction concept illustrated and sometimes even strengthened
self-control goals—again resembling the uses of original sin, which encouraged rather than discouraged moral injunctions concerning individual behavior. Discipline, though in principle contradictory to the idea of
addiction, was promoted in two senses. First, addiction as an explanatory
safety valve demonstrated the power of the norms applied to standard
behavior. Here, more frequent twentieth-century references reflected not
only the need to account for greater temptations—in gambling, for
example—but also the rigor of expectations leveled at the nonaddicted,
obliged to control their impulses. Addiction helped focus moral outrage
about excessive behavior and marked the fear of loss of control, often
leading to appeals for regulation but also reminding the nonaddicted of
the perils they were courting. Second, addiction rarely in fact excused
the afflicted from regaining control over their wills. A host of programs
were established, especially after the 1930s, to conquer addiction through
assisted discipline. Experts themselves treated addictions inconsistently,
arguing that diseases that by definition prevented control could be mastered by a combination of reasserted virtue and medical help. Rather than
excusing, addiction might merely increase the overall challenge.

The American Origins and Popularity of Addiction

The idea of addiction is a relatively modern one, at least in Western society. Several medical historians have already noted that the concept originated because of cultural necessity, not scientific discovery. The concept was first propounded by American doctors like Benjamin Rush, right before 1800. Its United States origins are revealing, for the nation was not at the time a hotbed of medical research or innovation—which helps confirm that the idea stemmed at least in part from a new kind of values dilemma.

Addiction was initially explored in relation to excessive drinking. Colonial Americans had worried periodically about heavy drinking and drunks—Cotton Mather fulminated against drunkards in 1673—but did not arrive at any special conclusions. Efforts to regulate, through limits on tavern time and public punishments for drunkards, did not significantly alleviate the problem. Some commentators emphasized "love" or "affection" for drink rather than overpowering compulsions, although a few ministers in the eighteenth century publicly wondered whether some drunkards had lost their ability to control their urges. Generally, moralists saw excessive drinking as a choice, albeit a sinful one, that some individuals made, not a diseased condition beyond the control of will; and many Americans did not even see the issue as a problem or a sin.

The earliest suggestion that total abstention was necessary to deal with drinking appeared in a pamphlet written in 1774 by Quaker Anthony Benezet. The idea reappeared in American temperance movements after the mid-nineteenth century. At the time, a few doctors first picked up the charge, for three reasons. First, they believed they had observed cases in which individuals could not control themselves. Although it was not clear that the level of drinking was growing, the alcoholic content of some beverages did increase with new manufacturing methods. Second, doctors were responding to professional advantage: it was useful to see problem drinking as a matter requiring physicians' attention. Finally, with the gradual but measurable decline of active Protestant beliefs in hellfire and original sin, more specific ideas about self-control were welcomed, and generalized explanations for bad behavior were dismissed. This was a context in which drinking seemed to be a greater problem than it had been before, whether or not it had actually increased, and in which the need to account for an inability to restrain the appetite grew noticeably.[4]

Benjamin Rush argued that drunkenness was a disease, not simply the enjoyment of alcohol. He believed it occurred at intervals, like other diseases, and increased in frequency, leading to a progressive inability to stop. His ideas fueled the temperance movement, even though his solution was not temperance but, rather, the medical institutionalization of drunkards into houses of sobriety where they could not drink at all. Thinking of this sort led to comments by former drinkers themselves, beginning in 1795, claiming an inability to control themselves. This obviously was a push for abstention as the only solution, although it also suggested that heroic self-discipline could in fact overcome the disease so that abstention might be possible. Various temperance movements in the nineteenth century, including the Washingtonians, sounded the same themes: drunkards operated under alcohol-induced compulsions, but they could be cured. In fact, a clear if not always explicit rift developed in reformist thinking, often in the same reformer. On the one hand, drinkers might be ill, requiring outside help to cure their affliction—in which case they were to be pitied, for they were victims of forces beyond their control. On the other hand, drinkers were immoral, dangers to themselves and others because of their shocking failure of self-control.

Some advocates tried to square the circle by arguing that serious drunks were blameless because they had no means of restraining their urges, whereas moderate drinkers were the guilty parties because they defied their own capacity for moral behavior. In fact, it was difficult not to blame the drunkard, and as a result, the disease concept—which could motivate efforts to ban drink altogether—commonly coexisted with the attributions of guilt and blame and has defined the ambiguity associated with the addiction concept ever since. The ambiguity was reinforced by middle-class social views: although the fear of middle-class drunks—of oneself or one's own potential for degeneracy—was quite real, most attacks on the problem were directed toward working-class and immigrant males, who were simultaneously seen as inferior (hence possibly victims of unrestrained appetite) and dangerously immoral (hence responsible for their acts and the punishments or degradations that they incurred).[5]

Ideas of addiction gained new attention and more publicity in the later nineteenth century as temperance efforts surged forward and medical research progressed. The National Temperance Society in 1873 repeated the central dilemma of the addiction concept: "The Temperance press has always regarded drunkenness as a sin and a disease—a sin first, then a disease." To deal with the disease, "well-appointed asylums" were needed for victims until "the disease and morbid appetite are effectually removed." And of course, the sale of liquor should be outlawed. In fact, however, the movement supported few efforts to set up asylums, believing that voluntary efforts and moral guidance should suffice. Their reluctance stemmed partly from expense and even more from the desire to highlight the need for legal attacks on all drinking, but it also reflected the continued commitment to personal fault, even sin, as the underlying culprit to be addressed through personal discipline. The growing number of attacks on drunkards as threats to their families and society at large enhanced the moral component of addiction claims, however illogical in principle. Temperance arguments became prime examples of an American insistence on self-control now removed from an explicitly religious framework. In this context, addiction might be an illness, but it was really a moral disease, not a result of uncontrollable external forces like physical disease.

The popularized commentary added another, equally ambiguous reason for attention to addiction, as it helped explain the ongoing, even increasing, problems with self-control amid general beliefs in social progress. An article in *Popular Science Monthly* in 1884 made this point in arguing against a purely moralistic approach to drunkenness. "If it were a moral disorder, it would diminish with the growth of morality and intelligence, but, not withstanding the advance in these directions, it is rapidly increasing." Purely hortatory strictures or punishments would not suffice, any more than punishing insanity used to do. Heredity was often involved—the principle was "well established." "Mental shock" might also play a role in uncontrollable drinking, although the phenomenon was admittedly unclear. Medical care and institutionalization were needed, but personal discipline remained essential during treatment and afterward, when people have "so far recovered as to be able to become good citizens and self-supporting."[6]

To some scientific researchers, the addiction concept was less problematic. The British Society for the Study of Addiction, established in 1884, made it clear that its first goal was to escape pervasive moralism and treat problems like alcoholism as diseases, allowing government and the medical profession to take the lead in recommending appropriate measures and remedies. Regarding alcoholism as hereditary—through what mechanism, however, remained unclear—encouraged this scientific approach. But even aside from the possible distortions stemming from professional self-interest, two related uncertainties persisted. First, was addiction a result of the substance—the qualities in alcohol itself— or of individual psychology? Alternatively, a combination might be involved, but the point is important and has not yet been resolved. A 1968 study unwittingly, but clearly, framed the problem concerning alcohol: "Alcoholic psychoses are psychoses caused by poisoning with alcohol. When a pre-existing psychotic, psychoneurotic or other disorder is aggravated by modest alcohol intake, the underlying condition, not the psychosis, is diagnosed." Second, was remediation possible, and if so, would it require self-control? Here, the psychological approach might both encourage and discourage optimism, as opposed to concentrating on the addictive qualities of a substance itself. The addiction researchers believed that some outside help was necessary, including appropriate medical attention. But they also contended that even hereditary addiction could respond to treatment, which would in turn restore the capacity for self-restraint which then had to be exercised to avoid a relapse. Though not inconsistent, this approach could maintain, at least in the public mind, the association of addiction with fault (even psychological fault) and with an avoidable lack of control that could be restored through intervention.[7]

Some research claims remained vague about the concept itself, apart from remediation. A German physician was the first, in 1877, to describe narcotic addiction in detail. He viewed addiction as a human passion, such as "smoking, gambling, greediness for profit, sexual excesses, etc." It was, in sum, a morbid habit or vice and might be widely applied beyond particular substances. The addiction concept thus described a substantial problem, but one that a proper individual should be able to control.[8]

Both scientific and popular ideas of addiction received a boost from the growing concern about drug use that began in the 1890s and accelerated after 1920. Here, too, were anomalies: previously, massive, middle-class opiate use had passed unnoticed, which ensured that an addiction model had to be invented rather than based on new behavior and new data. Indeed, the actual problem of drug addiction had begun to retreat once national and state legislation banned opiates without prescription and also moved against other forms of drug use. To be sure, concern about some new drugs, such as heroin, added an important empirical ingredient. But the principal reasons for extending the addiction model at this point seemed to flow from the larger process of medicalization, by which doctors claimed the right to define and deal with issues previously left untended, and from the larger symbolic utility of the addiction concept in an age of growing demands on self-control and also important redefinitions. A number of scholars have pointed out that despite widespread public beliefs, the addiction model does not apply to all drugs and does not explain the differences in withdrawal difficulties. Some drugs, like cocaine, long viewed as nonaddictive, were finally reclassified under the addiction model to add to the opprobrium and danger attached to their use.[9]

The final ingredient in installing addiction in popular consciousness came with the repeal of Prohibition and its symbolic consequences. Mainstream Americans now approved of drinking, and judged (overhastily) that Prohibition had failed. The reintroduction and dissemination of the nineteenth-century idea of addiction in the 1930s served three purposes in this context. First, most people could (and should) be able to control their drinking; abstention was a concept that applied only to the addictive minority. This was part of the revulsion against Prohibition's regulatory excess. Second, the concept helped focus moral anxieties about ending Prohibition by calling attention to an undeniable problem of self-control affecting at least some people. Here the ambiguities of the whole idea surfaced: if addiction reflected a prior personality disorder or a physical defect that simply seized on excessive drinking as an outlet or that was atypically vulnerable to the substance involved, then the addiction-free majority could go about its business. But if the problem was in the substance itself, then everyone must be wary. This led to addiction's third contribution: without requiring the condemnation of drinking, which was now unfashionable, it facilitated continued moral anxiety and widespread discussion—in effect, reminding many people that wariness was still essential lest addiction ensue, in a fashion that would reflect personal fault. As we will see, this complex rendering of alcohol addiction in a situation in which extensive regulation was no longer possible yielded an important therapy as cravings generated a new approach to remediation.

The largest consequence of the newly fearful response to drugs and the renewed attention to alcohol, along with the attendant popularization of the addiction model, was the growing reliance on addiction to explain a wide range of human behaviors. This was true whether the problem lay in substance or in psychology, although with drugs, the balance shifted more toward a psychological premise: "Drug addiction is usually symptomatic of a personality disorder," the American Psychiatric Association stated in 1952. As one observer, looking at the concept's reach by the 1970s, put the case: "Now, as much or more than ever, the science of addictionology has become a political, economic and religious tool" rooted in its professional utility but, even more, in its complex place amid pervasive demands for self-control in a consumer society. Addiction was an ideal instrument to remind people of their disciplinary needs, to supplement but also highlight individual effort, amid increasing temptation.[10]

The Gambling Addiction

Nothing illustrates the extension of addiction arguments better than the idea of a gambling addiction, first broached in the late nineteenth century as the concept spread from alcohol to drugs and beyond, but seriously discussed only after the 1930s. When addiction was seen as primarily reflecting a personal deficiency or disorder, rather than the qualities of a substance, its outreach inevitably widened. Twentieth-century experts thus increasingly opted for a definition "in terms of an unnatural drive towards the specific pleasure seeking goal"—with a growing range of "pleasure-giving activities."[11]

Gambling both resembled and differed from drink and drugs. The resemblance came from timing: as with open alcohol use, middle-class gambling expanded by the 1930s as regulations were dismantled. It remained easier for some groups to disapprove of gambling on conventional moral grounds than was the case for drink, but clearly the practice was gaining both popularity and respectability. In this sense, addiction, allowing warning and criticism without frontal assault, easily fit into the post-Prohibition climate. But gambling was not a substance and could not be regarded as inducing an incapacitating dependence because of inherent chemical properties. This fact—already suggested in nineteenth-century commentary on the subject—pushed this addiction category closer to the psychological side: something must be wrong with the makeup of the afflicted individuals. Addiction also incorporated the moral connotations of the concept: people who lost control must regain it, and their problem, though perhaps a disease in one sense, reflected badly on their disciplinary qualities.

The idea of addictive gambling developed in popular journalistic discourse before it became accepted by professionals. References during the 1930s began extending the basic idea, although not always through the explicit use of the term *addiction*. In 1938, a cautionary article in *Parents' Magazine* warned parents to teach their children about both the evils and the pervasiveness of gambling: "Some people are so weak that they keep on spending more and more money in the hope of winning, so that the whole family suffers because of the losses: . . . it cheapens the reputation of the community and invites many undesirable individuals into the village." By the early 1950s, references to addiction had become commonplace in the news media, usually in association with more diffuse moral condemnations, although the implications of addiction could also limit moral strictures. A 1957 article offered a questionnaire to identify "sick gamblers." *Newsweek* asked, "Is the weekend plunger a potential addict? Psychologists contend that the line between compulsive gambling and the recreational variety is rarely crossed unless a psychological problem already exists."[12]

By the 1960s, the recognition of compulsive gambling had entered common public discourse, but the concept was not formally recognized by the scientific community until 1980, when the American Psychiatric Association (APA) first fully described the symptoms. "The essential features are a chronic and progressive failure to resist impulses to gamble and gambling behavior that compromises, disrupts or damages personal, family or vocational pursuits. . . . Commonly these individuals have the attitude that money causes and is also the solution to all their problems." The disease often led to not only loss of family but also loss of job (because of absences and overspending) and even outright crime as a means of obtaining money. As adolescents, addicts disproportionately suffered a loss of parent or poor parental discipline plus exposure to gambling activities. The category was clearly clinical, but traditional moral factors easily entered. Thus addicts lacked the ability to budget or save, lapses in crucial self-control that Victorians could easily have recognized. Other disease symptoms were less obvious, although some addicts alternated between overconfidence and depression and might indicate suicidal impulses. Mostly, however, they got into trouble because of gambling.[13]

A later edition of the APA's *Diagnostic and Statistical Manual of Mental Disorders* changed the definition of addition somewhat, although the core issues remained. The changes may have reflected additional research and therapeutic experience, but moving the concept away from the damage done and toward personal characteristics increased both the moralistic and the purely psychological content. Furthermore, the shifting definitions confirmed the ambiguity of the subject: the experts might be right that disease was involved, but there was no question that it was hard to pin down, which in turn left space for independent cultural factors to be considered. Most crucially, expert wisdom replaced preoccupation with money as the leading symptom, with a desire for "action" (an "aroused euphoric state") that generated a constant quest for excitement in which money was actually secondary. Symptoms continued to include damage to family and possible crime but now were headed by being "preoccupied with gambling (e.g., preoccupied with reliving past gambling experiences, handicapping or planning the next venture, or thinking of ways to get money with which to gamble)."[14]

Expert evaluation remained closely intertwined with popular imagery. Story after story in the media told of people unable to control themselves, ruining careers and families in the process. Former football star Art Schlichter described his plunge. Otherwise "competitive, bright, charismatic," underneath he suffered from "loneliness and low self-esteem." He got hooked early, eventually losing his professional sports career and serving jail time for gambling-induced felonies. He was ultimately treated by a gambling-specialist doctor who tested him and found he was sick. Schlichter's response: " 'I'm so happy this is a disease. I thought I was just a bozo.' He [the doctor] told me: 'We can treat this. There's hope.' " When he was institutionalized, Schlichter began a cure that failed when his addiction caught up with him again; only jail time finally jolted him from his "fantasy world." As actual rates of gambling rapidly increased as part of America's consumerist leisure, articles on addiction became part of the moral response, describing a problem without usually sorting out what part disease played in the impressive numerical expansion of gambling outlays. This indeed was a classic self-control dilemma in the consumer age, even though neither the basic interest nor the moral critique was new. The addiction concept, loosely poised between excuses for lack of control and injunctions to take one's life in hand, uncomfortably bridged the divide between escapism and the quest for discipline.[15]

The gambling addiction literature was characteristic of twentieth-century responses when outright reproach seemed repressive but some discipline clearly had to be imposed. First, the problem was described in horrendous terms as a cancer on American society. Conventional wisdom argued that most addicts were hooked in adolescence before they had established rational controls: "Some experts believe problem gambling has become the fastest-growing teen addiction. . . . 'We will face in the next decade or so more problems with youth gambling than we'll face with drug use,' says the director of the Harvard Medical School Center for Addiction Studies."[16] Beyond the vulnerable youth argument, attacks on gambling addiction sought to expand the range of consequences. A rising crime rate was thought to follow from the surge in gambling (even though by the early 1990s, property crime rates were rapidly plunging). The scope of reputed crimes rose as well, particularly including domestic violence. Semirespectable behavior like stock trading was linked to gambling, with the same potential for debilitating addiction. Addiction rates were steadily inflated, with little support for the calculations. A widely cited 1977 figure contended that about 0.8 percent of the population was at least potentially addictive. By 1980 the rate had risen to 1 to 3 percent, which remained the estimate of the American Psychiatric Association. But popular articles were soon citing 6 percent ("and the percentage is higher among the teens") and stated that 10 percent of those who gambled at all would succumb. The spread of gambling sites obviously created more opportunities for addictive behavior, but popular claims were rarely based on specific findings, only vaguely attributed expert estimates.[17]

Finally, popularized treatments offered questionnaires that invited readers to identify their own symptoms, from clearly compulsive traits to habits less definitively associated with problem behaviors, the goal being moral self-scrutiny and firmer self-control, even though technically the disease label might seem to make remediation difficult. Thus, in addition to asking about types and frequency of gambling and problems such as loss of time at work or crime, typical self-help assessments asked readers: "Do people criticize your gambling habits? Do you ever feel guilty about gambling? Can you stop gambling if you want to? Was your childhood home troubled, with a parent who drank, gambled, or was abusive? Was lack of money a frequent topic of family discussion when you were young? Do you exhibit other signs of addictive, compulsive behavior, heavy drinking, drugs, extramarital sex, and the like? Do you sometimes trade or invest not because there is a sound reason for doing so but simply to elevate your mood? Do you often . . . exaggerate about how much money you have invested?" Clearly, in a society morally uncertain about gambling, with many ambivalent recreational gamers, a positive response might be far more common than an outright addiction, especially when other borderline behaviors were cited as codefendants. This reaction was, in a sense, the main point, when invocations of discipline outweighed any effort at diagnostic precision.[18]

This new preoccupation with addictive gambling had a predictable result: the growth of therapeutic services designed to help victims escape their affliction and the emergence of new attempts to regulate gambling opportunities in the name of preventing disease. Various professionals and professional groups offered assistance. Gamblers Anonymous was created in imitation of Alcoholics Anonymous. Efforts to attack gambling by law, though facing uphill battles against commercial interests and the governmental stake in lottery and casino proceeds, increased as well, and in 1994 a number of local citizen groups created the National Coalition Against Legalized Gambling, in a return to the late-Victorian approach to the issue.

The emergence and growth of the concept of addictive gambling responded to real issues and many personal agonies. The disease focus underwrote attempts to invoke legal remedies as the recollection of the fate of Prohibition faded and the notion of government controls over aberrant personal behavior revived. The concept also helped individuals see a way out of their dilemma, if only by insisting that outside help was both available and necessary. But as critics pointed out, there was also a self-fulfilling aspect to this and other emphases on addiction: some people were probably addicts only because the concept was culturally available. From a social standpoint, the concept stimulated concern but also revulsion, careful inquiry but also moral bombardment.[19]

Sexual Addiction

Given the concern about sex and the changes in sexual imagery and behavior, it was not surprising that addiction concepts were finally applied here, too, although with some additional complexities. Concern about compulsive sex predated ideas about addiction. In the later eighteenth century, attempts to explain nymphomania—extensive, presumably uncontrollable, sex drives in women—came when the cultural framework for female sexuality was shifting from being animal-like to naturally restrained. A French authority argued that women's yielding to sex drives was caused by physical irregularities—a "motion of the fibers in the internal parts of woman." Even here, comments about how these innate urges could be enhanced by wine, chocolate, and other hedonistic spurs complicated the issue, but the focus was on explaining a gross aberration, not concentrating on either treatment or control.

This kind of argument, seeking to explain sexual depravity through some largely innate urge, continued into the early twentieth century, bypassing the addiction approach. Then, for several decades, medical and popular commentary was further diverted from a straightforward addiction approach by the work of sex researchers like Krafft Ebbing and Freud and by growing anxieties about the deterioration of sexual standards. Krafft Ebbing proposed a disease approach to sexual excess, citing the need for surgery, medicine, or hypnosis, but was pessimistic about their success. Freud tended to explain sexual compulsions (including homosexuality, often discussed in the same terms as an excessive sex drive) as resulting from the distorted handling of natural childhood sexuality, leading to a failure to mature properly. The result might be alleviated by psychotherapy, and a disease model could certainly be applied, but the focus remained more on diagnosis than on remediation. Then in the 1920s and 1930s, experts and lay audiences alike began using the term *nymphomania* to explain female sexual voraciousness and particularly prostitution, which was often taken out of the social causation category and labeled as individual psychosis. Concerns about women's behavior in a time of change prompted a combination of public (particularly male) lust and disgust at the presumed qualities of the nymphomaniac, whose impulses seemed uncontrollable. As an *Esquire* article put it, "Again and again psychiatrists repeat that, no more than the kleptomaniac steals for love of stealing . . . does the nymphomaniac go to bed with you, me, and the elevator boy because she loves sex. . . . Instead of having a healthy attitude toward the sexual act, she is obsessed by it." And yet, so the article contended, doctors did not know what deep mental problems pushed toward this behavior; all they knew was that it was sick. Nymphomania thus continued to convey disapproval of sexually aberrant women using moral condemnation and the attendant titillation to explain embarrassing social phenomena such as prostitution and also less controversial issues such as married women who committed adultery or simply surpassed their husbands in sexual appetite. The catchall utility of the concept therefore detracted from a more standard addiction approach, despite shared components.[20]

In the 1960s and 1970s, medical professionals started to link these earlier approaches to nymphomania to a somewhat more subtle addiction model. Doctors began to discuss sexual obsessions, sometimes inventing terms like *hedonomania*. Links with earlier ideas continued the gender bias, however, with one account joining sexual excess to feminism and women's other revolts against conventional behavior. But men now came in for comment as well. A 1966 study focused on the male equivalent, satyriasis, arguing that female nymphomania, although a problem, was more purely physiological (and so less treatable) and that women were more likely to acknowledge their problem. In contrast, male excess could be treated because it resulted from "serious defects in character structure" despite a culturally determined male pride in the sex drive and the resulting unwillingness to admit to any difficulties.

The big shift, implied in the satyriasis study, was toward remediation, including new appeals to character along with invocations of individual and group therapy and, sometimes, supportive medication. Several authorities decried sex without love, describing in almost nineteenth-century terms (again, addiction concepts helped rescue many Victorian values) the spiritual, altruistic qualities of true affection. According to this view, sexual compulsion resulted from a spiritual breakdown, a "deterioration of human values and of our commitment to help others." But by the same token, it could be addressed, beginning by admitting to the problem and seeking help, leading to a rational attempt to shift beliefs. Sexual compulsion was a disease, in that it afflicted individuals who could not regulate themselves because of a combination of environmental and genetic factors, but these people could, indeed must, participate in their cure, which was designed to restore "self-regulation." In this new argument, addiction differed from the older nymphomania and satyriasis in that the latter were typically sudden in onset, whereas addiction was chronic but more closely intertwined with remediable aspects of character. Women thus could now be helped to build up their confidence and their capacity for restraint; persistent deviants were "simply not willing to do so," despite their psychological capacity. Rational training, sometimes repeated, could teach sufferers how to live a "saner existence." The older authorities, who had despaired of recovery through discipline, were wrong.[21]

By the 1970s, this transition was accompanied by appeals from potential patients for recognition of the addiction model. That is, troubled individuals wanted to see themselves as addicts. Greater sexual permissiveness revealed more instances of apparent compulsion and more anxiety about personal behavior, whether compulsive or not. The addiction concept, with its mixture of character references and assistance, seemed ideal in this context

The result, by the 1980s, was an array of sexual addiction messages. Sexual excess stemmed from poor personal values, including low self-esteem. It resulted from the same causes as other additions: the choice of sex was not in itself significant. The consequence might be disease in the sense that outside assistance was required—debate about the disease entity continued here as in other addiction categories—but individual capacity for reform was essential. Addicts must "accept responsibility for their actions and expect fair treatment from others," learning "the effect of their behavior on others" and understanding, like the Victorians before them, that real love was "unselfish, spontaneous, and healthy."[22]

By this point, sex had joined other behaviors in the commitment to the addiction model to explain and treat deviance. Lingering efforts to distinguish additional categories, such as nymphomania, continued, but on the whole, given the widespread approval of sex in principle, the phenomenon was not as frequently discussed as were addictions like gambling. When President Bill Clinton encountered a new barrage of sexual accusations in 1998, expert and armchair diagnosticians alike were ready to jump in with a claim of addiction. And true to the model, they offered a diagnosis, a suggestion that special help might be required, and a serious criticism of character. The president might need professional support to escape his presumed compulsion, but if he had had true self-discipline, he would have avoided the compulsion in the first place. Like other addicts, he was sick and not sick, blameless and deeply blamable.

Therapy for Addiction

The ambivalence of the addiction concept enabled a growing array of addictions to be identified, and after the 1950s, a variety of drug treatments and therapies were introduced, at great annual cost.[23] But the most striking initiative was lay-group therapy, as it demonstrated both the belief that addiction surpassed the individual capacity for control and the insistence that individuals, with group guidance and encouragement but mainly through their own resources, rediscover their capacity for personal discipline whose demands were all the greater in that a tragic vulnerability had been demonstrated. Many other therapies, as well as the larger public sentiment, shared this dualism despite important differences in specific treatments or attitudes. Alcoholism and other addictions might be diseases, but only faulty people succumbed, and they must learn, once punished by hardships in life, to rise above their faults. The scenario read like a classic Victorian morality play, with errant men redeemed through higher values and their own belated return to moral grace. The approach could work, but its success demonstrated the power of the cultural model.

Alcoholics Anonymous (AA) was launched in 1935, in Akron, Ohio, by a physician and a stockbroker with severe drinking problems. The incidence of drinking was rising in the wake of Prohibition, but systematic discussion of the problem was restricted by the failure of the regulatory effort. Individuals were on their own—indeed, it was not until the 1970s that government agencies and professional medical groups resumed systematic research and preventive advice, although academic study by groups such as the Yale University Center of Alcohol Studies had begun in the late 1930s. The AA founders, William Wilson and Dr. Robert Smith, had concluded from their own experience and from the revived availability of the addiction model that they were powerless in the face of alcohol, as were all alcoholics. They therefore carried a message of mutual support and self-help to other alcoholics, and the resulting network of local groups took the formal AA name in 1939.[24]

The organization was nonsectarian but permeated by the kind of diffuse religiosity that informed many other American efforts toward self-control. Members had to admit their powerlessness and lack of control over their lives. They then proceeded in successive steps to acknowledge the damage they had done and to apologize while recognizing their need for help from a higher power. Sustained by this belief and by active fellowship with other members, they could then regain control and pursue a life of sobriety while assisting sufferers in earlier stages of remediation. Even though addiction was not explicitly mentioned, the invocations of powerlessness and constant reminders that no one was ever cured echoed the definition. Pamphlets drew comparisons with diabetes, suggesting a disease that requried restraint in consumption. The AA treatment translated the ensuing ambivalence into a strikingly successful program. The result, assuming success, was the restoration of a person's ability to control the temptation of drink as part of a lifelong battle that, admittedly, ordinary people did not have to fight. Disease and discipline were ironically but often successfully combined.

In keeping with the augmented self-control approach, purists in the group resisted additional assistance from professional psychiatrists or supportive drugs such as antidepressants, although in fact, many individual alcoholics did combine these approaches.[25]

By the 1970s, more than half a million Americans had joined the AA, and allied family support groups had formed as well. The concept spread to drug addicts and gamblers and provided one of the key approaches to control overweight people's eating. Several sexual addiction groups were organized as part of the 1970s reaction to excess, all using the AA's twelve-step model. Sex and Love Addicts Anonymous and Sexual Addicts Anonymous provided collective and higher-power support for self-control within a range of normal sexual outlets, whereas Sexaholics Anonymous, closer to the AA model, permitted no sexual activity outside marriage. Experts lauded the disease therapy while admitting they did not fully understand how it worked. But even though doctors supported the removal of stigma, many recovering alcoholics, and those who dealt with them, valued the commitment to reparation and moral anxiety, plus the vow of lifetime control.[26]

This belief in the power of mental disorders and unconscious processes, along with the often related exploration of hereditary disorders, beginning in the late nineteenth century, dampened Victorian confidence in personal responsibility. Some historians have argued that this change was a fatal blow to the commitment to human willpower. However, the development of the addiction concept and the resulting therapeutic approaches confirm the importance of these innovations in American thinking as well as professional treatment but counter the idea of a sea change. As commonly understood, addiction allowed for forces beyond the self while insisting that control could be regained, provided that additional, often quite informal, assistance facilitated the transition. With a bit of help, or sometimes none at all except for a personal realization of the threat to life or success, addicts could rationally redirect their own lives. The biggest change, therefore, was the awareness that the moral battle was long term, not a simple facing down of some brief temptation. Victorians might have been embarrassed by the group confessions used in the most widely publicized approaches, but they would have understood the goal of reasserting character.

An Addiction to Stress?

The ambiguities in the addiction categories extended to other challenges to character by the late nineteenth century. Indeed, the popular understanding of mental illness continued to reflect an uncertain commitment to the idea of disease. The subtext here was that the mentally troubled were not really sick but could pull themselves together without the same dependence on a professional apparatus that a "real" physical disease required. Conflicts among treatments and the vagueness of connections between therapy and results reinforced the separation between mental and physical disease, but assumptions about the availability of self-discipline helped explain why both health policies and public attitudes kept mental health issues distinct from their physical counterparts, and less worthy of funded support.

An important cluster of concerns, widely discussed but on the borderline even of mental disease, entailed people's reactions to stress and its attendant nervous disorders. The concept of neurasthenia was developed in the final decades of the nineteenth century for people with a variety of physical symptoms that were caused by the pressures of daily existence on the nervous system. The idea was widely publicized and led to a variety of treatments, and it also bolstered the emerging psychiatric profession by furnishing clients in addition to the conventionally (often hopelessly) mentally ill.

The idea of neurasthenia was powerful but inherently fuzzy. Experts pointed to potentially contradictory situations that could lead to neurasthenia. Overworked businessmen formed one category, the most obvious; underworked, excessively idle, and self-indulgent middle-class housewives formed another; dissolute male workers a third; and overstressed, often abused working-class wives yet a fourth. Both work and the lack of it could produce nervous collapse, and the resulting gendering was complex.

Most important was the related disagreement about whether the causes of suffering resulted from forces beyond the individual's control. Leading experts like George Beard touted the work stress approach, calling the disease "American" because of the nation's generally commendable lead in devotion to the job—the suffering minority were not to blame in this construction. Attacks on excessive schoolwork made the same point: "overstudy" was "laying the foundation of all our nervous disorders." Although treatments could help people once they fell ill, systematic solutions must come from society at large. But the fact that most people could survive strenuous work without collapse made this assessment suspect. And when idleness was involved, the responsibility quotient almost inevitably shifted. Indeed, S. Weir Mitchell's rest cure approach for neurasthenic housewives was deliberately designed to induce so much boredom that the patients would rally in desperation, regaining appropriate control over their own lives and altering habits that had created the damaging idleness in the first place. Gradual changes in terminology confirmed the importance of self-help. Using engineering models and a mechanistic view of the body, nineteenth-century commentary had often referred to "strain," implying potent external forces that distorted human capacity. The rise of more specific terms like neurasthenia and ultimately the references to stress (which began in the 1920s but became commonplace only after World War II) suggested an internal disarray that might be corrected through effort of will.[27]

The ambiguity concerning nervous incapacity was also magnified with the advent of the concept of the nervous breakdown, first identified in 1901 and gradually replacing neurasthenia in popular parlance and in some professional commentary. The new construct, with its glitzier title, was still protean, but it did represent some new trends. The first was the gap between expert diagnoses and popular concern. Although the nervous breakdown received some psychiatric backing, it flourished particularly in popularizations and self-help therapeutic advice. Second, the work component prominent in neurasthenia, though still available, declined in favor of sudden crises, role confusions, and— still—excessive idleness. In response, the most commonly afflicted now were women, with one important exception. Third, following from the first two developments, individual ability as a whole to restrain or prevent collapse became the centerpiece. Work now was the principal remedy, which expanded the range of personal opportunities for self-control through discipline, and articles like "Ways to Work out Your Own Mind Cure" became staples of widely sold periodicals like the *Reader's Digest*.[28]

Needlessly anxious housewives were frequently castigated from the

1920s through the 1950s, in a commentary that helped set the basis for the later feminist rebellion spearheaded by Betty Friedan, who turned the analysis toward a more systematic plea for active engagement outside the home. In the more conventional, prefeminist rendering, women brought their problems on themselves, even though the resulting breakdown might render them seemingly incapable of restoring normal balance. "The problem of the nervous housewife is a problem of society because she gives her mood over to her family." "No less fantastic [is] your inability to make some reasonable adjustment to your husband's personality. . . . Ask yourself whether you don't cooperate in creating the 'unendurable tension..' . . . You should add: I suffer *consciously* under these tensions, and provoke and misuse these very tensions *unconsciously.*" In 1920, one of the first full treatments of breakdown, directed at the housewife, stated quite simply that hysteria was a "personality defect." In sum, people created the conditions for their own breakdowns, which is why a minority suffered despite living patterns that most people could handle without great difficulty. The unsystematic use of the Freudian idea of the unconscious could easily renew the emphasis on responsibility, for clearly this part of the mind could be brought under control.[29]

The same approach was widely applied to the male category most clearly vulnerable to the idea of a nervous breakdown. Beginning in World War I, soldiers whose nerves collapsed under the pressure of battle were widely held to have a flawed character. In fact, many soldiers and some doctors regarded "shell shock" as a ruse to escape combat duty. In reaction, the army attempted to set higher standards of mental health during the 1920s and 1930s: "Proper psychiatric screening of the mentally unfit at induction [is] the basic solution for eliminating the psychiatric disorder of military service." Despite the resulting belief that soldiers should now be able to manage their emotions, the same traumatic symptoms emerged again in World War II. And even though the idea of genuine disease advanced during this second modern war, the belief that what was then called "battle fatigue" denoted a "less strong personality" persisted. Only after the Vietnam War were professionals consistently careful (as in APA's *Diagnostic and Statistical Manual III*) to avoid implying that post-traumatic stress disorder victims had personalities that made them especially susceptible, and even here "several studies" were cited that assigned a more important role to "preexisting psychopathological conditions."[30]

Earlier, during the heyday of the popularity of the nervous breakdown idea, which crested in the 1950s, personal responsibility predominated. Popular articles might underscore the importance of modern-day faith as both preventive and cure, a reminder of the importance also of self-control as a moral statement in American life: "Fundamental to good emotional health is a basic philosophy of faith: faith in the ability of ourselves and others to improve and grow; . . . faith in spiritual and moral values, and in the essential decency of mankind. This faith will carry us through stresses that might otherwise shatter us"—and of course, it should be available to the right-thinking person. On one page, a popularized presentation might present a disease—hysteria triggered by a frightening event, no more a person's responsibility than shell shock—and on the next page declare: "*Hysteria has no cure, but control.* Many a wise, well-poised mature woman . . . has sternly disciplined what hysterical tendencies she had, into subjection to her good judgment." Neurotics, in sum, were "capable of improving themselves." "The most important element of treatment is moral control." That is, the only solution was to rescue oneself, and those who could not simply confirmed their deficient character.[31]

Although reactions to the concept of the nervous breakdown included a call for self-control, the concept's popularity also conveyed real problems and anxieties, including some people's desire to have a quasi disease that implied a sudden collapse due to forces beyond their control. Furthermore, even though breakdown suggested internal weakness, it could also be used as exculpation and as an explanation to oneself for failing to live up to the standard disciplinary forces of twentieth-century life. Again, this notion, like the addiction model, was double edged.

The nervous breakdown idea did create the conditions for its decline, however, and only in part because the psychiatric categories for stress and depression steadily became more detailed and sophisticated. Worry about a breakdown did ultimately push people to seek professional help, including medication. Although those who subscribed to the older notion of personal responsibility shunned this approach, those who expected or experienced crisis became more open to it. At the same time, the increasing use of medications, including tranquilizers which have been widely prescribed since the 1950s, reduced the sense of crisis (although they did nothing for, and indeed may have enhanced, longer-term depression). The massive number of women entering the work world in the 1950s and 1960s cut into the most widely perceived context for nervous breakdown but created new, work-related stress categories. In addition, the professional recognition in the Vietnam conflict of unavoidable combat stress drove another nail into the older approach. The whole concept had brought out a remarkably traditional set of beliefs in work, personal ability through discipline, and, often, male superiority. Its passing, like the failure of the posture campaign, showed a further remove from rearguard action in defense of essentially Victorian values.

Yet the ambiguity of the borderline, stress-related psychiatric disorder remained, although no explicit disease revived such literal Victorianism as the nervous breakdown had. The popular critique of personality types in the 1980s, for example, although widening the range of uncontrollability, nevertheless harked back to the possibility of self-restraint. Highly stressed type A's did not have to behave as they did, even if their task of moderation was more difficult than that of type B's: vacations, exercise, and meditation all were open to those who wanted relief. As with addiction, along with professional help and group support, most people had the power to prevent, limit, and overcome. Every new concept, including the chronic fatigue syndrome of the 1990s and more popularized terms like *burnout*, brought renewed commitment to the idea that sufferers were partly copping out. As the ambiguity between disease and control continued, so did the hesitation over whether objective stress should be embraced as a demonstration of superior character or modified in the interests of good sense and balance. Scorn for groups failing to accept maximum stress in college, for example, along with the collapse of the effort to attack work addiction as both undesirable and diseased, showed the ongoing commitment to challenge as a sign of moral capacity.[32]

Addiction and Disease

The complex concepts of addiction and nervous distress were supported by scientific research credentials, but the translations of the ideas remained amazingly varied. By the late twentieth century, the range of specific meanings was wide, and the number of remedies was large as well.

One variation, not new but now more prominent, entailed the degree of helplessness manifested and therefore the suitable social response. Drugs were commonly held to be hopelessly addictive and therefore appropriately outlawed. Skeptics, however, claimed that this blanket impression defied the actual research findings, which showed that some drugs such as cocaine were not normally addictive at all. Other addictions, however, such as to substances or activities normally approved (if ambivalently) and widely engaged in, like alcohol and gambling, were seen as based almost exclusively on personal fault or psychological deficiency or both. Moral control might be invoked in all cases, but when drugs were concerned, it must apply almost entirely to prevention— "just say no," as the slogan from the 1970s went—for cure was difficult and only halfheartedly supported given widespread bias against addicts, particularly those who also were members of racial minorities.[33]

Genetic and medical research provided another complication in the late twentieth century. It is important to remember that explanations based on human helplessness had ample precedent in American culture. Original sin had given way, to be sure. But in the late nineteenth century, in another period of tension between demanding standards and clear moral failures, many Americans placed great faith in inherited traits, which some sought to regulate quite brutally for eugenic reasons, thus seeking to prevent the reproduction of populations of drunkards, sexual degenerates, or other undesirable categories. The tension between reliance on education and self-control and alternative explanations and solutions resurfaced during the 1980s—the result of new scientific research along with public interest in approaches involving less personal responsibility during another round of the clash between indulgence and stiffening standards.

The discoveries of genetic proclivities to alcoholism, obesity, or even gambling—bolstering the older but vaguer hereditary beliefs—attracted attention in the United States because they fit the addiction model but with even less attribution of fault. Furthermore, genetic explanations might hold out hopes for remedies with no need for heroic discipline. In a climate of self-control amid constant temptation from potentially addictive materials and activities, this escape would be welcome, one reason for what Europeans noted was Americans' unusual national fascination.

The expansion of medical explanations showed also in the development of new categories, or at least more rigorous and widely applicable categories, for behavior difficulties not susceptible to simple pleas for discipline. Attention deficit disorder, formally labeled in the 1970s, is a case in point. The phenomenon is distinctive in that children are the focus, which makes it easier to rely on the disease label rather than combining treatment with moral promptings—for children are too young and perhaps too sick to respond. But moralism was injected into some of the explanations directed at parents, and the phenomenon has showed striking similarities to the common utilization of addiction in other respects, with many of the same ambivalences.

Attention deficit disorder is manifested mainly by restlessness and lack of attention, particularly in school, which helps explain why its identification awaited the twentieth century with its increase in the requirements for school time and focus. The discipline expected of children was strengthened, even as some adult-sponsored requirements for careful manners on special social occasions eased. The practice of labeling diseases corresponded to changes in behavior requirements, toward longer periods of self-control. At the same time, conventional adult rewards and punishments clearly did not suffice: labeling behavior problems did not necessarily correct the behavior, and the newfound emphasis on positive reinforcement rather than coercion for children complicated the issue still further.[34]

Children who could not concentrate and whose fidgeting surpassed manageable bounds were first identified in the early part of the century. The initial statements reflected Victorian thinking, as the children might be described as having "morbid defects in moral control." By the 1920s, labeling had moved toward medicalization, with terminology such as "restlessness syndrome," and in the 1940s and 1950s, the disorder merged with disease concepts based on assumptions about "brain injury syndromes"—whether or not actual brain injury could be determined. Problems with demonstrating "true brain damage" led to refinements by the 1960s, with distinctions such as "minimal brain dysfunctions."

Then in the 1970s, the renewed focus on behavioral designations and hyperactivity led to a characterization of deficits in attention and concentration abilities, with the official label—Attention Deficit Disorder with Hyperactivity—coming from the American Psychiatric Association in 1980. What initially was a strange problem in discipline, with children incapable of orderly self-control, had become a disease. The package was completed with the introduction of drugs, notably Ritalin, which often seemed to control the behavior.[35]

Medicalization was the most prominent feature of this whole evolution, but other character components were evident as well. Throughout the development of new categories of concern (originating first in Europe and then in the United States, particularly after the 1920s), the imposition of heightened control standards on children was an integral element, as the need to overcome restlessness reached unprecedented heights. But by the 1970s, the more traditional means used to produce this result—strict physical discipline—had become unacceptable, and so new methods of remediation were needed.

With all this in place, attention deficit disorder began to acquire many of the attributes already endemic in the moral-disease conceptualization of addiction, modified only by the focus on children and the frequent delight in a pharmacopoeia itself encouraged by drug companies and harassed teachers. First, explanations and treatments began to differ, with the disease orientation not rigorous but predominant. As in other instances, the disputes resulted in part from professional differences, with medical researchers emphasizing probable endocrine disorders (such as resistance to the thyroid hormone), possibly genetically caused, and psychologists adding a more environmental, familial component. The disputes also reflected real difficulties in measuring the disease and the reluctance to depend too much on medication for what in many respects seemed a lack of appropriate parental and teacher guidance. Parental responsibility, in particular, could not be fully dismissed, even when drug treatments seemed the logical remedy for afflicted children. Teachers were urged to downplay punishment in favor of rewards like praise, smiles, and special privileges—thus building on the more general emphasis on self-esteem in American education. More parental love was important, too, along with carefully defined behavioral limits. The results of this updated moral guidance might well replace drugs, depending of course on the specific problem and on how often the disease model was being invoked.[36]

As with addiction, the discovery of this new disorder generated much media attention; no responsible parent could be unaware of the need for concern. The inevitable questionnaires encouraged lay diagnosis, and although some warned that only prolonged behavior mattered, the list might easily cause anxiety through its generalized references to "restlessness." Indeed, one candid article noted that "some experts argue that there is nothing wrong with these children, it [the behavior] is not average but normal." Although experts usually argued that 3 to 5 percent of all children suffered from the newly identified disease, other estimates raised this to 10 percent, and one popularizer guessed 5 to 30 percent. Moreover, the stated impact pushed outward, and by the 1990s, popular articles were referring to adult attention deficit disorders under catchy titles like "Why Can't Your Husband Sit Still" and with references to general symptoms such as poor organizing skills. Skeptics noted that even for children, the disorder was "in the eye of the beholder," but clearly a new disease had been devised to deal with the area between enhanced disciplinary standards and the resulting deviance.[37]

The proliferation of disease candidates amid consumerist pressures on self-control extended well beyond attention deficits. The addiction concept could be extremely flexible. References to addictive sexuality became common, particularly after President Clinton's widely publicized difficulties in 1998, although the concept's currency suffered from the difficult tension between the quest for control, on the one hand, and the desire to demonstrate modern appetite and outlook, on the other. Other mechanisms, such as the attacks on rape and sexual harassment, did the job better. But references to addictive uses of electronic games in the 1980s were not uncommon, and by the 1990s, addiction to the Internet was generating therapeutic self-help books. Attacks on obesity were permeated with references to addiction. The pressure to increase the norms of self-restraint in the final decades of the twentieth century accelerated the popularity of explanations using genetics and addiction as a means of mitigating the challenge while appealing to moral responsibility. Some journalists derided the approach as a means of escaping the consequences of bad behavior. For example, by producing certificates of attention deficit disorder, several thousand adolescents won the right to be given longer examination periods. On the whole, however, these trends of medicalization continued to bear moral freight, particularly for adults, maintaining a modified idea of fault and expanding the publicity surrounding issues of self-discipline.

Political considerations, finally, played a growing role in the addiction patterns of the century's end. As had long been the case, invocations of addiction might not only reduce personal blame but also justify formal regulation precisely because reliance on individuals was demonstrably misplaced. By the 1990s, after several decades of emphasis on individual discipline, lawyers used the possibility of tobacco-induced addiction to seek massive damages from cigarette manufacturers, and the Clinton administration found a responsive public chord in urging the formal regulation of cigarette sales at least among adolescents, because of an addictive potential that surpassed normal capacities of self-restraint. Yet the moral ambiguities remained. Most Americans did not treat smokers as victims but as badly disciplined indulgers. The regulatory crusade, so reminiscent of Prohibition, was surrounded by moral fervor, not the dispassion of dealing with a purely medical problem. As with most uses of the interface between disease and morality over the past two hundred years, nicotine addicts were sick people who should get themselves in hand or be forced into compliance by legal restrictions.[38]

At the end of the 1990s, addiction thus continued its complex service, demonstrating the demands on self-control in a consumerist, sexualized society and promoting several service professions while also focusing moral outrage and disciplinary pressures on apparent victims and anxious bystanders alike. Afflicted individuals might need some help; the United States led the world in uses of therapy and the generation of support groups. Ultimately, however, the onus returned to the individual, who must use the help to reach a higher level of personal control. Those who were successful might be praised for their achievement: the media loved stories of people who shed 150 pounds or ended two decades of ruinous gambling. But even in the most adoring accounts, there were plenty of reminders that some moral flaw had led the victims to their "disease' in the first place.

The moral component of addiction further explained the continuing shame and embarrassment of needing therapy, which most "clients" (not patients) sought to conceal. It also explained the quintessential American delight in support groups. Sufferers had to acknowledge their failings to the group, but the advice and encouragement of like-minded others were worth the cost. At the same time, the group context helped recovering victims register their own disciplinary progress. Precisely, then, because fault and self-control remained fundamental to the concept of addiction, the opportunity for confession and open commitment to the reassertion of control was a vital asset. When a latter-day sin is involved, private warriors often seek group validation.

PART IV

Conclusions and Suggestions

| TEN |

Conclusions

Americans in the twentieth century remained highly aware of the need to keep themselves under control—or at least they were told to do so—even though the changes from Victorian standards were very real, with especially dramatic relaxations in manners and recreational culture. Assumptions about the responsibility for self-discipline not only endured but often broadened. Relaxations were usually counterbalanced by new requirements, with such trade-offs predominating over any trend toward greater ease. The result redefined some of the characteristic Victorian pressure points—areas in which standards and impulses particularly clashed—but it did not remove them. If anything, the experience of living in moral tension, between canons of emotional control and injunctions to be casual, between images of violence and the need to limit aggression at work, increased steadily.

Precision increased except in the area of manners. The number of rules taught to children and enforced on adults swelled advice manuals of all sorts. Generalized character references did diminish, which might reflect lessened confidence but more clearly followed from the need to specify amid informality plus the emergence of new categories of expertise.

The adjustments that produced the twentieth-century style of self-restraint have, on the whole, reduced protective arrangements and behavior laws, placing more responsibility on the individual for knowing and following the rules. The modernist desire to escape literal Victorianism plus the apparent failure to control behavior by legal means, as with gambling and drinking, have focused more attention on internalizing both old and new norms (with the exception of the new regulatory approach to drug use). At work, where economic as well as social pressures enforce new standards, and in driving, where novel technologies require a combined approach, individual efforts have been supplemented. On balance, however, well-adjusted people learn the rules themselves—hence the emphasis on detailed monitoring in early childhood. If an individual cannot quite measure up, he or she must try to conceal the shortcoming. The American tendency to hide emotions was then added to older interests in cloaking sexual excursions in a culture that reacted strongly to the judgment of others and also valued acting.

The idea of trade-offs reflects the assumption that collectively, Americans are uncomfortable with the increase in license and permissiveness and have deliberately, if often implicitly, formed compensatory disciplinary categories. In the twentieth century, the converse also is true, and more so than in Victorian times. That is, assertions of moralism now seem too rigid, or they have been couched in liberationist terms, or they are circuitous, or they have been matched by compensatory pleasure outlets, if only through symbolic performances available to spectators.

Yet the relationship of contemporary self-control to nineteenth-century character norms remains complex, as more survived than might be expected in an age of consumerist excess and fantasy and the collapse of specific strictures such as posture. Simple historical models, such as character yielding to personality, capture only part of the truth and err in ignoring continuities. Even addiction offers as much reinforcement to moral anxiety as release, reflecting and often advancing the pressure in contemporary America to maintain personal discipline.

While continuity combined with change, two shifts concealed older character goals. First, the escapist outlets clearly defied Victorian belief in a unified approach to good behavior, uniting norms and uplifting recreations. In this regard, the twentieth-century formula differed. Second, sexuality standards were less stringent compared with, say, body discipline or new kinds of emotional control on behalf of casual interpersonal smoothness. Because Victorianism was sometimes recalled in exaggerated fashion, both changes could appear conclusive—and dreadful. But shifting disciplinary priorities away from sex did not mean a collapse of discipline—even sex was still carefully hedged, merely used less often as a basis for judgmentalism. Escapist fare did not mean a disappearance of behavioral norms—indeed, it often indirectly reflected tighter norms, for example, governing boys' fistfights—even if it meant new complexity. Victorians would have been shocked by twentieth-century spectator leisure, but they also would have been surprised by the new restraints and new sources of self-criticism, as in the moral fervor now attached to dieting. There has been no collapse of impulse control or of the need for moral demonstrations, despite the shifts in form.

More character attributes survived than surface evaluations have revealed. It is easier to find and criticize relaxations than to note continuities or new disciplinary demands, but both old and new demands remain. Consumerism and the requirements of a service economy did move people away from classic Victorian definitions toward not only new indulgences but also a new concern for self and manipulative presentations of personality. Thus the idea of deliberately courting hardship as a means of self-improvement lost favor, although it continued in the redoubled attempts at body discipline. But even though character as a central concept changed, it did not disappear. Selling the personality was only added on. Indeed, demands on character persisted particularly in the stipulations that respectable people had to learn and conform to, from emotion to sex to hygiene. A number of settings revealed the reliance on sometimes superficial indices to indicate wider disciplinary capacities, that is, to indicate character. Thus job interviewers use hygiene, body control (including posture), and manners as signals of a wider ability to keep impulses in check, and personality tests do the same. Credit ratings use evidence about sex or drink (as well as outright financial probity) in assessing relevant moral attributes. Americans who seize on obesity or smoking as signs of moral fault also are attacking— however unfairly—symbols of greater disciplinary failure. The need for passive outlets has expanded, confusing conservative critics who assume that spectatorship and behavior are one. But the same indulgences have prompted more need for demonstrations of virtue, as in the daily weight-check or the emotional attack on sexual harassment. It now is, perhaps, harder to gain confidence that one has been good than it was in the heyday of Victorian character, but the desire for demonstration has remained intense. Even the rise of other-directness saw Americans checking their guilts with peers, not sidestepping the need for discipline.

New Year's resolution making was one index of continuity. The practice seems to have begun in the early nineteenth century when newspapers offered thoughts on the new year, although not necessarily directed toward character. By the 1830s, diarists and letter writers frequently took stock of the failings of the past year, moving gradually toward a resolve to improve in the coming year ("a new year commenced with a determination to do better . . ."). Americans continued the tradition in the twentieth century, simply becoming somewhat less religious, more body conscious in the resolutions themselves, and perhaps less detailed about what they had done wrong during the past year. References to work performance failures, common in the nineteenth century, also gave way to more personal measurements of character.[1] Even a free spirit like Woody Guthrie, in the 1940s, greeted a new year with impressively traditional resolutions ranging from "cleaning bed clothes more often" to the more character-relevant "work by a schedule."

Continuity showed further in the twentieth century's maintenance of standards (new or old) that allowed the identification and labeling of class, gender, or race "others" and also sinners who overate or lost their tempers as a means of maintaining the standards and gaining a sense of one's own virtue by contrast. Here also was the source of anxiety about the "others" who could not distinguish fantasy from reality, like adolescents who committed violent acts after seeing a violent film.

In a consumer age, the most powerful disciplinary statements came when products and moralism could unite, as in personal hygiene, because the resulting standards met both consumerist and disciplinary goals, often, as with nearly compulsive personal cleanliness, serving as symbols of a wider commitment to self-control. When there was a clash, accommodations were less predictable. A search for pleasure did not always predominate, hence the moral attack on smoking and the peddlers of cigarettes. Even when indulgence increased, as in food consumption, the result was frequently worry and self-criticism, along with a quest for other symbolic disciplinary targets. Many Americans were conducting a recurrent struggle with themselves.

This chapter looks at the broader implications of the twentieth-century evolution, especially social class and democratization, child rearing, and the intensification of control demands at the century's end— all in the context of the striking persistence of American moralism.

Democratization and Diversity

In the twentieth century, standards for self-control became less exclusive than they had been for the middle class in the nineteenth century. Although vestiges remained (as in attacks on the character of welfare recipients), the Victorian division between respectable and unrespectable people also eased, in two ways. First, the middle class's greater receptivity to escapist leisure and a new valuation of sexual enjoyment reduced their disagreements with lower-class elements and their criticism of many alternative behaviors. The avoidance of judgmentalism and the openness to diversity, although most pronounced after the 1960s, altered the context for evaluating self-control. Shared consumerism produced a common repertoire of material indulgence, despite considerable differences in economic means. Second, the standards that were maintained, whether old or new, were assumed to be universals, open to everyone. The Victorian ambivalence between urging the lower classes to act morally and using morality to condemn them subsided. At schools, particularly, the norms of decorum were pressed indiscriminately.

This process of democratization also extended to gender. Although gaps remained, as in sexuality, many of them reflecting Victorian precedents, standard setters spent less time on manners and child-rearing goals that distinguished between men and women and more time on shared issues of controlling excessive emotions or maintaining clean and sleek bodies or learning to enjoy sensuality.[2]

The trend toward democratization and the embrace of diverse behaviors should not be overemphasized, however. The process is complex precisely because many standards were maintained and because the defining signals were not always easy to access, as they depended on subtle socialization and experience in the middle-class world. Criticism on the basis of past norms continued in sexuality and other areas. Disputes about gambling also divided the middle class according to diverse moral codes. The central tension between discipline and indulgence in middle-class life included a battle among taste groups subscribing to different standards.

The twentieth century witnessed some sweeping exclusions as well. The feelings against homosexuals drew a bitter boundary that had not been emphasized in the nineteenth century, and despite political efforts by gays and appeals for tolerance by liberals after the 1960s, the hostility remained.

Still more important were the ongoing if subtle effects of class and race, even as claimed membership in the middle class soared toward its post–World War II total of 85 percent. Adherence to dominant self-control norms varied widely, as access to socialization remained uneven. Despite the greater informality, it was not easy to pick up the appropriate signals about emotion management, for example. The revived interest in etiquette at the century's end reflected this difficulty, along with concerns about real or imagined increases in incivility: definite rules were easier than demanding but flexible norms that depended on long experience and a knowledge of one's audience. Moreover, some groups were not shaped by predominantly middle-class standards; their experience derived from other sources.

The most successful new norms, those that embraced the largest populations, were, again, those for which restraint and consumerism went hand in hand, producing consistent messages in schools and advertisements alike. Standards of personal hygiene thus reached a wide audience. Defiance was most notable in the deliberate unkemptness of the hippies in the 1960s, but this was an indirect demonstration of the power of core values. Otherwise, regular bathing and deodorizing became American staples, modified only by the continuing distinction between manual and office labor. Lingering beliefs still held that certain minority races smelled different or were greasy, applying strict hygiene standards to key social groups. But even this pressure reflected the wide acceptance of middle-class norms plus the awareness of the extra challenge posed by prejudice.

Other body standards, however, continued to be more variable. Minority populations, mainly African Americans and Latinos, remained, on average, considerably heavier than Americans in general. *Ebony* magazine, an upscale publication aimed at middle-class African Americans, included mainstream diet and fashion advice but also an unusual tolerance of plumper models and articles on the sexiness of larger women. Thus one article quoted a black man as saying, "The only thing a thin woman can do for me is introduce me to a woman of size." This was a subculture not so much defying white middle-class standards as operating according to different values. Black women argued they had more important issues to worry about than weight, starting with race itself. Weight also could reflect the distinctive power position and work obligations that women held in African American family economies, including the ability to set their own beauty standards rather than, as with whites, receive them from the fashion industry and male-dominated authorities. The difference was important: black adolescent women were far more confident about their bodies than were whites, far less likely to suffer from eating disorders or depression. Though less studied, Latinos also resisted mainstream middle-class constraints and worries.[3]

Some aspects of recommended self-discipline contradicted the dynamics of subgroups. While the white middle class emphasized the control of anger, by the 1950s African American movements were calling for an abandonment of traditional deference—the elaborate controls needed for dealing with white America under slavery and Reconstruction—in favor of greater assertiveness. The result opened new possibilities for rhetoric and behavior, but it complicated racial interactions, especially in service-sector jobs. Changing African American male styles and the careful cheerfulness required of sales forces and office workers did not always mesh. Even in youth culture, defiant of adults standards in many respects, black and white patterns diverged, with black music more politically assertive in tone, volume, and vocabulary. White middle-class opinion, though varied and often marked by the older racism as well as newer cultural divides, frequently reflected disputes about self-control. Rarely as blatant as in the nineteenth century, when the improvidence and immorality of the poor required few circumlocutions, it was still possible to assume that different capacities of personal discipline and conformity produced different social results.

Democratization and diversity thus warred with other trends in twentieth-century American history, particularly after the 1960s. Even though outright exclusion became unfashionable—a constraint in itself for some people—definitions of deviation continued to be applied to people who did not conform to the prevailing sexual, body, and emotional norms. The division between older working-class immigrant groups and the middle class eased as a precondition for the latter's rapid growth, but prominent racial divisions combined with a different social structure to generate new confusions and implicit disputes.

Child Rearing and Children

For the middle class, twentieth-century patterns of self-control and consumer release generated tensions in and about children that mirrored—indeed, prepared them for—the anxieties of adulthood. Disputes about standards for raising children were carried into the social divisions regarding appropriate personal norms, with middle-class observers frequently despairing of the real or imagined lack of discipline of minority groups.

Early in the century, adult perceptions of children and adult-sponsored aspects of children's experience led to a new dualism, an interplay between constraint and release. This framework made sense to adults, as it was modeled on their own patterns. It also taught children the tantalizing balance between indulgence and control. On the one hand, nineteenth-century assumptions about children's strength and their considerable freedom from adult supervision yielded to new beliefs in inherent psychological flaws that required greater adult and expert guidance. On the other hand, the number and availability of opportunities for escape from anxious monitoring, particularly through new consumer outlets available for children and new forms of peer culture, increased. Childhood now oscillated between stricture and latitude, preparing an interaction that would be carried into adulthood. Subsidiary innovations in childhood, such as changes in familial work responsibilities, flowed from efforts to accommodate this tension.

Even as the rhetorical valuation of children rose at the end of the nineteenth century, discussions identified a range of disturbing issues, and the spate of novel child-rearing manuals reflected the need to explore a new paradigm. The ensuing adult anxiety took many forms, as in the targeting of jealousy among siblings. Here was the general theme: children harbored a variety of counterproductive emotions that they could not manage properly on their own. Helping them gain mastery was vital as the basis for an emotionally healthy adulthood.

Children also had to be taught regular habits of health and hygiene, even though they went against their inclinations—a task that occupied parents' and school authorities' time and attention. As the specialty of pediatrics gained respect, taking children for regular medical checkups became part of the standard routine. Children's bodies and emotions, then, were seen as vulnerable, requiring both protection and discipline by parents, schools, and other organizations. Special counseling might be needed when appropriate habits could not be formed. Like school programs, manuals and magazines turned away from the generalized morality typical of the nineteenth century; rather, a wider range of more specific problems now commanded attention. Overall, the basic approach to children, as suggested in the mainstream prescriptive literature, shifted. The dominant nineteenth-century middle-class advice relied on children's fundamental strength and innocence as long as misguided adult messages did not interfere. In the twentieth century, this confidence waned despite echoes of hoped-for innocence: children now were problems, or at least harbored an array of problems, even in the best environments. As a result, children needed greater supervision and control.[4] Oscillations in expert emphases—from behaviorism to somewhat greater permissiveness—added to the potential anxiety as it became harder to keep up with the latest wisdom but seemingly more imperative to do so.

One index of the combined impact of new expertise and new parental response was the growing pressure to monitor and train very young children. Concern about the emotional responses of toddlers—as in the sibling reactions of two-year-olds—and, of course, the necessity of inculcating habits of hygiene created unusual interest in the very young, compared with other cultures, even those in which upbringing was strict. Because children were now vulnerable, but the goals to instill complex, the young child became a new focus of anxiety and attention. Even Dr. Spock's work, by far the most widely sold book in the field and designed to ease parental burdens, continued to emphasize careful monitoring and subtle guidance, relaxing in only a few areas such as early toilet training.

For slightly older children, the new approach, based on vulnerability combined with ambitious disciplinary goals, encouraged a proliferation of programs to provide adult guidance of children's activities. In the century's early decades, efforts to use schools and settlement houses to create organized activities for immigrant children best represented this approach. Sports and other activities controlled potentially dangerous energies. The scouting movement, although it failed to be accepted by its initial adolescent targets, caught on strongly among boys and girls of grade school age, providing opportunities to learn skills and use time constructively. Organized lessons were popular, building on the nineteenth-century precedent of music training for girls. In addition, the pursuit of hobbies gained new energy in the 1920s. Leisure time could be used for self-improvement, with adult guidance providing the initial impetus for children, who could learn about the world by collecting stamps and coins or build radio sets from kits. Amid this barrage of guidance—headed by the intensification of schooling itself—middle-class children, particularly boys, lost much of their independence.[5]

The greatest change was the shift away from the nineteenth-century confidence in children's educability that had allowed moralists to assume that children could easily absorb adult standards during the prolonged period of youth. Complaints about children's deterioration peppered nineteenth-century commentary, to be sure, but child-rearing advisers assumed that children could learn the key norms. The new wisdom, however, argued that children were more troubled. Adolescence was now considered a separate, complex stage, not yet open to adult standards. Supplementary efforts, such as schools and sports programs, must help hold the line. All this made expertise both different and more important for parents, but it did not necessarily signal a relaxation of the standards themselves.[6]

This expertise was supported by other changes in context, without which it could not have found an audience. For example, the dramatic reduction in infant mortality after 1880, combined with the steadily declining birthrate, strengthened parents' attachment to individual children and made children's deaths less tolerable. This led, somewhat ironically, to a greater interest in health and hygiene. Safety concerns increased, partly because of new dangers from home appliances and automobiles and partly because of the new responsibilities associated with keeping children alive. In addition, changes in living arrangements, especially the move to the suburbs, made children rely more on adult transportation, which provided yet another reason to redefine controls.[7]

Another set of shifts contributed to the thirst for new advice. For three reasons, parents, and particularly mothers, now had greater contact than before with individual children, particularly in the middle classes. First, the use of live-in servants declined dramatically. Second, at a fairly steady rate beginning in the 1920s, grandparents began to move out of the homes of their adult children. Finally, smaller family size and more school obligations reduced the amount of child care available from older siblings. Middle- and upper-class fathers may have begun to provide a bit more help with children, although they usually acted as pals, which reduced their disciplinary authority. Overall, many parents began to find the task of dealing with young children more arduous than before, which heightened their receptivity to detailed advice and also made it easier to focus on the myriad problems of childhood. In addition, sibling rivalry increased with the falling birthrate, simply because there were fewer intermediaries between child and parent and more dependence on adult attention and affection.

Changes in adult policies also helped create new childhood experiences and problems. Dramatic shifts in sleeping arrangements followed from new concerns about individualism and adult leisure. Until the Civil War, infants usually slept in a cradle near an adult, either a parent or nursemaid, who could rock the baby if it stirred. Adult activities in evenings focused on family tasks that were compatible with this kind of attention. But by the 1890s, babies began to be put to sleep in separate bedrooms and in cribs rather than in the less structured cradles. By 1915, cradles were a fond memory, whereas cribs, in contrast, were widely approved for their safety and contributions to good posture and sleep. They had the advantage of allowing a young child to be safely placed in a separate room (something recommended earlier in the nineteenth century but not widely practiced), thereby freeing adults for other leisure or work activities; presumably, the child would learn more independent sleep habits in the process. After the crib years, children were more apt to sleep in separate bedrooms rather than the multiple-sibling rooms common even in the upper middle class during the nineteenth century. The custom of sleeping with other children grew less common, as part of the insistence on greater individuation and, probably, the growing concern about homosexuality. The result, not surprisingly, was that children's sleep deteriorated or at least sleep problems were more often identified. Interestingly, the amount of time recommended that children sleep was lengthened as well, consistent with the growing concern about their vulnerabilities. Though well intentioned, the result added up to fewer comforts and group ties available as part of growing up.[8]

Finally, adults in the early twentieth century seem to have projected onto their children some new concerns about their own lives. In an economy concentrating more and more on service-sector jobs and corporate management, it is not surprising that the resulting restraints were translated into less patience with children's anger. As men and women interacted more often socially, the additional constraints on adult jealousy contributed to the otherwise oddly intense concern with regulating this emotion in children. Even guilt over the rapidly falling birthrate, as parents sought consumer enjoyments, fed into the new protective stance toward children and the desire to provide more adult supervision.

Important changes in family and adult environments thus coalesced with a novel expertise that tried to heighten parental concerns in order to sell new advice and services. The result was a less confident, more problem-focused approach to children, with expert definitions and parental responses that stressed the difficulties. Accordingly, adults supervised even more vigilantly children's activities to make sure that goals and standards were being met in areas such as emotion, sleep, safety, and health. Unstructured children's groups gave way to organized activities—the school programs, scouting, sports and hobby clubs, and music and dancing lessons. Children's progress was now more closely monitored, along with formal and informal checkups. More precise school grading systems, another late-nineteenth-century innovation, displayed the same pattern.

Paralleling this development, however, was the targeting of children as consumers. Consumerism also underwrote new reasons for participating in peer groups devoted to similar consumerist or leisure activities. This was another trend initially sponsored by adults, but in directions designed to convince children to buy (or have bought for them) goods and services to enjoy rather than to be used to monitor and train. As part of this development, the idea of giving children more modest material items characteristic of the nineteenth century lost favor to hedonism, diversion, and entertainment.

In sum, nineteenth-century middle-class parents emphasized certain standards for children, mainly associated with manners, gender, and sexual restraint, which they reinforced by moralistic reading and uplifting recreation—while at the same time allowing children considerable latitude when playing. As the middle class expanded in the twentieth century, adults multiplied the number of goals attached to monitoring and guiding children while at the same time reducing the number of controls over consumption, thereby providing a world of fantasy and an alternative to reality.

The link between consumerism and childhood became closer in many ways. After the 1890s, the provision of allowances, designed to reward children and train them in the use of money, formed a crucial basis for separate consumer activities. Reading matter, including comics, was now inexpensive enough for children to buy on their own. Radio became an even more lucrative way to advertise items for children to acquire directly and for parents to buy for them.

Beginning in the 1920s, parental goals of emotional training depended more and more on consumer props. Advice materials urged parents to use purchased items to help distract children from fear—for example, putting a desired object near the frightening item. Separate goods for each child helped reduce jealousy; a common practice was to bring presents for the other siblings on a brother's or sister's birthday. Surrounding infants with soft dolls and other items was part of the movement toward using cribs. Habituated in infancy to having a variety of goods, children readily moved to greater attachments to acquisition and consumption as they matured.

The commercial media contributed to this pattern, as radio and movies designed explicitly for children evolved into children's programming on television, noteworthy for its routine violence even as middle-class children were being instructed not to fight and roughhouse. The schools participated as well, providing an array of leisure activities as part of their full-service approach to childhood. Textbooks, lavishly illustrated to please the eye, tried to combine learning and fun. Using children as a market, beginning in 1900, not only accelerated but also caused children themselves to define much of their lives in terms of acquisition and spectatorship.[9]

Childhood thus changed in two somewhat contradictory directions, with more detailed standards and parental controls vying with consumer diversions. At times, the two trends joined, marking some of the most striking changes in childhood. Both trends, for different reasons, encouraged new forms of indulgence. For instance, parents who worried about vulnerable children might buy items designed to make children's lives easier. This alliance may account for some otherwise odd exceptions to this regime of careful discipline. For example, American parents and experts alike have been notoriously lax in regulating children's eating habits, except to encourage them to eat more. As a result, particularly after the 1950s, American children grew fatter. Likewise, the relaxation of posture standards, after the many programs through the 1940s targeting schoolchildren, flowed from a desire not to add more burdens to childhood, plus the recognition that the new leisure activities required a more relaxed body style. Somewhat similarly, in merging anxiety and indulgence, efforts to regulate children at home often became loosely guided consumerism. Beginning in the 1920s, discussions of play turned to the idea of having playrooms in the home so that parents could supervise the toys and entertainments. But the result actually cleared the way for further purchases and interaction with media and goods, vaguely justified for some educational value.[10]

A decline in work expectations also followed from this strange alliance. Parents, worried about school demands and insistence on regulating children in other respects, steadily reduced the number of chores expected of them, though partly because the amount of domestic work itself had diminished. The 1930s depression briefly expanded children's obligations, which then fell back again. Lured by the media and consumer playthings, children eagerly joined in, becoming too busy as spectators to respond to work requests. The result was that school and lessons served as training for work rather than work itself.

Grade inflation, which began in the 1960s, reflected a similar combination of standards and indulgence. By the 1970s, parents were seeking higher grades to reduce their children's tensions, and the children themselves, as consumers, wanted an easier school experience, assuming, at the least, that any effort should be rewarded or, at the most, that school should be part of their entertainment package.

In other areas, however, the two trends of greater self-control and more consumer release clashed. Most apparently, parents and experts concerned about molding vulnerable children decried their lack of control over children's consumer culture. Early in the 1950s, attacks on comic books as promoting violence helped establish a recurrent theme among those responsible for children: that clear and demanding goals were being countered by many media presentations and violent toys. Subsequent battles focused on television and music. The conflict was clear, but it was never resolved, except in unusually strict households. From the children's standpoint, the result was an opportunity to distance themselves from demanding adults by pursuing consumer and spectator choices confined to their peer group, at once providing a common vocabulary with other children and eliciting adult disapproval.

Although objections to escapist media and music produced the clearest clash of trends—allowing children important wiggle room by insisting on tastes differing from their parents'—the media themselves played off parental strictures. As efforts to control children's anger and to prevent fights among young children intensified, radio and television violence escalated. A few control taboos were honored, homosexuality, for example, but in key areas, toys and shows were clearly if indirectly based on the new or heightened targets of discipline—deliberately courting audiences by presenting alternative fantasies.

This dualistic framework for childhood did not apply to everyone. Again, social class made a difference. During the first half of the century, parental goals tended to be similar, reducing social and ethnic differences. But the growing economic inequality and renewal of immigration after the 1950s opened the gaps wider, including greater differences in family size. Inner-city children might well experience differently from their middle-class counterparts the attraction of consumerism combined with subtle discipline and constraint.[11]

Overall, however, the tension between self-control and consumer release had a number of important consequences. Evidence of softness toward children, plus abundant signs of consumer devotion, led to recurrent claims that parents were losing control. Children, no longer simply ordered about, might seem to be defying authority. This view, however, was often exaggerated, because it ignored the greater efforts by parents and formal monitoring provided by expanded school programs and the greater rigor of key standards. But the view did make parents worry, who hoped to mold their children without repressing them, seeking to please through goods and entertainment while instilling controls over body presentation and emotion. Efforts to reduce, through concepts like attention deficit disorder, what could be an agonizing sense of responsibility might themselves be greeted by criticism from conservative observers who saw this as one more manifestation of softness and evasion.

An equally telling result of the effort at disciplining was teenagers' increasing if usually symbolic defiance of restraint. Precisely because younger children were so carefully shaped while coddled by means of leisure outlets and acquisitions, adolescents veered toward independence and submission to peer-based, rather than adult-prescribed, conventions. Above all, music was guided by its ability to shock adults, the shock in turn most commonly taking the form of obscene lyrics and sheer volume, a direct protest against a controlled and monitored childhood. By the late twentieth century, the fascination with body piercing was also revealing as an alternative to the disciplined, hygienic body fostered by vigilant parents. Indeed, only these controls can explain the specific directions that adolescents have taken, because of the need for contrasts with the constraint built into the leisure outlets of childhood itself. For the children themselves, the adolescent image was itself part of the fantasy release, the desire to grow up more quickly into alternative leisure and self-presentation, with behavioral adolescence reaching into younger and younger age groups.[12]

At the other end of adolescence, middle-class parents sought to reimpose controls by stressing (and often, however innocently, exaggerating) the difficulties of getting into a "good" college and the needs for careful behaviors to achieve collegiate success. For their part colleges, now ubiquitous middle-class institutions, tried to respond to demands for greater freedom and ongoing pressures to supervise—allowing cars and appliances in a response to ascending student consumerism, decreasing regulations over sexuality but responding to date rape concerns, tightening controls over student drinking in the 1900s, acquiescing for the most part in grade inflation.

In the largest sense, the conflicting trends of childhood and youth— the introduction of an early pattern of trade-offs between adult-prescribed reality and consumerist escape, capped by a usually brief but intense adolescent subculture—prepared children for the experience they would face as adults, tied to often demanding behavioral standards that were juxtaposed with fantasy leisure. To this extent, the dual trends of twentieth-century childhood were oddly consistent.

Intensification

In the 1980s and 1990s, the importance of demanding standards of self-control became apparent in the escalation of norms for both children and adults. The new trends reacted to impressions of a contemporary American culture mired in permissiveness. They built on older standards, with important innovations, and were accompanied by the crescendo of complaints about moral decay, which the conservative strictures were meant to counter even as they suggested a more complex reality.

Parenting sections in bookstores swelled in the 1990s. The new titles covered all sorts of situations—single parenting, grandparents serving as parents, fathering, adolescence, proper sleep, strong-willed children— all with the same underlying theme: children are not being handled right, especially in regard to parental and personal control. Most books had a lot to say about restraint: "Spoiled Rotten: Today's Kids and How to Change Them" and "Raising Self-Reliant Children in a Self-Indulgent World." The outpouring resembled the surge of the 1920s, and it signaled a widespread concern that appropriate disciplinary boundaries were being lost, along with parental guilt and uncertainty amid hardworking mothers and an absence of supporting adult kin. The ambivalences of twentieth-century parenting—the desire to avoid repressive strictness and to encourage appropriate consumerism without abandoning firm controls—almost guaranteed recurrent confusion and a quest for specialized expertise.[13]

The sense that American behavior was orbiting beyond restraint transcended child rearing. The interest in good manners surged as middle-class Americans sought new guidance in formal social behavior. The call for greater civility, though less prescriptive, also indicated a need for greater self-regulation, arguing that political habits, for example, had become destructive, preventing appropriate public discourse.[14]

More precise appeals for greater self-control began to be heard in the late 1970s. It was at this time that the new concepts of sexual harassment and date rape were publicized, both stemming from the revised feminism that sought to hold males to greater account. It was also at this time that the fierce campaign against smoking began, initially relying on highly moralistic appeals for self-mastery. New standards for drinking were established as well. The organization Mothers Against Drunk Driving (MADD) was formed in 1980, quickly winning 600,000 volunteers and donors and successfully soliciting, in nearly every state, tougher new laws against driving under the influence. The underlying moralism of these campaigns created strange unions in the late twentieth century: feminists and conservatives uniting against certain sexual expressions, liberal politicians vying with conservatives to censor music or films. The new disciplinary fervor blurred old boundaries.

Attacks on drinking spread to college campuses, and the tolerance of alcohol-related events declined markedly. At Penn State University, for example, a Phi Psi 500 race (jogging from bar to bar in bizarre costumes) and Gentle Thursday (a spring event with free beer provided) were outlawed. University administrators and local police collaborated in crackdowns on underage consumption, prompted by concerns about the health implications of binge drinking. By the late 1990s, one result was a series of campus riots, at Penn State and elsewhere, against further strictures. The riots seemed frivolous, but they suggested awareness of the larger contraints of latter-day moralism.

The intensification of constraints applied across the board to men and women alike, although there were gendered components. Men served as the primary targets for redefinitions of sexual propriety and drinking, with women drawn in occasionally. Women encountered new issues at work. Premenstrual syndrome (PMS), identified medically in the 1940s, began to gain wide currency in the 1970s. It served to explain some women's periodic emotional excess and also to constrain them, particularly on the job. Now having been given a label, PMS became something to watch out for, a danger for which women must take responsibility. Stigmas applied to menopause gained new medical precision, again highlighting problems that women might encounter in emotional control and, implicitly, standards of restraint that they should be able to uphold.

The creation of new organizations and concepts pushing for unprecedented levels of self-control in key areas was matched by the revival of interest in using the state to regulate behavior. Many of the end-of-century campaigns insisted on self-control yet wanted any lapses severely punished. Hence college men should be lectured about sexual responsibility, and they should also be prosecuted when they coerced a date. Smokers should quit, and by the 1980s many politicians were also declaring that opportunities to smoke should be limited by law. Movements against drunk driving simultaneously pushed for voluntary restraint and prosecution. Campaigns against gambling pressed for personal control and also legal limits. Proposals to tighten declarations of bankruptcy included personal responsibility. As a Colorado Republican put it, "If you can't afford it, don't buy it." No behavioral regulation as dramatic as Prohibition had yet been tried, but clearly some of the legal barriers to limiting behavior were being reconsidered.

There were other indices of escalating standards, many of them reflecting anxieties about the family and society. Ideas about Americans being out of control spread beyond generalized complaints over incivility and the campaigns concerning health, safety, and sex. Definitions of child abuse continued to expand, embracing not only lesser forms of violence and sexuality but also emotion. "The bruises don't show on the outside, so there are no statistics on how many children are victims," one authority noted in 1985: "But anyone who works with children knows that the problem is widespread." Abusers might come from any social class, a statement designed to provoke outrage and self-scrutiny from middle-class readers. Damage to a child's self-esteem by constant denigration was a key finding, but an unwillingness to console or actively show affection could be abusive as well. Popularized questionnaires urged parents to take stock of themselves and their anger, with therapy probably needed for parents enmeshed in the behaviors.[15]

Yet another excess was identified in 1997: road rage. Like all popularized problems of self-control, this was becoming a "runaway national problem," even though highway death rates were not rising. Questionnaires urged motorists to assess themselves: Have you honked at another driver simply because he annoyed you? Have you shouted, cursed, or gestured? Have you flashed your high-beam lights at someone driving too slowly? Or finally—phrased as if this were the logical culmination of the earlier measures—have you physically confronted another driver? Road rage became yet another self-measurement criterion, another social issue centered on personal control. It also picked up the characteristic twentieth-century view of human nature as composed of dangerous emotions threatening to erupt, whose every manifestation must be restrained lest the whole edifice crumble.

At the end of the twentieth century, Americans wanted to worry about themselves, or at least about others whose control was suspect. They identified (sometimes vague) new problems and applied greater rigor to certain behaviors, sometimes to the point of regulation. Of course, there were anomalies, for another characteristic of the twentieth century was the pattern of trade-offs, even faddishness, in the foci of control. Thus while maintaining strict body standards in principle— except for a small movement toward greater tolerance of the obese— the average American gained several pounds, height held constant, between 1985 and 1995. The lure of food as comfort as work tensions increased, plus the expansion of convenience foods as part of consumerism, overwhelmed many good intentions. Yet the larger point holds, as even less successful dieters became more self-critical. From manners to health to driving, a rising sense of precariousness spurred efforts toward restraint. In focusing on health and hygiene, anger and aggression, the basic patterns confirmed earlier trends in the century, although specific emphases varied at particular times.[16]

The question is why: what spurred at least two decades of self-discipline starting in the late 1970s? New technologies produced new control requirements in certain areas as the work realm expanded: more middle-class Americans learned to interrupt leisure and family time to respond to telephones and, later, pagers, and for many, the novel discipline of regularly checking one's e-mail became part of daily life. Certain problems of control became greater partly because of new discoveries— like smoking's damage to health. Some problems also may simply have increased. Road rage and sexual harassment may be examples, though the definitions were new and the behavioral data hard to assess over time. Claims of increased incidence, as in road rage, most obviously reflected the constructions of advocates, seeking to motivate new controls.

The measurement problem also applies to worries about public civility. Certain forms of nastiness have escalated, for instance, hate radio shows that insult and distort major political figures and their families. Yet negative, dirty political campaigning is not new; it flourished under Truman and Eisenhower in the 1940s and 1950s. In fact, Eisenhower is sometimes credited with conducting the first modern negative campaign, against Adlai Stevenson. The fact that reproved behaviors are not always new or increasing does not, of course, detract from efforts at greater control, but it does call for additional analysis.[17] Besides, some of the surge in negative political campaigning ironically displayed the larger interest in personal behavior standards. Character issues became more important and candidates more vulnerable. As policy debates between the two major parties receded, imposing moral tests gained greater currency.

Important elements of the new calls for discipline resulted from redefinitions of existing standards, not from deteriorating behavior. This is true for sexual abuse, as fondling uncles turned from being labeled annoying dirty old men to being deemed outright criminals. Redefinition also applied to the campaign against drunk driving, where problems had not been increasing measurably. It could be applied—at least in part—to the extent of moral anxiety about contagions such as second-hand smoke, for which vague research data were combined with a reformulation of appropriate personal space to label a long-tolerated situation as unacceptable.

So why, beyond behavior change, did these definitions shift? The answer may be found in two developments: new forms of social anxiety that sought targets for attack amid job insecurity and global competition, and an independent need for moral reaction. Social anxiety was crucial amid economic and international shifts. But even though it required expression, many options were available. It was the moral imperative that guided the direction of the new crusade.

Here, a national retreat from the real or imagined excesses of the 1960s was an important ingredient. In some respects, of course, some 1960s styles have persisted, amid disapproval and also a considerable degree of nonjudgmentalism. For example, although communes did not prove to be a wave of the future, couples living together before marriage became common, the fastest-growing census category into the 1980s. The replacement of conventional dating by group activities and somewhat more random sex has been another enduring trend, as has been the acceptability of sex before marriage for respectable women. Musical genres continued to evolve from their 1960s base. Recreational drugs form a more dubious category, but middle-class use has not fallen to pre-1960s levels. In sum, the phenomena of the 1960s have not simply faded away.[18]

Nonetheless, there have been reactions, with standard setters defining new limits. Feminists rethought their approval of freewheeling sexuality and, without attacking sexual pleasure directly, began defining additional boundaries. Baby boomers, regretting the excesses of their youth, sought subtly restrictive measures that would protect their own children and set more stringent limits. More generally, the move toward more rigorous definitions of self-control clearly followed from the previous movement toward unprecedented permissiveness.

Aging itself was involved: the same baby boom that triggered permissiveness in the 1960s provided a cohort of middle-aged reevaluators by the 1980s. We have discussed the possibility that second thoughts helped explain why the sexual adventures of the 1960s were revised in memory for the pollsters of the 1980s when Americans retold their stories about the numbers of sexual partners they had enjoyed.

Three other factors capped the process, adding causes like those that had helped usher in new control standards during the 1920s. First, moralism continued to respond to attractions in consumption and leisure styles that begged for personal and social redress. Specific compensatory leisure activities, like gambling and viewing sexually provocative films and shows, became more popular, and the interest in acquisition, if not always the capacity, remained high, providing good opportunities for groups to attack others for deficient self-control. For example, as tobacco companies continued to advertise cigarettes as part of the good life, a person's escape from smoking could demonstrate a virtuous restraint, an ability to defy omnipresent appeals to indulgence beyond the protection of health. The symbolic functions of self-control remained active, which is why ex-smokers are so complacent and so ready to demean the weaknesses of those still smoking.

Like the 1920s, the end-of-the-century decades succeeded a period of more active social reform interest (the Great Society years of the 1960s) that now seemed overblown. Confidence in using government to right social wrongs waned, just as the Progressive spirit had declined sixty years before. In 1965 two-thirds of all Americans polled believed government was a force for good; by 1995 the figure had dropped to 30 percent. Movements like the Jarvis campaign to cut back government by dramatically reducing taxes (California, 1978) translated sentiment into reality, making it more difficult, in fact, for government programs

to work. Americans may harbor a larger strain of antigovernment thinking than other Western societies, but the intensity clearly varies with
time. The final decades of the century unquestionably witnessed an
unusual peak, and the implications for attention to personal behavior
were profound.

Here, then, was another contemporary American oscillation: periods
of reformism alternated with more conservative times, when emphasis
was placed on personal responsibility, perhaps supplemented by regulations of some behavioral excesses, as the only escape from problems like
poverty, racism, or disease. If people could control themselves and their
bodies, a host of current dilemmas, immune to direct reform, might be
alleviated. Thus, in the 1990s, a Democratic administration that proved
unable to tackle health care reform turned to sermons and restraints on
the immorality of smoking. The same administration, incapable of con-
fronting the deepest urban poverty directly, urged school uniforms as an
encouragement to more disciplined behavior among young people.
Limitations on the use of government action to promote gender equity
was matched by new efforts to protect women through insistence on
greater sexual restraint. These emphases were not necessarily misplaced,
but they clearly substituted for the commitment to remediation through
government that had predominated three decades before. Apparent failure (sometimes due to underfunding and half-hearted commitment in
the first place) and loss of interest in one approach, abetted by a vigorous
conservative turn that attacked government programs across the board,
helped assure the new attention to personal discipline.

Finally, as in the century's beginning, the 1980s and 1990s were
shaped by the impact and confusion resulting from unprecedented levels
and varieties of immigrants, supplemented in this case by the higher
birthrates of racial minorities. The United States was becoming visibly
more diverse, which helped trigger a greater insistence on middle-class
behavioral standards and constraints. People again had to be measured
by their ability to discipline themselves. The growing interest in manners, sometimes adjusted to reflect social interactions with diverse
groups, clearly followed from a desire to teach habits that revealed
respectable breeding and identified outsiders whose lack of conformity
put them beyond the pale.

The needs for symbolic expiations amid ongoing consumerism, for new social cement amid challenges to majority values, and for an individualistic alternative to social programs combined to sustain the complaints about personal excesses and the resulting intensification of key standards. The causes collectively could even reverse the presumed lessons of Prohibition, renewing efforts to legislate certain facets of personal behavior. But the factors that led to the surge of moralism did not create it. Rather, they tapped an abundant cultural supply ready to do additional service when social conditions demanded. Here was the most important feature of the twentieth-century approach to self-control, building on Victorian values. Intensification was possible because of the continuing commitment to the idea that personal discipline demonstrated virtue.

The American Reservoir of Morality

Even as the interest in expressive sexuality advanced in the Western world, particularly after 1960, Americans visibly hesitated. Displays of nudity on television and advertisements continued to be prohibited, in contrast to the practice in Europe (and, ironically, to American advertising a century earlier). Topless beaches, standard in most of Western Europe, remained rare. American reticence about the body declined, without question, but evolution, not revolution, was the watchword.

Around 1990 an American advertising agency was hired by tobacco interests to work against pending French legislation limiting smoking in public places. Their strategy was to put selected political and media leaders on an American plane, on which smoking was prohibited, and to fly them to Los Angeles (a long way) where they would disembark in a smoke-free airport and take "please do not smoke" limousines to a hotel where smoking was banned. The conclusion? Severe limits on smoking was an American malady, the fruit of familiar moralistic excess—surely France would not fall victim as well. The legislation was watered down.[19]

The tendency of middle-class Americans to frame issues in terms of personal morality and responsibility for self-control periodically resurfaced during the twentieth century, helping differentiate the mainstream approaches from those in Europe and elsewhere. Dieting is a case in point, from the inception of the new code of slenderness in the 1890s. Preached for appearance and health, as it was in western Europe, American dieting also became a demonstration of character and ethical responsiveness. The later crusade against smoking had the same basis, in which sensible health arguments were embellished by moral overtones, making the cessation of smoking a major test of virtue and the failure to quit a sentence to pariah status. Even the emphasis on hygiene reflected a moralistically grounded penchant for excess. Despite its providing an important service to health and comfort, American-style hygiene was often carried to extremes, with multiple daily baths and concealments of odor—signs of uneasiness about pleasing others and a need to purge. Delight in talking about personal tests—the key to success of group-control approaches such as dieting clubs and Alcoholics Anonymous—reflected American gregariousness but also the compulsion to demonstrate moral commitments publicly. Deep-seated worry about failures, fueled by constant appeals to guilt through popularizations that typically exaggerated social trends or claimed new levels of excess with no real historical measurements, also flowed from the national preoccupation with moralism. The recurrent temptation was to turn from persuasion to regulation. The same moral intensity that had caused nineteenth-century temperance groups to advocate the cessation of drinking, rather than the moderation that their title implied, showed up in efforts to legislate new categories of sexual excess and in the legal isolation of smokers. Despite individual deviations and subcultures that did not accept the dominant approach, Americans continued to delight in moralization, and their late-century demonstration merely built on this penchant.

Why did this basic impulse, which seems better suited to Victorianism than to modernism, endure despite important redefinitions of specific moral targets? Some observers might point to the Puritan tradition, on the assumption that the emphasis on religious goals and fervor explains the push for moralistic self-control. This explanation is possible—along with other factors—but not obvious. Puritans did not insist on self-control across the board—they did not, for example, oppose alcohol, nor did they disapprove of sex in the proper context. Although their emphasis on sin and the need for redemption might have created a cultural substratum, the proximate causes of moralism lie closer, in the Victorian era and the transitional decades that succeeded it.[20]

Americans are accustomed to thinking of their society as undergoing rapid, often sporadic change—a factor in the unique national preoccupation with the decade as a historical unit with its own characteristics, yielding to another set of characteristics within a few years. Yet American society is in many ways—perhaps in reaction to this pervasive sense of disruption—highly conservative, as its politics normally demonstrates. Important cultural characteristics serve as a means of intergenerational transmission, the judgment and acculturation of newcomers, and basic identity. The insistence on moralism—only occasionally and temporarily overthrown in favor of some innovative consumerist or protest fad—is a vital example, blending with both the character definitions of the nineteenth century and the somewhat different but subtly demanding disciplinary demands of the twentieth century. Puritanism may have underwritten the moralistic formula, but its full flowering occurred in the nineteenth century, and we, despite our sense of unprecedented turmoil and devolution, are its direct heirs.

Several components intertwined. Moralism, religiously inspired but not denominational, helped compensate for the decline of traditional religion itself, save for an evangelical minority in the nineteenth and twentieth centuries. The attention to women as moral agents, to a spiritualized love as a control on sexuality, and to the transcendent virtues of temperance all were Victorian efforts to use the invocation of personal discipline as a surrogate for more conventional religious strivings as beliefs in hellfire and original sin lost favor. The use of moralistic supplements was all the greater in a society that prided itself on the lack of a church establishment and wide denominational divisions. Religious affiliation itself persisted more strongly in the United States than in most Western countries. In an unusually geographically mobile society without deep community roots, religion can be a force for cohesion and identity, and the same is true of religious-like moralisms. This is why, even though female virtue and temperance were invoked throughout the Western world in the nineteenth century, they had an unusually strong effect in the United States, providing cultural coherence; and this was why the invocation lasted as both supplement and surrogate for religious interest throughout the twentieth century—aided by the presence of an active fundamentalist minority eager to use moral causes to promote their particular agendas.

Self-discipline as religious surrogate was enforced by the Victorian belief—again unusually strong in the United States—in individuals as the creators of their economic fate. Emphasis on the nation as a land of opportunity and strong symbolic investment in education as society's principal obligation to its citizens, providing an equal start in life, had as an obvious corollary a common insistence on moral failings as the cause of poverty or immobility. These beliefs took shape clearly the 1830s. Entering into school programs, in reading lessons, and, later, in social studies courses, they were assured of continuity, at least in middle-class culture, well after formal Victorianism had ended. Americans' perception of themselves as a distinctive and superior nation supported the emphasis on moral judgments and injunctions to improve self-discipline over more social remedies. In regard to self-control, reliance on individual character was confirmed by the 1930s with the notorious failure of Prohibition; until the reversal of legalism at the century's end, character had to do the work once partially assigned to law.[21]

A second factor in the insistence on personal control and responsibility was the recurrent need to develop cultural baselines as a means of integrating diverse regions and immigrant populations. Lacking the readier cohesion of most European countries, where a kind of cultural cement was created from a shared history and residential persistence, American spokespeople—from politicians through educators and social workers to advice givers—underscored a few beliefs that could cut across otherwise divergent ethnic and religious patterns. This effort was frequently combined, especially around 1900 and again in the century's final decades, with anxiety about the moral capacity of some members of the diverse population. Stressing the need for self-control might simultaneously inculcate a shared belief package while calling attention to the need to master dubious impulses in order to gain respectability as Americans. (And should the latter effort fail, the same cultural package would justify the native middle class's scorning of the deviants; accordingly, there were gains in either alternative.)

The final, positive components shaping a commitment to the emphasis on self-control and its strong moral overtones came from recurrent success, real or imagined, and from the need for moral ballast in an inexpressive political culture. Early in the nineteenth century, one of the first invocations of a modern control ethic was applied to nonmarital sexuality, and it worked better in the United States than in western Europe. Sexual habits did change, and the rate of illegitimate births dropped. Efforts to attack drinking also achieved some success, although the stereotypic beliefs in the failure of Prohibition modified this particular reinforcement. Late in the twentieth century, widely publicized reductions in smoking constituted a clearer victory. Advances in the habits of hygiene were quite real, measurable, and satisfying. Periodic evidence from personal lives as well as more general social change thus confirmed the validity of the self-control message. The drop in teenage sex and pregnancy rates in the mid-1990s was similarly hailed as a success for moral education, with federal and local officials pointing to campaigns for abstinence and, sometimes, safe sex: "Our concerted effort . . . is succeeding," rejoiced the Secretary of Health and Human Services.

Attention to discipline helped compensate for the growing number of consumer temptations and other social issues in a nation committed to political moderation. Here, the contrast with most other industrial societies was clear. Socialism and communism could do the trick for some European countries, anti-Semitism and then fascism for others. These movements, however, did not fully take hold in American political culture because of the tremendous pressures against extremism and for a two-party system. Without such political outlets, the need for moral ballast in the twentieth century found expression in personal goals or at least in recommendations about personal compensations: hence the unusual moral enthusiasm attached to some aspects of bodily discipline and even sexual controls. To be sure, Americans politics was used recurrently to express moral uneasiness. This was a strong ingredient in responses to socialism in the 1920s and certainly during the cold war; indeed, the end of the cold war as an outlet for wider anxieties helped sustain the return to greater moralism at the century's end.[22] Throughout the century, more specialized political movements captured wider social concerns for certain groups. Even here, however, movements like the protest against abortion combined political fervor with an interest in heightening self-control through removing a key facilitator for recreational sex; and enthusiastic environmentalism could incorporate the theme of personal restraint along with wider economic regulations.

Overall, twentieth-century American politics—particularly during key periods in the gestation of the modern approaches to personal discipline, such as the 1920s, the 1950s, and the late-century decades—featured blandness and harmony—political self-restraint, in fact—over expressiveness. The result formed part of the context in which many Americans turned inward their concerns about wider trends and the temptations of consumerism. Social and political peace was purchased to some extent at the expense of self-comfort, as Americans, true to their individualism, used worry about personal discipline as expiation, avoiding the political attacks against aspects of modern consumer capitalism that stemmed from similar moral needs in other societies.

The point is clear: guilt reactions to advances in consumerism are standard in modern societies. They describe important impulses in France, Germany, and even Russia in the turn-of-the-century decades. The United States was no exception to the need to expiate signs of unaccustomed affluence and materialism (indeed, greater religiosity might have heightened the need). But expressions of this common reaction generally needed to be distinctive. The nation lacked a preconsumerist upper class that could help articulate alternative views, a role played by the European aristocracy before its conversion to jet-set role modeling. Leading in new consumerist forms and in commitment to capitalism, Americans found it harder to blame foreigners or domestic groups for inciting degeneracy (a feature of German attacks on French influence and later of anti-Americanism or anti-Semitism). American racism was vigorous, but it did not express consumerist guilt. So moral concerns pressed on individuals, as already had been suggested in the moral-uplift movements against commercialization in the 1830s and 1840s. The resulting emphasis on individual discipline was linked to other national cultural staples, notably the tendency to highlight individual effort (as opposed to social determinants) as a cause of economic success or failure, with failure attributed to individual fault and not to social or economic barriers.[23]

The personal need to display virtue thus reflected powerful cultural pressures tied to the ways that most middle-class Americans explained outcomes and the ways they assessed worthiness and abundance alike. The same context made it difficult for Americans to recognize the source of their need for moral compensation beyond vague, often inaccurate, references to Puritanism. The more politicized anticonsumerism possible in other societies, although often burdened with unsavory social overtones, clarified these needs and reduced the insistence on personal demonstrations of control. This, above all, is why American moralism remained distinctive, even in—indeed, because of—a hedonistic consumer culture.

This was the cultural setting in which children were early introduced to the varied demands of whatever self-discipline targets were most fashionable at the time. In some cases, as we have seen, child rearing not only reflected adult self-control concerns but also were cathartic, as adult anxieties were displaced onto arrangements designed to defuse childish emotion. Schools continued the message of moral individualism usually launched in the early years. Socialized to resonate for appeals for self-control, sometimes taught to carry messages back to parents about new hygiene standards or the dangers of drink, middle-class children not surprisingly grew up to replicate much of the same moral concern.

The same continuity created a ready audience for the often poorly documented tales of excess—from drink and drugs to sexuality to incivility and road rage. Despite their optimism and national pride, Americans liked to be told that they were not behaving well, that serious problems threatened unless they strengthened their willpower. This vulnerability to free-floating warnings was the counterpart of the belief that social problems could be alleviated by more disciplined conduct.

Moralism did not, of course, prevent change and tension. Even as attention to discipline remained fixed, behaviors did change and consumerist leisure did provide even more outlets for symbolic release. Americans did show a new concern for "self" and personality, even though the results complicated rather than contradicted a real attachment to standards. The result added to the disciplinary worries: surrounded by affluence and entertainments replete with symbolic violence and sexual innuendo, it was easy to feel the need for yet another demonstration of personal sacrifice and control, particularly when spurred by critics who confused change with reversal of standards. It was the tension between alternatives that many Americans sought, opting for neither indulgence nor asceticism. The inner conflict helped reconcile diverse impulses, including the drive to demonstrate a capacity for restraint, but it also was demanding. The results, precisely because they defy more common generalizations about moral deterioration, demand a final assessment.

ELEVEN

An Agenda for Evaluation and Change

Historians usually are uncomfortable moving from a presentation of past developments, of changes and continuities, to an evaluation of their quality. Yet the recent history of self-control invites questions about the results: Is the basic American disciplinary system, modified by exceptions and symbolic compensations, working well for individuals and for society as a whole?

This book has looked at the evolution of beliefs about self-control and the influence of these beliefs on American behaviors, because we need to understand the past in order to understand the present. Beliefs and values—cultures—can be amazingly persistent as they pass from one generation to the next and adapt to changing circumstances while still providing a sense of identity and continuity. The heritage of Victorian moralism in twentieth-century goals for personal discipline is a major example. But by definition, cultures can change and be changed. One of the roles of cultural history is to decide what we should reconsider, given a fuller understanding of our values, so that we do not become passive victims of beliefs that shape important aspects of our lives. This reviewable and changeable aspect of culture cannot be ignored, even by historians more comfortable with analysis than with recommendation.

Is it useful, for example, to assume that adolescents lie, as if we simply must wait for them to grow up while we are privately seething? Might some new approach strike a balance between overrigid Victorian codes and contemporary indulgence? Can we reconsider our insistence that politicians be role models for private character as well as public policy?

Were we not better off in terms of government effectiveness just three decades ago when the peccadilloes of a Kennedy or a J. Edgar Hoover were concealed and judgments based their political behavior? Have we, in sum, trapped ourselves in a sense of inevitability, that this media excess cannot be stopped, that this character judgment is absolutely vital lest the national edifice collapse? Moving into a new century, even amid mounting pressures for moral regulation, it is time to reflect on our constraints.

History and Comparison

This book is not concerned simply with lessons for our time. It also seeks to demonstrate the richness of the newer kind of cultural-behavioral history, promoting a better appreciation of the unexpected reaches of historical inquiry by tracing standards of conduct and the persistence and adaptability of American moralism. We have already seen the significant relationship between politics and self-control, because the deterioration of political interest promotes greater efforts at personal discipline. Disciplinary standards, in turn, affect the political process. Since the time of Woodrow Wilson, observers have commented on the rigidities in the United States' foreign policy generated by American moralism, the inflexibility that results from our judgments about foreign excesses, and our tendency to insist on apology as well as emendation. On a more personal political level, Americans have developed an inclination to judge politicians and even foreign leaders by their manner more than by the substance of their policies. Moreover, many Americans seem more interested in their leaders as symbolic representations of personal virtue than for any other quality, and partisan politicians both echo and amplify this mood by endless comments about personal as well as political ethics. For instance, the debate about Clarence Thomas's professional qualifications for the U.S. Supreme Court was overshadowed by the furor over his real or imagined sexual sins. Even when the American public decides to be nonjudgmental, as was long the case in reactions to reports about the sex scandal surrounding President Bill Clinton, its attention was on his personal behavior, not policy issues. Which is worse, his having consensual sex with an adult woman not his wife or failing to deal constructively with a painfully anomalous health care system? For their part, politicians have also learned to pander to the nation's disciplinary concerns, often using them to distract from their lack of constructive programs in more substantive areas.[1] Clearly, an unconventional historical net focused on self-control not only explains much of Americans' personal behavior but also illuminates key aspects of their national political life.

The fascination with tensions concerning self-control has narrowed essentially political discussions at work as well as in political life. By the 1990s, identification of the problems that women encountered in the workplace increasingly focused on sexual harassment because of the challenge of this disciplinary symbol. The result was greater difficulty in discussing possibly more significant issues of work style and advancement patterns: that is, the problems that could be defined morally crowded out other, often more systematic concerns. Here, as in politics more generally, a greater awareness of the control demands in our culture might create a more engaged and relevant political climate. Bringing too many concerns into the realm of personal discipline risks an inadequate assessment of policy needs. A historically informed understanding of why we zero in so quickly on personal behaviors and how we have come to do so may clear a path to more constructive and wide-ranging initiatives.

The process of understanding through historical exploration must continue, of course. The recent amplification of moral concerns needs further probing, including attention to any signs that the current phase is beginning to yield to a different balance between the social and the personal, as ultimately it must. Comparative issues need more inquiry. Americans' approach to morally charged disciplinary issues such as dieting or hygiene leans toward excess, by wider Western standards, and unusual sexual prudery endures despite change. Lacking abundant political outlets to express their anxieties about affluence and new leisure time, Americans have turned inward compared with their European counterparts. Ironically, the result has been both a different and a more permanent set of concerns. To take an extreme case, after decades of fighting modern lifestyles, Germans became the world's leisure leaders. Not so middle-class Americans, whose interest in tightening personal standards and judging the inadequacy of individual response seems a more durable concomitant of affluence and compensatory leisure.

National patterns are already sufficiently clear to highlight the utility of behavioral history in exploring the relationship between past and present and also to offer some recommendations. We know enough about how current concerns are shaped by past trends and what these trends have been and what they have answered to, to be able to assess our own condition. It is essential to consider at least moderate change and greater license for skepticism and critique. What this book has delineated is a potent and nationally distinctive cultural system, and power always warrants evaluation.[2]

Improving the Terms of Debate

The first task is to do a better job of sorting out the facts and to use more relevant criteria when presenting moral complaints. As the following items suggest, what is needed is a sort of character reform encompassing more restraint and decorum from a range of self-appointed advocates of self-restraint, along with firmer guidelines for evidence and analysis. Conservatives make many claims that are worth considering, but the tendency, particularly on the political and religious right, toward misleadingly simple generalizations actually limits the claims' potential impact. To clear the way for a more productive debate, several guidelines emerge from the historical record.

Point 1. Do not accept blanket statements about American moral deterioration. For example, a newspaper comment about Dr. Laura Schlessinger, a syndicated radio commentator pushing the idea of character, urges: "In a Me-Me-Me Age awash with immorality, hedonism and runaway irresponsibility," Dr. Schlessinger fights "our national plague of entitlement." The commentary—not necessarily authorized by the radio personality—is silly. It ignores the constraints routinely, sometimes unwittingly, accepted by most Americans. Certain groups, or certain behaviors, may need attention, but an across-the-board assertion is ridiculous. Audience rejection should point journalists toward a more sophisticated approach, one more likely to gain attention by recognizing the important areas in which Americans attempt, and often achieve, considerable self-discipline.

What we need, as opposed to facile invocations of guilt, is an active historical perspective. This is a concept often evoked but whose meaning is not always apparent. In fact, it suggests some combination of three principal analytical strategies: first, knowledge of a wide range of relevant history so that similarities with current situations can aid our understanding, not through misleadingly precise analogies, but through orientation and guidance. Second, awareness of which past factors continue to cause current behaviors. And third, a grasp of contemporary history so that we can identify change but not exaggerate it. All three of these strategies form a more sophisticated approach to issues of personal discipline and avoid excessive, potentially counterproductive claims. In 1997, for example, fourteen states announced that students would be required to participate in character education programs designed to teach the importance of such traits as honesty, obedience, respect, loyalty, and enthusiasm. Backed by media blitzes, advocates nevertheless had the good sense to acknowledge that the initiative comprised mainly warmed-over elements long present in both twentieth- and nineteenth-century school programs. The approach might or might not generate useful results—asking grade schoolers to identify "character words" might seem far removed from the stated goals—but the honesty of its presentation was refreshing. The promotion of character is not new in the twentieth century: reform efforts derive from a rich past, shaped by decades of tension between American moralism and the pressures of abundance.

Point 2: Do not accept statements implying a deterioration from some past time that offer no historical justification. In addition, be aware of groups—like the road safety enthusiasts behind the poorly documented road-rage claims—that stand to benefit from assertions of decline. Remember that as it has developed historically, our national culture leaves us exceptionally vulnerable to the vocabulary of the moral crusade or jeremiad.

An attempt to portray the present as a specially tainted moment should be supported by a demonstration that some moment in the relevant past was far less tainted, in measurable respects. Any claim of deterioration is a historical claim and should be historically supported—or simply ignored. For all the belief in progress, Americans are oddly gullible when it comes to the good old days. Again, on specific points our behaviors may be open to criticism because of a harmful slide from the past—although in other areas, such as smoking, we may also have "improved." It is not even clear, as we have seen, that constraints are less burdensome in the late twentieth century than they were in the heyday of Victorianism. Rather, they are different, involving a distinctive set of tolerances and restrictions and, in some ways, demanding greater vigilance.

The greatest lurch toward permissiveness in modern society has been the compensatory leisure culture, which most Americans enjoy as passive spectators seeking some release but not as a source of day-to-day behavioral guidelines. This point needs to be taken into account, as does the recurrent movement toward intensifying both standards and their enforcement. Checkups, actuarial reports, work supervision, and anxiety-provoking media commentary all serve to remind most Americans of significant boundaries, usually marked by moral implications. We accept more standards than we realize and we have more imposed on us, and our evaluation of contemporary trends and contemporary reality must recognize these burdens.

Point 3: Reject efforts to generalize from a few behaviors—the typical ploy of commentators seeking an audience by implying widespread moral vulnerability. Most of us, to refer to an earlier example, do not need to worry about becoming road ragers, even if we show signs of mild anger when driving. A teenage mother who killed her newborn in order to return to a dance may well merit condemnation, but this is not typical behavior—nor in fact is it new or increasing, for the number of infanticides has almost certainly dropped since the late nineteenth century.[3] Despite sexually loose films and music, most teenagers do not kill infants, their own or others'. Similar cautions must be directed to moralisms coming more frequently from liberals. Domestic violence merits concern, but it is not rampant. Few women are treated in emergency rooms as a result of battering (about 0.3 percent of all visits, or 1 percent of all visits owing to injuries—even though well-intentioned cautionary literature often cites rates of 30 percent). Exaggeration can harm others— like men too readily regarded as beasts in custody cases—and, equally to the point, risks losing an audience that senses the distortion. It is time to move the debate about our disciplinary condition to a level at which we can grapple with real problems. The moral deterioration argument is a red herring.

Point 4: Reject zealotry. This book pleads for a better appreciation of the trends in self-control that surround us. Urging understanding may seem bland or even academic. Certainly, people caught in one of the dilemmas that our standards encourage—like girls carrying diet enthusiasms to anorectic extremes—may find little utility in pleas for greater knowledge and sophistication. In the long run, however, we will improve our cultural context only by grappling with its bases and then translating our conclusions into more moderate child-rearing advice and more responsible journalism. A crucial step is recognizing our national propensity toward moral extremism. Most Americans, to be sure, already discount the most obvious zealotry, acknowledging its excesses or simply not wanting to bother with such demanding goals. Yet residual guilt and anxiety remain, and some people are deeply ensnared into all-or-nothing thinking—whether about dieting, or smoking, or celibacy—that pushes them to unrealistic extremes and also unduly harsh judgments of others. Moderation is an old plea. In the American context, we must recognize our tendency to try to match potential excess in indulgence with even greater excess in discipline.

Moderation needs to balance some faddish enthusiasms. Americans are fond of symbolic intensities that satisfy a moral thirst at the expense of careful empiricism. This vulnerability increases when the symbolism is attached to claims of deterioration or morally linked health concerns. The attacks on secondhand smoke provide targets for outrage, but to date, the data on effects run well behind the furor: what we really are after is expressing our health fears and our resentment of undisciplined others. Zealous crusades against drugs deal with real problems but also, often, statistically modest ones. We have seen that our beliefs regarding addiction outpace the available evidence concerning several kinds of drugs. Some observers urge a calmer approach even to measurably addictive substances, noting that far fewer deaths result from drugs than from other forms of substance abuse and that a less character-based remedial program that provides more legal outlets for drug users might work better than current abolitionary efforts do. Issues of this sort need to be discussed, of course, but we can talk about them more constructively if we understand, and control, our own historically conditioned need for moral crusades.

The Legitimate Targets

The pattern of trade-offs in disciplinary emphases—relaxing strictures against laughter while tightening those on hygiene—can be evaluated in terms of the soundness of choice. As long as we acknowledge the general maintenance of discipline, we can appropriately question specific latitudes introduced into sexual standards, depending on our value system and judgment of social results. Worrying more about dieting than media sexuality as a moral index, for example, may simply be misplaced, not because we have abandoned our standards, but because our reshuffled priorities reflect a more debased taste (which must be defined and defended, not just asserted) and a less acute sense of social impact (which must be demonstrated). The relaxation of concern about lying merits attention as the most blatant distortion of Victorian standards. Because contemporary capitalism and politics depend on light-fingered truth, a reversal here would be challenging, but we might give it some thought.

It is possible that we should discipline spectator offerings more and ease up on the regulation of emotions at work. Here, too, it would be the trade-off, not some misassigned degeneracy, that would be targeted. The broader tendency to avoid judgmentalism, although it does not reflect an absence of standards, might also be rethought, as some philosophers and conservative commentators have suggested.[4] Some Americans, particularly the young, may need to become more conscious of what values they do hold and when tolerance may be inappropriate. Shorn of their tendency toward exaggeration, people who worry about certain aspects of American morality deserve a voice. We might make some norms more stringent, and we could also consider relaxing others that do not work well, like the excessive rigor applied to body fat, and that may distract us from more important goals. Clearly, we have moved away from some Victorian standards—though not from all standards— and a careful historical comparison of the resulting adequacy of personal and social behaviors is warranted. We must emphasize the care required, however: fantasy Victorianism without the spitting, the sexual titillation, the frequent anger, and the sweat is an irrelevant historical measurement

Historical understanding could serve to recast the discussion of staples such as pornography, without eliminating the subjective variable of tastefulness. Increasingly available pornography has not undermined normal sexual restraint or a nuanced prescriptive culture. Except for a small minority, the problem is not behavioral. Indeed, in a consumer society, pornography may enforce restraint. From 1992 to 1998, as sexual behavior became more cautious, rentals of video pornography increased by 100 percent. A culture that relies so heavily on fantasy distortions may well deserve review. But we need to get the reasons straight, particularly if we seek to persuade those whom the complex culture currently ensnares. Too often we argue off the mark, claiming damage that goes beyond the facts and thereby failing to convince those whom the culture seemingly satisfies.

The same invitation to more precise critiques could apply to a certain faddism apparent in American disciplinary exercises in the twentieth century. Even though the basic need to claim self-control has not really wavered despite some modest oscillations, targeting has proved a bit fickle, open to the latest generation of popularized expertise. In this respect, goals reflect some of the inherent tendencies of consumerism itself, even though they are designed to compensate, and the result may be needlessly confusing and at times superficial. There is a crusade-of-the-decade flavor to twentieth-century patterns, and the results may be less serviceable than a more consistent, less helter-skelter focus. Faddism also affects judicial balance. Harassment claims by the late 1980s were driving anxious, mostly male, administrators to accept accusations without much careful inquiry: sexual smoke must mean fire. By the late 1990s, these excesses, punished by heavy damage payments in several cases, caused a reversal, and what had been known about the problem of harassment and the difficulties faced by women bringing charges risked being forgotten entirely. Case-by-case inquiry, the obvious judicial recourse, tended to be overwhelmed by fad reactions to sexual symbolism. Here, as in other areas, American society can do better.

The distractions generated by cultural compensations for disciplinary rules also deserve scrutiny. Critics of American license, from the late-nineteenth-century action stories through comic books to television and rock music, have often argued that the presence of violent or sexual images risks misleading the audience, particularly when they are directed toward impressionable youth. Their arguments have not prevailed, however, despite modest gestures toward rating systems. And the arguments probably are not correct, just as they miss the mark on pornography: American habits, overall, have not become disastrously degenerate. When new areas of permissiveness in actual behavior have opened up, they usually have been balanced by enhanced regulations in other categories. Nor, of course, is it historically unusual for recreational or literary cultures to provide imaginary vistas that actually help audiences accept more limited realities, although this was not the dominant Victorian pattern. But compensatory cultures can mislead certain individuals and smaller groups toward believing that the representations of license authorize licentious behavior. It is thus possible that deviant lyrics and images can cause some people to go astray. Again, if carefully phrased (and not carried over into more general standards, which have not eased so much), this point is well worth evaluating.

In our general reassessment, we might also consider taste issues more closely, without trying to cloak them in erroneous statements about trends and behaviors. That is, we have trouble controlling bad judgments in lyrics or journalism, often leading to the assumption that whatever is sexual and commercial must be at the cutting edge. For instance, many commentators have noted the tackiness of a public and political culture that delights in commenting on the characteristics of an American president's private parts. We, or at least many groups of Americans in a society culturally divided, have become accustomed to excess as a means of counterbalancing real-life constraints. This trade-off is not inevitable. If we can confront somewhat more frankly our proclivity to urge restraint in our daily behavioral standards, we might also be more successful at dealing with rhetorical and visual excess in our compensatory outlets. If we depended less on spectator fantasies for release from constrained realities, we might be able to persuade the media to reconsider what they present—in the sexual innuendos of the sitcoms or the unnecessary regaling of the details of politicians' private lives. Less frustrated by rules that we often only vaguely perceive, we might withdraw audience support from the more tasteless compensations. The revision would be difficult but well worth considering in a society that looks far more seedy than it actually is.

Finally, now that we are more aware of Americans' moral needs and their relationship to consumerism, we might also attempt to improve their articulation. A society concerned about self-discipline in some respects remains profligate with goods, disposable products, and quick obsolescence. This is a case in which the enjoyment of abundance and a symbolic dependence on the nation as an inexhaustible "land of plenty" have outstripped moral reactions. We should study the failures of moralization efforts in this area, in a highly moralistic society. As consumers, we might usefully work harder on environmental controls—reducing our massive per capita world lead as creators of garbage—while easing up in some other obsessive areas, like needlessly frequent bathing and other body controls. The moral gain might hold steady, with superior social results.

The Flip Side

Our evaluation must not be confined, however, to areas of possible latitude. It also is important to ask about excessive rigor and limitation. We may be trying to tame the beast too much, with counterproductive results—as in gaining weight partly in response to worrying about slimming down—and, above all, with a needless loss of spontaneity and fun.

First, is a culture of fantasy outlets truly adequate? Pundits and scholars have been debating the human quality of twentieth-century leisure for some time.[5] On the one hand, people seem to like what is available: they watch television regularly, go to sanitized vacation spots where spontaneity is carefully limited, sit as spectators at an endless procession of sports events. If they like what they see, often noting how sports or television helps them cope with normal constraints, it may seem elitist to carp. But too much passive spectatorship surely has drawbacks, by inhibiting more careful consideration of real-life constraints and even detracting from constructive protest. It might be better, for example, to encourage and tolerate more anger against mindless work routines and less passive reliance on images of violence and sports aggression. Detractions aside, the limits in a normal life may not be sufficiently balanced by meaningful, expressive leisure. The problem warrants continued attention.

The late twentieth century did coin a meaningful phrase: Get a life. The term might apply simply to someone too preoccupied by work activities to find any pleasure away from the job. More commonly, "get a life" refers to a combination of work restraints and passive leisure interests that leave no time for spontaneity or unpredictable human contact (often including expressive sex). The phrase captures the increasing loneliness in which many Americans live, impelling the reassessment of a society far less filled with fun than its inhabitants are wont to claim.

American moralism itself has some drawbacks apart from its role in pushing a hedonism too often channeled into largely passive directions. This moralism also creates harmful political and diplomatic effects, isolating the nation in world opinion at crucial junctures and generating frivolous criteria for assessing politicians. More broadly, it risks becoming counterproductive. In explaining American moralism in the previous chapter, we noted that it has had some exemplary successes to its credit over the past two centuries. But it also can fail. Strictures in childhood can lead to teen rebellions. For instance, even as adults stopped smoking in the moralistic 1980s, its incidence among teenaged white girls rose. More recently still, smoking has been rising once again: cigars for prosperous adults and much higher cigarette use by high school and college students. Excessive pressure to lose weight, to measure down to impossible body images, has been part of the "eating rebellion" over the past fifteen years. Too much preaching regarding too many categories, backed by clearly exaggerated warnings, almost ensures reactions. The current phenomenon of behavioral rebellion has its counterparts earlier in the nineteenth and twentieth centuries. Excessive moralism can lead to unnecessary recklessness or a helpless surrender in light of impossible goals: a more balanced approach would work better.

The American approach to control surely tends toward excessive worry and self-denigration. Historians have discussed particular "ages of anxiety" in American history. At the personal level, many aspects of both the Victorian era and the twentieth century seem filled with unnecessary, or at least overly rigorous and numerous, alarms. By the end of the century, "persistent anxiety" had even become a disease category, open to doctors' diagnosis and treatment through medication.[6] Some Americans at least—there is no need to exaggerate the problem, pending further analysis—may impose so many standards on themselves that enjoyment and release become excessively difficult. We may not, to put the case bluntly, have enough fun—even as we divert ourselves by buying another product or watching another show. Judging a society by its capacity for pleasure is inherently inexact and risks seeming frivolous, particularly in the present period in which Americans are urged to consider yet again how they are failing to measure up to a new set of disciplinary demands. Even sex, for which Victorian standards—never fully imposed in any event—were obviously eased, may be needlessly surrounded by distracting guilts and self-doubts. We might consider lightening up on ourselves.

The reach of American moralism and the desire to rely on character go beyond personal calculations. The nation is noteworthy, for example, for policies that delay the approval of medicinal drugs and that refuse to accept European or other evidence of beneficial effects. There are many reasons for this, but one is the suspicion of remedies, especially psychiatric medications, that might undermine appeals to character. To be sure, Americans take a lot of drugs, and the number of prescriptions filled has risen exponentially. But both the amounts and the available range of drugs are eclipsed by those in countries like France and Germany. This is another area in which our character standards may be making our lives needlessly difficult. Addictions might be rethought in a society less bent on character correction. The concept describes some horrendous compulsions in a consumer age, but its wider role in explaining deviance, providing therapeutic redemption, and defining normalcy adds to the national anxiety. It would be interesting to see whether we could narrow the concept's scope.

Another issue to reconsider: value systems amid new diversity, a vital point in recent decades as Americans' moral reservoir was highlighted in new ways. Historians will look back on the ways would-be opinion shapers in the later twentieth century sought desperately, if not always explicitly, to promote a unitary disciplinary culture to counter the real or imagined effects of new immigration and the growing African American presence. The effort is understandable, but in insisting on restrictive values, deriving from past culture, it is miscast. It will not effectively override diversity but rather creates additional strains in the larger society; and it puts too much pressure on the coventional middle class itself. We need a more open search for the necessary minimum consensus, not the insistence on personal discipline alone.

Should we also address our larger cultural commitment to an ethic of self-help and personal responsibility? (And given its deep roots, *can* we address it?) It seems clear that at the end of the twentieth century, our insistence on character as the key to personal and social issues has fallen out of balance, though not for the first time in American history. We expect too many results from regulating individual behavior. Americans can remain committed to self-improvement while also recognizing the importance of larger issues, such as poverty or organizational constraints. Even self-help depends on a better knowledge of social realities than we currently encourage: working on character alone will not suffice. Sometimes we should protest our personal deficiencies less and the larger structural issues more. Our targets would be more accurate, and we would have a livelier, less fantasy-dependent society.

It is possible, of course, that Americans on balance not only enjoy but also benefit from the existing tensions and restrictions. Opportunities to move between beliefs in basic addictions and claims about the need for control over the same impulses create some latitude, as does the space between consumer temptation and moral critiques. Because of their very complexity, the formulas help accommodate diversity in a diverse society, even though extremists at both ends detest each other. But for those in the middle, the resulting confusions and occasions for excess or guilt may be disorienting, leading to behaviors that then must be regretted and expiated, from food binges to a midlife sexual excursion. Worrying both about having enough fun (the consumer requirement) and having too much fun (the moral legacy) may be historically inevitable, but perhaps it might be rethought.

The historian can offer no final judgments but should instead encourage a more informed and open debate about the effects of the contemporary version of self-control. Both critics of undue restriction (on the run, however, after the 1960s) and critics of inadequacies can contribute if the discussion is framed around real patterns and not oversimplified deteriorations from an imagined past. Furthermore, many Americans would profit from some probing debate of their own, with the starting point being an understanding of the impact of history in imposing standards on modern life. The standards are powerful, for in some cases they have been at work for two centuries, but we constructed them ourselves so they are not irretrievable. Even health and longevity goals, seemingly objective and closely associated with moral worth, are not sacrosanct. Twentieth-century Americans are more bounded than they often imagine, for their standards are compared with those of a partially mythical repressive past. All societies repress, but not all repress in the same ways or to the same degrees. We have our own history to assess when formulating or reevaluating our goals. We may decide that more control is needed, or different control, or less. Using recent history sensibly means stepping back from current standards to see how they have changed and what effects they have had—and what might profitably be altered. A generation can never shake off the hand of the past, but it can become more aware of it and begin, should it so decide, to modify it. The modern history of self-control, properly understood, enables choice, starting with the realization of how many standards most of us accept and how deep the impulse is to respond to affluence with guilty discipline. In this regard, government is not the only threat, and perhaps not the most pervasive threat, to responsible American freedom.

The targets most open to assessment include the current balance between escapist fantasy, commercially manipulated and subject to few definite boundaries, and workaday commitments to discipline. Many people would be better off extending the daily boundaries a bit—allowing themselves and others some emotional leeway, for example—while relying less on the consumption of passive alternatives (and possibly subjecting the alternatives themselves to clearer standards of taste). Constraints on children might be reassessed, including the effort to complicate access to birth control while presenting an unpleasurable picture of sex: with a more pragmatic, less moralistic approach, we might get better birth control results and also happier people. The interest in keeping down weight or smoking might be divested of the symbolic moralism that leads to counterproductive pressures and outright intolerance. Shifts of this sort would be difficult: a serviceable culture, now more than a century old, would change slowly at best. But just as it was constructed, so it can be revised. The first step is simply to acknowledge the restraints and trade-offs that have come to frame much of contemporary life.

NOTES

Notes to Chapter 1

1. C. Dallett Hemphill, "Middle Class Rising in Revolutionary America: The Evidence from Manners," *Journal of Social History* 30 (1996): 317–44; John Adams, *The Diary and Autobiography of John Adams*, vol. 1, ed. L. H. Butterfield (New York, 1964), pp. 68–69; Nancy Cott, "Religion and the Bonds of Womanhood," in J. E. Freedman, W. G. Shade, and M. J. Capozzoli, eds., *Our American Sisters* (Lexington, Mass., 1987), p. 139; quoting John Gregory, *A Father's Legacy to His Daughters* (London, 1822), and Daniel Chaplin, *A Discourse* (Andover, Mass., 1814).

2. Ben B. Lindsey, *The Revolt of Modern Youth* (New York, 1925), p. 216; Paul Robinson, in *The Modernization of Sex* (New York, 1976) coined the term *sex enthusiast* for some of the anti-Victorian spokespeople.

3. Robert M. Ireland, "Insanity and the Unwritten Law," *American Journal of Legal History* 32 (1988): 157–72, and "The Libertine Must Die: Sexual Dishonor and the Unwritten Law in the Nineteenth-Century United States," *Journal of Social History* 23 (1989): 27–44; *Burger v. State*, 238 Ga. 171, 172, 231 S.E. 2d 769, 771 (1977); Joshua Dressler, "Rethinking Heat of Passion: A Defense in Search of a Rationale," *Journal of Criminal Law and Criminology* 73 (1982): 421–34; Peter N. Stearns, *Jealousy: The Evolution of an Emotion in American History* (New York, 1989), chap. 3.

4. *Oxford English Dictionary*, 2d ed. (Oxford, 1989), s.v. "Judgmental"; I am grateful to Dr. Roger Wertheimer for these insights and for his own work on the ethical implications of the shifting evaluation of judgments. See his working paper "Constraining Condemning" (1996): "Ours is a culture conflicted about condemnation. Though much condemned, it's rarely much understood. Unsympathetic ethics instructors, frustrated by pandemic student queasiness at condemning that paralyzes moral judgment, dismissively diagnose the condition as ill-digested anti-objectivism, some virulent strain of relativism" (p. 2). See also his working paper "The Right to Judge Others" (1997).

5. Adam Bryant, "America's Latest Fad: Modesty It's Not," *New York Times Week in Review*, February 9, 1997, p. 3; George Will, "Our Whatever World," *Pittsburgh Post Gazette*, December 22, 1996, p. E-3.

6. Robert Bork, *Slouching toward Gomorrah: Modern Liberalism and American Decline* (New York, 1996).

7. Richard Bushman and James Morris, "The Rise and Fall of Civility in America," *Wilson Quarterly* (Autumn 1996): 13–46; Christopher Lasch, *The Culture of Narcissism: American Life in an Age of Diminishing Expectations* (New York, 1979), and *Haven in a Heartless World: The Family Besieged* (New York, 1977). On youth values, see Paula S. Fass, *The Damned and the Beautiful: American Youth in the 1920s* (New York, 1977), pp. 329–34. On current standards, see Alan Wolfe, *One Nation after All* (New York, 1998).

8. David Peterson del Mar, *What Troubles I Have Seen: A History of Violence against Wives* (Cambridge, Mass., 1996); John Burnham, *Bad Habits: Drinking, Smoking, Taking Drugs, Gambling, Sexual Misbehavior, and Swearing in American History* (New York, 1992).

9. Burnham, *Bad Habits,* chap. 8; see also Timothy Jay, *Cursing in America* (Philadelphia, 1992).

10. From http.wellsfargo,comn/ftr/ftrsty/ch11.

11. Alfred Kinsey, W. B. Pomeroy, and C. E. Martin, *Sexual Behavior in the Human Male* (New York, 1948), p. 670. Though the least common sexual contact, 8 percent of American males participated in bestiality at least once to the point of orgasm (4 percent urban, 17 percent rural), and even more had preorgasmic sexual contact with animals. Elisabeth Kübler-Ross, *Death: The Final Stage of Growth* (Englewood Cliffs, N.J., 1979), esp. pp. 5–6, 19–21; Daniel A. Fiore, " 'Grandma's Through': Children and the Death Experience from the 18th Century to the Present" (honor's thesis, Carnegie Mellon University, 1992).

12. William H. Whyte Jr., *The Organization Man* (New York, 1961). For an important recent study of one set of growing constraints, see Martin Wain, *Freud's Answer: The Social Origins of Our Psycho-Analytic Century* (Chicago, 1998).

13. Susan Porter Benson, *Counter Cultures: Saleswomen, Managers, and Customers in American Department Stores, 1890–1940* (New York, 1988); Arlie Russell Hochschild, *The Managed Heart: Commercialization of Human Feeling* (Berkeley and Los Angeles, 1983); Dale Carnegie, *How to Win Friends and Influence People* (New York, 1940), pp. 2, 27, 68, 70, 156; Peter N. Stearns, *American Cool: Constructing a Twentieth-Century Emotional Style* (New York, 1994).

14. Elizabeth Lasch-Quinn, "Race and Etiquette: Advice on Interracial Conduct since the 1960s," *Journal of Social History* 32 (1998). I am most grateful to Prof. Lasch-Quinn for access to this stimulating work.

15. Martin Bruegel, " 'Time That Can Be Relied Upon.' The Evolution of

Time Consciousness in the Mid-Hudson Valley, 1790–1860," *Journal of Social History* 28 (1995): 547–64.

16. Peter Gay, *Education of the Senses*, vol. 1: *The Bourgeois Experience, Victoria to Freud* (New York, 1984); Jed Dannenbaum, *Drink and Disorder: Temperance Reform in Cincinnati from the Washington Revival to the WCTU* (Urbana, Ill., 1984); Ellen Rothman, "Sex and Self Control: Middle-Class Courtship in America, 1770–1870," *Journal of Social History* 15 (1982): 409–25.

17. Gay, *Education of the Senses*.

18. Peter Filene, *Him/Herself: Sex Roles in Modern America*, 2d ed. (Baltimore, 1986); Stearns, *American Cool*, chap. 2.

19. John Kasson, *Rudeness and Civility: Manners in Nineteenth-Century Urban America* (New York, 1990); Ellen Rothman, *Hands and Hearts: A History of Courtship in America* (New York, 1989); Dannenbaum, *Drink and Disorder;* W. J. Rorabaugh, *The Alcoholic Republic: An American Tradition* (New York, 1981).

20. E. Anthony Rotundo, "Boy Culture: Middle-Class Boyhood in Nineteenth-Century America," in Mark Carnes and Clyde Griffen, eds., *Meanings for Manhood* (Chicago, 1990), pp. 15–36; Stearns, *American Cool*, chaps. 2, 3.

21. Karen Lystra, *Searching the Heart: Women, Men and Romantic Love in Nineteenth-Century America* (New York, 1989); Jon Butler, *Awash in a Sea of Faith: Christianizing the American People* (Cambridge, Mass., 1992); Roger Finke, "An Unsecular America," in Steven Bruce, ed., *Religion and Modernization* (Oxford, 1992), pp. 145–69.

22. Ruth Cowan, *More Work for Mother: The Ironies of Household Technology from the Open Hearth to the Microwave* (New York, 1953).

23. Cas Wouters, "Developments in the Behavioral Codes between the Sexes: The Formalization of Informalization, in the Netherlands, 1930–1985," *Theory, Culture, and Society* 4 (1987): 405–27, and "On Status Competition and Emotion Management," *Journal of Social History* 24 (1991): 699–717; Jürgen Gerhards, "The Changing Culture of Emotions in Modern Society," *Social Science Information* 28 (1989): 737–54.

24. For an excellent assessment of Prohibition and its collapse, see Burnham, *Bad Habits*, chap. 2.

25. "The Abolition of Death," *Current Opinion* 62 (April 1917): 270–71; Sarah N. Cleghorn, "Changing Thoughts of Death," *Atlantic Monthly*, December 1923, p. 812; Milton Weldman, "America Conquers Death," *American Mercury* 10 (February 1927): 216–27; Margaret Stroebe et al., "Broken Hearts in Broken Bonds," *American Psychologist* 47 (1992): 1205–12.

26. David Tyack and Elisabeth Hansot, *Learning Together: A History of*

Coeducation in American Public Schools (New Haven, Conn., 1990); Stearns, *Jealousy*, chaps. 3–5.

27. Hillel Schwartz, *Never Satisfied: A Cultural History of Diets, Fantasies, and Fat* (New York, 1983); Peter N. Stearns, *Fat History: Bodies and Beauty in the Western World* (New York, 1997).

28. Robert L. Rabin and S. D. Sugarmann, eds., *Smoking Policy: Law, Politics and Culture* (New York, 1993).

29. Peter N. Stearns, *Be a Man! Males in Modern Society*, 2d ed. (New York, 1990); Marc Fasteau, *The Male Machine* (New York, 1974); Jack Nichols, *Men's Liberation: A New Definition of Masculinity* (New York, 1975).

30. Sally McNall, "American Children's Literature, 1880–Present," in Joseph Hawes and N. Ray Hiner, eds., *American Childhood: A Research Guide and Historical Handbook* (Westport, Conn., 1988), pp. 377–411.

31. Benjamin Rader, "Compensatory Sports Heroes: Ruth, Grange and Dempsey," *Journal of Popular Culture* 19 (1983): 11; Allen Guttmann, *Sports Spectators* (New York, 1986).

32. Frederick Wertham, who wrote *The Seduction of the Innocent* (New York, 1954), was the great crusader. For a riposte, blasting Wertham's sentimental-Victorian evaluation of children, see also George N. Gordon, "Can Children Corrupt Our Comics," in D. M. White and A. H. Abel, eds., *The Funnies: An American Idiom* (New York, 1963), pp. 158–59.

33. Joel Pfister and Nancy Schnog, eds., *Inventing the Psychological: Toward a Cultural History of Emotional Life in America* (New Haven, Conn., 1997). The volume contains an essay by John Demos that explains the rapid and extensive American middle-class receptivity to psychology and psychoanalysis as a result of the intense, privatized family life of the nineteenth century. This is plausible, but new demands of self-control, building just as psychology popularizations hit the streets, provided a spur as well.

Notes to Chapter 2

1. For a discussion of the now-abandoned modernization/liberation approach to emotions history, see Steven L. Gordon, "The Sociology of Sentiments and Emotion," in Morris Rosenberg and R. H. Turner, eds., *Social Psychology: Sociological Perspectives* (New York, 1981), pp. 562–96.

2. John Demos, "Shame and Guilt in Early New England," in Carol Z. Stearns and Peter N. Stearns, eds., *Emotion and Social Change* (New York, 1988), pp. 69–86; John Kasson, *Rudeness and Civility: Manners in Nineteenth-Century Urban America* (New York, 1990).

3. Norbert Elias, *The Civilizing Process: The History of Manners*, trans. Ed-

mund Jephcott (New York, 1979); Kasson's *Rudeness and Civility* applies the theory to the United States, implicitly noting that the process began a bit later than in Europe. For a recent evaluation of the materials on the decline in homicides, see Jeffrey S. Adler, " 'My Mother-in-Law Is to Blame, but I'll Walk on Her Neck Yet': Homicide in Late Nineteenth-Century Chicago," *Journal of Social History* 31 (1997): 293–96.

4. Scott Sandage, "Creating the Modern Businessman: Credit Reporting and the Commodification of Character," chap. 4 of his "Deadbeats, Drunkards, and Dreamers: A Cultural History of Failure in America, 1819–1893" (Ph.D. diss., Rutgers University, 1995).

5. Cas Wouters, "Etiquette Books and Emotion Management in the 20th Century: The Integration of Social Classes," *Journal of Social History* 29 (1995): 107–24; Roy Rosenzweig, *Eight Hours for What We Will: Workers and Leisure in an Industrial City, 1870–1920* (Cambridge, 1985).

6. Cas Wouters, "Emotion Management in the 20th Century: The Integration of the Sexes," *Journal of Social History* 29 (1996): 325–40. See also this book, chap. 1, n. 21.

7. Jürgen Habermas offers another, related, model in his *The Structural Transformation of the Public Sphere: An Inquiry into a Category of Bourgeois Society* (Cambridge, Mass., 1991). His emphasis on a distinction between public and private spaces as a precondition for much of nineteenth-century discipline also combines continuities and shifts in the twentieth century, when different spaces overlap more confusingly, particularly with the advent of new public leisure areas but also the invasion of the home by outside voices and images from radio and television.

8. Cas Wouters, "Emotion Management in the 20th Century," pp. 325–40.

9. Michel Foucault, *History of Sexuality*, vol. 2 (New York, 1990). Although Foucault's popularity has declined somewhat, his insistence on the power of cultural constraints informs my own study. See also John D'Emilio, *Sexual Politics, Sexual Communities: The Making of a Homosexual Minority in the United States, 1940–1970* (Chicago, 1984).

10. David Riesman, with Nathan Glazer and Reuel Denney, *The Lonely Crowd: A Study of the Changing American Character* (New Haven, Conn., 1961); see also Christopher Lasch, *The Culture of Narcissism: American Life in an Age of Diminishing Expectations* (New York, 1979). Lasch uses a model similar to Riesman's, though with more perjorative judgments about the current incarnation. For empirical findings on clearly other-directed behavior in the United States, contrasted with European patterns, see Peter Salovey, ed., *The Psychology of Jealousy and Envy* (New York, 1991).

11. Warren Susman, *Culture as History: The Transformation of American*

Society in the Twentieth Century (New York, 1985), pp. 271–85; T. J. Jackson Lears, *No Place of Grace: Antimodernism and the Transformation of American Culture* (Chicago, 1994).

12. G. Stanley Hall, "A Study of Fear," *American Journal of Psychology* 8 (1897): 147–248; Lears, *No Place of Grace*. But on congenital arguments, see chapter 9 of this book.

13. Cesar Grana, *Bohemian versus Bourgeois* (New York, 1964).

14. Philip Rieff, *The Triumph of the Therapeutic: Uses of Faith after Freud* (New York, 1966); David Yankelovich, *New Rules: Searching for Self-Fulfillment in a World Turned Upside-Down* (New York, 1981).

15. A recent comment on the continuity of Victorian character concerns, as opposed to a personality replacement, is David Wickberg's *The Senses of Humor: Self and Laughter in Modern America* (Ithaca, N.Y., 1998).

16. R. P. Neuman, "Masturbation, Madness and the Modern Concepts of Childhood and Adolescence," *Journal of Social History* 8 (1975): 1–27.

17. Peter N. Stearns, *American Cool: Constructing a Twentieth-Century Emotional Style* (New York, 1994); Kevin White, *The First Sexual Revolution: The Emergence of Male Heterosexuality in Modern America* (New York, 1993); Jan Lewis and Peter N. Stearns, eds., *An Emotional History of the United States* (New York, 1998).

18. Christopher Clark, *The Roots of Rural Capitalism in Western Massachusetts, 1780–1960* (Ithaca, N.Y., 1990).

19. Robert Wells, "Family Size and Fertility Control in Eighteenth-Century American Society: A Study of Quaker Families," *Population Studies* 25 (1971): 73–82.

20. Alfred Chandler, *The Visible Hand: The Managerial Revolution in American Business* (Cambridge, Mass., 1977); Michael Grossberg, "Institutionalizing Masculinity: The Law as a Masculine Profession," in Mark Carnes and Clyde Griffen, eds., *Meanings for Manhood* (Chicago, 1990), pp. 133–51; T. J. Jackson Lears, "From Salvation to Self-Realization: Advertising the Therapeutic Roots of the Consumer Culture, 1880–1930," in R. W. Fox and T. J. Jackson Lears, eds., *The Culture of Consumption* (New York, 1983), pp. 1–38. On changes in work goals in child rearing amid the persistence of the rhetoric of character, see Daniel Rodgers, *The Work Ethic in Industrial America, 1850–1920* (Chicago, 1979).

21. Steven Seidman, *Romantic Longings: Love in America, 1830–1980* (New York, 1991), and "The Power of Desire and the Danger of Pleasure: Victorian Sexuality Reconsidered," *Journal of Social History* 24 (1990): 47–68; Clelia Mosher, *The Mosher Survey: Sexual Attitudes of Forty-Five Victorian Women* (New York, 1980).

22. Mark Thomas Connelly, *The Response to Prostitution in the Progressive Era* (Chapel Hill, N.C., 1980).

23. Peter N. Stearns, *Fat History: Bodies and Beauty in the Modern West* (New York, 1997).

24. Stanley Coben, *Rebellion against Victorianism: The Impetus for Cultural Change in 1920s America* (New York, 1991); Peter N. Stearns, *Be a Man! Males in Modern Society*, 2d ed. (New York, 1990); Leonard J. Moore, *Citizen Klansmen: The Ku Klux Klan in Indiana, 1921–1928* (Chapel Hill, N.C., 1991).

25. Felix Adler, *The Moral Instruction of Children* (New York, 1893); the book was reissued into the early 1900s. After a pause in significant new child-rearing literature, medical authors began to move in, initially using Victorian-sounding titles: for example, William Forbush, M.D., *The Character- Training of Children*, 2 vols. (New York, 1919). On the dominant nineteenth-century prescriptive styles, see Bernard Wishy, *The Child and the Republic* (Philadelphia, 1968).

26. Jennifer Scanlon, *Inarticulate Longings: The Ladies' Home Journal, Gender, and the Promises of Consumer Culture* (New York, 1995).

27. Jay Mechling, "Advice to Historians on Advice to Mothers," *Journal of Social History* 9 (1977): 44 ff.

28. Timothy Kelly and Joseph Kelly, "American Catholics and the Discourse of Fear," in Lewis and Stearns, eds., *Emotional History*, pp. 259–82.

Notes to Chapter 3

1. Horace Mann, *On the Education of Free Men* (New York, 1987; originally published 1843); see also Lindley Murray, *An English Reader* (Cooperstown, N.Y., 1829).

2. R. P. Neuman, "Masturbation, Madness and the Modern Concepts of Childhood and Adolescence," *Journal of Social History* 8 (1976): 1–27; G. J. Barker-Benfield, *Horrors of the Half-Known Life: Male Attitudes toward Women and Sexuality in Nineteenth-Century America* (New York, 1976); Mark West, "A Spectrum of Spectators: Circus Audiences in Nineteenth-Century America," *Journal of Social History* 15 (1981): 265–70.

3. Carol Z. Stearns and Peter N. Stearns, *Anger: The Struggle for Emotional Control in America's History* (Chicago, 1986).

4. L. Crocker, *An Analysis of Lincoln and Douglas as Public Speakers and Debaters* (Springfield, Ill., 1968); J. Podell and S. Anzoven, eds., *Speeches of the American Presidents* (New York, 1988), pp. 121–24.

5. John Demos, "Shame and Guilt in Early New England," in Carol Z.

Stearns and Peter N. Stearns, eds., *Emotion and Social Change* (New York, 1988), pp. 69–85; Bertram Wyatt-Brown, *Southern Honor* (New York, 1982).

6. Charles Rosenberg, *The Cholera Years* (Chicago, 1987).

7. Susan Sontag, *Illness as Metaphor* (New York, 1978).

8. John S. Haller Jr. and Robin Haller, *The Physician and Sexuality in Victorian America* (Urbana, Ill., 1974).

9. John Kasson, *Rudeness and Civility: Manners in Nineteenth-Century Urban America* (New York, 1990).

10. Karen Halttunen, *Confidence Men and Painted Women: A Study of Middle-Class Culture in America, 1830–1870* (New Haven, Conn., 1982); Scott Sandage, "Deadbeats, Drunkards, and Dreamers: A Cultural History of Failure in America, 1819–1893" (Ph.D. diss., Rutgers University, 1995).

11. Robert L. Griswold, "The Evolution of the Doctrine of Mental Cruelty in Victorian American Divorce," *Journal of Social History* 20 (1986): 127–48.

12. Paul Johnson, *The Shopkeepers' Millennium: Society and Revivals in Rochester, New York, 1815–1837* (New York, 1978) Mary K. Catyon, "Who Were the Evangelicals?: Conservative and Liberal Identity in the Unitarian Controversy in Boston, 1804–1833," *Journal of Social History* 31 (1997): 85–108.

13. Diary of Rachel Willard Stearns, July 19, 1835, cited in Nancy Cott, "Religion and the Bonds of Womanhood," in Jean Freeman, W. G. Shade, and M. J. Capozzoli, eds., *Our American Sisters* (Boston, 1987).

14. Christopher Clark, *The Roots of Rural Capitalism: Western Massachusetts, 1780–1860* (Ithaca, N.Y., 1990).

15. John Spurlock, *Free Love: Marriage and Middle-Class Radicalism in America, 1825–1860* (New York, 1988); Stephen Nissenbaum, *Sex, Diet and Debility in Victorian America: Sylvester Graham and Health Reform* (Westport, Conn., 1980).

16. Barbara Welter, "The Cult of True Womanhood, 1820–1860," *American Quarterly* 18 (1966): 151–74.

17. D. F. Musto, "Evolution of American Attitudes toward Substance Abuse," *Annals of the New York Academy of Science* 562 (1989); J. S. Blocker, *American Temperance Movements: Cycles of Reform* (Boston, 1989); J. R. Gusfield, *Symbolic Crusade: Status Politics and the American Temperance Movement* (Urbana, Ill., 1986); Edward Hitchcock, "Dyspepsy Forstalled and Resisted: or, Lectures on Diet, Regimen, and Employment," *Journal of Health* (1830): 312–13; S. Worcester, *The Drunkard Destroyed* (Boston, 1817); "Speech of Mr. Graham," *Graham Journal of Health and Longevity* (1939): 234–35.

18. David A. Johnson, *Policing the Urban Underworld: The Impact of Crime in the Development of the Police in America, 1800–1887* (Philadelphia, 1978).

19. Horace Bushnell, *Views of Christian Nurture* (Hartford, 1847); John

James, *The Family Monitor, or a Help to Domestic Happiness* (Concord, N.H., 1829); *Oxford English Dictionary* (Oxford, 1989), s.v. lying.

20. William H. Leffingwell and E. M. Robinson, *Textbook of Office Management* (New York, 1950); Margery Davies, *Woman's Place Is at the Typewriter: Office Work and Office Workers, 1870–1920* (Philadelphia, 1982); R. C. Borden and Alvin Busse, *How to Win a Sales Argument* (New York, 1926); Walter Dill Scott et al., *Personnel Management* (New York, 1941); Edward Kilduff, *The Private Secretary* (New York, 1915).

21. Peter N. Stearns, *American Cool: Constructing a Twentieth-Century Emotional Style* (New York, 1994), chaps. 2, 3; Kasson, *Rudeness and Civility*.

22. Susan J. Matt, "Frocks, Finery, and Feelings: Rural and Urban Women's Envy, 1890–1930," in Peter N. Stearns and Jan Lewis, eds., *Emotional History of the United States* (New York, 1998), pp. 377–95. Ida Tarbell, "A Woman and Her Raiment," *American Magazine* 74 (1912): 474; Mrs. James Cox, "The Council Chamber: A Special Talk with Girls," *Ladies Home Journal*, June 1903, p. 18.

23. Stearns and Stearns, *Anger;* Peter N. Stearns, *Jealousy: The Evolution of an Emotion in American History* (New York, 1989).

24. James Reed, *From Private Vice to Public Virtue: The Birth Control Movement and American Society since 1830* (New York, 1978); Clelia Mosher, *The Mosher Survey: Sexual Attitudes of Forty-Five Victorian Women* (New York, 1980).

25. State Medical Institute (Fort Wayne, Ind.), *A Friend of Mankind* (Fort Wayne, Ind., n.d. [1910–20]).

26. Neuman, "Masturbation"; Michel Foucault, *History of Sexuality*, vol. 2 (New York, 1990).

27. Peter N. Stearns, *Be a Man! Males in Modern Society*, rev. ed.(New York, 1990); Steven Seidman, "The Power of Desire and the Danger of Pleasure: Victorian Sexuality Reconsidered," *Journal of Social History* 24 (1990): 47–68.

28. Karen Lystra, *Searching the Heart: Women, Men and Romantic Love in Nineteenth-Century America* (New York, 1989); John Spurlock, "The Problem of Modern Married Love for Middle-Class Women," in Stearns and Lewis, eds., *Emotional History*, pp. 319–32; Byron Caldwell Smith, *The Love-Life of Byron Caldwell Smith* (New York, 1930), pp. 4, 9, 49, 74, 141–42; Gilbert Barnes and Dwight Dumon, eds., *Letters of Theodore D. Weld, Angelina Grimke Weld, and Sarah Grimke* (New York, 1934), pp. 588, 625.

29. Lisa M. Sigel, "Name Your Pleasure: The Transformation of Sexual Language in Nineteenth Century Pornography," unpublished article, Millsaps College, 1997.

30. Jacqueline S. Wilkie, "Submerged Sensuality: Technology and Percep-

tions of Bathing," *Journal of Social History* 19 (1986): 649–65; William Harvey Allen, *Civics and Health* (Boston, ca. 1909); Luther Gulick, *The Efficient Life* (New York, 1907), pp. 141, 148; Catharine Beecher, *A Treatise on Domestic Economy* (Boston, 1841), pp. 270–95; J. H. Walsh, *A Manual of Domestic Economy* (London, 1857), pp. 541–43.

31. Martha Verbrugge, *Able-Bodied Womanhood: Personal Health and Social Change in Nineteenth-Century Boston* (New York, 1988); Francis G. Gosling, *Before Freud: Neurasthenia and the American Medical Community* (Urbana, Ill., 1987); Alain Corbin, *The Foul and the Fragrant: Odor and the French Imagination* (Cambridge, Mass., 1986); Richard Schoenwald, "Training Urban Man," in H. J. Dyos and Michael Wolff, eds., *The Victorian City*, vol. 2 (London, 1973), pp. 669–92.

32. David Yosifon, "Laughter in Nineteenth-Century America," unpublished paper, Carnegie Mellon University, 1997; Philip Stanhope, fourth Earl of Chesterfield, *Letters of Advice to His Son* (1774; repr. New York, 1950), p. 35; J. Hamilton Moore, *The Young Gentleman and Lady's Monitor* (New York, 1802), pp. 216–17; Nancy Walker, *A Very Serious Thing: Women's Humor and American Culture* (Minneapolis, 1988). Mme. Celnart, *The Gentleman and Lady's Book of Politeness* (Boston, 1833), pp. 125–26; Cecil Hartley, *The Gentlemen's Book of Etiquette and Manual of Politeness* (Boston, 1860), p. 12.

33. David Yosifon and Peter N. Stearns, "The Rise and Fall of American Posture," *American Historical Review* 103 (1998): 1057–95; L. Dallett Hemphill, "Middle-Class Rising in Revolutionary America: The Evidence from Manners," *Journal of Social History* 30 (1996): 317–44; Emma Parker, *Important Trifles: Chiefly Appropriate for Females on Their Entrance into Society* (London, 1817); Edward Turner, *The Young Man's Companion* (Brattleboro, Vt., 1866), pp. 17, 19; Sharon Darling, *Chicago Furniture: Art, Craft and Industry* (New York, 1984), pp. 81–85; William B. Carpenter, *Principles of Human Physiology* (Philadelphia, 1850), p. 84.

34. Lewis Perry, "Progress, Not Pleasure, Is Our Aim: The Sexual Advice of an Antebellum Radical," *Journal of Social History* 12 (1979): 354–66.

35. Daniel Cohen, *Pillars of Salt, Monuments of Grace: New England Crime Literature and the Origins of American Popular Culture* (New York, 1993); Michael Barton, "Journalistic Gore: Disaster Reporting and Emotional Discourse in the New York Times, 1852–1956," in Stearns and Lewis, eds., *Emotional History*, pp. 155–72; Catherine Lutz and Jane Collins, *Reading National Geographic* (Chicago, 1993).

36. Jan Lewis, "Mother's Love: The Construction of an Emotion in Nineteenth-Century America," in Andrew Barnes and Peter N. Stearns, eds., *Social History and Issues in Human Consciousness* (New York, 1989), pp. 209–29.

37. Jeffrey Steele, "The Gender and Racial Politics of Mourning in Antebellum America," in Stearns and Lewis, eds., *Emotional History*, pp. 91–108; Robert Wells, "Taming the 'King of Terrors'; Ritual and Death in Schenectady, New York, 1844–1860," *Journal of Social History* 27 (1994): 717–34; Maris Vinovskis, "Angels' Heads and Weeping Willows: Death in Early America," *American Antiquarian Society, Proceedings* 86 (1976): 273–302.

38. Leslie Fischbein, "Harlot or Heroine? Changing Views of Prostitution, 1870–1920," *The Historian* 43 (1980): 23–36; David J. Pivar, *Purity Crusade: Sexual Morality and Social Control, 1868—1900* (Westport, Conn., 1973).

39. Harriet Beecher Stowe, 1845 letter quoted in Edmund Wilson, *Patriotic Gore* (New York, 1966), p. 22; Nancy Cott, "Passionlessness: An Interpretation of Victorian Sexual Ideals," *Signs* 4 (1978): 217–36.

40. Carroll Smith Rosenberg, "The Female World of Love and Ritual: Relations between Women in Nineteenth-Century America," *Signs* 1 (1975): 1–29; E. Anthony Rotundo, "Romantic Friendship: Male Intimacy and Middle-Class Youth in the Northern United States, 1800–1900," *Journal of Social History* 23 (1989): 1–28.

41. Stearns, *American Cool.*

42. Kasson, *Rudeness and Civility;* Emily Post, *Etiquette* (New York, 1922); Catharine Sedgwick, *Home* (Boston, 1834); Beecher, *Treatise on Domestic Economy.*

43. T. S. Arthur, *Advice to Young Ladies* (Boston, 1848), and *Advice to Young Men* (Boston, 1848); see also T. S. Arthur, *The Young Wife* (Philadelphia, 1846); William Alcott, *The Young Husband* (Boston, 1841).

44. Yosifon and Stearns, "Rise and Fall"; John W. Bright, *The Mother's Medical Guide: A Plain, Practical Treatise on Midwifery, and the Diseases of Women and Children* (Louisville, Ky., 1844), pp. 323–24; Francis D. Condie, M.D., *Practical Treatise on the Diseases of Children*, 3d ed. (Philadelphia, 1850), pp. 47, 50; R. W. Tamplin, *Lectures on the Nature and Treatment of Deformities* (Philadelphia, 1846), p. 257.

45. Mark Carnes, *Secret Ritual and Manhood in Victorian America* (New Haven, Conn., 1989); Rotundo, "Romantic Friendship." For comparable changes in women's companionship patterns, see Linda W. Rosenzweig, " 'Another Self'? Middle-Class American Women and Their Friends," in Stearns and Lewis, eds., *Emotional History*, pp. 357–76.

46. Edith Spencer, *The Spencers of Amberson Avenue* (Pittsburgh, 1983), pp. 121–24; D. P. Del Mar, *What Trouble I Have Seen: A History of Violence against Wives* (Cambridge, Mass., 1996).

47. Carroll Smith Rosenberg, *Disorderly Conduct: Visions of Gender in Victorian America* (New York, 1985); Mary Grew, Providence, R.I., to Isabel

Howland, Sherwood, N.Y., April 27, 1892, Howland Correspondence, Sophia Smith Collection, Smith College.

48. E. Anthony Rotundo, "Boy Culture: Middle-Class Boyhood in Nineteenth-Century America," in Mark Carnes and Clyde Griffen, eds., *Meanings for Manhood* (Chicago, 1989), pp. 15–36.

49. Joseph Kett, *Rites of Passage: Adolescence in America, 1790 to the Present* (New York, 1977); Wayne K. Durrill, "New Schooling for a New South: A Community Study of Education and Social Change, 1875–1885," *Journal of Social History* 31 (1997): 155–81.

50. Tamara K. Hareven and Randolph Langenbach, *Amoskeag: Life and Work in an American Factory City* (New York, 1978), p. 352; L. G. Lindahl, "Discipline One Hundred Years Ago," *Personnel Journal* 28 (1949): 246; Peter N. Stearns, "Emotional Change and Political Disengagement in the 20th-Century United States," in A. Kofler, ed., Special Issue on Emotion and Culture, *Innovation — The European Journal of Social Science* 10 (1997): 361–80; Mary Blewett, "Passionate Voices and Cool Calculations: The Emotional Landscape of the Nineteenth-Century New England Textile Industry," in Stearns and Lewis, eds., *Emotional History*, pp. 109–25.

51. Michael Katz, *In the Shadow of the Poorhouse: A Social History of Welfare in America* (New York, 1986).

52. Ellen Rothman, "Sex and Self Control: Middle-Class Courtship in America, 1790–1870," *Journal of Social History* 15 (1982): 409–26; Peter Gay, *The Bourgeois Experience, Victoria to Freud*, 2 vols. (New York, 1984–86).

53. Peter Filene, *Him/Herself: Sex Roles in Modern America*, 2d ed. (Baltimore, 1986).

54. Elizabeth Fox-Genovese, *Within the Plantation Household: Black and White Women of the Old South* (Chapel Hill, N.C., 1989), pp. 250–51; Elizabeth Parsons-Channing, *Autobiography* (Boston, 1907); Lydia Sigourney, *Lucy Howard's Journal* (New York, 1858), pp. 6–7; Charlotte Gilman, *Recollections of a Southern Matron* (New York, 1852), pp. 296–98.

55. Margaret Marsh, *Suburban Lives* (New Brunswick, N.J., 1990).

56. Ellen Rothman, *Hands and Hearts: A History of Courtship in America* (Cambridge, Mass., 1987); Annie Cox to Winan Allen, October 20, 1863, and March 1, 1865, Cox-Allen Papers, Newberry Library.

57. David M. Katzman, *Seven Days a Week: Women and Domestic Service in Industrializing America* (New York, 1987); Daniel Sutherland, *Americans and Their Servants: Domestic Service in the United States from 1809 to 1920* (Baton Rouge, La., 1981); Tera Hunter, *To Joy My Freedom* (Cambridge, Mass., 1997).

58. Smith Rosenberg, *Disorderly Conduct;* Steven Mintz and Susan Kellogg,

Domestic Revolutions: A Social History of American Family Life (New York, 1988).

59. James Mohr, *Abortion in America: The Origins and Evolution of National Policy, 1800–1900* (New York, 1978); Robert V. Wells, *Revolutions in Americans' Lives: A Demographic Perspective on the History of Americans, Their Families, and Their Society* (Westport, Conn., 1982) pp. 64–66, 83–86, and *passim;* Maris A Vinovskis, *Fertility in Massachusetts from the Revolution to the Civil War* (New York, 1981), pp. 117–51 and *passim;* Robert V. Wells, "Illegitimacy and Bridal Pregnancy in Colonial America," in Peter Laslett et al., eds., *Bastardy and Its Comparative History* (Cambridge, Mass., 1980), pp. 349–61; Daniel Scott Smith, "The Long Cycle in American Illegitimacy and Prenuptial Pregnancy," in Laslett et al., eds., *Bastardy*, pp. 362–78; D. S. Smith and Michael S. Hindus, "Premarital Pregnancy in America 1640–1971: An Overview and Interpretation," *Journal of Interdisciplinary History* 5 (Spring 1975): 537–70.

Notes to Chapter 4

1. Peter N. Stearns and Timothy Haggerty, "The Role of Fear: Transitions in American Emotional Standards for Children, 1850–1950," *American Historical Review* 96 (1989): 63–94; Mrs. Theodore Birney, *Childhood* (New York, 1906), pp. 24–29; Dorothy Canfield Fisher and Sidonie Gruenberg, *Our Children: A Handbook for Parents* (New York, 1932), pp. 134–37; Timothy Kelly and Joseph Kelly, "American Catholics and the Discourse of Fear," in Peter N. Stearns and Jan Lewis, eds., *Emotional History of the United States* (New York, 1998), pp. 259–82.

2. Mark Thomas Connelly, *The Response to Prostitution in the Progressive Era* (Chapel Hill, N.C., 1980).

3. Lawrence Levine, *Highbrow/Lowbrow: The Emergence of Cultural Hierarchy in America* (Cambridge, Mass., 1988); Ann Douglas, *Terrible Honesty: Mongrel Manhattan in the 1920s* (New York, 1995); Kathy Peiss, *Cheap Amusements: Working Women and Leisure in Turn-of-the-Century New York* (Philadelphia, 1986); Robert Toll, *On with the Show. The First Century of Show Business in America* (New York, 1976).

4. Elaine S. Abelson, *When Ladies Go A-Thieving: Middle Class Shoplifters in the Victorian Department Store* (New York, 1989); Vincent Vinikas, *Soft Soap, Hard Sell: American Hygiene in an Age of Advertisement* (Ames, Iowa, 1992); Richard W. Fox and T. J. Jackson Lears, eds., *The Culture of Consumption* (New

York, 1983); "Lucky Strike," *American Magazine* 81 (1916): 85; "Shredded Wheat," *Harper's* 47 (1903): 681.

5. Lindy Aron, *Ladies and Gentlemen of the Civil Service: Middle-Class Workers in Victorian America* (New York, 1987); Susan Porter Benson, *Counter Cultures: Saleswomen, Managers and Customers in American Department Stores, 1890–1940* (Urbana, Ill., 1986).

6. Stephen H. Norwood, *Labor's Flaming Youth: Telephone Operators and Worker Militancy, 1878–1923* (Urbana, Ill., 1990); Emily Post, *Etiquette* (New York, 1922), pp. 441–48; Claude Fischer, *America Calling: A Social History of the Telephone to 1940* (Berkeley and Los Angeles, 1992).

7. John D'Emilio and Estelle Freedman, *Intimate Matters: A History of Sexuality in America* (New York, 1988), part 3; Beth Bailey, "Scientific Truth . . . And Love: The Marriage Education Movement in the United States," *Journal of Social History* 20 (1987): 711–32; Mark Carnes, *Secret Ritual and Manhood in Victorian America* (New Haven, Conn., 1989); David Tyack and Elisabeth Hansot, *Learning Together: A History of Coeducation in American Public Schools* (New York, 1990).

8. Stephen Baker, *Visual Persuasion* (New York, 1961); Lois Banner, *American Beauty* (New York, 1983); D'Emilio and Freedman, *Intimate Matters;* Stuart Ewen and Elizabeth Ewen, *Channels of Desire: Mass Images and the Shaping of American Consciousness* (New York, 1982), pp. 125–40; T. J. Jackson Lears, *Fables of Abundance: A Cultural History of American Advertising* (New York, 1994), p. 149.

9. Susan J. Matt, "Frocks, Finery and Feelings: Rural and Urban Women's Envy, 1890–1930," in Stearns and Lewis, eds., *Emotional History*, pp. 377–95; Woods Hutchinson, "The Sin of Homeliness, the Duty of Every Woman to Be Well Dressed," *Saturday Evening Post* 183, no. 39 (1911): 45; *Ladies Home Journal*, June 1919, p. 153, and July 1928, p. 6; David Horowitz, *The Morality of Spending: Attitudes toward the Consumer Society in America, 1875–1940* (Baltimore, 1985).

10. Christy Callahan, "Body Hair Removal in the United States from a Social Historical Perspective," *Oakland Review* 23 (1996): 74–83; Christine Hope, "Caucasian Female Body Hair and American Culture," *Journal of American Culture* 5 (1982): 94–147; Susan Brownmiller, *Femininity* (New York, 1994), pp. 142–48; Kathy Peiss, *Hope in a Jar: The Making of America's Beauty Culture* (New York, 1998).

11. Peter N. Stearns, *Fat History: Bodies and Beauty in the Modern West* (New York, 1997); Hillel Schwartz, *Never Satisfied: A Cultural History of Diets, Fantasies and Fat* (New York, 1983); Emma Walker, "Pretty Girl Papers," *Ladies Homes Journal*, June 1904, p. 365, and January 1905, p. 33; Mrs. S. T.

Rorer, "Dietetic Sins and their Penalties," *Ladies Home Journal*, January 1906, p. 42.

12. Joy Ruth Ashmore, "Side-Talks with Girls," *Ladies Home Journal*, December 1896, p. 345, and May 1897, p. 29; "Mrs. Roper's Answers to Questions," *Ladies Home Journal*, January 1898, p. 31; *Physical Culture*, November 1918, p. 36, and February 1919, p. 15; Harold Wentworth and Stuart Flexner, eds., *Dictionary of American Slang* (New York, 1975), s.v. "slob."

13. David G. Phillips, *Susan Lenox: Her Fall and Rise* (New York, 1900); Edith Lowry, *The Woman of Forty* (Chicago, 1919), p. 33; Francis Benedict, "Food Conservation by Reduction of Rations," *Nation* 101 (1918): 355–57; Amelia Summerville, *Why Be Fat?* (New York, 1916), pp. 218–19.

14. Peter N. Stearns, *American Cool: Constructing a Twentieth-Century Emotional Style* (New York, 1994), pp. 148–64; Margaret Stroebe et al., "Broken Hearts in Broken Bonds," *American Psychologist* 47 (1992): 1205–12; Amy Vanderbilt, *New Complete Book of Etiquette* (New York, 1952), pp. 121, 126; "Grieving," *Independent* 64 (1908): 476–77; H. B. Marriott-Watson, "Some Thoughts on Pain and Death," *North American Review* 173 (1901); 540–53.

15. David Yosifon and Peter N. Stearns, "The Rise and Fall of American Posture," *American Historical Review* 103 (1998): 1057–95; Katherine C. Grier, *Culture & Comfort: People, Parlors, and Upholstery 1850–1930* (New York, 1988).

16. D. F. Lincoln, *School and Industrial Hygiene* (Philadelphia, 1880), pp. 31–37; Tait Mackenzie, M.D., "The Influence of School Life on Curvature of the Spine," *American Physical Education Review* 3 (1898): 274–80; George Muller, M.D., *Spinal Curvature and Awkward Deportment* (New York, 1894), pp. 3–4, 20, 24, 39.

17. Jessie H. Bancroft, "New Efficiency Methods of Training the Posture of School Children," *American Physical Education Review* 18 (1913): 309–13; Ethel Perrin, "Methods of Interesting School Children in Good Postural Habits," *American Physical Education Review* 19 (1914): 503–6; Yosifon and Stearns, "Rise and Fall."

18. James Martin and Mark Lender, *Drinking in America* (New York, 1982); see also chap. 3, n. 17; David Musto, "Evolution of American Attitudes toward Substance Abuse," *Annals of the New York Academy of Science* 502 (1989) and *The American Disease: Origins of Narcotic Control* (New York, 1987).

19. Lawrence Cremin, *The Transformation of the School: Progressivism and American Education, 1876–1957* (New York, 1961); Paul Chapman, *Schools as Sorters: Lewis M. Terman, Applied Psychology, and the Intelligence Testing Movement* (New York, 1988).

20. Harvey Green, *Fit for America: Health, Fitness, Sport and American*

Society (Baltimore, 1986); James C. Whorton, *Crusaders for Fitness: The History of American Health Reformers* (Princeton, N.J., 1982); David MacLeod, *Building Character in the American Boy: The Boy Scouts, YMCA, and Their Forerunners* (Madison, Wis., 1983); Mary Odem, *Delinquent Daughters: Protecting and Policing Adolescent Female Sexuality in the United States* (Chapel Hill, N.C., 1995); Steven Schlossman, *Love and the American Delinquent: The Theory and Practice of "Permissive" Juvenile Justice* (Chicago, 1977).

21. Stanley Coben, *Rebellion against Victorianism: The Impetus for Cultural Change in 1920s America* (New York, 1991).

Notes to Chapter 5

1. Scott Sandage, "Deadbeats, Drunkards, and Dreamers: A Cultural History of Failure in America, 1819–1893" (Ph.D. diss., Rutgers University, 1995); Joan Jacobs Brumberg, *Fasting Girls: The Emergence of Anorexia as a Modern Disease* (Cambridge, Mass., 1988); Edward Shorter, "Paralysis: The Rise and Fall of a 'Hysterical' Symptom," in Peter N. Stearns, ed., *Expanding the Past: A Reader in Social History* (New York, 1988), pp. 215–48; G. J. Barker-Benfield, *Horrors of the Half-Known Life: Male Attitudes toward Women and Sexuality in Nineteenth-Century America* (New York, 1976).

2. Robert Wiebe, *The Search for Order, 1879–1920* (New York, 1967); John Burnham, *Bad Habits: Drinking, Smoking, Taking Drugs, Gambling, Sexual Misbehavior, and Swearing in American History* (New York, 1992).

3. John Kasson, *Rudeness and Civility: Manners in Nineteenth-Century Urban America* (New York, 1990), conclusion; Cas Wouters, "On Status Competition and Emotion Management," *Journal of Social History* 24 (1991): 699–717, and "Human Figurations: Essays for Norbert Elias," *Amsterdams Sociologisch Tijdschrift* (1977): 438, 446; Abram de Swaan, "The Politics of Agoraphobia: On Changes in Emotional and Relational Management," *Theory and Society* 10 (1981): 373.

4. David Lewis, *The Secret Language of Success* (New York, 1989); Robbie Kaplan, *The Whole Career Sourcebook* (New York, 1991), p.154 (an American Management Association publication).

5. Carol Z. Stearns and Peter N. Stearns, *Anger: The Struggle for Emotional Control in America's History* (Chicago, 1986), chap. 5; Elton Mayo, *The Human Problems of Industrial Civilization* (New York, 1933), pp. 84 ff.

6. Peter Filene, *Him/Herself: Sex Roles in Modern America*, 2d. ed. (Baltimore, 1986).

7. Daniel Cohen, *Pillars of Salt, Monuments of Grace: New England Crime*

Literature and the Origins of American Popular Culture (New York, 1993), and "The Beautiful Female Murder Victim: Literary Genres and Courtship Practices in the Origins of a Cultural Motif, 1790–1850," *Journal of Social History* 31 (1997): 277–306.

8. C. Dallett Hemphill, "Class, Gender and the Regulation of Emotional Expression in Revolutionary-Era Conduct Literature," in Peter N. Stearns and Jan Lewis, eds., *Emotional History of the United States* (New York, 1998), pp. 33–51.

9. Nancy Cott, "Passionlessness: An Interpretation of Victorian Sexual Ideology, 1790–1850," *Signs: A Journal of Women in Culture and Society* 4 (1978): 219–36; Carl N. Degler, "What Ought to Be and What Was: Women's Sexuality in the Nineteenth Century," *American Historical Review* 79 (1974): 1467–90.

10. David J. Pivar, *Purity Crusade: Sexual Morality and Social Control, 1868–1900* (Westport, Conn., 1973); Leslie Fishbein, "Harlot or Heroine? Changing Views of Prostitution, 1870–1920," *The Historian* 43 (1980): 23–36; Nancy Cott, *The Grounding of American Feminism* (New Haven, Conn., 1987).

11. Burnham, *Bad Habits*, chap. 2.

12. T. J. Jackson Lears, *Fables of Abundance: A Cultural History of Advertising* (New York, 1995); Roland Marchand, *Advertising the American Dream: Making Way for Modernity, 1920–1940* (Berkeley and Los Angeles, 1985).

13. Stanley Coben, *Rebellion against Victorianism: The Impetus for Cultural Change in 1920s America* (New York, 1991).

14. Paul Robinson, *The Modernization of Sex* (New York, 1976).

15. A. Michael Sulman, "The Freudianization of the American Child: The Impact of Psychoanalysis in Popular Periodicals in the United States, 1919–1939" (Ph.D. diss., University of Pittsburgh, 1992).

16. Coben, *Rebellion;* Robert Lynd and Helen M. Lynd, *Middletown: A Study in Contemporary American Culture* (New York, 1929).

17. Judith Merkle, *Management and Ideology: The Legacy of the International Scientific Management Movement* (Berkeley and Los Angeles, 1980); Frederick W. Taylor, *Shop Management* (New York, 1911); Loren Baritz, *Servants of Power: A History of the Use of Social Science in American History* (Middletown, Conn., 1960); Stephen Meyer, *The Five-Dollar Day: Labor, Management and Social Control in the Ford Motor Company* (Albany, N.Y., 1981).

18. G. Stanley Hall, "A Study of Fear," *American Journal of Psychology* 8 (1897): 147–248; Sybil Foster, "A Study of the Personality Makeup and Social Setting of Fifty Jealous Children," *Mental Hygiene* 11 (1927): 533–71; Mabel Sewall, "Some Causes of Jealousy in Young Children." *Smith College Studies in*

Social Work 1 (1930–31): 6–22; for an assessment of the old sibling studies, see Juy Dunn and Carl Kendrick, *Siblings: Love, Envy, and Understanding* (Cambridge, Mass., 1982).

19. Regina Kunzel, "The Professionalization of Benevolence," *Journal of Social History* 22 (1988): 21–43; Beth Bailey, "Scientific Truth . . . And Love: The Marriage Education Movement in the United States," *Journal of Social History* 20 (1987): 711–32.

20. Leone Kell and Jean Aldous, "Trends in Child Care over Three Generations," *Marriage and Family Living* 22 (1960): 176–77; Celia Stendler, "Sixty Years of Child Training Practices," *Journal of Pediatrics* 36 (1950): 122–34; Martha Wolfenstein, "Trends in Infant Care," *American Journal of Orthopsychiatry* 23 (1953): 120–30.

21. Christopher Lasch, *Haven in a Heartless World: The Family Besieged* (New York, 1977).

22. On the role of middle-class occupations on the reception of new child-rearing ideas, see Daniel Miller and Guy Swanson, *The Changing American Parent* (New York, 1958).

23. Alfred Chandler, *The Visible Hand: The Managerial Revolution in American Business* (Cambridge, Mass., 1977); Michael Grossberg, "Institutionalizing Masculinity: The Law as a Masculine Profession," in Mark Carnes and Clyde Griffen, eds., *Meanings for Manhood* (Chicago, 1990), pp. 133–51.

24. William Chafe, *Women and Equality* (New York, 1990); Susan Householder Van Horn, *Women, Work and Fertility, 1900–1986* (New York, 1988).

25. Daniel Rodgers, *The Work Ethic in Industrializing America, 1850–1920* (Chicago, 1978); Susan Porter Benson, *Counter Cultures: Saleswomen, Managers and Customers in American Department Stores, 1890–1940* (Urbana, Ill., 1986); Stearns and Stearns, *Anger;* Peter N. Stearns, *Fat History: Bodies and Beauty in the Modern West* (New York, 1997); Reinhard Bendix, *Work and Authority in Industry: Ideologies of Management in the Course of Industrialization* (Berkeley and Los Angeles, 1956), chap. 7.

26. T. J. Jackson Lears, "From Salvation to Self-Realization: Advertising and the Therapeutic Roots of the Consumer Culture, 1880–1930," in Richard Wightman Fox and Lears, eds., *The Culture of Consumption* (New York, 1983), pp. 1–38; Peter N. Stearns, *Be a Man! Males in Modern Society,* rev. ed. (New York, 1990); Leonard J. Moore, *Citizen Klansman: The Ku Klux Klan in Indiana, 1921–1928* (Chapel Hill, N.C., 1991).

27. Francis G. Gosling, *Before Freud: Neurasthenia and the American Medical Community* (Urbana, Ill., 1987); Tom Lutz, *American Nervousness, 1903: An Anecdotal History* (Ithaca, N.Y., 1991).

28. *Presbyterian Banner*, June 7, 1876, January 15, 1879, July 28, 1875; Peter N. Stearns, "Consumerism and Childhood: New Targets for American Emotions," in Stearns and Lewis, eds., *Emotional History*, pp. 396–416; Francis G. Couvares, *The Remaking of Pittsburgh: Class and Culture in an Industrializing City, 1877–1919* (Albany, N.Y., 1984); Marchand, *Advertising the American Dream*; Vincent Vinikas, *Soft Soap, Hard Sell: American Hygiene in an Age of Advertisement* (Ames, Iowa, 1992). William Waits, *The Modern Christmas in America* (New York, 1993); Viviana Zelizer, *Pricing the Priceless Child* (Newport, 1986); Miriam Formanek-Brunell, "Sugar and Spice: The Politics of Doll Play in Nineteenth Century America," in Elliot West and Paul Petrik, eds., *Small Worlds: Children and Adolescents in America, 1850–1950* (Lawrence, Kans., 1992), pp. 107–24; Elaine S. Abelson, *When Ladies Go A-Thieving: Middle Class Shoplifters in the Victorian Department Store* (New York, 1989); Patricia O'Brien, "The Kleptomania Diagnosis: Bourgeois Women and Theft in Late Nineteenth-Century France," in Stearns, *Expanding the Past*, pp. 105–17; Mark Swiencicki, "Consuming Brotherhood: Men's Culture, Style, and Recreation as Consumer Culture, 1880–1930," *Journal of Social History* 31 (1998): 723–808; Stephen Nissenbaum, *The Battle for Christmas* (New York, 1997).

29. Larry May, *Screening out the Past: The Birth of Mass Culture and the Motion Picture Industry* (New York, 1980); Norman Katkov, *The Fabulous Fanny: The Story of Fanny Brice* (New York, 1953), pp. 58–59.

30. Deeply appreciated rituals and recreations that clash with normal manners are not unusual. At the end of the Middle Ages, lance-swinging knights pretended to make war in an aristocracy becoming less violent; presumably the contrast with courtly manners was a relief. The Balinese cockfight described by anthropologist Clifford Geertz diverged from a rather subdued daily ethic. But the initial movement to a compensatory culture, as occurred in the shift from Victorianism's confirmatory to the twentieth century's escapist fare, deserves a close analysis of its causes and functions.

31. *Pittsburgh Post-Gazette*, June 25, 1997.

32. Christine Ruane, "Clothes Shopping in Imperial Russia: The Development of a Consumer Culture," *Journal of Social History* 28 (1995): 765–82; Warren G. Breckman, "Disciplining Consumption: The Debate about Luxury in Wilhelmine Germany, 1890–1914," *Journal of Social History* 24 (1991): 485–506; Rosalind Williams, *Dream Worlds: Mass Consumption in Late Nineteenth-Century France* (Berkeley and Los Angeles, 1982); Emile Zola, *Au bonheur des dames* (Paris, 1871).

33. Thorstein Veblen, *Theory of the Leisure Class: An Economic Study of Institutions* (New York, 1912); Stephen Nissenbaum, *Sex, Diet and Debility in*

Jacksonian America: Sylvester Graham and Health Reform (Westport, Conn., 1980).

34. Jürgen Kocka, *White Collar Workers in America, 1890–1940: A Social-Political History in International Perspective* (Beverly Hills, Calif., 1980).

35. Simon Patten, "Overnutrition and Its Social Consequences," *Annals* 10 (1897): 44–46, and *New Basis of Civilization* (1907; repr., Cambridge, Mass., 1969); Daniel M. Fox, *The Discovery of Abundance: Simon N. Patten and the Transformation of Social Theory* (New York, 1976).

36. James T. Patterson, *The Dread Disease: Cancer and Modern American Culture* (Cambridge, Mass., 1987).

37. James Reed, *From Private Vice to Public Virtue: The Birth Control Movement and American Society Since 1830* (New York, 1978); Linda Gordon, *Woman's Body, Woman's Right: A Social History of Birth Control in America* (New York, 1976).

38. Steven Seidman, *Romantic Longings: Love in America, 1830–1980* (New Brunswick, 1992); Kevin White, *The First Sexual Revolution: The Emergence of Male Heterosexuality in Modern America* (New York, 1993).

39. On the moral impact of the declining birthrate, see Rudolph Binion, "Fiction as Social Fantasy: Europe's Domestic Crisis of 1879–1914," *Journal of Social History* 27 (1994): 679–700.

40. John D'Emilio, *Sexual Politics, Sexual Communities: The Making of a Homosexual Minority in the United States, 1940–1970* (Chicago, 1983); George Chauncey Jr., "Christian Brotherhood or Sexual Perversion? Homosexual Identities and the Construction of Sexual Boundaries in the World War One Era," *Journal of Social History* 19 (1985): 189–211.

41. Margaret Mead, *Blackberry Winter: My Earlier Years* (New York, 1972), pp. 102–9.

42. Peter N. Stearns, *Jealousy: The Evolution of an Emotion in American History* (New York, 1989).

Notes to Chapter 6

1. Jeffrey Adler, " 'My Mother-in-Law Is to Blame, but I'll Walk on Her Neck Yet': Homicide in Late Nineteenth-Century Chicago," *Journal of Social History* 31 (1997): 253–76; Elizabeth Pleck, *Domestic Tyranny: The Making of Social Policy against Family Violence from Colonial Times to the Present* (New York, 1987).

2. John Dollard et al., *Frustration and Aggression* (New Haven, Conn., 1939); Donald A. Laird and Eleanor Laird, *The Strategy of Handling Children* (New York, 1949), p. 78; Harold W. Bernard, *Toward Better Personal Adjust-*

ment (New York, 1951), p. 170; B. E. Schwarz and B. A. Ruggieri, *Parent-Child Tensions* (Philadelphia, 1958), p. 48.

3. Angelo Patri, *Talks to Mothers* (New York, 1929), pp. 38–39; Norma Cutts and Nicholas Moseley, *Better Home Discipline* (New York, 1950), pp. 116–23; Frank Richardson, "Quarrelsomeness," *Parents' Magazine* 7 (1927): 19; Fritz Redl, "What Do You Do When They Fight," *Parents' Magazine* 32 (1957): 42; Ernest Grove, *Whole Childhood* (Boston, 1931), pp. 139–40; Gary Myers, *The Modern Family* (New York, 1934), pp. 200–1.

4. Pleck, *Domestic Tyranny;* "When They're Angry," *Newsweek*, April 16, 1962, p. 74; "Battered Child Syndrome, *Time*, July 20, 1962, p. 60; "Medics," *People*, November 8, 1982.

5. "Medics."

6. J. L. Bernstein, "Is the Bankruptcy Act Bankrupt?" *American Mercury*, October 1960, pp. 66–75; "Why Are So Many People Going Bankrupt?" *U.S. News and World Report*, April 3, 1967, pp. 83–85; "Bankruptcy: One Way Out," *U.S. News and World Report*, December 30, 1974, pp. 49–50; "Behind the Surge in Personal Bankruptcies," *U.S. News and World Report*, May 25, 1981, pp. 87–88; "Deadbeat Nation," *Newsweek*, April 14, 1997, p. 50; William Hotchkiss, "Two Years of the Federal Bankruptcy Law," *North American Review*, April 1901, pp. 573–83.

7. Edward Kilduff, *The Private Secretary* (New York, 1915), pp. 50, 57; see also later editions to 1935; Harry W. Hepner, *Human Relations in Changing Industry* (New York, 1938), p. 96; Annette Garrett, *Counseling Methods for Personnel Workers* (New York, 1944), p. 71.

8. Luella Cole and John Morgan, *Childhood and Adolescence* (New York, 1947), pp. 373–82; William Bauer, *Stop Annoying Your Children* (Indianapolis, 1947), pp. 121–33; Hornell Hart and Ella Hart, *Personality and the Family* (Boston, 1941), pp. 413–16; Rev. George Kelly, *The Catholic Family* (New York, 1959), pp. 48–50.

9. Amy Vanderbilt, *Etiquette* (New York, 1952), p. 755; Irma Black, *Off to a Good Start, a Handbook for Parents* (New York, 1953), pp. 50–52; David Goodman, *A Parent's Guide to the Emotional Needs of Children* (New York, 1969), p. 241; Benjamin Spock and Michael Rothenberg, *Dr. Spock's Baby and Child Care* (New York, 1985), pp. 569–71; Joseph Teich, *Your Child and His Problems* (Boston, 1953), p. 146; Alan Fromme, *The Parents Handbook* (New York, 1956), pp. 148–51; Homer Lane, *Talks to Parents and Teachers* (New York, 1969); Haim Ginott, *Between Parent and Child* (New York, 1965), pp. 58–63; Nancy Samalin and Patricia McCormick, "The Truth behind Lying," *Parents' Magazine* (November 1955): 121; Esther Davidowitz, "Is Honesty the Best Policy?" *Parents' Magazine* (April 1990): 84; William Sayres, "The Lighter

Side of Lying," *Parents' Magazine* (June 1989): 131; Jane Marks, "Why Kids Lie," *Parents' Magazine* (June 1987): 112.

10. Paul Boyer, *Enduring Vision* (New York, 1996), p. 783. Note that this figure was more than 50 percent above the 1996 level, despite vastly fewer people and drivers.

11. Joel W. Eastman, *Styling versus Safety: The American Automobile Industry and the Development of Automotive Safety 1900–1966* (New York, 1984). I am grateful to Joel Tarr and particularly John Thomas for appropriate references in this area.

12. U.S. House Committee on Interstate and Foreign Commerce, Traffic Safety, *Hearings* 1956, pp. 225, 863; James Ridgeway, "Car Design and Public Safety," *New Republic*, September 19, 1964, p. 9; "How Accidents Are Caused," *Newsweek*, April 13, 1953, p. 81; Harry DeSilva, *Why We Have Automobile Accidents* (New York, 1942), pp. vii, xiv; Eastman, *Styling versus Safety*, pp. 148–49; American Automobile Association, Safety Responsibility Committee, *Safety Responsibility Bill* (n.p., 1931); American Management Association, *Compulsory Automobile Insurance* (n.p., 1936); Automobile Club of Michigan, Safety and Traffic Division, "Lecture on Uniform Traffic Law and the Safety Responsibility Bill for Use in Senior and Junior H.S." (n.p., 1934); American Association of Motor Vehicle Administrators, *Procedure for the Minimum Standard Examination for Drivers* (n.p., 1939); E. W. Jones, *Improving Driver Responsibility* (New York, 1939); Automobile Club of Southern California, Public Safety Department, *Course of Study in Safety* (Los Angeles, 1928); California Department of Motor Vehicles, *Guide for Instructors of Traffic Schools for Violators* (Los Angeles, 1936); New Hampshire Department of Motor Vehicles, *An Elective Non-Unit Course in Automobile Driving in Secondary Schools, Designed to Prepare for a Driver's License* (n.p., 1935); National Safety Council, Education Division, *A Program for Organizing a High School Senior Traffic Club* (Washington, D.C., 1932); California Department of Education, *Manual on Traffic Safety for the California Secondary Schools* (Sacramento, 1936); American Automobile Association, *Sportsmanlike Driving: A Teachers' Outline for a Course in Traffic Safety and Driving for High Schools* (Chicago, 1935).

13. Katherine Fisher, "A Man's Job," *National Safety News* 36 (1937): 40.

14. Joel Tarr and Mark Tebeau, "Managing Danger in the Home Environment, 1900–1940," *Journal of Social History* 29 (1996): 797–816; John Burnham, "Why Did Infants and Toddlers Die? Shifts in Americans' Ideas of Responsibility for Accidents—From Blaming Mom to Engineering," *Journal of Social History* 29 (1996): 817–38.

15. *Pittsburgh Post-Gazette*, July 20, 1997, p. A5.

16. Dorothy Canfield Fisher and Sidonie Gruenberg, *Our Children* (New

York, 1932), pp. 119, 177; Carl Renz and Mildred Renz, *Big Problems on Little Shoulders* (New York, 1934), pp. 84–87; Benjamin Spock, *The Common Sense Book of Baby and Child Care* (New York, 1946), pp. 195–96.

17. Fritz Redt, *When We Deal with Children* (New York, 1966), pp. 136–37.

18. Renz and Renz, *Big Problems*, p. 84; Peter N. Stearns, *American Cool: Constructing a Twentieth-Century Emotional Style* (New York, 1994), chaps. 4, 5.

19. Ruth Benedict, *The Chrysanthemum and the Sword* (Boston, 1946); Robert I. Watson, *The Psychology of the Child* (New York, 1959), p. 460.

20. Brian Mendelez, "Honor Code Study," *Harvard University Report*, September 1985; (Bryn Mawr) *College News*, May 12 and December 9, 1953, and February 10 and April 14, 1954. My thanks to Clio Stearns for these references.

21. My thanks for this observation, inherently impressionistic, to Dr. Natalia Basovskaya, vice-rector of the Russian State University for the Humanities.

22. Colin Campbell, *The Romantic Ethic and the Spirit of Modern Consumerism* (London, 1989); Roland Marchand, *Advertising the American Dream: Making Way for Modernity, 1920–1945* (Berkeley and Los Angeles, 1985); Vincent Vinikas, *Soft Soap, Hard Sell: American Hygiene in an Age of Advertisement* (Ames, Iowa, 1992); Francis Couvares, *The Remaking of Pittsburgh: Class and Culture in an Industrializing City, 1877–1919* (Albany, N.Y., 1984).

23. Susan J. Matt, "Frocks, Finery and Feelings: Rural and Urban Women's Envy, 1890–1930," in Peter N. Stearns and Jan Lewis, eds., *Emotional History of the United States* (New York, 1998), pp. 377–95; *Ladies Home Journal*, editorial 40, no. 1 (1923): 24.

24. *Ladies Home Journal* 36, no. 6 (1919): 153; 42, no. 11 (1925): 132; and 45, no. 7 (1928): 6; *Saturday Evening Post*, November 19, 1921, p. 49.

25. D. H. Thom, *Child Management* (Washington, D.C., 1925), pp. 9–12; Peter N. Stearns, *Jealousy: The Evolution of an Emotion in American History* (New York, 1989); U.S. Department of Labor, Children's Bureau, *Are You Training Your Child to Be Happy?* (Washington, D.C., 1930), p. 31; Child Study Association of America, *Guidance of Children and Youth* (New York, 1926), pp. 100–1; Herman Vollmer, "Jealousy in Children," *American Journal of Orthopsychiatry* 16 (1946): 187; Ada Hart Arlitt, *The Child from One to Twelve* (New York, 1931).

26. Gordon Clanton, "Jealousy in American Culture, 1945–1985; Reflections from Popular Literature," in D. Franks and E. D. McCarthy, eds., *The Sociology of Emotions* (Greenwich, Conn., 1989), pp. 179–93; Evelyn Duvall, *Facts of Life and Love for Teenagers* (New York, 1950), pp. 210, 231; Alexander

Magoun, *Love and Marriage* (New York, 1956), pp. 301–6; Judson Landis and Mary Landis, *A Successful Marriage* (Englewood Cliffs, N.J., 1958), p. 82; Lear J. Saul, *Fidelity and Infidelity, and What Makes or Breaks a Marriage* (Philadelphia, 1961), p. 73; John Levy and Ruth Monroe, *The Happy Family* (New York, 1962), p. 89.

27. Mendelez, "Honor Code Study"; Walter B. Kolesnick, *Education Psychology* (New York, 1963), p. 458; John R. Ban, "A Lesson Plan Approach for Dealing with School Discipline," *Clearinghouse* 55 (1982): 345; Robert Geiser, "What to Do If You Can't Stand That Kid," *Teacher* 91 (1973): 14–16.

28. E. E. Le Masters, *Modern Courtship and Marriage* (New York, 1957), pp. 132–33; Ernest A. Smith, *American Youth Culture* (Glencoe, Ill., 1962); Willard Waller, "The Rating and Dating Complex," *American Sociological Review* 2 (1937): 727–34; Beth Bailey, *From Front Porch to Back Seat: Courtship in Twentieth-Century America* (Baltimore, 1988).

29. Richard H. Smith, Sung Hee Kim, and W. Gerrod Parrott, "Envy and Jealousy; Semantic Problems and Experimental Distinctions," *Personality and Social Psychology Bulletin* 14 (1988): 401–9; Stearns, *Jealousy*, pp. 219–20.

30. Marchand, *Advertising the American Dream;* Peter Salovey, ed., *The Psychology of Jealousy and Envy* (New York, 1991).

31. Adler, " 'My Mother-in-Law Is to Blame' "; Roger Lane, *Violent Death in the City* (Cambridge, Mass., 1979); Eric Monkkonen, "New York City Homicides: A Research Note," *Social Science History* 19 (1995): 201–14.

32. Leon Baritz, *The Servants of Power: A History of the Use of Social Science in American Industry* (Middletown, Conn., 1960); Stanley M. Herman, *The People Specialists* (New York, 1968), pp. 245 ff; Stephen Meyer, *The Five Dollar Day: Labor Management and Social Control in the Ford Motor Company, 1908–1921* (Albany, N.Y., 1981); Daniel Nelson, *Managers and Workers: Origins of the New Factory System in the United States, 1880–1920* (Madison, Wis., 1975).

33. Elton Mayo, *The Human Problems of an Industrial Civilization* (New York, 1933), pp. 84 ff; F. J. Roethisberg and William J. Dickson, *Management and the Worker* (Cambridge, Mass., 1941), pp. 180 ff; Walter Dill Scott et al., *Personnel Management: Principles, Practice and Point of View* (New York, 1941); R. C. Borden and Alvin Busse, *How to Win a Sales Argument* (New York, 1926), p. 7.

34. Garrett, *Counseling Methods;* Baritz, *Servants of Power;* Nathaniel Cantor, *Employee Counseling: A New Viewpoint in Industrial Psychology* (New York, 1945), pp. 64–73; Helen Baker, *Employee Counseling* (Princeton, N.J., 1944).

35. G. W. Wadsworth, "How to Pick the Men You Want," *Personnel Journal* 14 (1935): 334; Doncaster Humm and G. W. Wadsworth, "Temperament in

Industry," *Personnel Journal* 21 (1942): 314–22; D. L. Kirkpatrick, "How to Select Foremen," *Personnel Journal* 47 (1968): 262–70; Kilduff, *The Private Secretary*, pp. 50, 57.

36. Roethisberger and Dickson, *Management and the Worker*, pp. 212, 348; Rexford Hersey, *Better Foremanship* (Philadelphia, 1961), p. 10; Glenn Gardiner, *Better Foremanship* (New York, 1941), pp. 53–54; Garrett, *Counseling Methods*, p. 120. Jai Ghorpade and J. R. Lackrits, "Influences behind Neutral Responses in Subordinate Ratings of Supervisors," *Personnel Psychology* 34 (1981): 511–22; Charles W. Walker and Robert Guest, *The Man and the Assembly Line* (Cambridge, Mass., 1952), pp. 92–99.

37. Paul W. Johnson and J. C. Bledsoe, "Morale as Related to Perceptions of Leadership Behavior," *Personnel Psychology* 26 (1973): 581–91; M. L. Gross, *The Brain Watchers* (New York, 1962); William Leffingwell and E. M. Robinson, *Textbook of Office Management* (New York, 1950), pp. 386–92; Judith Merkle, *Management and Ideology: The Legacy of the International Scientific Management Movement* (Berkeley and Los Angeles, 1980).

38. Studs Terkel, *Working* (New York, 1976), pp. 30, 81, 265, 285, 547; C. Wright Mills, *White Collar: The American Middle Classes* (New York, 1953), p. 184; Arlie Hochschild, *The Managed Heart: Commercialization of Human Feeling* (Berkeley and Los Angeles, 1983), pp. 25, 33, 115. Barbara Ehrenreich, *The Hearts of Men: American Dreams and the Flight from Commitment* (New York, 1983).

39. Dale Carnegie, *How to Win Friends and Influence People* (New York, 1940), pp. 2, 27, 68, 70, 156; Borden and Busse, *How to Win a Sales Argument*, p. 7; Todd A. Postol, "Creating the American Newspaper Boy: Middle-Class Route Service and Juvenile Salesmanship in the Great Depression," *Journal of Social History* 31 (1997): 327–45.

40. Hochschild, *Managed Heart*; Carol Z. Stearns and Peter N. Stearns, *Anger: The Struggle for Emotional Control in America's History* (Chicago, 1986), chap. 5; P. J. Andersini and M. B. Shapiro, "Women's Attitudes toward Their Jobs," *Personnel Psychology* 31 (1978): 23.

41. Mary Blewett, "Passionate Voices and Cool Calculations: The Emotional Landscape of the Nineteenth-Century New England Textile Industry," in Stearns and Lewis, eds., *Emotional History*, pp. 109–25.

42. E. L. Miller, "Job Attitudes of National Union Officials," *Personnel Psychology* 19 (1966): 395–410; on unions and strikes, see U.S. Department of Labor, Bureau of Labor Statistics, *Analysis of Work Stoppages* (Washington, D.C., 1941–80).

43. Burt Scanlan, "Sensitivity Training: Clarification, Issues, Insights," *Personnel Journal* 540 (1970): 549–52; Chris Argyris, *Interpersonal Competence*

and Organizational Effectiveness (Homewood, Ill., 1962), pp. 23–30, 137, 174, 255; Xerox/Carnegie Mellon University, *Basic Quality Training: Prework* (Stamford, Conn., 1992).

44. For the work-leisure convergence thesis, see Steven M. Gelber, "Working at Playing: The Culture of the Work Place and the Rise of Baseball," *Journal of Social History* 16 (1983): 3–20. Assessing the thesis, Melvin L. Adelman ("Baseball, Business and the Work Place: Gelber's Thesis Reexamined," *Journal of Social History* 23 [1989]: 285–301) sensibly argues that sports supplied both contrast and convergence. The other argument here is that the convergence motif was stronger at first than after the 1920s, when the sports role changed. See also John P. Robinson and Geoffrey Godbey, *Time for Life: The Surprising Ways Americans Use Their Time* (State College, Pa., 1996).

45. Steven M. Gelber, "A Job You Can't Lose: Work and Hobbies in the Great Depression," *Journal of Social History* 24 (1991): 741–66.

46. Roger Munitz, *An Economic and Social History of Gambling in Britain and the United States* (Manchester, 1994).

47. Munitz, *Economic and Social History of Gambling;* Mark H. Haller, "Policy Gambling, Entertainment and the Emergence of Black Politics: Chicago from 1900 to 1940," *Journal of Social History* 24 (1991): 719–40; John C. Burnham, *Bad Habits, Drinking, Smoking, Taking Drugs, Gambling, Sexual Misbehavior, and Swearing in American History* (New York, 1993), chap. 6.

48. Benjamin Rader, *American Sports: From the Age of Folk Games to the Age of Spectators* (Englewood Cliffs, N.J., 1983); Stearns, *American Cool,* chap. 9; K. C. Constantine, *The Man Who Liked Slow Tomatoes* (New York, 1983), pp. 85–86; Allen Guttmann, *Sports Spectators* (New York, 1986), pp. 149 ff; on the symbolic functions of wrestling, see Bruce Lincoln, *Discourse and the Construction of Society: Comparative Studies of Myth, Ritual, and Classification* (New York, 1989); Claude Fischer, "Change in Leisure Activity, 1870–1940," *Journal of Social History* 24 (1994): 453–75; W. A. Cragsie and J. A. Hulbert, eds., *A Dictionary of American English* (Chicago, 1942), vol. 2, p. 93a.

49. Larry May, *Screening out the Past: The Birth of Mass Culture and the Motion Picture Industry* (New York, 1980); Otto Friedrich, "Up, up, and Awaaay," *Time,* March 14, 1988, p. 66; Gillian Avery, *Childhood's Patterns: A Study of the Heroes and Heroines of Childhood Fiction, 1770–1950* (London, 1975).

50. On the quick turning away from unduly serious films, see Martin S. Pernick, *The Black Stork: Eugenics and the Death of "Defective" Babies in American Medicine and Motion Pictures since 1915* (New York, 1996).

51. Tania Modleska, *Loving with a Vengeance: Mass-Produced Fantasies for Women* (Hamden, Conn., 1982), pp. 82, 86; Elizabeth G. Traube, *Dreaming*

Identities: Class, Gender, and Generation in 1980s Hollywood Movies (Boulder, Colo., 1992); John Kasson, *Amusing the Millions: Coney Island at the Turn of the Century* (New York, 1978); Kathy Peiss, *Cheap Amusements: Working Women and Leisure in Turn-of-the-Century New York* (Philadelphia, 1985).

52. Louis Ehrenberg, *Steppin' Out: New York and the Transformation of American Culture, 1890–1930* (New York, 1981); Marshall Stearns and Jean Stearns, *Jazz Dance: The Story of American Vernacular Dance* (New York, 1994).

53. Frederic Wertham, *The Seduction of the Innocent* (New York, 1954); Frederic Wertham, *Testimony at Hearing before the Subcommittee to Investigate Juvenile Delinquency of the Committee on the Judiciary of the United States Senate*, 83rd Cong. (Washington, D.C., 1954), pp. 81–86; George N. Gordon, "Can Children Corrupt Our Comics," in D. M. White and A. H. Abel, eds., *The Funnies: An American Idiom* (New York, 1963), pp. 158–59.

54. Munitz, *Economic and Social History of Gambling*, p. 175.

55. May, *Screening out the Past*.

56. Stearns, *American Cool*, pp. 279–80; Edna Barth, *Witches, Pumpkins, and Grinning Ghosts* (New York, 1981).

57. David Yosifon, "Laughter and Humor in the American Emotional Style," working paper, Carnegie Mellon University, 1996. I am very grateful to Mr. Yosifon for permission to use and cite his work.

58. Maud C. Cooke, *Social Etiquette* (Boston, 1896), pp. 43, 48; Mrs. Charles Harcourt, pseud., *Good Form for Women* (Philadelphia, 1907), pp. 112–13.

59. "Mrs. Humphry," *Manners for Women* (New York, 1897), pp. 11–17; Mary Stanton, *The Encyclopedia of Face and Form Reading* (New York, 1895), pp. 1054–57; Jessie Fowler, *A Manual of Mental Science for Teachers and Students* (New York, 1897), pp. 118–19.

60. Mabel Cox, "Propagation of Laughter," *Cosmopolitan Magazine*, June 1906, pp. 22–23; Hjalmar Boyessen, "The Plague of Jocularity," *North American Review*, November 1895, pp. 528–35; F. Treudley, "The Place of Humor," *Educational Review* 40 (1910): 92–93; Jerome Jerome, "You Can't Be Funny All the Time," *Cosmopolitan Magazine*, May 1906, pp. 110–12; Henry Jenkins, *What Made Pistachio Nuts?: Early Sound Comedy and the Vaudeville Aesthetic* (New York, 1992), chap. 2; Carolyn Wells, "First Lessons in Humor," *Century Illustrated Monthly Magazine*, May 1902, pp. 78–83. See also, for the twentieth century, the important recent study by Daniel Wickberg, *The Senses of Humor: Self and Laughter in Modern America* (Ithaca, N.Y., 1998).

61. Walter Blair and Hamlin Hill, *America's Humor: From Poor Richard to Doonesbury* (New York, 1978).

62. Grace Mulvihill, "Big Girls Don't Cry," *Parents' Magazine* 61 (1986): 106; Ruth Mason, "Why You Should Let Kids Cry," *Parents' Magazine* 70 (1995): 26.

63. Yosifon, "Laughter and Humor"; Robert Grimshaw, *The Modern Foreman* (New York, 1921), pp. 155, 198.

64. H. D. Ward, *Sensible Etiquette of the Best Society* (Philadelphia, 1878), p. 141; John Kasson, *Rudeness and Civility: Manners in Nineteenth Century Urban America* (New York, 1990).

65. Cas Wouters, "Etiquette Books and Emotion Management: Part Two— The Integration of the Sexes," *Journal of Social History* 29 (1995): 325–40.

66. Emily Post, *Etiquette in Society, in Business, in Politics, and at Home* (New York, 1922), p. 1.

67. Emily Post, *Etiquette* (New York, 1937), p. 307; Cas Wouters, "Etiquette Books and Emotion Management: Part One—The Integration of Social Classes," *Journal of Social History* 29 (1995): 107–24.

68. Amy Vanderbilt, *Etiquette* (New York, 1952), p. 755.

69. Mary D. Chambers, *Table Etiquette, Menus, and Much Besides* (Boston, 1929), p. 173; Sidney Morse, *Household Discoveries: An Encyclopedia of Practical Recipes and Processes* (New York, 1909); Katherine C. Grier, *Culture and Comfort: Parlor Making and Middle-Class Identity, 1850–1930* (Washington, D.C., 1997).

70. Gerald Carson, *The Polite Americans* (Westport, Conn., 1966); Timothy Jay, *Cursing in America: A Psycholinguistic Study of Dirty Language in the Courts, in the Movies, in the Schoolyards, and on the Streets* (Philadelphia, 1992). On changes in language acceptability on a larger scale, see Rochelle Gurstein, *The Repeal of Reticence: A History of America's Cultural and Legal Struggles over Free Speech, Obscenity, Sexual Liberation, and Modern Art* (New York, 1996).

71. Post, *Etiquette* (1937), pp. 32, 34.

72. Emily Post, *Etiquette* (New York, 1965), p. 17. Amy Vanderbilt agreed, terming the practice "barbaric" even in her 1963 edition (p. 553).

73. Judith Martin, *Miss Manners' Guide to Excruciatingly Correct Behavior* (New York, 1979), p. 417.

74. Lois Banner, *American Beauty* (New York, 1983).

75. David Hogan, *Selling 'Em by the Sack: White Castle and the Creation of American Food* (New York, 1998); Harvey Levenstein, *Paradox of Plenty, a Social History of Eating in Modern America* (New York, 1993).

76. Emily Holt, *Everyman's Encyclopedia of Etiquette* (New York, 1920), p. 179.

77. Lilian Eichler, *The Book of Etiquette* (New York, 1921), vol. 2, pp. 104–5.

78. Matthews Hamabata, *Crested Kimono: Power and Love in the Japanese Business Family* (Ithaca, N.Y., 1990).

79. Judith Martin's book was published in New York, 1996; she also comments on the lack of civility, as well as her expectations of imminent redress in *Manners for the Turn-of-the-Millennium* (New York, 1990).

80. Elisabeth Post, *Emily Post's Etiquette* (New York, 1992); John Sedgwick, "Putting on Good Graces at the Ritz," *US Airways Attaché*, August 1997, pp. 40–41.

81. "The Marketing Value of Good Telephone Skills," http://www.gactr.uga.edu/GC/at/MIM/MIMmay95.html (Business95 magazine website); Mary Bell Anderson, "Good Telephone Manners: How to Teach Them to Your Child," *Parents' Magazine* 27 (1953): 37.

82. Elisabeth Lasch-Quinn, "Race and Etiquette: Advice on Interracial Conduct since the 1960s," forthcoming in the *Journal of Social History;* Sheila Rush and Chris Clark, *How to Get Along with Black People: A Handbook for White Folks, and Some Black Folks Too* (New York, 1971); Amoja Three-Rivers, *Cultural Etiquette: A Guide for the Well-Intentioned* (Indian Valley, Va., 1990).

83. Martha Wolfenstein, "Fun Morality. An Analysis of Recent American Child Training Literature," in Margaret Mead and Martha Wolfenstein, eds., *Childhood in Contemporary Cultures* (Chicago, 1955).

84. Esther Lloyd-Jones and Ruth Fedder, *Coming of Age* (New York, 1941), p. 35; Dorothy Baruch, *New Ways in Discipline* (New York, 1949); William C. Menninger, ed., *How to Be a Successful Teenager* (New York, 1954), p. 141.

85. Jan Lewis, "The American Doctrine of Motherhood in the Nineteenth and Twentieth Centuries," paper presented at the eighth Berkshire Conference on the History of Women, Douglass College, June 1990; Linda W. Rosenzweig, " 'The Anchor of My Life': Middle-Class American Mothers and College-Educated Daughters, 1880–1920," *Journal of Social History* 25 (1991): 5–25; E. S. Martin, "Mothers and Daughters," *Good Housekeeping*, May 1917, p. 27; Gabrielle Jackson, *Mother and Daughter* (New York, 1905), pp. 3, 81–86, 129; M. V. O'Shea, *First Steps in Child Training* (Chicago, 1920), p. 128; John B. Watson, *Psychological Care of Infant and Child* (New York, 1928), chap. 3; Ernest R. Groves and Gladys Groves, *Wholesome Childhood* (Boston, 1931), pp. 12–13, 98–101; Anna Wolf, *The Parents' Manual: A Guide to the Emotional Development of Young Children* (New York, 1941), p. 81; Lillian Gilbreth, *Living with Our Children* (New York, 1928), pp. 106–7.

86. Stearns, *Jealousy;* Ayala Pines and Eliot Aronson, "Antecedents, Correla-

tions, and Consequences of Sexual Jealousy," *Journal of Personality* 51 (1983): 126–40; Bailey, *Front Porch to Back Seat;* Ete. Le Masters, *Modern Courtship and Marriage* (New York, 1957), pp. 132–33; Shula Sommers, "Reported Emotions and Conventions of Emotionality among College Students," *Journal of Personality and Social Psychology* 46 (1984): 214; Willard Waller, *The Family* (New York, 1938), p. 586; Carolyn Symonds, " 'Sexual Mate-Swapping' Violation of Norms and Reconciliation of Guilt," in J. M. Hensher, ed., *Studies in the Sociology of Sex* (New York, 1971), pp. 87–88.

87. "Editor's Diary," *North American Review*, October 1907, pp. 307–8; Marian Castle, "Decent Christian Burial," *Forum*, April 1934, pp. 253–55; "The New Mien of Grief," *Literary Digest*, February 1916, p. 292; Milton Weldman, "America Conquers Death," *American Mercury*, February 1927, pp. 216–17; Stearns, *American Cool*, chap. 5.

88. Vanderbilt, *Etiquette*, pp. 121, 126.

89. Margaret Stroebe et al., "Broken Hearts in Broken Bonds," *American Psychologist* 47 (1992); "No End to the Quest for Closure," *Los Angeles Times*, August 18, 1997, p. A14. My thanks to Baruch Fischhoff and Roger Werthei-mer for relevant references. On emotion generally, see J. M. Bartelet, *Evolution, Social Theory and Social Structures: A Macrosociological Approach* (Cambridge, 1998); Lynn Jamieson, *Intimacy: Personal Relationships in Modern Societies* (New York, 1998).

90. R. Marie Griffith, " 'Joy Unspeakable and Full of Glory': The Vocabulary of Pious Emotion in the Narratives of American Pentecostal Women, 1910–1945," and Kimberley L. Phillips, " 'Stand by Me': Sacred Quartet Music and the Emotionology of African American Audiences, 1900–1930," both in Stearns and Lewis, eds., *Emotional History*, pp. 218–58.

91. Robert Reich, *Locked in the Cabinet* (New York 1997), p. 39; Peter N. Stearns, "Emotional Change and Political Disengagement in the 20th-Century United States," in A. Kofler, ed., Special Issue on Emotion and Culture, *Innovation—The European Journal of Social Sciences* 10 (1997): 361–80.

92. Peter N. Stearns, "Consumerism and Childhood: New Targets for American Emotion," in Stearns and Lewis, eds., *Emotional History*, pp. 396–416; Lisa Jacobson, "Revitalizing the American Home: Children's Leisure and the Reevaluation of Play, 1920–1940," *Journal of Social History* 31 (1997): 581–96; Sarah Canstock, "The Significance of Playthings," *Good Housekeeping*, December 1918, p. 35; Ruth Frankel, "Choosing the Rights Toys," *Hygeia*, December 1931, p. 1106; John Burroughs, "Corrupting the Innocents," *Independent*, December 1906, p. 1424; Lillian N. Reid, *Personality and Etiquette* (Boston, 1950), pp. 242–52.

93. E. Anthony Rotundo, "Romantic Friendship: Male Intimacy and Mid-

dle-Class Youth in the Northern United States, 1800–1900," *Journal of Social History* 23 (1989): 1–26; Lillian Rubin, *Just Friends: The Role of Friendship in Our Lives* (New York, 1985); Mark Carnes, *Secret Ritual and Manhood in Victorian America* (New Haven, Conn., 1989); Linda W. Rosenzweig, " 'Another Self'? Middle-Class American Women and Their Friends, 1900–1960," in Stearns and Lewis, eds., *Emotional History*, pp. 357–76; Dolores Avelleyra Murphy, ed., *In Red Hats, Beads, & Bags: 1908 Graduates Sharing Their Lives through Letters* (Morrison, Colo., 1990), p. 73; Lillian Hellman, *An Unfinished Woman: A Memoir* (Boston,. 1969), pp. 29–30; Doris Faber, *The Life of Lorena Hickock: E. R.'s Friend* (New York, 1980); Jamieson, *Intimacy*.

94. *Oxford English Dictionary*, 2d ed. (Oxford, 1989); William and Mary Morris, *Dictionary of Contemporary Usage* (New York, 1958), p. 201; Stearns, *American Cool*, p. 250. The word was coined in English early in the twentieth century and was extensively used in the United States only after 1950, when its meaning shifted from deep artistic appreciation to sharing in the feelings of others. It was dubbed a "vogue word" in the 1980s.

95. For a characteristic statement, see Marc Fasteau, *The Male Machine* (New York, 1974); see also Elizabeth Pleck and Joe Pleck, eds., *The American Man* (Englewood Cliffs, N.J., 1980).

96. Steven Mintz and Susan Kellogg, *Domestic Revolutions: A Social History of the American Family* (New York, 1987); Willard Waller, *The Old Love and the New* (New York, 1930); Ben B. Lindsay and Wainwright Evans, *The Companionate Marriage* (New York, 1927).

97. Peter Willmott and Michael Young, *The Symmetrical Family* (London, 1973).

98. Henry Morton Robinson, "This Brave New Love," *Esquire*, February 1934, p. 56; Joseph Kessel, "Sleepless Night," *Esquire*, May 1936, p. 69; Alfred Adler, "Love Is a Recent Invention" *Esquire*, May 1936, p. 56; Beth L. Bailey, "Scientific Truth . . . and Love: The Marriage Education Movement in the United States," *Journal of Social History* 20 (1987): 711–32; Theodore Van de Velde, *Ideal Marriage: Its Physiognomy and Technique* (1930; repr. Westport, Conn., 1950); Ernest W. Burgess, "Proposal for Marriage Study," handwritten draft, n.d., Burgess papers, University of Chicago, box 31, 11-b-12, 16; John Spurlock, "The Problem of Modern Married Love for Middle-Class Women," in Stearns and Lewis, eds., *Emotional History*, pp. 319–32.

99. Modleska, *Loving with a Vengeance;* Sandy Rousma, "Soap Operas and Anger," *Washington Post*, May 5, 1991; Eva Illouz, *Consuming the Romantic Utopia: Love and the Cultural Contradictions of Capitalism* (Berkeley and Los Angeles, 1987).

100. David Shumway, "Something Old, Something New: Romance and

Marital Advice in the 1920s," in Stearns and Lewis, eds., *Emotional History*, pp. 305–18; Fransesca Cancian, *Love in America; Gender and Self-Development* (Cambridge, 1987); Elaine Tyler May, *Great Expectations: Marriage and Divorce in Post-Victorian America* (Chicago, 1980); Elinor Glyn, *The Philosophy of Love* (New York, 1923); Marie Stopes, *Married Love: A New Contribution to the Solution of Sex Difficulties* (New York, 1931).

101. Anne Morrow Lindbergh, *Hour of Gold, Hour of Lead: Diaries and Letters of Anne Morrow Lindbergh, 1929–1932* (New York, 1973), pp. 53, 64, 69; Ernest Groves et al., *The Family and Its Relationships* (Chicago, 1932), pp. 165, 174; Spurlock, "Problem of Married Love"; Steven Seidman, *Romantic Longings: Love in America, 1830–1980* (New York, 1991); John C. Spurlock and Cynthia A. Magistro, *Feeling Women: Women's Emotions and American Culture, 1915–1930* (New York, 1998).

102. Arlie Hochschild, "The Time Bind: When Work Becomes Home and Home Becomes Work," *New York Times Magazine*, May 11, 1997; Lewis Terman, *Psychological Factors in Marital Happiness* (New York, 1938), pp. 142–66; David Buss, "Conflict between the Sexes: Strategic Interference in the Evocation of Anger and Upset," *Journal of Personality and Social Psychology* 56 (1989): 235–47.

103. Guy Oakes, *The Imaginary War* (New York, 1994), p. 40. My thanks to Halil Damar for the reference. On legal instructions, my thanks to Richard Johnson.

104. The concealment impulse is striking in a culture that claims to value authenticity but in fact requires careful emotion management. See Stearns, *American Cool;* Sommers, "Reported Emotions"; Shula Sommers, "Adults Evaluating Their Emotions: A Cross-Cultural Perspective," in Carol Malatesta and Carroll Izard, eds., *Emotions in Adult Development* (Beverly Hills, Calif., 1984), pp. 319–38.

Notes to Chapter 7

1. Paula Fass, *The Damned and the Beautiful* (New York, 1977); Estelle Freedman and John D'Emilio, *Intimate Matters: A History of Sexuality in America* (New York, 1988); Daniel Scott Smith, "The Dating of the Sexual Revolution: Evidence and Interpretations," in Michael Gordon, ed., *The American Family in Socio-Historical Perspective* (New York, 1973); Steven Seidman, *Romantic Longings: Love in America, 1830–1980* (New York, 1991); Paul Robinson, *The Modernization of Sex* (Ithaca, N.Y., 1989); Kevin White, *The First Sexual Revolution: The Emergence of Heterosexuality in Modern America* (New

York, 1992); Beth Bailey, *From Front Porch to Back Seat: Courtship in Twentieth-Century America* (New York, 1992).

2. Cindy Aron, *Ladies and Gentlemen of the Civil Service: Middle-Class Workers in Victorian America* (New York, 1987); James Reed, *The Birth Control Movement and American Society: From Private Vice to Public Virtue* (New York, 1993); Lewis Erenberg, *Steppin' Out: New York Nightlife and the Transformation of American Culture, 1890–1930* (Westport, Conn., 1981); Larry May, *Screening out the Past: The Birth of Mass Culture and the Motion Picture Industry* (New York, 1980).

3. Marie Stopes, *Married Love* (London, 1918), p. 19; Margaret Sanger, *Happiness in Marriage* (New York, 1926), p. 17; Isabel Hutton, *The Sex Technique in Marriage*, 3d ed. (New York, 1932), p. 26; Seidman, *Romantic Longings*, chap. 3.

4. Bailey, *Front Porch;* John Modell, "Dating Becomes the Way of American Youth," in Leslie Page Moch and Gary Stark, eds., *Essays on the Family and Historical Change* (College Station, Tex., 1983); E. L. Clark, *Petting, Wise or Otherwise* (New York, 1939).

5. Lisa Duggan, "The Social Enforcement of Heterosexuality and Lesbian Resistance in the 1920s," in Amy Swedlow and Hanna Lessinger, eds., *Class, Race and Sex: The Dynamics of Control* (Boston, 1983); David Greenberg, *The Construction of Homosexuality* (Chicago, 1988); Jonathan Katz, *Gay/Lesbian Almanac* (New York, 1988); George Chauncey Jr., "From Sexual Inversion to Homosexuality: Medicine and the Changing Conceptualization of Female Deviance," *Salmagundi* 58–59 (1983).

6. Roland Marchand, *Advertising the American Dream: Making Way for Modernity* (Berkeley and Los Angeles, 1985), p. 180); *Life*, October 5, 1942, p. 128; Lois Banner, *American Beauty* (New York, 1983).

7. Alfred Kinsey et al., *Sexual Behavior in the Human Male* (Philadelphia, 1947), and *Sexual Behavior in the Human Female* (Philadelphia, 1953); Beth Bailey, "Prescribing the Pill: Politics, Culture and the Sexual Revolution in America's Heartland," *Journal of Social History* 30 (1997): 827–56.

8. Bailey, "Prescribing the Pill"; Morton Hunt, *Sexual Behavior in the 1970s* (Chicago, 1974); Barbara Ehrenreich, *The Hearts of Men* (New York, 1983); Seidman, *Romantic Longings;* U.S. Commission on Obscenity and Pornography, *The Report of the Commission on Obscenity and Pornography* (New York, 1970); Wilt Arnytage, R. Chester, and John Reel, eds., *Changing Patterns of Sexual Behavior* (New York, 1980). Also see the important recent study by Sharon Ullman, *Sex Seen: The Emergence of Modern Sexuality in America* (Berkeley and Los Angeles, 1997).

9. Robinson, *Modernization of Sex;* Bertrand Russell, *Marriage and Morals* (New York, 1929), pp. 78–92, 153–55.

10. A. Herbert Gray, *Men, Women and God* (New York, 1922), pp. 5–13, 85, 95, 150–54.

11. Sanger, *Happiness in Marriage*, pp. 15 19–20, 39, 90–91, 123–24, 132, 139, 146. On the ongoing love theme, see Francesca Cancian, *Love in America* (Cambridge, 1987).

12. Stopes, *Married Love*, pp. 27–30, 32–33, 60–67, 76; June Rose, *Marie Stopes and the Sexual Revolution* (London, 1992); Ruth Hall, *Passionate Crusader: The Life of Marie Stopes* (New York, 1977).

13. Ben B. Lindsey, *The Revolt of Modern Youth* (New York, 1925), pp. 63, 94,117–18, 127.

14. Paul Popenoe, *The Conservation of the Family* (Baltimore, 1926), pp. 3–6, 25–32, 51, 56, 57–58, 66, 81–90, 113.

15. William J. Fielding, *Sex and the Love-Life* (New York, 1927), pp. 112–44.

16. Peter Laipson, " 'Kiss without Shame, for She Desires It': Sexual Foreplay in American Marital Advice Literature, 1900–1925," *Journal of Social History* 29 (1996): 507–26; Frederic Gerrish, *Sex-Hygiene: A Talk to College Boys* (Boston, 1917); William J. Fielding, *Sanity in Sex* (New York, 1920); Walter Robie, *The Art of Love* (Boston, 1921), p. 97, and *Rational Sex Ethics* (Boston, 1922); Harland Long, *Sane Sex Life and Sane Sex Living* (Boston, 1919), p. 68.

17. Theodore H. Van de Velde, *Ideal Marriage: Its Physiology and Technique* (New York, 1930), pp. 8–9, 131, 134.

18. Phyllis Blanchard and Carlyn Manasses, *New Girls for Old* (New York, 1930), pp. 51–61, 111; Ray Barber, *Marriage and the Family* (New York, 1939), pp. 266–69, 561; Ernest Burgess, Paul Wallin, and Gladys Schultz, *Courtship, Engagement and Marriage* (Philadelphia, 1954), pp. 22–35, 52–63, 65–66, 73, 111–12; Paul Popenoe, *Modern Marriage: A Handbook for Men* (New York, 1946).

19. Sybil Neville-Rolfe, ed., *Sex in Social Life* (New York, 1950); Henry Bowman, *Marriage for Moderns* (New York, 1942), pp. 420–21, 433; Burgess et al., *Courtship*, p. 414.

20. Bowman, *Marriage for Moderns;* Dorothy Baruch and Hyman Miller, *Sex in Marriage: New Understandings* (New York, 1962), pp. 51, 106–7; Albert Ellis, *Sex without Guilt* (New York, 1958), pp. 21–52, 178–84.

21. Ellis, *Sex Without Guilt;* Annette G. Godow, *Human Sexuality* (St. Louis, 1982), pp. 102–3. On the tolerance of homosexuality before Ellis, see White, *First Sexual Revolution.*

22. Alex Comfort, ed., *The Joy of Sex* (New York, 1970), pp. 15–48; in addition, see "M," *The Sensuous Man* (New York, 1971); "J," *The Sensuous Woman* (New York, 1969); Alex Comfort, ed., *More Joy of Sex* (New York, 1977); Hugh Hefner, "The Playboy Philosophy," *Playboy*, December 1962, p. 169. Some titles, however, implied the briefly popular permissiveness while actually falling back to a largely medical-factual approach, including health warnings as well as technical encouragement: David Reuben, *Everything You Always Wanted to Know about Sex (But Were Afraid to Ask)* (New York, 1969). Reuben urged new findings on sexual pleasure and declared active sexuality to be indispensable to a person's potential ("maximum pleasure from sexual activity without doing damage to anyone," p.48). But he also insisted on love and deep emotional bonds as the best context for sex; he criticized homosexuality; he attacked adultery (this was "damage" in the same category as rape and homosexuality); and he warned against trying to emulate media representations of sex, which too often implied superhuman qualities that were misleading and even dangerous.

23. Jay Gale, *A Young Man's Guide to Sex* (New York, 1984); Ted McIlvena, ed., *The Complete Guide to Safer Sex* (Fort Lee, N.J., 1987 (primarily aimed at gay sexuality); Domeena Renshaw, *Seven Weeks to Better Sex* (New York, 1995).

24. William Masters and Virginia Johnson, *The Pleasure Bond: A New Look at Sexuality and Commitment* (Boston, 1970), pp. 3–15, 80, 114–15, 138, 166–80. The book was implicitly sequenced, with an anything-goes approach predominating in the early sections and greater emphasis on individual regulation about 160 pages into the text. See also Kenneth Walker and Peter Fletcher, *Sex and Society* (Westport, Conn., 1975).

25. Ruth Westheimer, *Dr. Ruth's Guide for Married Lovers* (New York, 1986), pp. 3, 21, 33–34, 146, 196.

26. Helen Gurley Brown, *Sex and the Single Girl* (New York, 1962); Alan Soble, *Pornography* (New Haven, Conn., 1986).

27. "Shocker on Sex," *Newsweek*, December 1, 1947, p. 52; "Kinsey," *Saturday Review of Literature*, March 13, 1948; "Behavior after Kinsey," *Time*, April 12, 1948; "Effects Weighed of Kinsey Report," New York *Times*, April 1, 1948, p. 50. On magazine materials, see Lynn Jamieson, *Intimacy: Personal Relationships in Modern Societies* (New York, 1998); and Rochelle Gorstein, *The Repeal of Reticence* (New York, 1995).

28. Alfred Adler, "Training School for Lovers," *Esquire*, September 1936, pp. 57, 197–98; Albert Treynor, "Women—How to Break and Train," *Esquire*, February 1934, pp. 30–31; George Nathan, "The Sex Appeal Myth," *Esquire*, August 1934, pp. 23, 135; George Nathan, "Sweet Faces and Foul Minds,"

Esquire, November 1934, pp. 43, 140; W. M. Marston, "Running Wild without Men," *Esquire*, February 1936, pp. 72, 130; Marcel Desage, "She's No Longer Faithful If—," *Esquire*, May 1936, p. 52; Alan MacDonald, "You Can't Sleep with Women," *Esquire*, November 1936, p. 84; Lawrence Gould, "The Great American Delusion," *Esquire*, June 1938, pp. 35, 156; Fred Kelly, "Cupid Is a Hypocrite," *Esquire*, January 1942, pp. 34–35, 167; E. S. Woodhead," Should I Marry the Girl," *Esquire*, October 1942, pp. 32–33; Betty South, "The Trouble with Women Is Men," *Esquire*, April 1952, pp. 51, 128–29.

29. Miriam Lincoln, "The Male Sex in Middle Life," *Esquire*, February 1952, pp. 32, 103; Nicholas David, "Careless Love Can Kill You," *Esquire*, January 1958, pp. 103–5.

30. Marion Magid, "A Last Word: The Public Fantasy versus the Private Act," *Esquire*, May 1966, pp. 128–29; C. D. B. Bryan, "Sex and the Married Man," *Esquire*, June 1984, pp. 235–45; George Leonard, "The End of Sex," *Esquire*, December 1982, pp. 76–80; Laurence Shames, "Wolves Mate for Life," *Esquire*, November 1982, pp. 25–28; Colette Dowling and Patricia Fahey, "The Calculus of Sex," *Esquire*, May 1966, pp. 123, 165–66; Harry Stein, "How I Spent the Sexual Revolution," *Esquire*, June 1986, pp. 147–56; Terry McMillan, "McMillan," *Esquire*, July 1988, pp. 100–4.

31. Mildred Gilman and David Loth, "Are You Frigid?" *Mademoiselle*, February 1952, pp. 140–41, 176–77; Mary Scott Welch, "How to Get a Man," *Mademoiselle*, September 1953, pp. 150–51, 180–85; Jane Whitbread and Vivian Cadden, "What's on Your Mind? Dating and Marriage," *Mademoiselle*, August 1954, pp. 245, 330–40; Jane Shortbread, "A Report on Current Views toward Chastity," *Mademoiselle*, July 1959, pp. 37–40; Ellen Willis, "The Birth Control Pill," *Mademoiselle*, January 1961, pp. 54–55, 112–13; June Bingham, "Sexual Morality and the Young," *Mademoiselle*, September 1963, pp. 126, 184–85.

32. David Newman and Robert Benton, "Man Talk: Man and Superwoman," *Mademoiselle*, February 1965, pp. 88–89; David Newman and Robert Benton, "Man Talk: Sex Appeal and the Single Girl," *Mademoiselle*, March 1965, p. 26; David Newman and Robert Benton, "Man Talk: The Disguise," *Mademoiselle*, May 1965, p. 52; Jean Collins, "Battle of the Sexes," *Mademoiselle*, December 1965, pp. 93, 150–51; David Newman and Robert Benton, "Man Talk: Your Secret Life," *Mademoiselle*, March 1967, p. 90; Vernon Grant, "An Opinion: On Virginity," *Mademoiselle*, February 1968, pp. 76–78; David Newman and Robert Benton, "Man Talk: Wish You Were Here," *Mademoiselle*, October 1968, pp. 96, 201; Linda Goodman, "A Sexy Sort of Horoscope," *Mademoiselle*, January 1969, pp. 91, 136–38; Lilian Roxon, "The Intelligent Woman's Guide to Sex," *Mademoiselle*, April 1973, p. 20.

33. Lillian Roxon, "The Intelligent Woman's Guide to Sex," *Mademoiselle*, May 1973; the column was taken over by Karen Durbin, 1975–1977.

34. Karen Durbin, "Sex: The New Definition of Normal," *Mademoiselle*, January 1977, pp. 84, 120; Gretchen, Kurz, "Sexual Freedom: Is It Worth the Hassle?" *Mademoiselle*, August 1977, p. 207; Carol Mithers, "The Intelligent Woman's Guide to Sex," *Mademoiselle*, June 1983, p. 62; Lynda Schor, "It's All Right to Talk about Oral Sex," *Mademoiselle*, September 1983, p. 158; Shere Hite, "True Love and Great Sex," *Mademoiselle*, November 1983, pp. 120–1; C. D. B. Bryan, "Too Much Sex, Too Little Love," *Mademoiselle*, November 1985, p. 134. See also Shere Hite, *The Hite Report* (New York, 1976).

35. *Penthouse*, 1980s–1990s; Carol Tavris and Susan Sadd, *Redbook Report on Female Sexuality* (New York, 1977); Linda Wolfe, *The Cosmo Report* (New York, 1982).

36. Sybil Neville-Rolfe, ed., *Sex in Social Life* (New York, 1950), p. 211.

37. C. W. Saleby, "The Price of Prudery," *Forum*, March 1911, pp. 311–19; Solomon Schindler, "Innocence at the Price of Ignorance," *Arena*, July 1893, pp. 185–90; Laura Scammon, "Knowledge the Preserver of Purity," *Arena*, November 1893, pp. 702–9; "Religion and Ethics: Sex Education as Its Friends and Its Foes View It," *Current Opinion* 85 (1913): 261–62; "The Havoc of Prudery," *Current Literature*, February 1911, pp. 174–75.

38. Mary Ware Dennet, "Sex Enlightenment for Civilized Youth," in V. F. Calverton and S. D. Schmalhausen, eds., *Sex in Civilization* (New York, 1929), pp. 97–108.

39. W. H. Burger, *Growing up with Our Children* (New York, 1932), pp. 17–20; Florence Mather, *Just Normal Children* (New York, 1929); Alfred Adler, *Guiding the Child* (New York, 1930); Arthur Payne, *My Parents: Friends or Enemies?* (New York, 1932), pp. 124–38; Ernest Groves, *Wholesome Childhood* (Boston, 1924); Anna Wolf, "How Will They Learn about Sex?" *Woman's Home Companion*, January 1947, p. 58; Floyd Dell, "Preparing Them for Hard Realities," *Parents' Magazine*, October 1937, p. 36; Caroline Zachry, "Sex Facts Boys and Girls Need to Know," *Parents' Magazine*, April 1941, pp. 24–25; Mae Solomon Tilles, "Start Sex Education Early," *Parents' Magazine*, December 1942, p. 25; A. S. English and C. J. Foster, "Sex Education for the School Age Child," *Parents' Magazine*, May 1950, pp. 36–37.

40. Hornell Hart and Ella Hart, *Personality and the Family* (Boston, 1941), pp. 417–22; Marion Faegre et al., *Child Care and Training* (Minneapolis, 1958); David Goodman, *The Emotional Needs of Children* (New York, 1959), p. 239; ; Ruth Strang, *An Introduction to Child Study* (New York, 1959).

41. Dolores Curran, "Sexeducation: A 12-Letter Word for Parents," *New*

Catholic World 218 (1975): 165–69; George A. Kelly, *The Catholic Family Handbook* (New York, 1959), chap. 6.

42. Neville-Rolfe, *Sex in Social Life*, pp. 154–55.

43. Robert Lynd and Helen Lynd, *Middletown: A Study in American Culture* (New York, 1929), p. 145; "An Outline for Sex Education in the High School," *School and Society* 15 (1922): 650–52; Barbara Goodheart, "Sex in the Schools: Education or Titillation?" *Today's Health*, February 1971, pp. 28–30.

44. Judith Ann Metz, "Teaching Young Teenagers about Sex," *Parents' Magazine*, March 1966, pp. 60–61; Mortimer Smith, "Some Reservations about Sex Education," *Parents' Magazine*, November 1969, pp. 66–67.

45. John Tebbel, "Sex Education: Yesterday, Today, and Tomorrow," *Today's Education*, January–February 1976, pp. 70–72; Sol Gordon, "What Our Children Need from Sex Education," *Education Digest*, May 1985, pp. 46–49.

46. John Passmore, "Sex Education," *New Republic*, October 4, 1980, pp. 27–30; Barbara Whitehead, "The Failure of Sex Education," *Atlantic Monthly*, October 1994, pp. 55, 70, 80.

47. "The Push for Sex Education," *Newsweek*, special issue, Summer 1990, p. 52; Madelon Finkel and Steven Finkel, "Sex Education in High School," *Society*, November 1985, pp. 48–49; Richard Nadler, "Abstaining from Sex Education," *National Review*, September 15, 1997, pp. 50; "Circle of Jerks," *The Nation*, January 2, 1995, p. 4; Jeff Stryker, "Abstinence or Else!" *The Nation*, June 16, 1997, pp. 19–20; Lynn Langway, "Sex Education 101 for Kids—And Parents," *Newsweek*, September 1, 1980, pp. 50–51.

48. "Teaching Children Sex," *Hygeia*, March 1927, pp. 148–49; "Teaching about Sex," *Hygeia*, November 1926, p. 653; "Sex Education," *Newsweek*, July 14, 1935, p. 25; "Information, Please!" *Collier's*, June 17, 1939, p. 82; Paul Woodring, "What Is Sex Education?" *Saturday Review*, December 18, 1965, pp. 55–56.

49. Lynd and Lynd, *Middletown*, p. 112; Anne-Marie Sohn, "The Golden Age of Male Adultery: The Third Republic," *Journal of Social History* 28 (1995): 469–90. The French evidence suggests that adultery was increasing as disapproval eased.

50. Dorothy Bromley and Florence Britten, *Youth and Sex* (New York, 1938); Burgess et al., *Courtship*, pp. 116, 155, 533; Gilbert Hamilton, *A Research on Marriage* (New York, 1929), pp. 147 and *passim*; "Survey," *Fortune* (1943); Freedman and D'Emilio, *Intimate Matters* (New York, 1988), chap. 11; Smith, "The Dating of the American Sexual Revolution," pp. 321–35; Winston Ehrmann, *Premarital Dating Behavior* (New York, 1959); Ira Reiss, *Premarital Sexual Standards in America* (Glencoe, Ill., 1960); John

Modell, *Into One's Own: From Adolescence to Adulthood in America 1920–1975* (Berkeley and Los Angeles, 1989).

51. Maris Vinovskis, *An "Epidemic" of Adolescent Pregnancy? Some Historical and Policy Considerations* (New York, 1987); John Kantner and Melvin Zelnik, *Sex and Pregnancy in Adolescence* (New York, 1979).

52. Freedman and D'Emilio, *Intimate Matters*, chap. 11; Kinsey, *Sexual Behavior in the Human Female*, pp. 356–65.

53. Lewis Terman, *Psychological Factors in Marital Happiness* (New York, 1938); John Spurlock, "The Problem of Married Love," in Peter N. Stearns and Jan Lewis, eds., *Emotional History of the United States* (New York, 1998), pp. 319–32.

54. Samuel Janus and Cynthia Janus, *The Janus Report on Sexual Behavior* (New York, 1993), p. 36; Hite, *Hite Report;* Anthony Pietropinto, *Beyond the Male Myth: What Women Want to Know about Men's Sexuality: A Nationwide Survey* (New York, 1977); George O'Neill and Nena O'Neill, *Open Marriage: A New Life Style for Couples* (New York, 1984).

55. Edward O. Laumann, John Gagnon, Robert Michael, and Stuart Michaels, *The Organization of Sexuality: Sexual Practices in the United States* (Chicago, 1994). The book's painstaking methods are discussed in the first section, the polling data throughout. Whether the methods fully cut through some ambivalences in cultural winds may still be questioned, but most key findings seem solid. John Billy, Koray Tanfer, William Grady, and Daniel Klepinger, "The Sexual Behavior of Men in the United States," *Family Planning Perspectives* (1994): 52–60, largely confirms the Laumann group's findings. Focused on men aged twenty to thirty-nine, the study indicates that the frequency of engagement with multiple partners may be rising still, amid great variety among racial groups and between men currently married (lowest number of lifetime partners) and men never or formerly married (the latter the highest number).

56. Daniel Cohen, "The Beautiful Female Murder Victim: Literary Genres and Courtship Practices in the Origins of a Cultural Motif, 1590–1850," *Journal of Social History* 31 (1997): 253–76.

57. Franny Nudelman, "Beyond the Talking Cure: Listening to Female Testimony of 'The Oprah Winfrey Show'," in Joel Pfister and Nancy Schnog, eds., *Inventing the Psychological: Toward a Cultural History of Emotional Life in America* (New Haven, Conn., 1997), pp. 297–316; Joshua Gamson, *Freaks Talk Back: Tabloid Talk Shows and Sexual Nonconformity* (Chicago, 1998).

58. David Allyn, "Private Acts/Public Policy: Alfred Kinsey, the American Law Institute and the Privatization of American Sexual Morality," *Journal of American Studies* 30 (1996): 405–28.

59. John Burnham, *Bad Habits: Drinking, Smoking, Taking Drugs, Gambling, Sexual Misbehavior, and Swearing in American History* (New York, 1993), chaps. 2, 7.

60. Freedman and D'Emilio, *Intimate Matters;* Rochelle Gurstein, *The Repeal of Reticence: A History of America's Cultural and Legal Struggles over Free Speech, Obscenity, Sexual Liberation, and Modern Art* (New York, 1996); U.S. Commission on Obscenity, *Report.*

61. Seidman, *Romantic Longings*, chap. 5, Burnham, *Bad Habits*, chap. 7.

62. Kathy Newman, "A View from the Couch," (on "McBeal"), *Pittsburgh City Paper*, February 4, 1998; Ehrenreich, *Hearts of Men.*

63. Lillian Faderman, "The Mordification of Love between Women by 19th-Century Sexologists," *Journal of Homosexuality* 4 (1978): 73–90; Katz, *Gay/ Lesbian Almanac;* Kenneth Plummer, ed., *The Making of the Modern Homosexual* (London, 1981); James Kiernan, "Classification of Homosexuality," *Urologic and Cutaneous Review* 20 (1916): 350; John D'Emilio, *Sexual Politics, Sexual Communities: The Making of a Homosexual Minority in the United States, 1940–1970* (Chicago, 1983); Chauncey, "From Sexual Inversion"; George Chauncey, "Christian Brotherhood or Sexual Perversion? Homosexual Identities and the Construction of Sexual Boundaries in the World War One Era," in Peter Stearns, ed., *Expanding the Past* (New York, 1988), pp. 169–92.

64. David Gollaher, "From Ritual to Science: The Medical Transformation of Circumcision in America," *Journal of Social History* 28 (1994): 5–36.

65. On the move away from treating homosexuality as a disease, see American Psychiatric Association, *Diagnostic and Statistical Manual of Mental Disorders*, 3d ed. (Washington, D.C., 1980). Note that psychiatry continued to cite the potential for treatment in some cases. This kind of ambivalence about certain near-disease entities is further discussed in chapter 9.

66. Maris Vinovskis, "Development of Policy for Adolescent Issues," Netherlands Institute for Advanced Study in the Humanities and Social Sciences Conference, "Are We at the End of the Century of the Child?" February 1998; Alan Guttmacher Institute, *11 Million Teenagers: What Can Be Done about the Epidemic of Adolescent Pregnancies in the United States* (New York, 1979); Else Jones et al., *Pregnancy, Contraception and Family Planning Services in Industrialized Countries* (New Haven, Conn., 1989).

67. On the shift in abuse categories and its popularization, see "My Daughter Was Molested," *Good Housekeeping*, September 1971, p. 14. On therapeutic uses and their problems, see Mark Pendergast, ed., *Victims of Memory: Incest Accusations and Shattered Vows* (Hinesburg, Vt., 1995); Richard Ofshe and Ethan Watters, *Making Monsters: False Memories, Psychotherapy, and Sexual Hysteria* (New York, 1994). My thanks to Robyn Dawes for his work in this area.

See also Philip Jenkins, *Moral Panic: Changing Concepts of the Child Molester in Modern America* (New Haven, Conn., 1998).

68. Karen Barrett, "Date Rape: A Campus Epidemic?" *Ms.* 11 (1982): 48–53; "When the Date Turns to Rape," *Time*, March 23, 1957, p. 77; "The Date Who Rapes," *Newsweek*, April 9, 1984, p. 91.

69. " 'Roofies': The Date-Rape Drug," *Newsweek*, February 26, 1996, p. 54; David Carlin Jr., "Date Rape Fallacies, *Commonweal*, February 25, 1994, p. 11; Nancy Gibbs, "When Is It Rape?" *Time* (cover story), June 3, 1991, pp. 48–55; Ellen Sweet, "Date Rape: The Story of an Epidemic," in Adele Stano, ed., *Debating Sexual Correctness: Pornography, Sexual Harassment, Date Rape, and the Politics of Sexual Inequality* (New York, 1995), pp. 10–20.

70. Robin Warshaw, *I Never Called It Rape: The Ms. Report on Recognizing, Fighting and Surviving Date and Acquaintance Rape* (New York, 1988), pp. 20, 120 ff.

71. Letty Cottin Pogrebin, "Sex Harassment," reprinted in Stano, *Debating Sexual Correctness*, pp. 4–9; "Scorecard," *Sports Illustrated*, October 8, 1990, p. 21; "Sexual Harassment Lands Companies in Court," *Business Week*, October 1, 1979, p. 120; Jill Smolowe, "Betrayed by His Kiss" (on Senator Robert Packwood), *Time*, September 18, 1995, pp. 42–46; "Retreat for Advances: The Fight against Sexual Harassment Reaches the Supreme Court," *Time*, April 7, 1986, p. 62; on Anita Hill's harassment allegations against Supreme Court nominee Clarence Thomas, see "The Untold Story," *U.S. News and World Report*, October 12, 1992.

72. Pogrebin, "Harassment," p. 6; Joan Faer, "Sexual Harassment on the Job," *Harper's Bazaar*, August 1979, pp. 90–91; Elizabeth Powell, *Talking back to Sexual Pressure: What to Say. . . to Resist Persuasion . . . to Avoid Disease. . . to Stop Harassment . . . to Avoid Acquaintance Rape* (Minneapolis, 1991), p. 116.

73. On the Tailhook harassment scandal and military harassment more generally, see Powell, *Talking Back;* "What's Wrong with the Navy?" *U.S. News and World Report*, July 13, 1992, pp. 22–26. The year 1997 saw another major outbreak, particularly in the army, of harassment charges and the resulting revisions in training guidelines.

74. Powell, *Talking Back*, pp. 116–17; Michelle Ingrassia, "Virgin Cool," *Newsweek*, October 17, 1994, p. 59.

75. Philip Elmer DeWitt, "Making the Case for Abstinence," *Time*, May 24, 1993, p. 64; "Viewpoint," *Glamour*, June 1981, p. 80; Vernon Grant, "An Opinion: On Virginity," *Mademoiselle*, February 1968, p. 76; Sarah Crichton, "Sexual Correctness: Has It Gone Too Far?" *Newsweek*, October 25, 1993, pp. 52–56.

Notes to Chapter 8

1. "Studies of Blood Pressure," *Scientific American Supplement*, October 31, 1903; C. C. Guthrie and F. H. Pike, "Relation of Pressure in the Coronary Vessels to the Activity of the Isolated Heart," *Science*, July 1906, pp. 52–54; W. R. Tyndale, "Blood Pressure as an Indication of Condition," *Journal of Proceedings and Addresses of the Fifty-First Annual Meeting of the NEA*, 1913, pp. 703–6.

2. Carole Haber, *Beyond Sixty Five: The Dilemma of Old Age in America's Past* (Cambridge, 1983); James T. Patterson, *The Dread Disease: Cancer and Modern American Culture* (Cambridge, Mass., 1987).

3. Lillian N. Reid, *Personality and Etiquette* (Boston, 1950), pp. 176–95, 255–57. My sincere thanks to Scott Sandage for thoughts and references on the nineteenth century. *Remarks on the Bankrupt Law; to Which Are Added, the Projected Amendments of Hopkinson and Webster* (New York, 1819); "The Bankrupt," *The Debtor's Journal* 1 (1820): 16; Karen Lystra, *Searching the Heart: Women, Men and Romantic Love in Nineteenth-Century America* (New York, 1989), p. 64, citing a letter of 1873.

4. Vincent Vinikas, *Soft Soap, Hard Sell: American Hygiene in the Age of Advertisement* (Ames, Iowa, 1992). Kathy Peiss, *Hope in a Jar: The Making of America's Beauty Culture* (New York, 1998).

5. Vincent Vinikas, "Lustrum of the Cleanliness Institute, 1927–1932," *Journal of Social History* 22 (1989): 613–30; "Another Order of the Bath," *New York Times*, August 17, 1927, p. 23; W. W. Peter, Dr. P. H. Hallock, and Grace Hallock, *Hitchhikers: Patrolling the Traffic from the Mouth and Nose* (New York, 1930), pp. 47–50; Roscoe Edlund, "Lave and Learn: Study Made by Cleanliness Institute Reveals That Hands of America's 25,000,000 School Children Are Not Washed as Often as Health and Decency Demand" (Albany, N.Y., n.d.), pp. 1–3.

6. Vinikas, "Lustrum," citing materials in the Soap and Detergent Association Archives, New York; Grace Hallock, *A Tale of Soap and Water, The Historical Progress of Cleanliness*, 2d ed. (New York, 1937); Mary Kimball and Mary Alden, *The Judd Family: A Story of Cleanliness in Three Centuries* (New York, 1932).

7. "Skin Troubles in Industry: What Personal Cleanliness Can Do for the Worker" (New York, n.d.); Vinikas, "Lustrum," p. 621; Roland Marchand, *Advertising the American Dream: Making Way for Modernity, 1920–1940* (Berkeley, Calif., 1985), p. 211.

8. T. J. Jackson Lears, "From Salvation to Self-Realization; Advertising and the Therapeutic Roots of the Consumer Culture, 1880–1930," in Richard Fox

and T. J. Jackson Lears, eds., *The Culture of Consumption; Critical Essays in American History* (New York, 1983), pp. 1–38.

9. Ernest R. Groves and Gladys Groves, *Wholesome Childhoods* (Boston, 1931); Norma Cutts and Nicholas Moseley, *Better Home Discipline* (New York, 1952), pp. 64–67.

10. "Toothbrush and Toothpaste," http://www.catalog.com/dentist/den-his.html, 1997; Pauline E. Warner, "No More Toothache," *Parents' Magazine*, March 1937, p. 22; Charles Stolff, "Transforming Ugly Mouths," *Parents' Magazine*, November 1933, p. 26; *Parents' Magazine*, 1933–1943, advertisements for Ipana and Pepsodent products.

11. David Yosifon and Peter N. Stearns, "The Rise and Fall of American Posture," *American Historical Review* 103 (1998): 1057–95; Katherine Grier, *Culture and Comfort: Parlor-Making and Middle Class Identity, 1850–1930* (Washington, D.C., 1997).

12. D. F. Lincoln, *School and Industrial Hygiene* (Philadelphia, 1883), pp. 31–37; Tait Mackenzie, "The Influence of School Life on Curvature of the Spine," *American Physical Education Review* 3 (1898): 274–80; Edmund Shaftesbury, *Cultivation of the Chest, or, the Highest Physical Development of the Human Form* (Washington, D.C., 1895), pp. 7, 10; Walter Truslow, *Body Poise* (Baltimore, 1943), pp. viii, 136.

13. Truslow, *Body Poise*, p. 136; Shaftesbury, *Cultivation*, p. 10; John M. Keating, *Cyclopedia of the Diseases of Children* (Philadelphia, 1890), vol. 3, pp. 355, 357, 1002.

14. Walter Truslow, "The Relation of Corsets, Shoes and Gymnastics to Posture," *American Physical Education Review* 18 (1913): 313–18; Truslow, *Body Poise;* G. E. Thomas, "Postural Defects of the Toddler," *The Practitioner* 172 (1954): 257–66.

15. Walter Truslow, "A Method of Recording and Charting Cases of Scoliosis," *American Physical Education Review* 6 (1901): 226–30; M. B. Howarth, "Posture in Adolescents and Adults," *American Journal of Nursing* 56 (1956): 34–36.

16. Keating, *Cyclopedia*, vol. 3, p. 990; A. Jacobi, *Therapeutics of Infancy and Childhood* (Philadelphia, 1898).

17. Thomas, "Postural Defects," p. 264.

18. Lillian C. Drew, "Ways and Means of Overcoming Inefficient Posture," *American Physical Education Review* 28 (1933): 3–8; Jessie H. Bancroft, "New Efficiency Methods for Training the Posture of School Children," *American Physical Education Review* 18 (1913): 309–13.

19. Bancroft, "New Efficiency Methods"; Dorothy Brock, "Some Practical Ideas about Posture Training," *American Physical Education Review* 28 (1923):

330–35; Ellen Kelly, *Teaching Posture and Body Mechanics* (New York, 1949), p. 17.

20. *Manners and Conduct in School and Out* (Chicago, 1921), pp. 6–7.

21. Children's Bureau, *Infant Care* (Washington, D.C., 1914 and 1929). See also 11th ed. (Washington, D.C., 1963), p. 64.

22. Children's Bureau, *Good Posture in the Little Child* (Washington, D.C., 1933, repr. 1946); M. Robinow, V. L. Leonard, and Margaret Anderson, "A New Approach to the Quantitative Analysis of Children's Posture," *Journal of Pediatrics* 22 (1943): 655–63; Winifred Rand, Mary Sweeny, and E. L. Vincent, *Growth and Development of the Young Child* (Philadelphia, 1940); Florence Sherbon, *The Child* (New York, 1934), p. 252; C. Sweet, "The Teaching of Body Mechanics in Pediatric Practice," *Journal of the American Medical Association* 110 (1938): 419–25; Billie Crook, "The Posture of the Young Child," *Childhood Education* 13 (1937): 317–21.

23. D. H. Thom, *Guiding the Adolescent* (Washington, D.C., 1933), pp. 7, 9; Zella van Ornum Glimm, "This Way to Good Posture," *Parents' Magazine*, November 1931, p. 28.

24. Benjamin Spock, *The Common Sense Book of Baby and Child Care* (New York, 1956), pp. 364–65. See also Benjamin Spock and Michael Rothenburg, *Dr. Spock's Baby and Child Care* (New York, 1985), pp. 473–74; Josephine Kenyon, *Healthy Babies Are Happy Babies* (Boston, 1945), pp. 192, 256; Gertrude Chittenden, *Living with Children* (New York, 1944); Sidonie Gruenberg, ed., *The Encyclopedia of Child Care and Guidance* (New York, 1954); Elizabeth Hurlock, *Child Growth and Development* (New York, 1956), p. 128; Willard Olson, *Child Development* (Boston, 1949), p. 82; Lois H. Meck, *Your Child's Development and Guidance* (Philadelphia, 1951); Harold Stuart and Diane Pugh, eds., *The Healthy Child* (Cambridge, Mass., 1960), p. 112; Marian Breckenridge and E. Lee Vincent, *Child Development* (Philadelphia, 1960), pp. 296, 298; Martha May Reynolds, *Children from Seed to Sapling* (New York, 1951), p. 113; Catherine MacKenzie, *Child Development* (New York, 1949), p. 166.

25. Margaret Beery, *Manners Made Easy* (New York, 1949), pp. 17, 50–54.

26. Janet Lane, "Does Your Child Slump?" *Parents' Magazine*, January 1945, pp. 23, 56; Marguerite Angiel, "Overcoming That Teenage Slouch," *Parents' Magazine*, September 1930, pp. 26–27; Helen Kaufman, "Cultivating Good Looks," *Parents' Magazine*, February 1930, pp. 22, 64; E. T. Wilkes, "Start Early for Good Posture," *Parents' Magazine*, February 1942, pp. 29, 68–70; Mary B. Noel, "Improving Your Child's Posture," *Parents' Magazine*, June 1935, pp. 33–34, 75; Lillian Montanye, "Good Posture Can Be a Habit," *Parents' Magazine*, November 1937, pp. 22–23, 74–76; Metropolitan Life Insurance, "Toes Straight Ahead," *Parents' Magazine*, March 1932, p. 5; Phoebe

Radcliffe, "Posture Present and Future," *Parents' Magazine*, January 1944, p. 22.

27. Theodosia C. Hewlett and Olive P. Leiter, "Measuring Introversion and Extroversion," *Personnel Journal* 6 (1927): 358.

28. Kelly, *Teaching Posture and Body Mechanics*, pp. iii, 17. Kelly was chair of the physical education department at the University of Oklahoma. See also Armin Kelin, "What Price Posture Training," *Journal of Health and Physical Education* 10 (1932): 3; K. Hansson, "Posture and Body Mechanics," *Journal of Health and Physical Education* 16 (1943): 549; J. E. Goldthwaite, L. T. Brown, L. T. Swan, and J. G. Kirkus, *Body Mechanics in Health and Disease* (Philadelphia, 1941), p. 241; Ellen D. Kelly, "Taking Posture Pictures," *Journal of Health and Physical Education* 17 (1946): 464.

29. For various data, insights, and materials from the Vassar archives, I am greatly indebted to Professor Elizabeth Daniels.

30. Ron Rosenbaum, "The Great Ivy League Nude Posture Photo Scandal," *New York Times Magazine*, January 15, 1993.

31. Eastern Society of College Directors of Physical Education for Women, seventh annual meeting, minutes, April 22–23, 1921.

32. Memorandum on the Need for a New Physical Education Building at Vassar College, September 12, 1930, Vassar College archives.

33. *The Thistle* (Carnegie Institute of Technology yearbook), 1910–1964.

34. Mattress advertisements were checked for at least a two-month span during the fifth year in each decade from the 1920s through the 1970s, in the *New York Times*, the *Pittsburgh Post-Gazette*, and the *Pittsburgh Press*. See *Pittsburgh Post-Gazette*, September 3, 1965, p. 7; *Pittsburgh Press*, October 17, 1965, p. 19; *Pittsburgh Press*, March 16, 1975, p. A-24; *New York Times*, March 23, 1975, p. 28.

35. Elizabeth Post, *The New Emily Post's Etiquette* (New York, 1975), pp. 158–59, 396, 656; the same points were repeated in a 1984 edition. Letitia Baldridge, *Complete Guide to the New Manners for the '90s* (New York, 1990), p. 132, and *Complete Guide to a Great Social Life* (New York, 1987), pp. 148–49.

36. Judith Martin, *Miss Manners' Guide to Excruciatingly Correct Behavior* (New York, 1992), p. 128; Amy Vanderbilt, *New Complete Book of Etiquette* (Garden City, N.Y., 1963).

37. Stuart and Pugh, *The Healthy Child;* Louis Thorpe, *Child Psychology and Development* (New York, 1955), p. 125; Ernest H. Watson and G. H. Lowry, *Growth and Development of Children* (Chicago, 1951), pp. 78, 80. Poor posture is bad only when it results *from* a health problem and body forms are "highly variable." William Sheldon, *The Varieties of Temperament* (New York, 1942);

Francis Ilg and Arnold Gesell, *Child Behavior* (New York, 1955); Karl Garrison, *Growth and Development* (New York, 1952).

38. D. M. Doran, "Mechanical and Postural Causes of Chest Pain," *Proceedings of the Royal Society of Medicine* 62 (1969): 876–80; M. B. Menelaus, "Posture and Gait in Children," *Medical Journal of Australia* 1 (1969): 1312–13; J. G. Williams, "Impact of Television on Medicine: Posture and Physical Fitness," *Proceedings of the Royal Society of Medicine* 62 (1969): 683–85; M. E. Tavel, "Straight Back—'Nonsyndrome,' " *Annals of Internal Medicine* 79 (1970): 335–36.

39. J. P. Kevve, " 'Fitness,' 'Posture,' and Other Selected School Health Myths," *Journal of School Health* 37 (1967): 8–15.

40. My thanks to Dr. David Stone for information about current orthopedic thinking.

41. Haim Ginott, *Better Parents and Children* (New York, 1965); Penelope Leach, *Your Baby: From Birth to Age Five* (New York, 1990). For a typical no-comment approach, see B. E. Schwartz and G. A. Ruggieri, *You Can Raise Decent Children* (New Rochelle, N.Y., 1971). See also T. B. Brazelton, *Doctor and Child* (New York, 1970); M. T. Lewis, *Parents' Books of Physical Fitness* (New York, 1975).

42. Edith Stern, "Relax about Your Child's Posture" *Parents' Magazine*, January 1958, pp. 36, 56; Benjamin F. Miller, "Posture Changes," *Parents' Magazine*, October 1959, p. 120.

43. The Nirvana song was entitled "Pennyroyal Tea." Thanks to Cordelia and Clio Stearns for the reference and assistance in interpretation.

44. Yosifon and Stearns, "Rise and Fall"; Robbie Kaplan, *The Whole Career Sourcebook* (New York, 1991), p. 154 (an American Management Association publication); David Lewis, *The Secret Language of Success* (New York, 1989); Thomas E. Cyrs, *Teaching at a Distance with the Emerging Technologies* (Las Cruces, N.M., 1997), pp. 345–53.

45. William R. Emerson, "The Over-Weight Child," *Women's Home Companion* (1920): 31; James S. McLester, "Obesity, Its Penalties and Treatment," *Southern Medical Journal* 21 (1928): 196; Gavin Fulton and Edward Humphrey, "The Management of Obesity," *Kentucky Medical Journal* 37 (1939): 110; Emily Post, *Etiquette* (New York, 1940), p. 208; Alan Guttmacher, *Pregnancy and Birth* (New York, 1962); Naomi Wolf, *The Beauty Myth: How Images of Beauty Are Used against Women* (New York, 1991); Rosalyn Meadows and Lillie Weiss, *Women's Conflicts about Eating and Sexuality* (Binghamton, N.Y., 1993); Marcia Millman, *Such a Pretty Face: Being Fat in America* (New York, 1980); Brett Silverstein and Deborah Patrick, *The Cost of Competence: Why*

Inequality Causes Depression, Eating Disorders and Illness in Women (New York, 1995).

46. Hillel Schwartz, *Never Satisfied: A Cultural History of Diets, Fantasies and Fat* (New York, 1983); Peter N. Stearns, *Fat History: Bodies and Beauty in the Modern West* (New York, 1997); Elmer Wheeler, *The Fat Boy's Downfall, and How Elmer Learned to Keep It Off* (New York, 1952); Kay Barth, "From Man Mountain to the Mountain Climber," *Today's Health,* July 1954, pp. 41–70; Jesse Berrett, "Feeding the Organization Man: Diet and Masculinity in Postwar America," *Journal of Social History* 30 (1997): 805–25; Molly O'Neill, "The Morality of Fat," *New York Times Magazine,* March 10, 1996, p. 39. Also see the important recent treatment of body discipline by Joan Jacob Brumberg, *The Body Project: An Intimate History of American Girls* (New York, 1997).

47. M. B. Green and Max Beckman, "Supplement Protein in Weight Reduction" *American Practitioner and Digest of Treatment* 1 (1950): 1239; G. J. Warnshuis, "Individualizing the Treatment of Obesity," *Medical Review of Reviews* 37 (1931): 676; Schwartz, *Never Satisfied,* pp. 200 ff.; Kim Chernin, *The Obsession: Reflections on the Tyranny of Slenderness* (New York, 1981), p. 44.

48. Emma Seifrit Weigly, "Average? Ideal? Desirable? A Brief Overview of Weight Tables in the United States," *Journal of the American Dietetic Association* (April 1984): 417–23; "1983 Met Life Height & Weight Tables," *Statistical Bulletin of the Metropolitan Life Insurance Company* (January–June, 1983): 3–9; Stearns, *Fat History,* pp. 111–15.

49. Sharlene McEvoy, "Fat Chance: Employment Discrimination against the Overweight," *Labor Law Journal* 43 (1992): 3–19; Regine Herzlinger and David Calkine, "How Companies Tackle Health Care Costs," *Harvard Business Review* (1986): 70–80; Stanley Siegelman, "Employers Fighting Battle of the Bulge," *Business and Health* 9 (1991): 62–63; Jack Friedman, "Those Hidden Pounds: Executive Enemy No. 1," *Dun's Review and Modern Industry,* April 1961, pp. 42–44.

50. Schwartz, *Never Satisfied,* p. 246; Ernest Havemann, "The Wasteful, Phony Crash Dieting Craze," *Life,* January 19, 1959, p. 102; Roberta Seid, *Never Too Thin: Why Women Are at War with Their Bodies* (New York, 1989); Stearns, *Fat History.*

51. Hilde Bruch, "Psychological Aspects of Reducing," *Psychosomatic Medicine* 14 (1952): 338, and *The Importance of Overweight* (New York, 1957); Jane Lincoln, "I'm to Blame That My Husband Died Young," *Cosmopolitan,* August 1954, pp. 84–89; "Obesity the Enemy," *Newsweek,* October 20, 1947, p. 54.

52. Stephen Nissenbaum, *Sex, Diet, and Debility in Jacksonian America: Sylvester Graham and Health Reform* (Westport, Conn., 1980).

53. Judy Shields, "Problems of the Fad Diet Freak," *Seventeen*, June 1973, p. 116; Abigail Wood, "Why Do I Make Myself Fat?" *Seventeen*, March 1973, p. 28; "Ladies Home Journal Diet Club," *Ladies Home Journal*, April 1969, p. 98; Robert Linn, *The Last Chance Diet Book* (New York, 1976); "Reduced 53 lbs. in Nine Weeks" (advertisement), *Ladies Home Journal*, January 1924, p. 108; Murray Siegel, *Think Thin* (New York, 1971), pp. 28, 103; Theodore Rubin, *The Thin Book* (New York, 1966), pp. 11, 46, 54; Sidney Petrie, *The Lazy Lady's Easy Diet* (West Nyack, N.Y., 1968); Frank Wilson, *Glamour, Glucose and Glands* (New York, 1956).

54. "Size-Wise Diet," *Seventeen*, October 1969, p. 26; Louise Paine Benjamin, "I Decided to Reduce," *Ladies Home Journal*, November 1935, p. 28; Maz R. Tarnoff, "I Cut My Weight by 150 Pounds," *Ladies Home Journal*, October 1958, pp. 146–47.

55. Stearns, *Fat History*, chap. 8; Jacques Decourt and Michel Perin, *L' Obésité* (Paris, 1962), pp. 63–65; Marguerite Duvel, *Je veux maigrir, je veux grossir* (Paris, 1956), pp. 15–16; Elie Azaral, *Lettres à un ami obèse* (Paris, 1970), pp. 7–8, 45, 55–57.

56. Stearns, *Fat History*, chaps. 4, 6.

57. James G. Hughes, *Pediatrics in General Practice* (New York, 1952), p. 144; I. N. Kugelmass, *Superior Children through Modern Nutrition* (New York, 1942), p. 291; Mary S. Ross, *Feeding the Family* (New York, 1955), p. 185; Flanders Dunbar, *Your Child's Mind and Body* (New York, 1949), p. 386; Stearns, *Fat History*, chap. 6; Waverly Root and Richard de Rochemont, *Eating Well in America* (New York, 1976), pp. 124, 125; Richard Cummings, *The American and His Food* (Chicago, 1940); Harvey A. Levenstein, *Revolution at the Table* (New York, 1988).

58. M. F. Najj and M. Rowland, *Anthropometric Reference Data and Prevalence of Overweight, 1976–80*, National Center for Health Statistics, Vital and Health Statistics Series, report no. DHH5/PUB/PHS-87–1688 (Hyattsville, Md., 1987): David F. Williamson, "Descriptive Epidemiology of Body Weight and Weight Change in U.S. Adults," *Annals of Internal Medicine* (1953): 646–49; "Trends in Average Weights, Insured Men and Women," *Statistical Bulletin of the Metropolitan Life Insurance Company* (1970): 1–3; "Trends in Average Weights and Heights of Men: An Insurance Experience," *Statistical Bulletin of the Metropolitan Life Insurance Company* (1970): 6–7; Society of Actuaries and Association of Life Insurance Medical Directors of America, *Build Study 1979* (New York, 1980); Edward A. Lew, "Mortality and Weight: Insured Lives and the American Cancer Society Studies," *Annals of Internal Medicine* (1989): 1024–29; Robert Kuczmarski et al., "Increasing Prevalence of Overweight

among US Adults," *Journal of the American Medical Association*, July 20, 1994, pp. 205–11.

59. Richard Klein, "Big Country: The Roots of American Obesity," *New Republic*, September 19, 1994, pp. 32, 34; Stearns, *Fat History*.

60. Cited in *New York Times*, November 20, 1996.

61. Arlene Eisenberg, *What to Expect When You're Expecting* (New York, 1991); Arlie Russell Hochschild, *The Managed Heart: Commercialization of Human Feeling* (Berkeley and Los Angeles, 1983); "What Strong Emotions Do to Us," *Harper's Monthly Magazine*, July 1922, pp. 235–41; Frank Hoffman, *Psychology and Common Life* (New York, 1903), p. 161; William Sadler, "What You Need to Know about Your Blood Pressure," *American Magazine*, May 1926, pp. 46–47, 212–16.

62. Ronald J. Troyer and Gerald Markle, *Cigarettes: The Battle over Smoking* (New Brunswick, N.J., 1983).

63. Troyer and Markle, *Cigarettes;* John Burnham, *Bad Habits: Drinking, Smoking, Taking Drugs, Gambling, Sexual Misbehavior, and Swearing in American History* (New York, 1993), chap. 4.

64. U.S. Department of Agriculture, Economic Research Service, *Food Consumption, Prices, and Expenditures* (annual reports, 1970–1985); U.S. Treasury Department, Internal Revenue Service, annual reports, *Alcohol and Tobacco Summary Statistics*, 1901–1956.

65. Troyer and Markle, *Cigarettes;* Robert L. Rabin and S. D. Sugarman, eds., *Smoking Policy: Law, Politics and Culture* (New York, 1993), pp. 61, 83, 106, 171.

66. U.S. Office of the Surgeon General, Office on Smoking and Health, *Preventing Tobacco Use among Young People* (Washington, D.C., 1994); Jordan Goodman, *Tobacco in History: The Cultures of Dependence* (London, 1993); Robert Goodin, *No Smoking: The Ethical Issues* (Chicago, 1989); National Research Council, Committee on Passive Smoking, *Environmental Tobacco Smoke: Measuring Exposures and Assessing Health Effects* (Washington, D.C., 1986); Richard Carney, ed., *Risk-Taking Behavior: Concepts, Methods, and Applications to Smoking and Drug Abuse* (Springfield, Ill., 1971); Stanton Glantz, ed., *The Cigarette Papers* (Berkeley and Los Angeles, 1986); Elizabeth Whelan, *A Smoking Gun: How the Tobacco Industry Gets Away with Murder* (Philadelphia, 1984); U.S. Department of Health and Human Services, Public Health Service, Office on Smoking and Health, *The Health Consequences of Smoking: Nicotine Addiction: A Report of the Surgeon General* (Rockville, Md., 1988); Robert Tollison, ed., *Smoking and Society: Toward a More Balanced Assessment* (Lexington, Mass., 1986); U.S. Department of Health and Human Services, Public

Health Service, Office on Smoking and Health, *Tobacco-Control Activities in the United States* (biennial report) (Rockville, Md., 1992–93); U.S. Department of Health and Human Services, Office on Smoking and Health, *Smoking and Health, a National Status Report* (biennial report) (Rockville, Md., 1986—).

67. David Keogh, *Smoking: The Artificial Passion* (New York, 1991), pp. 15, 18, 97, 141, 155; Tollison, *Smoking and Society;* Rabin and Sugarman, *Smoking Policy;* Barbara Lyrich and R. J. Bonnie, eds., *Growing up Tobacco Free* (Washington, D.C., 1994), pp. 77, 98.

Notes to Chapter 9

1. For current research on control issues, see George Loewenstein, "Out of Control: Visceral Influences on Behavior," *Organizational Behavior and Human Decision Processes* 65 (1996): 272–92. Americans routinely downplay the power of impulses, what Loewenstein calls "visceral factors." This may be a common human problem, but the American quest for control might exacerbate it. This is an intersection where the addiction concept proved to fit.

2. Harry Gene Levine, "The Discovery of Addiction: Changing Conceptions of Habitual Drunkenness in America," *Journal of Studies on Alcohol* 39 (1978): 143–69; Stanton Peele, "Addiction as a Cultural Concept," *Psychology: Perspectives and Practice. Annals of the New York Academy of Sciences* 602 (1990): 205–20.

3. Janet Golden, " 'An Argument That Goes Back to the Womb': The Demedicalization of Fetal Alcohol Syndrome, 1973–1992," forthcoming in the *Journal of Social History.* In addition to the useful model of demedicalization, this essay shows how as part of the increased moral regulation pressures of the time, late-twentieth-century Americans turned away from the disease explanation in favor of blaming both the mother and the child-victim. The result can be compared with other addiction dilutions and with the ambivalent use of attention deficit disorder.

4. Levine, "Discovery."

5. Levine, "Discovery"; Peele, "Addiction"; Leonard Bacon, *Total Abstinence from Ardent Spirits* (New Haven, Conn., 1829); Leonard Blumberg, "The Significance of the Alcohol Prohibitionists from the Washington Temperance Societies," *Journal of Studies on Alcohol* 41 (1980): 37–87.

6. Joseph Gusfield, *Symbolic Crusade: Status Politics and the American Temperance Movement* (Urbana, Ill., 1963); W. J. Rohrabaugh, *The Alcoholic Republic: An American Tradition* (New York, 1979); "Treatment for Inebriate Patients," *Popular Science Monthly*, August 1884, p. 571; E. F. Arnold, "Inebriety

from a Medical Standpoint," *North American Review* 6 (1893): 756–61; J. H. Follergill, "Effects of Alcoholic Excess on Character," *Popular Science Monthly*, January 1879, pp. 379–88; Thomas Pegram, *Battling Demon Rum: The Struggle for a Dry America* (Chicago, 1998).

7. Virginia Berridge, "The Society for the Study of Addiction 1884–1988," *British Journal of Addiction* 85 (1990): 987–1066; M. M. Glatt and J. Marks, eds., *The Dependence Phenomenon* (Ridgewood, N.J., 1982).

8. Cited in Peele, "Addiction," p. 207; V. Berridge and G. Edwards, *Opium and the People. Opiate Use in Nineteenth-Century England* (New Haven, Conn., 1987); A. R. Lindesmith, *Addiction and Opiates* (Chicago, 1968); David Court-wright, *Dark Paradise: Opiate Addiction in America before 1940* (Cambridge, Mass., 1982).

9. Peele, "Addiction," pp. 215–16; for an example of dubious claims about cocaine, see S. Cohen, "Reinforcement and Rapid Delivery Systems: Under-standing Adverse Consequences of Cocaine," in U.S. Department of Health and Human Services, N. J. Kozel and E. H. Adams, eds., *Cocaine Use in America: Epidemiological and Clinical Perspectives* (Washington, D.C., 1984).

10. Peele, "Addiction," p. 218; Francis Seeburger, *Addiction and Responsi-bility: An Inquiry into the Addictive Mind* (New York, 1993).

11. Glatt and Marks, eds., *Dependence*, p. xi; see also Stanton Peele, *Diseasing of America: Addiction Treatment out of Control* (Lexington, Mass., 1989).

12. L. J. Hauser, "A Short Course in Gambling," *Parents' Magazine* (1938): 31, 74; "Morals of Gambling," *Newsweek*, April 9, 1951, p. 72; "Everyone in the Pool," *Newsweek*, April 18, 1966, p. 106; R. L. Heilbrier, "Are You a Gambler?" *American Mercury* 84 (1957): 55–60.

13. American Psychiatric Association, *Diagnostic and Statistical Manual of Mental Disorders III* (Washington, D.C., 1980), pp. 291–93.

14. American Psychiatric Association, *Diagnostic and Statistical Manual of Mental Disorders IV* (Washington, D.C., 1993), pp. 615–18.

15. "Hope for Victims of Another Addiction," *Fortune* 15 (1981): 26; "The Addict: Even When You Win, You Lose," *U.S. News and World Report* 94 (1983) : 31; A. Finlayser, "A Compulsive Gambler's Secret Life," *Macleans* 97 (1984): 56; A. H. Rosenfeld, "Brain Chemicals and the Gambler's High," *Psychology Today* 19 (1985): 8; "I Was a Compulsive Gambler," *Good House-keeping* 200 (1985): 76; F. White III, "Gambling Addicts: How to Tell If You Are Hooked," *Ebony* 41 (1986): 108; L. Worner, "My Husband Is Irresponsi-ble," *Ladies Home Journal* 104 (1987): 12; Suzanne Sataline, "Increase in Gambling Addiction Worries Asian Community," Knight-Rider/Tribune News Service, May 7, 1996, p. 507K8487; Timothy Morgan, "The Invisible Addic-tion," *Christianity Today* 40 (1996): 12; Judith Valente, "A Long Road to

Daylight: A Fallen Football Hero Fights to Break Free of the Gambling Addiction That Sacked His Career," *People Weekly* 45 (1996): 81; Hugh Drummond, "Hope and Addiction" *Boston Magazine* 81 (1989): 98.

16. Cited in Morgan, "The Invisible Addiction," p. 12.

17. Gordon Williams, "Investor or Gambler," *Financial World* 163 (1994): 70; J. H. Skolnick, "Compulsive Gambling: Talking to the Examples," *Psychology Today* 13 (1979): 52; Bernard Horn, "Is There a Cure for America's Gambling Addiction?" *USA Today Magazine*, May 1997, p. 34.

18. Williams, "Investor or Gambler"; White, "Gambling Addicts."

19. Horn, "Cure," p. 34.

20. D. T. de Bienville, *Nymphomania, or a Dissertation Concerning the Furor Uterinus* (London, 1775); Max Huhner, *A Practical Treatise of Disorders of the Sexual Function in the Male and Female* (Philadelphia, 1916); Louis London, *Abnormal Sexual Behavior* (New York, 1937); Allen Churchill and Pierre Rube, M.D., "Nymphos Have No Fun," *Esquire*, August 1954, pp. 21–23.

21. Wallace Irving, *The Nympho and Other Maniacs* (New York, 1971); Charlotte Kasl, *Women, Sex and Addiction* (New York, 1989); Franklin Klaf, *Satyriasis: A Study of Male Nymphomania* (New York, 1966); Albert Ellis, *Nymphomania: A Study of the Oversexed Woman* (New York, 1965); Charles Wahl, *Sexual Problems* (New York, 1967); Sandor Lorand, *Perversions* (New York, 1956).

22. Jim Orford, *Excessive Appetites: A Psychological View of Addiction* (New York, 1985); A. Goodman, "Sexual Addiction: Designation and Treatment," *Journal of Sex and Marital Therapy* 18 (1992): 303–14; D'Arcy Jenish, "Obsessed with Sex," *Maclean's* 104 (1991): 44–46; C. Moster, "A Response to Aviel Goodman's 'Sexual Addiction: Designation and Treatment,' " *Journal of Sex and Marital Therapy* 19 (1993): 220–24; A. Goodman, "Diagnosis and Treatment of Sexual Addiction," *Journal of Sex and Marital Therapy* 19 (1993): 225–51; E. S. Nelson, D. Hill-Barlow, and J. O. Benedict, "Addiction versus Intimacy as Related to Sexual Involvement in a Relationship," *Journal of Sex and Marital Therapy* 20 (1994): 35–45.

23. Dwight B. Heath, ed., *International Handbook on Alcohol and Culture* (Westport, Conn., 1995), p. 306.

24. Mark Lender and James K. Martin, *Drinking in America: A History* (New York, 1982), pp. 182–90; *Alcoholics Anonymous: The Story of How Many Thousands of Men and Women Have Recovered from Alcoholism*, 3d ed. (New York, 1976); Robert Thomsen, *Bill W.* (New York, 1975); Ernest Kurtz, *Not-God: A History of Alcoholics Anonymous* (Center City, Minn., 1979).

25. *Alcoholics Anonymous;* Kurtz, *Not-God.*

26. E. M. Jellinek, *The Disease Concept of Alcoholism* (Highland Park, N.J., 1960); Jenish, "Obsessed," pp. 44–46.

27. F. G. Gosling, *Before Freud: Neurasthenia & the American Medical Community, 1870–1910* (Champaign, Ill., 1988); Thomas Read, "The American Secret," *Reader's Digest*, April 1927, pp. 721–22; Agnes Repplier, "The Nervous Strain," *Atlantic Monthly* 105 (1910): 198–201; Edward Shorter, *A History of Psychiatry: From the Age of the Asylum to the Age of Prozac* (New York, 1997); Robert Kugelman, *Stress: The Nature and History of Applied Grief* (Newport, Conn., 1992).

28. Tom Lutz, " 'Sweat or Die': The Hedonization of the Work Ethic in the 1920s," *American Literary History* 8 (1996): 259–82; O. Henry, *Let Me Feel Your Pulse* (New York, 1910); Joseph Jastrow, *Sanity First! The Art of Sensible Living* (New York, 1935).

29. Abraham Myerson, *American Women: Images and Realities* (Boston, 1920); Edmund Bergler, *Tensions Can Be Reduced to Nuisances* (New York, 1960), pp. 24–25; Albert Adams, *Nervous Breakdown* (New York, 1901).

30. Frederick Painton, "There Is No Such Thing as Shell Shock," *Reader's Digest*, October 1943, p. 59; Roger Spiller, "Shell Shock," *American Heritage* 41 (1990): 75–87

31. George Stevenson, "How to Deal with Your Tensions," *Reader's Digest*, March 1969, pp. 89–92; Jastrow, *Sanity First!* pp. 181, 182; Gladys Rush Alexander, *I'm Glad I Had a Nervous Breakdown* (New York, 1966), pp. 4–5; Boris Sides, "The Secret of Sound Sleep," *Reader's Digest*, January 1923, pp. 763–64; Frank Caprio, *How to Avoid a Nervous Breakdown* (New York, 1969), pp. 5, 12, 22; Vanessa Ochs, "Taking the Cure," *Tikkun* 10 (1995): 47. "The modern treatment for Nervous Disorders is not rest. Fatigue . . . does not break us down—on the contrary, we have in us a sort of electric battery that charges by running. . . . People have an unusual font of energy because they work hard" (Eleanor Kelly, "The Fashionable Subconscious," *Reader's Digest*, August 1923, p. 340).

32. Gerald Gurrin, Joseph Vernoff, and Sheila Feld, *Americans View Their Mental Health* (New York, 1960); Richard Omark, "Nervous Breakdown as a Folk Illness," *Psychological Reports* 47 (1980): 862; John Reinhold, "Users and Nonusers of College Counseling and Psychiatric Services," *Journal of the American College Health Association* 21 (1973): 201–8; Joseph Vernoff et al., *Mental Health in America: Patterns of Help-Seeking from 1957 to 1976* (New York, 1981); "Office Hours," *Fortune*, June 23, 1986, p. 160; Cynthia Crossen, "Nervous Breakdowns, by Any Name, They Aren't What They Used to Be," *Wall Street Journal*, December 3, 1996, p. 1.

33. H. Wayne Morgan, *Drugs in America: A Social History* 1800–1980 (Norman, Okla., 1981); Peele, "Addiction."

34. Anastaria Toufexis, "Worries about Overactive Kids: Are Too Many Youngsters Being Misdiagnosed and Medicated?" *Time* 133 (1989): 65; "Handling Kids with Attention Disorders," *USA Today Magazine* 122 (1993): 9; "Hyperactive Heredity," *Time* 141 (1993): 23; "How Active Is Hyperactive?" *Family Circle* 105 (1992): 47; Alfie Kohn, "Suffer the Restless Children," *The Atlantic* 264 (1989): 90.

35. American Psychiatric Association, *Diagnostic and Statistical Manual of Mental Disorders III*; Stephanie Weiss, "Attention Deficits: What We Know Now," *NEA Today* 12 (1994): 17.

36. E. Carpenter, "New Measures of Attention," *Psychology Today* 19 (1985); Holly Matthews, "Fidgety Phil and Beyond: Attention Deficit Disorder," honors thesis, Carnegie Mellon University, 1998.

37. Sally Stich, "Why Can't Your Husband Sit Still," *Ladies Home Journal* 110, no. 9 (1993): 74; "What's Wrong with My Child," *Ladies Home Journal* 109, no. 4 (1990): 98; "What Makes Hyperactive Kids Hyper," *U.S. News and World Report* 109, no. 21 (1990): 18; Stephanie Garber, Marianne Garber, and Robyn Spizman, "Is Your Child Hyperactive? Inattentive? Impulsive? Distractible?" *Redbook* 175, no. 6 (1990): 32; Sally Shaywitz and Bennet Shaywitz, "Increased Medication Use in Attention-Deficit Hyperactivity Disorder: Regressive or Appropriate?" *Journal of the American Medical Association* 260 (1988): 2270.

38. Roberta Ferrence, *Deadly Fashion: The Rise and Fall of Cigarette Smoking in North America* (New York, 1989).

Notes to Chapter 10

1. My thanks to Scott Sandage for the nineteenth-century references. Diary of Jonathan Henry Hill, American Antiquarian Society, Worcester, Mass., entry of December 31, 1847; diary of Edward Neufville Tailer Jr., New York Historical Society, vol. 12, entry of January 7, 1855; diary of Albion W. Clark, New York Public Library, vol. 4, entry of January 1867; diary of Charles William Dabney, Virginia Historical Society, vols. 1 and 2, entries of January 4, 1832, December 31, 1836, January 7, 1838, January 5, 1839, December 31, 1847, December 30, 1848 ("I feel a solemn spirit of retrospection always at the end of a year, and in my farming matters, I have generally much to recollect with regret, but little with pleasure").

2. Cas Wouters, "Etiquette Books and Emotion Management in the 20th Century: Part One—The Integration of Social Classes," *Journal of Social His-*

tory 29 (1995): 107–24, and "Part Two—The Integration of the Sexes," *Journal of Social History* 29 (1995): 325–39.

3. Peter N. Stearns, *Fat History: Bodies and Beauty in the Modern West* (New York, 1997), chap. 4; "When Bigger Is Better," *Ebony*, July 1994, pp. 102–4; "Big Can Be Beautiful," *Ebony*, October 1978; S. K. Kumanyika, F. F. Wilson, and M. Guildford-Davenport, "Weight-Related Attitudes and Behaviors of Black Women," *Journal of the American Dietetic Association* 93 (1993): 416–22.

4. Peter N. Stearns, "Historical Perspectives on 20th-Century Childhood," paper presented to Netherlands Institute for Advanced Study in the Humanities and Social Sciences, ed. W. Koops and M. Zuckerman, Wassenaar, Netherlands, February 1998.

5. Christopher Lasch, *Haven in a Heartless World: The Family Besieged* (New York, 1977); Dorothy Ross, *G. Stanley Hall: The Psychologist as Prophet* (Chicago, 1972); Joseph Kett, "Reflections on the History of Adolescence in America," paper presented at Netherlands Institute for Advanced Study in the Humanities and Social Sciences Conference, "Are We at the End of the Century of the Child?" Wassenaar, Netherlands, February 1998.

6. Anthony Platt, *The Child Savers: The Invention of Delinquency* (Chicago, 1969); Dominick Cavallo, *Muscles and Morals: Organized Playgrounds and Urban Reform, 1880–1920* (Philadelphia, 1981); Lisa Jacobson, "Revitalizing the American Home: Children's Leisure and the Revolution of Play, 1920–1940," *Journal of Social History* 30 (1997): 581–96; Glen Elder Jr., *Children of the Great Depression: Social Change in Life Experience* (Chicago, 1974); David Tyack and Elisabeth Hansot, *Learning Together: A History of Coeducation in American Public Schools* (New Haven, Conn., 1990); Steven Gelber, "A Job You Can't Lose: Work and Hobbies in the Great Depression," *Journal of Social History* 24 (1991): 741–66.

7. Joel Tarr and Mark Tebeau, "Managing Danger in the Home Environment, 1900–1940," *Journal of Social History* 29 (1996): 797–816; John Burnham, "Why Did the Infants and Toddlers Die? Shifts in Americans' Ideas of Responsibility for Accidents—From Blaming Mom to Engineering," *Journal of Social History* 29 (1996): 817–37.

8. On fathering, see Margaret Marsh, *Suburban Lives* (New Brunswick, N.J., 1990); Richard Sennett, *Families against the City: Middle Class Homes of Industrial Chicago, 1872–1910* (Cambridge, Mass., 1970); Peter N. Stearns, *Jealousy, The Evolution of an Emotion in American History* (New York, 1989); Peter N. Stearns, "Children's Sleep: Sketching Historical Change," *Journal of Social History* 30 (1996): 345–66.

9. Susan Matt, "Frocks, Finery, and Feelings: Rural and Urban Women's

Envy, 1890–1930," in Jan Lewis and Peter N. Stearns, eds., *Emotional History of the United States* (New York, 1998), pp. 377–95; Peter N. Stearns, "Consumerism and Childhood: New Targets for American Emotions," in Lewis and Stearns, eds., *Emotional History*, pp. 396–416; Sally McNall, "American Children's Literature, 1880–Present," in Joseph Hawes and N. Ray Hiner, eds., *American Childhood: A Research Guide and Historical Handbook* (Westport, Conn., 1982).

10. Lisa Jacobson, "Revitalizing the American Home: Children's Leisure and the Revolution of Play, 1920–1940," *Journal of Social History* 30 (1997): 581–96.

11. Urie Bronfenbrenner, "Socialization and Social Class through Time and Space," in E. Maccoby, T. Newcomb, and E. Hartley, eds., *Readings in Social Psychology* (New York, 1958), pp. 400–25; John Modell and Robert Siegler, "Child Development and Human Diversity," in Glen Elder, J. Modell, and R. Parke, eds., *Children in Time and Place: Developmental and Historical Insights* (Cambridge, 1993), pp. 73–106.

12. John Modell, *Into One's Own: From Youth to Adulthood in the United States, 1920–1975* (Berkeley and Los Angeles, 1989).

13. Fred Gosman, *Spoiled Rotten: American Children and How to Change Them* (Andersen, Ind., 1993); H. S. Glenn and Jane Nelsen, *Raising Self-Reliant Children in a Self-Indulgent World* (Rocklink, Calif., 1988).

14. Elizabeth Lasch-Quinn, "Race and Etiquette: Advice on Interracial Conduct since the 1960s," forthcoming in the *Journal of Social History*.

15. Susan Jacoby, "Emotional Child Abuse: The Invisible Plague," *Reader's Digest*, February 1985, pp. 186–89; Emily Martin, *The Women in the Body: A Cultural Analysis of Reproduction* (Boston, 1992), pp. 120–21.

16. Stearns, *Fat History*, chap. 6.

17. Ed Rollins, with Tom DeFrank, *Bare Knuckles and Back Rooms: Life in American Politics* (New York, 1996); Darrell M. West, *Air Wars: Television Advertising in Election Campaigns, 1952–1992* (Washington, D.C., 1993); Bruce E. Grombeck, "Negative Political Ads and American Self Images," in A. H. Miller and B. Grombeck, eds., *Presidential Campaigns and American Self Images* (Boulder, Colo., 1994); Stephen Ansolabehere and Shanto Iyengar, *Going Negative: How Attack Ads Shrink and Polarize the Electorate* (New York, 1995); Irwin Ross, *The Loneliest Campaign: The Truman Victory of 1948* (New York, 1968); Edwin Diamond and Stephen Bates, *The Spot: The Rise of Political Advertising on Television* (Cambridge, Mass., 1992).

18. William O'Neill, *Coming Apart, an Informal History of America in the 1960s* (Chicago, 1971).

19. From a Burson-Marstellar (advertising agency) presentation at Carnegie Mellon University, 1994.

20. Julius H. Ruben, *Religious Melancholy and Protestant Experience in America* (New York, 1994).

21. Stephan Thernstrom, *Poverty and Progress: Social Mobility in a Nineteenth Century City* (Cambridge, Mass., 1964). For an intriguing comparative assessment of the symbolic importance of education in the United States in ensuring equal opportunity for individual effort, in contrast to more social approaches in western Europe, see Arnold Heidenheimer, *Comparative Public Policy: Policies of Social Choice in Europe and America* (New York, 1975).

22. Elaine Tyler May, *Homeward Bound: American Families in the Cold War Era* (New York, 1989).

23. Rosalind H. Williams, *Dream Worlds: Mass Consumption in Late Nineteenth-Century France* (Berkeley and Los Angeles, 1982); Warren Breckman, "Disciplining Consumption: The Debate about Luxury in Wilhelmine Germany, 1890–1914," *Journal of Social History* 26 (1993): 327–54; Ellen Furlough, "Selling the American Way in Interwar France," *Journal of Social History* 26 (1993): 501–20; R. W. Fox and T. J. Jackson Lears, eds., *The Culture of Consumption* (New York, 1983), chap. 1.

Notes to Chapter 11

1. For example, Maris Vinovskis noted that since the 1970s, symbolic, and statistically misleading, invocations of the problems of teenage pregnancy—even as pregnancy rates were declining—have detracted from efforts to do much about the problems involved for adolescent parents or their offspring. See Maris Vinovskis, "Development of Policy for Adolescent Issues," paper delivered at Netherlands Institute for Advanced Study in the Humanities and Social Sciences Conference, "Are We at the End of the Century of the Child?" Wassenaar, Netherlands, February 1998.

2. Part of the assessment issue involves culture as a tool of authority and order, which the culture of self-discipline certainly is. This book has avoided some of the more formal musings about what culture means and general theories of cultural manipulation under capitalism. The new cultural studies have explored issues of hegemony and commodification, which unquestionably relate to this book, even though what follows invokes less theory and more ruminations about the difficulty of getting people to see how they are controlled. See Guy Debord, *The Society of the Spectacle* (New York, 1995); Stuart Hall, ed., *Representation: Cultural Representations and Signifying Practices* (Thousand

Oaks, Calif., 1997); Michael Denning, *The Cultural Front: The Laboring of American Culture in the Twentieth Century* (New York, 1997).

3. George Will, "The Barbarian at the Prom," *Pittsburgh Post-Gazette*, June 15, 1997.

4. David Gelernter, *Drawing Life: Surviving the Unabomber* (New York, 1997).

5. See, for example, Christopher Lasch, *The Culture of Narcissism* (New York, 1976).

6. Advertisement for BuSpar, *New York Times*, December 9, 1996, p. A-11.

INDEX

abortion, 90–91, 225, 240, 243, 249, 350
abstinence. *See* celibacy
abuse, 9, 62, 84, 137, 244–45, 310, 341, 343, 358
accountants, 139
Action on Smoking and Health, 286
Adams, John, 3, 43, 75
addiction, 186, 288, 291–320, 359, 365, 366
Adolescent Health Series and Pregnancy Prevention Act, 243
adultery, 4, 14, 50, 87, 188, 226, 230, 231, 238, 250, 305
advertising, 45, 68, 94–95, 97–98, 99, 103, 112, 119–20, 121, 141, 149–53, 192, 235–36, 257, 259, 271, 287, 335
African Americans, 49, 78, 86, 94, 110–11, 174, 226, 231, 280, 328–29, 337, 345, 365
aggression, 136
AIDS, 216, 224, 233, 243, 285, 286
alcohol. *See* drinking
Alcoholics Anonymous, 287, 303, 308–20, 347
alcoholism. *See* addiction
allowances, 355
Ally McBeal, 238
American Cancer Society, 288
American Medical Association, 192
American Physical Education Review, 103
American Posture League, 104, 264
American Psychiatric Association, 299, 300, 301, 303, 312, 317
Americanization, 115, 154
amusement parks, 163

anal sex, 233
anger, 15, 27, 57, 67, 69, 79, 85, 89, 95, 110, 135, 174, 175, 187, 244, 329, 334, 337, 341, 363
Antioch College, 249
anti-Semitism, 119, 124–25, 350–51
anxiety, 364
Asians, 94
Associated Advertising Clubs of the World, 98
Attention Deficit Disorder, 316–17, 337
automobiles, 24, 96, 121, 141–44, 194, 252, 338, 340
Automotive Safety Foundation, 142

Baldridge, Letitia, 272
Ballantine, Harriet, 268
Bancroft, Jessie, 103–4, 264
Bancroft test, 267
bankruptcy, 121, 139, 256, 341
Baruch, Dorothy, 207
baseball, 10, 56, 163
bathing, 19, 73–74, 257–58, 347
bathrooms, 255–56, 259
battered child syndrome, 137
Baywatch, 191
beds, 270–71, 333
Benedict, Ruth, 146
Benezet, Anthony, 254
Bernhardt, Sarah, 100
birth control, 44, 60, 64, 69, 90, 106, 127, 128, 192, 195, 198–205, 223, 224, 226, 228, 230, 243, 332, 367
birth control pill, 195, 215, 230
body, 73–77, 252–90
body odor, 257, 260, 328

ABOUT THE AUTHOR

Peter N. Stearns is dean of the College of Humanities and Social Sciences and Heinz Professor of History at Carnegie Mellon University. He has won several teaching awards at Carnegie Mellon, where he offers an introductory world history survey as well as advanced courses in social and cultural history. He has served as vice-president of the American Historical Association and has been active in the College Board, the National Association for Professional Teaching Standards, several school districts in Pennsylvania and Virginia, and a variety of other organizations. He founded and still edits the *Journal of Social History*.

Peter Stearns's books deal with many topics in European social history and world history. Since 1983, his research has focused on the history of emotions and body discipline in the United States, sometimes in a comparative context. He is married, with four children and several stepchildren, and enjoys the discipline of racket sports and finds it interesting to monitor his reactions to self-control standards in other areas. He believes deeply that history contributes to the understanding of what life has to offer.